St Antony's Series

General Editor: **Jan Zielonka** (2004–), Fellow of St Antony's College, Oxford

Recent titles include:

Valpy FitzGerald, Frances Stewart and Rajesh Venugopal (*editors*)
GLOBALIZATION, VIOLENT CONFLICT AND SELF-DETERMINATION

Håkan Thörn
ANTI-APARTHEID AND THE EMERGENCE OF A GLOBAL CIVIL SOCIETY

Lotte Hughes
MOVING THE MAASAI
A Colonial Misadventure

Fiona Macaulay
GENDER POLITICS IN BRAZIL AND CHILE
The Role of Parties in National and Local Policymaking

Stephen Whitefield (*editor*)
POLITICAL CULTURE AND POST-COMMUNISM

José Esteban Castro
WATER, POWER AND CITIZENSHIP
Social Struggle in the Basin of Mexico

Valpy FitzGerald and Rosemary Thorp (*editors*)
ECONOMIC DOCTRINES IN LATIN AMERICA
Origins, Embedding and Evolution

Victoria D. Alexander and Marilyn Rueschemeyer
ART AND THE STATE
The Visual Arts in Comparative Perspective

Ailish Johnson
EUROPEAN WELFARE STATES AND SUPRANATIONAL GOVERNANCE OF SOCIAL POLICY

Archie Brown (*editor*)
THE DEMISE OF MARXISM-LENINISM IN RUSSIA

Thomas Boghardt
SPIES OF THE KAISER
German Covert Operations in Great Britain during the First World War Era

Ulf Schmidt
JUSTICE AT NUREMBERG
Leo Alexander and the Nazi Doctors' Trial

Steve Tsang (*editor*)
PEACE AND SECURITY ACROSS THE TAIWAN STRAIT

C. W. Braddick
JAPAN AND THE SINO–SOVIET ALLIANCE, 1950–1964
In the Shadow of the Monolith

Isao Miyaoka
LEGITIMACY IN INTERNATIONAL SOCIETY
Japan's Reaction to Global Wildlife Preservation

Neil J. Melvin
SOVIET POWER AND THE COUNTRYSIDE
Policy Innovation and Institutional Decay

Julie M. Newton
RUSSIA, FRANCE AND THE IDEA OF EUROPE

Juhana Aunesluoma
BRITAIN, SWEDEN AND THE COLD WAR, 1945–54
Understanding Neutrality

George Pagoulatos
GREECE'S NEW POLITICAL ECONOMY
State, Finance and Growth from Postwar to EMU

Tiffany A. Troxel
PARLIAMENTARY POWER IN RUSSIA, 1994–2001
A New Era

Elvira María Restrepo
COLOMBIAN CRIMINAL JUSTICE IN CRISIS
Fear and Distrust

Ilaria Favretto
THE LONG SEARCH FOR A THIRD WAY
The British Labour Party and the Italian Left Since 1945

Lawrence Tal
POLITICS, THE MILITARY, AND NATIONAL SECURITY IN JORDAN, 1955–1967

Louise Haagh and Camilla Helgø (*editors*)
SOCIAL POLICY REFORM AND MARKET GOVERNANCE IN LATIN AMERICA

St Antony's Series
Series Standing Order ISBN 0–333–71109–2
(*outside North America only*)

You can receive future titles in this series as they are published by placing a standing order. Please contact your bookseller or, in case of difficulty, write to us at the address below with your name and address, the title of the series and the ISBN quoted above.

Customer Services Department, Macmillan Distribution Ltd, Houndmills, Basingstoke, Hampshire RG21 6XS, England

---

Globalization, Violent Conflict and Self-Determination

Edited by

Valpy FitzGerald

Frances Stewart

and

Rajesh Venugopal

palgrave
macmillan

First published 2006 by
PALGRAVE MACMILLAN
Houndmills, Basingstoke, Hampshire RG21 6XS and
175 Fifth Avenue, New York, N.Y. 10010
Companies and representatives throughout the world

PALGRAVE MACMILLAN is the global academic imprint of the Palgrave Macmillan division of St. Martin's Press, LLC and of Palgrave Macmillan Ltd. Macmillan® is a registered trademark in the United States, United Kingdom and other countries. Palgrave is a registered trademark in the European Union and other countries.

ISBN-13: 978–1–4039–8794–5
ISBN-10: 1–4039–8794–7

This book is printed on paper suitable for recycling and made from fully managed and sustained forest sources.

A catalogue record for this book is available from the British Library.

Library of Congress Cataloging-in-Publication Data
Globalization, violent conflict and self-determination / edited by Valpy FitzGerald, Frances Stewart, and Rajesh Venugopal.
p. cm. — (St. Antony's series)
Includes bibliographical references and index.
ISBN 1–4039–8794–7 (cloth : alk. paper)
1. Political violence—Developing countries. 2. Self-determination, National. 3. Globalization. I. Fitzgerald, E. V. K. (Edmund Valpy Knox), 1947– II. Stewart, Frances, 1940– III. Venugopal, Rajesh, 1970– IV. St. Antony's series (Palgrave Macmillan (Firm)).
JC328.65.D48G56 2006
303.609172'4—dc22 2005056577

10 9 8 7 6 5 4 3 2 1
15 14 13 12 11 10 09 08 07 06

Printed and bound in Great Britain by
Antony Rowe Ltd, Chippenham and Eastbourne

Contents

Preface

Violent conflict in the developing world is a critical issue for the twenty-first century, threatening the livelihoods and futures of millions. Largely because the security of the states that dominate the world system are believed to be threatened by these conflicts, increasing international effort and resources are dedicated to trying to prevent them. Yet these interventions – whether by force, diplomacy or aid – do not appear to be very effective. This is due in considerable part to the fact that the economic, political and cultural roots of the conflicts are poorly understood and studied as if they were simply an extreme dimension of historical backwardness and failure to modernise. Moreover, the global sources and trajectories of such conflicts are often neglected.

Previous work at Queen Elizabeth House on the consequences of conflict for poor countries revealed both the international dimension of the problem and the central role of self-determination movements. This led us to question the 'received view' on the roots of conflict, and to plan further research on the context of global economic and cultural forces and local responses to them. We are very grateful therefore to the International Peace and Security Program of the Carnegie Corporation for supporting this critical work, and to Stephen Del Rosso for his help and encouragement in the design and execution of the project. We also would like to thank the participants at the project workshops in Oxford, London and Pomona for their constructive comments.

Building on the project reported in this volume, work continues at Queen Elizabeth House into the wider context of the consequences of 'horizontal inequality' between social groups for vulnerable people in developing countries at the Centre for Research on Inequality, Human Security and Ethnicity (CRISE) funded by the UK Department for International Development.

VALPY FITZGERALD
FRANCES STEWART
RAJESH VENUGOPAL

Notes on the Contributors

Sandra Dudley is Lecturer in Interpretive Studies in the University of Leicester's Department of Museum Studies. Her research concerns ethnicity and cultural identity, displacement and forced migration, material culture and corporeal experience, people–objects networks, and issues of interpretation and representation. She is co-editor with Elizabeth Dell of *Textiles from Burma* (2003) and is completing a monograph on materiality and corporeal experience amongst Karenni refugees.

Pierre Englebert is Associate Professor of Politics at Pomona College, Claremont, California. He is the author of *State Legitimacy and Development in Africa* (2000). His research interests include the political economy of weak-state reproduction in Africa, separatist movements, and institutional dimensions of development.

Valpy FitzGerald is Reader in International Economics and Finance at the Department of International Development, Oxford University and Professorial Fellow of St Antony's College, Oxford. He also holds visiting chairs in economics at the Institute of Social in The Hague and the Universidad Complutense in Madrid, and acts as an adviser to UNCTAD, the UN Department of Economic and Social Affairs and the UK Government. Recent books include *War and Underdevelopment*, with Frances Stewart (2000), *Global Markets and the Developing Economy* (2003) and *The Transmission of Economic Ideas in Latin America*, with R. Thorp (2005).

Cathie Lloyd is Senior Research Officer at the Department of International Development, University of Oxford. Her work in political sociology covers gender relations, social movements, civil society and democratization with a regional focus on North Africa.

William Reno is Associate Professor of Political Science at Northwestern University, Ohio. He has written extensively on the political economy of conflict and the organization of armed groups in the context of state collapse. His publications include *Corruption and State Politics in Sierra Leone* (1995) and *Warlord Politics and African States* (1998). His forthcoming book is called *The Evolution of Warfare in Independent Africa*. His current research, based on fieldwork in Africa and the Caucasus, focuses on explaining the causes of differences in the behaviour of non-state armed groups in wider conflicts.

Frances Stewart is Director of the Centre for Research on Inequality, Human Security and Ethnicity (CRISE) in the University of Oxford and fellow of Somerville College. She was director of the University's International Development Centre from 1993 to 2003. Books include *Adjustment with a Human Face*, with Giovanni Cornia and Richard Jolly (1987), *War and Underdevelopment*, with Valpy Fitzgerald and others (2000), and *Group Behaviour and Development* (with Judith Heyer and Rosemary Thorp). She is a Board member and Vice-Chairman of the International Food Policy Research Institute (IFPRI), and an Overseer of the Thomas Watson Institute, Brown University.

Rajesh Venugopal is Research Officer at the Department for International Development, University of Oxford. He is completing a doctoral dissertation at Oxford on the ethnic conflict in Sri Lanka, and his research interests cover the political economy of nationalism, development and security, and market reforms in African agriculture.

1
Introduction

Valpy FitzGerald, Frances Stewart and Rajesh Venugopal

Globalization, self-determination and violent conflict

Economic and cultural globalization is the defining characteristic of our world in the early twenty-first century. Yet in the closing decades of the previous millennium the apparent end to conflicts between the major powers was accompanied by continued and increasing pressure for 'self-determination' in developing and transition countries – usually accompanied by violent conflict. The opening years of this new century have already seen similar events, ranging from the conflicts in Bolivia, Chechnya, Ivory Coast and Sudan to the attacks by Al Qaeda and similar groups in the US, Indonesia, Spain and the UK. This process has not been halted – and indeed may be stimulated – by the temporary dominance of a single super-power technically capable of military interdiction across the globe in a 'unipolar moment'.

This book explores the connections between these three phenomena of our time: that is, how global factors have affected violent conflict and movements for self-determination. In doing so we seek both cultural and economic explanations, focusing particularly on how these two interact to affect the politics of self-determination. Our central propositions are three:

- that the global economic and cultural dimensions of 'self-determination movements' (SDMs) are far more important than previously recognized, and cannot simply be reduced to the 'criminal greed' of rival local elites or to age-old 'ethnic rivalries';
- that SDMs have an essentially political dimension that involves both the contestation of state power and the construction of legitimacy, both of which have international dimensions and that cannot simply be condemned as 'terrorism';
- and that both concerted action from the international community and extensive institutional change are essential in order to reduce the violence of both SDMs and incumbent states, of which the main victims are the poor and vulnerable.

This book aims to provide the evidence upon which these propositions are based, while this chapter provides the analytical framework within which the individual contributions should be understood. We start by explaining how the concept of self-determination has been constructed in the specific historical context of changing global institutional conventions, which have moved from colonial and territorial concepts towards a definition based on human rights and the representation of peoples. Our own definition extends and clarifies this logic in order to encompass movements aspiring to fundamental social transformation as well as territorial autonomy. The history of SDMs is bound up with the successive geopolitical phases of colonialism, the cold war and the present unipolar hegemony that seems to have reduced the space for self-determination. However, the processes of economic and cultural globalization have also tended to strengthen SDMs both by weakening existing states and generating spontaneous popular reaction to change. We thus explore the nature of violence as an inherent dimension of self-determination, the way that this dimension has changed over time, and how globalization itself has altered the political and cultural role of violent conflict. Such a discussion also demands a clear conceptualization, which we attempt to provide, of the form that war takes in developing countries, in terms of the way in which it is waged and the consequences for the population.

This chapter also summarizes the arguments of the four cross-cutting studies in this book of the mechanisms by which the spread of a single global trading, financial and cultural system affects self-determination movements. We show that the relationship is not simple, and that global hegemonic forces are effectively contested and undermined at the local level, while SDMs find ways to turn global tensions and rivalries to their own advantage. Our five country studies of the Democratic Republic of Congo, Somalia, Algeria, Burma, and Sri Lanka are not representative of all SDMs or even of their geographic spread. This is for two reasons: first, because the cases of the Balkans and Palestine have been studied in great depth in the academic and policy literatures; and second, because our chosen cases illustrate the central economic, social and cultural characteristics of self-determination and violent conflict in developing countries subject to the pressures and constraints of globalization. In consequence, it should be possible to generalize our findings to other regions.

In order to address such a complex issue, we have combined a number of scholarly disciplines and research methodologies. On the one hand, the research team combined backgrounds in development economics, social anthropology, political sociology and political science. On the other hand, we have combined selected country cases from across the globe with cross-cutting thematic studies of global influences. This approach has a number of obvious strengths, but we are also conscious of a number of problems that it creates in comparability, and in drawing simple inferences from our case studies. The various streams of academic literature on globalization that have emerged across the social sciences have developed quite distinct conceptual categories to address their specific theoretical, methodological, and empirical preoccupations. The explanation that follows of what we understand by key concepts such as 'self determination', 'globalization' and 'violence' thus serves to clarify not only the way they are used in this book, but also how distinct disciplinary approaches to these issues can be reconciled.

Self-determination

The concept of self-determination can be understood at two very different levels. The first is drawn from the reality of existing *movements* for self-determination, which have been among the most dynamic and important factors in the reshaping of world politics over the past century. The second relates to the way the term self-determination has itself been abstracted and interpreted, often with great ambiguity and inconsistency, within the conservative realm of international power politics and international law. Our focus here is predominantly on the former aspect, although the latter forms an important part of the global dimensions that we seek to explore.

We understand an SDM to be an organized popular movement which aims to institute fundamental structural changes bearing ideological, representational and/or territorial consequences for an existing state or states. This change may take the form either of the creation of a new sovereign state entity from within existing empires or multi-national states, or that of the substantial replacement of the constitutional structure and social functions of the state within its present territory. In many cases the two are combined.[1]

The first type relates to the issue of self-government for groups defined by distinct linguistic, cultural, ethnic or religious identities. For the most part, such SDMs have emerged either in the context of colonial rule or representing dissatisfied minority groups within large multi-ethnic states. The second type of 'replacement' refers to movements that seek to institute radical ideo-political transformations in societies that may or may not be already considered self-governing. During much of the twentieth century this form of self-determination involved revolutionary socialist movements that sought the transformation of state power in order to institute far-reaching socio-economic changes. Such movements continue to form the basis of a number of contemporary insurgent wars, for example in Colombia and Nepal. However, other types of 'replacement' have since arisen, and the end of the twentieth century was marked by the replacement of 'real socialism' by capitalism (Eastern Europe), the overthrow of dictatorships in favour of liberal democracy (Ukraine, Philippines, Chile) and the transformation of states that institutionalized the racial supremacy of a colonial–settler minority (South Africa, Zimbabwe). Finally, the establishment of theocratic states (Iran, Afghanistan) has returned as an objective, most vividly under the rubric of 'political Islam' in its many forms.

For both types, self-determination implies changes at the level of the state, not just a change of government. The very fundamental nature of the socio-political or territorial agenda of self-determination movements means that they are almost by definition pitted in sharp and often violent political conflict against an existing state or states. Indeed, unresolved disputes over self-determination have formed the basis for the vast majority of violent conflicts in the world since 1945, mostly in the developing regions of Asia, Africa and Latin America. Some examples of varying duration over these six decades are: Indonesia (1945–50), Vietnam (1948–75), Kenya (1952–6), Cuba (1952–9), Algeria (1954–62), Mozambique (1962–92), Angola (1962–02), Colombia (1964–), Nigeria (1967–70), East Pakistan (1971), Zimbabwe (1971–9), Ethiopia (1974–91) and Sri Lanka (1983–02). After the end of the cold war, such processes of self-determination and state-transformation in the developing world continued and even accelerated, as is evident in a number of new conflicts that have erupted since 1990, such as in Algeria (1992), Democratic Republic of Congo (1996), Chechnya (1994), various parts of Indonesia (1997) and Bolivia (2004).

As an explicitly recognized internationally legitimate claim, the concept of self-determination is usually attributed to US President Woodrow Wilson at the Versailles negotiations after the First World War. Self-determination was intended to be a new democratic principle for the definition of states and their political borders, in explicit contrast to territorial conquest, dynastic inheritance or diplomatic treaty, and was one of the cornerstones upon which the League of Nations was established. The League itself, of course, foundered on the reefs of renewed global war, but it did mark a clear historical break from the previous system of *de facto* recognition of territorial conquest by states independently of the wishes of the populations concerned. In the aftermath of the Second World War, the UN Charter recognized the 'principle' of self-determination and the duty to support legitimate claims. Later, the UN General Assembly Resolution on the Granting of Independence to Colonial Territories and Peoples (1960) made an even more explicit recognition of self-determination as a right under international law, further confirmed in subsequent covenants over the following decade.

However, these apparently radical advances in international law[2] had important limitations and ambiguities that meant that they were in effect extending support to only one category of SDM (anti-colonial movements), and that too, at a time when decolonization was already a *fait accompli*. Although 'all peoples' were held to have the right to self determination, there remains to this day no clear sense of who or what could comprise such a people, and which, if any, agency would enforce such a right. This ambiguity in itself did not lead to any subsequent clarification of the requisite criteria, but rather to a blanket limitation on the right to self-determination in cases where they interfered with the territorial integrity of existing states. In effect, the prestige of the title 'self-determination', and the weight of international legitimacy, support, and advocacy came to apply not to 'all peoples' as such, but to 'all territories'. Self-determination thus came to describe the formalistic process by which 'non-self governing territories' were converted into 'self-governing territories', irrespective of the depth of popular participation, or the extent of state transformation that this process actually embodied.

Since 1945, more than 80 territories held under colonial rule and trusteeship have achieved independence, and at the turn of the century, there remained only a handful of 'non-self governing territories' left on the agenda of the UN Decolonization Committee – most of which are small, thinly populated islands in the Caribbean and Pacific.[3] With the substantial completion of the decolonization process, the predominantly territorial aspect of self-determination has effectively been exhausted, and international law has come under pressure to reflect better the reality of actual SDMs and their demands.

The limitations imposed on the applicability of self-determination were first breached by the separation of Bangladesh from Pakistan in 1971, and then even more definitively by the unilateral declarations of independence by Yugoslavia's constituent units in 1991. Furthermore, with the dramatic change in the international superpower equation following the end of the cold war, the consensus on issues such as self-determination is shifting still further through the challenges to state sovereignty posed by the human rights agenda, the doctrines of humanitarian intervention and pre-emptive military action. We would also argue that this changing consensus and the reshaping of norms should take into account the claims of SDMs. As we shall argue in Chapter 11, these evolving issues are central to the policy proposals derived from our study.

Globalization and self-determination

Contemporary explanations for violent conflict have tended to be rooted in local events, often presented as the product of the economic aspirations of some and the losses of others ('greed and grievance')[4] or else simply ethnic rivalry.[5] When global developments are considered, it is cultural explanations that predominate in the so-called 'clash of civilisations'.[6] In contrast, we argue that both cultural and economic factors are involved, at both local and global levels, and that a better understanding of the relationship between globalization and self-determination is essential in order both to reduce the human costs of conflict and promote sustainable development.

While the external dimensions of an internal conflict are more readily visualized in terms of such diplomatic or military interventions by outside powers, localized conflicts are increasingly networked to the outside world through a plethora of less visible forms of external intervention.[7] We do not argue that such conflicts are uniquely and directly caused by globalization, but rather that it is essential to take the global into account in understanding contemporary conflicts and developing policies towards them.

We understand globalization as the process by which a single market system spreads across the world and integrates all societies into a single system of production and exchange. This process has been under way for many centuries, and was one of the main products of colonialism and imperialism. It was, however, interrupted for some seventy-five years between 1914 and 1989 by the two world wars and the installation of regimes antagonistic to this process from both the left and right of the political spectrum. In consequence, although the renewed integration process in recent decades is often seen as something new, in fact it is not.

This overtly economic process of globalization is most evident in patterns of trade and investment. Trade in goods is now virtually liberalized worldwide, with few import quotas and trade taxes remaining. A new system of international trade law and arbitration has been established under the auspices of the World Trade Organization to regulate this system, and all countries are now members or aspire to become so. There are of course exceptions, particularly in areas of interest to developing countries such as agricultural and textile products, where developed countries still protect their declining industries and low productivity employment. Interestingly, trade in services is less integrated because distinct legal and regulatory systems are exercized by national states, so that much of the integration in this field is in fact implemented thorough foreign investment.

A similar, but less institutionalized process is under way with respect to capital flows. The spread of multinational corporations out of their traditional natural resource enclaves in developing countries, into industry, banking, transport, public utilities and entertainment has made their presence much more apparent, and their influence on local societies much greater than in the past. There is no global regulator for this flow as there is for trade, but international financial institutions such as the International Monetary Fund, the World Bank and the Bank for International Settlements in effect ensure that capital is able to move freely and that investment contracts are enforced.[8] As in the case of trade, all countries are now committed to freedom of capital flows, although the degree of regulation varies with considerations such as national security and macroeconomic stability.

The implications of this renewed and accelerating globalization of trade and finance for SDMs are considerable. First, the establishment of a single world system of rules has the effect of constraining the ability of developing states to direct the domestic economy in support of their own legitimacy and stability, by protecting specific production sectors (and thus regions of the country) or directing public expenditure towards particular social groups. In the case of those middle-income countries classified as 'emerging markets' these rules are reinforced by the sensitivity of international capital flows to any policy not approved by the IMF. These constraints are strengthened by the conditionality imposed by 'donors' of development assistance led by the World Bank in the case of less-developed countries.

Second, the increased visibility of multinational corporations in developing countries and the support for liberalization from domestic elites tends to mobilize opposition among trades unions and small producers who are (or feel) threatened by the rapid modernization of production systems and the exposure to world markets. Third, the liberalization of world trade and reduced transport costs have also facilitated cross-border smuggling and international transactions in 'unregulated' products, ranging from narcotics and gems to arms and timber, creating a large and porous informal trading system in which SDMs can generate their own funds without relying on the exploitation of the local population. A similar process has taken place with financial flows, where unregulated channels such as offshore tax havens and informal transfer systems provide SDMs with the means to fund international operations.

The cultural dimension of globalization is closely linked to market integration. At the most immediate level, the spread of global consumer brands and explicitly cultural products has a direct and visible impact on local cultures. Such images also transform the aspirations of the young and portray a 'modern' view of social values – particularly gender roles. The communications technology revolution – first radio, then television and now the internet – allow people in developing countries not only to consume new images, information and ideas but also to communicate directly with the world without the intermediation of local authorities. This is not just an incidental product of economic globalization: it is a necessary foundation. Advertising is crucial to market integration and thus access to the media is intrinsic to globalization. The effect, in some cases, is to reduce the appeal of cultural nationalism – particularly among urban youth – and, in other cases, to intensify the attempt to protect 'traditional values'. This latter has been a potent source of legitimacy for some SDMs – particularly those associated with religious movements.

Because globalization is as much an ideological as an economic concept, for it to become legitimate – particularly in the form of open markets and liberal democracy – there must be a cultural shift in the national elite of developing countries, if not the population as a whole. Such a cultural shift does not occur naturally. To be effective, dedicated institutions such as universities, the media and international development agencies must deliberately transfer the new liberal economic doctrine.[9] This transfer generates social reactions rooted in the dislocations and vulnerability associated with globalization, which may take a variety of forms ranging from new political opposition movements to religious fundamentalism. These in turn cross frontiers and become in effect globalized through international non-governmental organizations (INGOs) which have become the main 'informal' and unregulated transmission mechanisms for non-hegemonic ideas. These INGOs, of course, include not only those concerned with poverty reduction and human rights, but also religious organizations and political parties, and have become a vital link between SDMs and the outside world.

Finally, while the market in goods, capital and ideas has become increasingly globalized, the global labour market is still very asymmetric. Fundamentally, there is global freedom of movement for citizens of industrialized economies only. However, the domestic elites of poorer countries can and do send their children to study abroad, and they can then move freely if they become employees of multinational corporations or international agencies. The poor cannot move so easily, except as temporary workers to a limited number of richer countries, although the informal flow of international 'economic' migrants is clearly increasing. Although the flows of 'forced migrants' from conflict zones are allowed to move on humanitarian grounds, the vast majority of these only reach neighbouring poor countries. Nonetheless, the accumulated size of these 'diaspora communities' is considerable both in developed countries and within developing regions. These communities provide a means for SDMs not only to raise funds but also to get information to the press and civil society in other countries.

In sum, the political history of SDMs is bound up with the successive geopolitical phases of colonialism, cold war and the present unipolar hegemony. This last would seem to have reduced the space for self-determination. In contrast, the process of economic globalization seems to have the opposite effect. It tends to strengthen SDMs both by weakening the ability of the state to control its own economy and by providing means of funding armed conflict and generating international political support. However, by generating spontaneous yet complex popular reaction to change through the spread of universal cultural concepts such as human rights, democratic representation and gender equality on the one hand, and through defensive response to the impact of global culture on local values on the other, the cultural effect of globalization on SDMs is more ambiguous.

The changing role of violence in self-determination movements

We have sought to direct the analytical focus of our study to those cases where movements for self-determination are combined with situations of violent conflict. While these share many of the characteristics of those operating in more peaceful environments, the atmosphere of violent conflict and civil war significantly affects the character and operations of many self-determination movements: for example, much of their political and economic activity is illegal and underground; they generate special financial needs for the support of military activities; they generally give rise to forced migration which leads to diasporas; and they have a more disruptive economic and social impact.

Almost all political conflicts relating to self-determination in developing countries are embroiled in violent conflict, or contain a latent potential for an escalation to violence – hence our focus on this phenomenon. Our understanding of violence in this context is not restricted to killing or wounding (whether of civilians or soldiers) or indeed the use of arms, but extends to the coercion of civilians by threat of force, imprisonment or even starvation to do the bidding of particular groups – whether by the incumbents of the state apparatus or those in opposition to it. This violence is by definition non-democratic but can exist in nominal democracies where representation – or even basic human rights – is denied to particular subordinate groups. Indeed, self-determination movements are often excluded *ab initio* from the political process, or become so because the majority (or even a minority) consider their claims for autonomy to be illegitimate, 'unconstitutional' and 'unpatriotic'. Thus violence – real or potential, by state or opposition – is likely to occur among self-determination movements.

Violent conflicts over self-determination in developing countries do not involve formal military operations in the usual sense of pitched battles for specific territorial positions and the objective of forcing formal military surrender of the enemy. They are thus not easily fitted into the formal rules of war established in international law in general and the Geneva Conventions in particular. Armed conflict in developing countries today – leaving aside military intervention by foreign powers – involves lightly armed ground troops in small units, few if any pitched battles and extensive involvement of civilians and paramilitaries on both sides. These wars are relatively inexpensive in the sense that weapons are assault rifles and mortars, communications technology is based on cellular phones, transport relies on civilian-type vehicles and both sides 'live off the land' to a considerable extent. The main victims are civilians, but not (apart from some thankfully rare incidents of genocide) by direct involvement, but mainly through hunger and sickness due to the disappearance of commercial networks, forced migration and the collapse of public services.[10]

These 'low intensity conflicts' may seem like a new phenomenon to aid agencies and academics whose point of reference is the Second World War. But they were well known as 'small wars' by colonial administrators (in order to distinguish them from 'proper wars' between the Great Powers) before 1939, and as 'counter-insurgency' during the cold war. Moreover in developing countries (as in developed countries in the past) everyday life is intrinsically violent, and the borderline between 'peace' and 'conflict' is thin and hazy. Over a lifetime, a person's direct experience of violence may cover the whole spectrum from robbery and rape, through forced eviction from land and housing, and police repression of strikes and demonstrations, to military coups and regional uprisings to full-scale civil war and foreign intervention. Only this last pair is usually classed as 'conflict' by researchers, but from the point of view of ordinary people (both rich and poor) violence and the threat of violence is an endemic aspect of social and political relations.

We obviously reject the simplistic view that all political violence is irrational (or criminal and simply motivated by personal gain) but we have tried to avoid the opposite danger of seeing it in merely instrumental terms as a Clausewitzian extension of politics by another means. This is for two reasons. First, because the use of violence by an SDM or incumbent state is never a simple choice or even strategy – rather, it is the outcome of specific historical circumstances that build up over time to produce (and legitimize) the armed confrontation. Second, because violence cannot be employed by either side without a considerable degree of social support – in the form of either political legitimacy for military repression by the incumbent or the provision of support networks for the rebels. It is true that any one point in time both sides may choose non-violent or violent means to pursue their ends, but effectiveness of either depends on specific circumstances.

Violence has generally been central to the construction of 'national' cultures. In the history of almost all societies (European ones in particular)[11] the imagined national identity is closely related to a collective picture of a violent past, whether as state expansion, collective defeat or individual heroism. In SDMs as well as national liberation movements and anti-colonial struggles, military gestures and selfless martyrs are usually an integral part of the iconography, literature and songs passed on from one generation to the next. It is essential therefore not to underestimate the symbolic role of violence, which often has a far greater political effect than any direct military damage. On the one hand, dramatic acts of violence against the state – of which the attacks on the Twin Towers and Pentagon are only the latest examples – are intended to undermine the sense of invulnerability of those in power and hearten the opposition. On the other hand similarly symbolic acts of torture and repression – of which Abu Ghraib and Guantanamo are only the latest in a long tradition – are intended to do the exact opposite.[12] Both have been illuminatingly termed 'the theatre of violence'.[13]

The persistent use of violence clearly has a corrupting effect on both sides in the conflict for a number of reasons. The sense of impunity generated by the repeated breaking of social rules can frequently become a justification for criminal behaviour and repressive leadership within both state and SDM. The individuals concerned become psychologically conditioned to violent behaviour, which they find difficult to abandon subsequently. Last but not least, the mounting toll of victims on both sides makes it difficult to agree to a compromise settlement that might, as it were, betray the dead.

It is, of course, the case that 'non-violent' movements based on mass mobilization and civil disobedience can be very effective in achieving change, but this is only true when the incumbent state is already very weak and unable to repress the movement, or where in fact only a change in government (as opposed to a major social change or a territorial separation) is involved. Important examples in recent decades have been the collapse of communist regimes in Central Europe on the one hand and the transition from military dictatorship to parliamentary democracy in Latin America on the other. However, in the case of territorial separation in particular, the armed forces will usually defend the status quo even if they will not defend a particular government, because their own corporate cohesion and identity are in question. Again, while the regime change itself can be relatively peaceful, it is usually preceded by armed conflict, which has resolved the issue by making change inevitable – as in the case of South Africa.

Moreover, there is some reason to believe that the role of violence in SDMs has changed in recent times. The Enlightenment concept of human rights has been a long time in taking root, but has gradually spread from the industrialized democracies to the developing world – and to the interventions of the former in the latter. The establishment of the United Nations was a key step in this process, and the recent international recognition of human rights over and above state rights has profound implications for the use of violence by SDMs.[14] While the cold war (and now the 'war on terror') made progress difficult, the defence of human rights has increasingly been taken up by non-governmental organizations, trades unions and other social organizations. This has undoubtedly curtailed the ability of many governments to use overt violence against civilians, and limited the legitimacy of SDMs to do the same. In this context, the modernization and globalization of the media – starting with the radio but particularly television and internet – have allowed such human rights pressure to be exercised more effectively. On the one hand, television – much more than newspapers, its predecessor in this respect – has allowed the nature of violence to be conveyed dramatically and directly to voters in the industrialized countries. On the other hand, the internet – whose predecessor in this context was the radio – has allowed SDMs and other subordinate groups in developing countries to communicate directly with other news media, and indeed with the electorate of the developed world. This means that acts of violence by either side can be used as propaganda almost in real time.

From global to local

In Chapter 2, an overview on the global economic dimensions of self-determination, Stewart examines how the global economy interacts with the fundamental political causes of SDMs, and the subsequent effects of the global economy on the resourcing of conflict. Two opposing views are considered: that globalization reduces the probability of conflict due to the economic opportunities it offers to opposing groups and the democratization that international culture promotes; or that globalization promotes conflict due to the economic marginalization of groups without financial or human capital, and the reduced ability of the state to redistribute resources domestically. She concludes that globalization has both positive and negative effects, but the balance varies in different parts of the world, so that those areas that have been negatively affected have seen high and rising levels of violent conflict. Moreover, the growth of the global economy generally provides easier access by contending parties to arms and finance through diverse sources such as natural resource rents, emergency aid and diaspora remittances.

Economic conditions of stagnation, high inequality, widespread unemployment, and cutbacks in social services occurred in many countries: but not all experienced violent conflict. Where they did so, it was generally because cultural, political and ideological factors were also present, serving to mobilize large numbers of people. Strong and developing horizontal inequalities – where the gains from aid, natural resources or growth are unevenly distributed among different groups – have been particularly likely to generate violent conflict. Stewart notes that international efforts have been mainly targeted at the interdiction of financial resources such as 'conflict diamonds', with less attention to addressing fundamental economic factors such as economic stagnation, poverty and inequality. Measures to control the financial sources are not only inherently difficult to institute and monitor, but they are highly unlikely to be effective in preventing or stopping SDMs without measures to address the structural causes of conflict.

In Chapter 3, Dudley and Lloyd consider the principal 'pathways' for global influences on SDMs, including diasporas, transnational movements and the global media. The objectives and methods of SDMs are continually being redefined and renegotiated. Crucial to this process are power, education, language and culture that together shape the channels through which ideas about identity and purpose are communicated. Migration and transnational solidarities, strengthened by the new media, are pathways of multidirectional cultural influence between the local, regional and global. They suggest that although the pathways themselves are broadly common to all SDMs, the global cultural influences that travel along them are myriad, while the self-image and contested vision of the world constructed by the SDMs themselves is similarly complex. Dudley and Lloyd show that an essential component of this self-image is the notion of a shared bond of suffering. Nationalism and religion exert a powerful hold over certain social groups and play a key role in these processes of identity formation and reformation. They can also have major impact upon how outsiders conceive and interact with members of SDMs, and thus ultimately upon the strategy and trajectory of SDMs themselves. Global media networks thus play important roles in this process of SDM identity formation by shaping perceptions of, and responses to, SDMs in a transnational context, and thus become in turn the object of political control by powerful states.

FitzGerald explores conflict finance further in Chapter 4, examining the difficulties experienced by the international community in policing such flows due to systemic features inherent in the global financial system. Conflict-related funds are easily transmitted within international unregulated (or 'informal') systems, such as offshore financial centres used by global wealth holders and *hawala* transfer networks that service expatriate and migrant worker populations. There also exist numerous weak links – such as correspondent banks – within the regulated financial networks that have historically been exploited for money laundering and other clandestine 'civil' purposes, and also thus provide cover for conflict finance.

In the period following the 9/11 attacks in the USA, international regulatory authorities sought to monitor both formal and informal networks as a means to interdict potential terrorist finances, imposing much more stringent reporting requirements on financial institutions. However, FitzGerald shows that systemic features of the international financial system resulting from the process of globalization render this effort ineffective. Multilateral regulatory efforts in this direction have had limited success largely because of the economic disincentives involved in the disclosure of transactions by wealthy individuals (who seek to evade tax) and the high cost of international banking to migrant workers (who use informal transfer mechanisms) – both of which, along with the narcotics and arms trades, underpin the 'global informal financial sector' within which clandestine conflict funding can move. Established and broad-based SDMs with known and visible international networks of sympathisers and representatives are a much easier target for financial interdiction – which leads in turn to undemocratic governments exploiting the tide of international anti-terrorism in order to neutralize popular opposition movements.

In Chapter 5 Venugopal shows how the profusion of state collapse and civil wars since the end of the cold war has been largely blamed on internal causes, or due to an absence of adequate external integration or intervention. Instead, he argues that such conflicts should be viewed as a result of the way in which countries and groups have been integrated into the global system. First, global circumstances and developments can contribute towards (or inhibit) the rise and sustenance of self-determination movements through economic, cultural, ideological, or other means. Second, the global dimensions of self-determination relate to how the actual content of statehood is defined, fashioned and constrained globally in economic, political and normative terms, and how this in turn determines the shape and scope of self-determination movements. The first mechanism is illustrated by the case of Colombia, where the dynamics of a long-standing rural insurgency are closely embedded within the global drug economy and global political–military interventions. The second is exemplified by East Timor, which underwent 'self-determination from above' under UN auspices, followed by the construction of new state institutions by the international aid community.

From local to global

In contrast to the first five chapters, designed to assess the importance of global influences on SDMs, the next five contain in-depth country studies designed to distinguish external from internal factors and thus understand how the interaction between the global and the local works out in different historical contexts. The five case studies – three in Africa and two in Asia – were chosen in order to reflect the multiple dimensions of SDMs, including: religious (Algeria) and ethnic (Sri Lanka, Burma) drivers in strong states; weak states that have broken up (Somalia) or survived (Congo); and the quest for democratic representation (Algeria, Burma). To the extent that these countries have all been exposed to broadly similar global economic and cultural forces, these case studies allow us to identify the interaction between these forces and domestic dynamics.

In Chapter 6, on the Democratic Republic of Congo, Englebert explores the relationship between global norms and self-determination by examining the paradox of the Congolese state. Despite a history of secessionist insurgencies with numerous ethnic divisions, the military occupation of large areas by regional powers, and a bankrupt state offering almost no public services, security or economic development there are as yet no serious movements that seek to pursue political independence either through secession or fundamental replacement. Rather, a fragile state persists and is reproduced in weak, dysfunctional form. It lacks authority or territorial control and yet it still commands the support both of predatory political elites and the large mass of Congolese.

The explanation Englebert suggests for this paradox lies in global cultural norms of statehood and global flows of aid and investment. Despite lacking territorial control or functioning institutions, the Congolese state continues to enjoy the prerogatives of international recognition, and the attendant benefits of a sovereign state. Sovereignty grants the weak state a powerful source of external legitimacy that is a valuable resource for state elites as it both provides them with access to foreign aid and legitimizes their plunder of Congo's resources, obviating the need to cultivate domestic legitimacy. Ethnic elites realize that they stand little chance of gaining international recognition for a secessionist state, and have instead found it more beneficial to negotiate for the spoils arising from the monetization of international sovereignty within a weak state. Thus, the violent conflicts in the Congo's periphery revolve around the terms of the rebels' integration with the state rather than over the nature or composition of the state itself.

Does the example of Congo suggest that there is a trade-off between external recognition and internal substance? In Chapter 7, Reno presents a compelling counter-factual to the Congo that might answer this question in the affirmative. Following the violent collapse of Somalia in 1991, the south remained embroiled in violence and uncertainty while an apparently enduring, stable and peaceful political authority has arisen in the far north under the self-declared state of Somaliland. What accounts for these divergent post-collapse outcomes?

Reno argues that Somaliland's success in re-establishing order is due precisely to its marginality in the colonial and post-colonial periods. The continuing violence in the south is a legacy of the centralized patronage politics of the 1970s and 1980s, based on the selective distribution of economic opportunities arising from the export trade and foreign aid. But northern entrepreneurs and clan leaders remained largely marginalized from the failing regime's political and economic networks. Consequently, northern clan leaders were forced to preserve local sources of legitimacy that later proved useful in exerting authority over armed groups. Northern entrepreneurs developed clandestine business opportunities outside the regime's patronage networks, and forged early links with local clan leaders and local armed groups to protect themselves. Reno argues that the differences between the north and south relate to the social control of violence and economic opportunity. International economic links can be disruptive to this relationship as can international mediation efforts.

In Chapter 8 Lloyd identifies two distinct forms of cultural global influence in Algeria as new axes of conflict opened between the West and the Muslim world after the cold war. On the one hand, the world-wide movement of political Islam inspired and sustained the rise of the *Front Islamique du Salut* (FIS). On the other, Western (predominantly French) identities influenced the perceptions, objectives and actions of both the military backed government and the ethnic Berber movement. Algeria's search for a post-colonial and post-cold war identity has thus engendered tensions that cannot be understood without reference to these global forces. Gender relations, language and religion all reinforce the cultural roots of conflict; but behind these lies an acute economic crisis. Algeria's vast gas and oil resources have cushioned the regime but the impact of rapid demographic growth and economic liberalization on youth unemployment and reduced standards of living for unskilled groups have proved fertile ground for mobilizing protest.

Lloyd demonstrates that global cultural forces heavily influence the identities constructed or strengthened by local leaders in Algeria. The single most important global cultural force has been political Islam, which spread through a variety of 'informal' channels, such as Standard Arabic teachers from Egypt who were influenced by the Muslim Brotherhood. However, while culture and ideology defined the contested arenas of conflict, popular disillusion arising from mass unemployment and deterioration of social and economic conditions undermined the legitimacy of the regime and thus its ability to contain or resolve these conflicts.

The problematic impact of external sources of legitimacy upon domestic actors also informs Dudley's analysis of the relationship between the state and the pro-democracy movement in Burma in Chapter 9. Since the cancellation of the 1988 election results, Burma's military government has come under world-wide condemnation, while the opposition pro-democracy movement has enjoyed strong world-wide recognition and support: its leader, Daw Aung Sang Suu Kyi, has become a global media icon. The growth of electronic media and the expansion of international civil society groups in the past decade have fuelled international activism from exiled Burmese and non-Burmese solidarity activists against the military regime. In response the Burmese government has sought to capitalize on the international popularity and legitimacy of their opponents by stigmatizing them as foreign in inspiration and support.

Dudley also discusses the role of international non-governmental organizations on Burma's ethnic separatist movement, particularly with respect to refugee camps on Burma's borders. Foreign aid workers in these camps have provided refugee populations with a window to the outside world that has heightened awareness of their own identity and of their place in the larger world. The presence of INGOs lends authority and legitimacy to the Karenni political groups in charge of the camps, while on a more subtle level it is influencing and changing the perceptions of what it means to be Karenni. Paradoxically, the spread of electronic media has increased the distance between those outside groups who have gained legitimacy from it and those on the inside who lack almost all access to world opinion and support.

In Chapter 10, Venugopal shows how the ethnic conflict in Sri Lanka spanned a number of distinct historical phases in global and regional politics, all of which played an important role in its dynamic. He locates the trajectory of the conflict within different phases in the integration of the Sri Lankan economy into the global market, from the dirigisme of 1956–77 to the subsequent market reforms of the 1980s, and the way that these have affected the advancement of the political conflict through a variety of mechanisms. The Sri Lankan conflict was also affected by regional developments in the South Asian subcontinent in a number of ways, particularly in the 1970s and 1980s. In 1971, India's support for the secession of East Pakistan changed the geopolitics of South Asia, and triggered anticipation that a similar scenario could unfold for Sri Lanka's Tamils, who enjoyed close cultural ties with India's much larger Tamil population. With the onset of civil war in 1983, hundreds of thousands of Tamil refugees sought refuge in India, and this led to a massive escalation of India's role in the conflict – both as war-maker and peace-maker – that ended in much rancour in 1990.

In the post-cold war period, India's abrupt withdrawal from Sri Lanka dramatically changed the internal and external dimensions. For this entire period, the remaining Tamil insurgent organization, the Liberation Tigers of Tamil Eelam (LTTE) survived without any overt state patronage by tapping into new sources of external economic, diplomatic and military support. An important element was the huge Sri Lankan Tamil diaspora, accounting for almost a quarter of all Sri Lankan Tamils, comprising substantial communities in countries such as Canada, Britain, USA, France and Australia. At the same time, the Sri Lankan government worked hard to disrupt the LTTE's external network and has benefited more recently from the growing force of international anti-terrorism, as a result of which the LTTE was proscribed in the US and UK.

The international policy response to self-determination and violent conflict

As the previous two sections have demonstrated, the studies in this book are designed to assess the importance of global influences on violent SDMs, to explore the mechanisms through which these influences operate, and to analyse the interaction between the economic and the cultural. However, our aim as researchers is not just to establish the truth – or at least a convincing version of it – but also to identify realistic policies that are derived from our findings and that might reduce the human costs among vulnerable peoples in countries and regions with contested SDMs. Global influences are already so pervasive – or to put it another way, SDMs form such an integral part of the global polity – that we cannot frame international policies in terms either of avoiding any global influence, or only in terms of local outcomes.

A new approach is thus likely to require both institutional reforms and changed objectives at the global level and these are the topic of the concluding chapter of this book. Chapter 11 argues that although local conditions are critical in the development of SDMs, global forces – economic and cultural – condition the resulting trajectory as much as overt political or military interventions, even though the latter have appeared to be dominant since 9/11. Potentially, global actors can help contain and channel the conflicts over self-determination towards less violent means, and reduce the incidence of violence on the poor and vulnerable. But this will require major changes in international institutions, particularly a more central role for the United Nations as the only representative global institution. Above all we argue that it will be necessary to influence attitudes and beliefs in the North as well as the South, and to do so requires challenging official discourse and shifting the dominant paradigm, a long-term task which has as much to do with education and culture as with policy choice and global governance.

Notes

1. For instance, the indigenous movement in the Andes is mobilized around both the creation of separate territorial state (*Collasuyo* – one of the regions of the Inca empire comprising parts of Bolivia, Peru, Argentina and Chile) and a distinct social, economic and political organization based on pre-capitalist communitarian principles.
2. On this complex topic, see Dixon (1993), Duursma (1996) and Falk (2002).
3. With the notable exception of Western Sahara.
4. See Keen (1998), Berdal and Malone (2000), Collier and Hoeffler (2000).
5. DfID (2001).
6. Huntington (1996).
7. Such as those mapped by Duffield (2001) or Kaldor (1999).
8. See FitzGerald (2001).
9. For a study in depth of how liberal economic doctrine has been transmitted over the last two centuries in Latin America and then contested and embedded, see FitzGerald and Thorp (2005).
10. See Stewart and FitzGerald (2000).
11. Schoolbook 'national heroes' such as Washington and Lincoln, or Nelson and Wellington, or Napoleon and de Gaulle were all military commanders of course.
12. The bombing campaign against Iraq before the 2003 invasion was officially named 'Shock and Awe' (Woodward 2004).
13. See Foster and others (2005) on this interpretation of violence in South Africa.
14. It also has profound implications for the role of international organizations in protecting the victims of conflict, as we shall argue in Chapter 11.

References

Berdal, M. and D. Malone (2000) *Greed and Grievance: Economic Agendas in Civil Wars*. Boulder, CO: Lynne Rienner.

Collier, P. and A. Hoeffler (2000) 'Greed and Grievance in Civil War', Washington, DC: World Bank.

DfID (2001) *The Causes of Conflict in Sub-Saharan Africa*. London: Department for International Development.

Dixon, M. (1993) *Textbook on International Law*. London: Blackstone Press.

Duffield, M. (2001) *Global Governance and the New Wars*. London: Zed.

Duursma, J. C. (1996) *Fragmentation and the International Relations of Micro-States: Self-Determination and Statehood*. Cambridge: Cambridge University Press.

Falk, R. (2002) 'Self-Determination under International Law' in W. Danspeckgruber (ed.) *The Self-Determination of Peoples: Community, Nation and State in an Interdependent World*. Boulder, CO: Lynne Rienner.

FitzGerald, V. (2001) 'Developing Countries and Multilateral Investment Negotiations' in E. C. Nieuwenhuys and M. M. T. A. Brus (eds) *Multilateral Regulation of Investment*. The Hague: Kluwer Law Internatonal.

FitzGerald, V. and R. Thorp (eds) (2005) *Economic Doctrines in Latin America*. Basingstoke: Palgrave Macmillan.

Foster, D. P. Haupt and M. de Beer (2005) *The Theatre of Violence*. Cape Town: Institute for Justice and Reconciliation, and Oxford: James Currey.

Huntington, S. P. (1996) *The Clash of Civilizations and the Remaking of World Order*. New York: Simon & Schuster.

Kaldor, M. (1999) *New and Old Wars: Organized Violence in a Global Era*. Stanford, CA: Stanford University Press.
Keen, D. (1998) *The Economic Functions of Violence in Civil Wars*. Oxford: Oxford University Press for the International Institute for Strategic Studies.
Stewart, F. and V. FitzGerald (2000) *War and Underdevelopment Vol. I*. Oxford: Oxford University Press.
Woodward, B. (2004) *Plan of Attack*. New York: Simon & Schuster.

2

Global Economic Influences and Policies towards Violent Self-Determination Movements: An Overview

Frances Stewart[1]

Introduction

This chapter explores the major global economic influences on violent self-determination movements and identifies policies which might help reduce the incidence of violence. Two types of global economic influence are analyzed, one longer term, the other short-term: the first covers the way global economic forces may contribute to, or moderate, underlying causes of violence; the second consists in the processes by which the global economic and financial system facilitates and motivates violent movements, once conflict has broken out, through trade and finance.

Most policy has been directed towards the shorter-term factors – the way the system facilitates violence through trade and finance. Less attention has been paid to the way global influences affect the long-term propensity to violence. Yet these long-term aspects are of more fundamental importance, since as long as they continue eruptions of violent conflict will continue; global efforts to cut off the oxygen of finance and trade are not likely to be effective in the long run if the more fundamental causes remain.

The first section of this chapter reviews the various hypotheses that have been advanced as to the major long-term economic causes of large-scale violent conflict. The next section considers how these are affected by global economic forces; the following section analyses major global economic factors that facilitate wars in the shorter term by financing and motivating them, and policies towards these factors. The final section considers the nature of global policies likely to moderate the long-term causes of violent struggles for self-determination.

Fundamental economic causes of violent conflict

Three economic hypotheses that have been put forward to explain current intra-state wars are: group motivation associated with group inequalities; private motivation and incentives; and a failure of the social contract, stemming from economic failure and poor government services.

Group motivation

Group motives, resentments and ambitions form one of the basic motivations for struggles for self-determination (Horowitz 1985; Gurr 1993; Stewart 2001, 2002). Resentments that lead to violent conflict frequently arise in situations where cultural divisions based on ethnicity, race, or religion coincide with sharp economic and political differences. As Cohen (1974) stated:

> Men may and do certainly joke about or ridicule the strange and bizarre customs of men from other ethnic groups... But they do not fight over such differences alone. When men *do*... fight across ethnic lines it is nearly always the case that they fight over some fundamental issues concerning the distribution and exercise of power, whether economic, political, or both.

Group differences of an economic, political and social nature, termed *horizontal inequalities*, thus can form a fundamental cause of war. These are often provoked by the relative deprivation suffered by individual groups, but can also arise from relatively privileged groups who fight in order to protect their position (Horowitz 1985). There is abundant case study evidence showing the existence of sharp horizontal inequalities between groups in conflict (Nafziger, Stewart *et al.* 2000). Horizontal inequalities appear to be most likely to lead to conflict where they are significant, consistent across dimensions, and widening over time. Gurr (1993) and Ostby (2004) have provided supporting evidence using international data, Barrows (1976) provides evidence for a group of African countries, and Mancini (2005) shows a statistically significant relationship between some socio-economic HIs and conflict across districts in Indonesia. Case studies suggest that HIs are particularly likely to lead to violence where political exclusion accompanies economic inequality (Langer 2005).

Private motivation

War confers *benefits* on individuals, as well as costs. The 'private motivation' hypothesis argues that the net economic advantages of war to particular individuals motivates them to fight (Keen 1994, 1998; Collier and Hoeffler 2000). Keen (1998) lists many ways in which war confers individual benefits. For example, it provides employment for soldiers and offers opportunities to loot and profiteer from shortages and from relief aid, to trade arms, and to carry out illicit production and trade in drugs, diamonds, timber and other commodities. The 'greed' hypothesis of Collier and Hoeffler suggests that the incidence and duration of wars is greater where alternative opportunities are few and the possibilities of enrichment by war considerable (Hirshleifer 1994; Collier and Hoeffler 2000).

Individual motivation is rarely the main explanation of conflicts over self-determination. Although the achievement of greater autonomy can be expected to generate some economic advantages, such gains are usually remote considering the costs inflicted by the conflict. Moreover, greed is essentially individualistic and therefore unlikely to provide sustained support for a lengthy struggle fought by groups with political objectives.

Private profiteering does play a role in most conflicts, while it is dominant in some situations, as case studies of the Sudan, Sierra Leone, and Liberia (Reno 1998; Keen 1994; Keen 2001a,b) describe very powerfully. For example, Reno (2000) has argued that in weak states as official revenue falls and patronage politics is thereby weakened, control over natural resources becomes a new source of patronage, and the struggle for control of natural resources consequently becomes a driving force for war. A UN Report found that conflict in the DRC 'has become mainly about access, control and trade of five key mineral resources: coltan, diamonds, copper, cobalt and gold'. (UN, 2001). However, Guttierez (2005) has shown that most leaders and foot soldiers in Colombia did not improve their economic positions by joining the armed struggle. Collier and Hoeffler test the 'greed' hypothesis, with a rather crude measure of resource riches and find a significant association with conflict,[2] which peaks at an intermediate level.[3] De Soysa and Neumayer (2003) find that while the overall per capita availability of natural resources is unrelated to civil war, a highly significant association is found when only mineral resources are included.

Failure of the social contract

This argument derives from the view that social stability is premised on a social contract between the people and the government. People accept state authority so long as the state delivers services and provides reasonable economic conditions (employment and incomes). With economic stagnation, decline and worsening state services such as in failing states (for example, Vayrynen 2000), the social contract breaks down, and promotes the rise of violent conflict. Hence high (and rising) levels of poverty and a decline in state services would be expected to cause conflict (Nafziger and Auvinen 2000). A general indicator of a failed state is a low level of revenue. For example, Uganda's revenue declined to 5 per cent of GDP during the Amin years – but we should note that, as with many other variables, this is as much a result as a cause of violence.

A breakdown of the social contract can be a powerful motive for both types of self-determination struggle – as people seek self-determination or

Table 2.1 Variables associated with violent conflict

Economic variable associated with conflict	*Evidence of association with conflict*	*Hypotheses*
Decline/stagnation in per capita incomes	Cross-country and case study support	Failure of social contract; environmental degradation; low opportunity costs of war – private motive.
Horizontal inequality	Cross-country and case study support	Group motives for conflict (horizontal inequalities)
Vertical inequality	Conflicting evidence	Failure of social contract
High poverty	Same evidence as for per capita incomes	Failure of social contract.
Reduced government revenue and social expenditure	Case study evidence. Limited statistical investigation. No evidence for association with IMF programmes	Failure of social contract; weak government ability to suppress conflict – failed state.
High levels of natural resources	Support for mineral resources only	Private motives (and financing)

control over the state to replace what appears as a dysfunctional exercise of power. This is a convincing explanation of the breakdown in consensus in Algeria (Roberts 2001).

Considerable evidence from econometric studies shows that conflict incidence is higher among countries with lower per capita incomes, life expectancy and economic growth (Nafziger and Auvinen 2000; Elbadawi and Sambanis 2002; Collier and Hoeffler 2000). Yet numerous statistical investigations of the association between vertical income distribution and conflict produce inconsistent results (Lichbach 1989; Nafziger and Auvinen 2000; Collier and Hoeffler 2000).

Table 2.1 provides a summary of the variables that are associated with each hypothesis. The next section will consider how these variables are affected by globalisation.

How global influences affect the fundamental economic causes of conflict

At a general level, two contradictory views have been advanced on the connection between *globalization* (that is, the growth of global influences, particularly through greater international trade, financial flows and increasing global communication) and the incidence of conflict. On the one hand the neo-liberal view is that globalization reduces the likelihood of conflict because it raises incomes and spreads democratization (Hegre and Gleditsch 2001). On the other hand, it is argued that globalization increases inequality and marginalization, while greater emphasis on local identities is likely to occur as a reaction to cultural homogenization, making internal wars more likely (Duffield 2001). According to Willett:

> *one* of the major structural causes of current patterns of violence and conflict is to be found in the general failure of neoliberal policies, underpinning the current phase of globalisation, to deliver more equitable patterns of development to large parts of the world. (Willett 2001, p. 36)

Before commenting on these contradictory positions, we will discuss how global influences affect the variables identified above as being associated with conflict.

Income growth

In general evidence suggests that slow growth (and especially economic stagnation) is likely to be associated with a higher propensity to conflict. The uneven growth rates among countries across the world, all facing broadly the same global environment, show that the impact of global influences depends in part on conditions and policies within countries. Despite this, attempts have been made to reach some general conclusions regarding the impact of increased globalization on economic growth in two ways: by comparing the growth rates of countries with different degrees of openness, and by looking at the growth record over time, with particular emphasis on the post-1980 period when the rate of globalization accelerated.

Some empirical assessments have concluded that greater openness leads to faster growth, for example Sachs and Warner (1995). The methodology of this and other studies, however, has been effectively criticised by Rodriguez and Rodrik (1999), particularly in relation to the measure of openness. A cross-section study by Rodrik (1997) of the relationship between capital market liberalization in developing countries, 1975–1989, and per capita GDP growth rate found no relationship.

Evidence of change in growth rates over time does not support the view that increased globalization has been associated with increasing growth rates – in fact the reverse seems true, with the growth rates of the 1980s and 1990s significantly less than in the previous more inward-looking decades (Table 2.2). A slowdown occurred in all regions of the world, with the important exceptions of India and China, the two largest countries, where growth accelerated. In Sub-Saharan Africa there was a serious deterioration in growth in many countries. Only eight countries increased their growth

Table 2.2 Global growth rates: 1965 2000

Region	*Growth in GDP*		
	1965–1980	*1980–1990*	*1990–1999*
World	4.1	3.4	2.5
Low-income economies		4.7	3.2
Low-income economies, ex-India and China	4.8	2.9	
China	6.8	10.1	10.7
India	3.6	5.8	6.0
Middle income economies	6.3	3.3	3.5
Latin America	6.0	1.7	3.4
Sub-Saharan Africa	4.2	1.7	2.2
South Asia	3.6	5.6	5.6
East Asia and Pacific	7.3	8.0	7.5
High-income economies	3.8	3.4	2.3

Source: World Bank, World Development Indicators (UNDP 2001).

rate in the period 1980–2000 compared with 1965–1980 while 25 experienced a worsening. Particularly serious was the fact that two-thirds of the countries had falling per capita incomes in the latter period. While many countries in the region suffered severe conflict over these years, and their poor growth performance is partly due to this, the growth rate of quite a number of countries without significant conflict deteriorated, partly as a consequence of worsening commodity prices and tough adjustment policies – for example, Kenya, Malawi and Zambia.

Globalization thus has clearly had mixed effects on growth: it has enabled some parts of the world to grow rapidly, as they can borrow internationally, attract foreign investment and sell their goods on the world market. Yet, in a large number of poor countries, globalization has been associated with worsening commodity prices, rising debt, declining industry and falling incomes. It is precisely in these areas that conflict has been particularly likely to break out. While global forces can take much credit for the economic successes of South and East Asia, those same forces have been associated with prolonged economic failure in many other countries, which then become more vulnerable to conflict. There then follows a vicious cycle as conflict worsens economic regression.

Inequality

Violent SDMs could arise as a result both of rising horizontal and of worsening vertical inequality. Rising horizontal inequality acts as a powerful incentive for groups to seek independence, or control over the state; while increasing vertical inequality can give rise to movements that seek transformation of the state in order to promote redistribution of assets (as in the case of land distribution in Colombia and Zimbabwe).

The era of accelerated globalization has been associated with rising vertical inequality in the majority of individual countries (Wade 2001; Cornia 2004). In general, the evidence suggests that more open economies and ones with greater foreign direct investment tend to have rising inequality (Lundberg *et al.* 2000; Wang 2001). Although, the question of whether there has been a parallel rise in horizontal inequality has been less well-researched, there is accumulating evidence that globalization contributes to rising horizontal inequality. Horizontal inequalities generally have their origin in historic circumstances – often colonial policy which privileged some groups over others. An initial advantage then leads to long-term cumulative advantage, as resources and education allow the more privileged groups to secure further advantages. In many contexts, particular regions (often associated with particular ethnic groups) gain cumulative advantage. In general, increasing global opportunities increase such horizontal inequality, as any group or region with an initial advantage (for example, of education or location) finds this accentuated by global competition. For example, in South-East Asia, ethnic Chinese minorities have historically accumulated educational and entrepreneurial advantages that can be further exploited in the global economy. Moreover, countries which have succeeded in the global economy almost invariably find high regional inequalities in development. Manufacturing exports in China have been concentrated in the south-east of the country, which has grown rapidly, leaving the rest of the country far behind. In Mexico the rapid industrial expansion resulting from NAFTA has been concentrated in the north of the country.

It is clear that horizontal inequalities have been widening in many of the areas where conflict is threatened or has occurred, as some groups are able to take advantage of global opportunities while others are left behind. For example:

- Widening economic differentials between the Western and Islamic world. From 1975–99, annual growth in per capita incomes in Arab States was 0.3 per cent, while that of high-income OECD countries was 2.2 per cent. In 1999, PPP adjusted per capita incomes in the high-income OECD countries was nearly six times that of the Arab states.
- More specifically, there has been a widening gap in per capita incomes between Israel and Palestine; Israeli per capita incomes have been growing at about 5 per cent p.a. (1990–99), while the CIA estimate that GDP in Palestine has been declining at a rate of 7.5 per cent (dates not specified).
- Uneven regional growth has occurred in most countries participating successfully in the global economy creating tensions, sometimes leading

to struggles for self-determination. These can be initiated by successful regions which wish to jettison the backward regions, or by the backward regions which resent domination by the more successful. The Khalistan movement in India during the 1980s and the Biafra war of the late 1960s in Nigeria are examples of relatively more prosperous areas seeking independence. The political rebellion in the state of Chiapas in Mexico, in contrast, is an example of a backward region seeking autonomy.

In sum, global economic influences have tended to result in uneven development across classes and groups tending to accentuate both horizontal and vertical inequalities. Government action to counter sharp inequalities has sometimes been successful in maintaining peaceful co-existence (as in Malaysia), but elsewhere has provoked the rise of SDMs among the more privileged groups that wished to preserve their position (such as in parts of Indonesia and Sri Lanka).

Poverty

Absolute numbers of people in poverty, defined as people on incomes below $1 (PPP) a day, have been rising in Sub-Saharan Africa, Eastern Europe, Central Asia, Latin America and the Caribbean. Numbers in poverty as a proportion of the population rose in Sub-Saharan Africa and Eastern Europe and Central Asia (the latter from a very low ratio). In Sub-Saharan Africa nearly 50 per cent of the population are below this poverty line, and other indicators of poverty (life expectancy, infant mortality and educational enrolment) have also been worsening. The high and rising levels of poverty in Sub-Saharan Africa certainly predisposes many countries to conflict. While there are many local factors accounting for this poverty – notably poor levels of education, weak governance structures and AIDs – global influences have not been favourable. The terms of trade have been deteriorating; there is a huge burden of external debt; tough adjustment policies imposed from outside have generally not succeeded in restoring growth and have led to cuts in social services; until recently aid has been declining; and African countries have attracted only miniscule amounts of private capital.

Social service provision

Failure of the state to provide people with services and to protect against risks can reduce loyalty to the state and increase the likelihood of conflict. Globalization affects social protection in two ways; on the one hand, it increases the need for protection because of the increased risks associated with greater openness. On the other hand, it reduces the state's ability to tax and supply social protection. Increased global competition for capital and highly skilled manpower puts downward pressure on tax rates, especially direct taxes. To the extent that these downward pressures are not compensated for by rises in other taxes, total tax revenue may decline, undermining governments' ability to finance the social sectors (Rodrik 1997; Grunberg 1998).

For developed countries, Rodrik has concluded:

> the evidence suggests three things: globalisation reduces the ability of governments to spend resources on social programmes, it makes it more difficult to tax capital, and labour now carries a growing share of the tax burden. (Rodrik 1997, p. 64)

Governments' ability and willingness to provide universal social services in developing countries has similarly been weakened by a variety of global influences – including problems in raising revenue, increased emphasis on the need for budgetary balance, increased debt servicing requirements pre-empting budgetary resources and the model of service provision advanced by the International Financial Institutions in which the private sector, NGOs, and within the government, local authorities, take an increasing role.

For low-income developing countries total current revenue as a percentage of GDP has been declining from an estimated 16.5 per cent in 1980–1, to 14.8 per cent in 1999. Among African economies government revenue as a share of GDP held up in the 1980s (though GDP per capita was falling so that revenue per capita fell), but fell in the 1990s. For ten African countries for which data are available, government revenue as a percentage of GDP was 15.5 per cent in 1990 and had fallen to 11.4 per cent by 1998,[4] although experience varied – for example, Kenya and Zimbabwe increased their revenue share over these years. In half the African economies for which data is available current government revenue is at or below 10 per cent of GDP – a level at which it is impossible to meet social sector needs. In these countries, the social contract is evidently being undermined.

Levels of social expenditure per capita in African countries fell sharply in the 1980s (Stewart 1995a), reflecting falling incomes and revenue share. In the 1990s, the average fall was less. For the period 1980–97 the share of GNP going to education decreased in nine, and increased in seven, African countries for which evidence is available.

In summary, globalization has not had uniform effects on the variables associated with conflict. In some countries – such as China – it has contributed to accelerating growth and reduced poverty. In such countries, the growth and poverty impact of globalization has reduced the likelihood of conflict, yet at the same time the uneven impact of this growth across regions and populations enhancing horizontal inequalities, and the sharp economic fluctuations (for example, as experienced in South East Asia in the late 1990s) may have raised the probability of political disturbances. For many countries, globalization has not led to the acceleration of economic growth predicted by those who hypothesize that it would tend to diminish conflict. For the world as a whole, indeed, globalization has been associated with a slowdown in growth. In some countries – especially in Africa – globalization has been associated with prolonged stagnation and rising poverty. For Africa as a whole, there has been declining per capita income during this era. In many low-income countries, particularly those suffering declining incomes, there has also been a cutback in the role of the state and very high unemployment, especially among male youth, all elements which tend to make movements for self-determination and violent conflict more likely.

On the political side, globalization has been associated with a transition to democracy. According to the UNDP: 'Since 1980, 81 countries have taken significant steps towards democracy, with 33 military regimes replaced by civilian governments'. (UNDP 2002, p 10). This has put more countries into the dangerous 'intermediate' position between dictatorship and stable democracy where conflict is most likely. Indeed, the UNDP reports that only 47 of the 81 new democracies are 'fully democratic'. The transition to democracy of the remainder has either stalled or they have lapsed back into authoritarian regimes or conflict. In the longer run, these transitional states may turn into stable democracies – but in the medium term they are more vulnerable to conflict.

We see, therefore, that the two positions put forward at the beginning of this section are both over-simplistic. Globalization does not systematically reduce the likelihood of conflict but in important respects, and in certain conditions, increases it. On the other hand, it does not invariably provoke conflict. Where it is associated with well-distributed economic growth and increasing social provision, the probability of conflict is reduced. The major issue is then what international and national policies are most likely to generate conditions which reduce the potential for violence. These will be considered later after consideration of global influences on the financing of conflicts.

Private profiteering and global financing of conflicts

The presence of resources that can generate large profits for particular individuals or groups plays a double role in generating and sustaining conflict. The likelihood of making considerable fortunes from war enhances the motives for war, as noted above; at the same time some of these profits contribute to the finance of the wars. Resources suitable for this dual role need to be internationally marketable – because local markets rarely produce large profits, and never in sought-after foreign exchange. They also need to offer rents (that is, returns substantially higher than the costs of production) and thus, large profits. Obvious candidates that fulfil this role are oil, diamonds, timber and drugs. Two other types of global resource should also be considered – aid flows and remittances from diasporas – as they contribute to the finance of conflict and in a sense offer rents since they are provided on a non-exchange basis, without corresponding activities or costs.

Several points should be noted about these resources. First, non-rent producing commodities such as cotton, tobacco, coffee or tea for which there are no supply restrictions do not offer large profits – and hence are not major sources of war motivation or finance. Second, profits are made from trading and trafficking these commodities as well as production. For example, conflicting groups in Northern Ireland are said to have profited from drug trading, while timber trading has financed conflict in Thailand and Sierra Leone. Third, the possibility of gaining personal fortunes and of financing wars through the sale of such commodities is by no means confined to rebels. In many cases revenues are most easily accessed by governments and provide motives and finance for repressing opposition. For example, timber has been a major source of finance for governments in Liberia, Burma and Cambodia; oil has provided the government with finance in the Sudan and Angola.

Fourth, in most cases the complicity of major companies is needed. In the case of diamonds, the trade was implicitly sanctioned by De Beers which bought diamonds from countries in conflict. In timber, it is argued that the 'same companies... crop up again and again in different countries...' (Global Witness 2002, p. 12). Fifth, not all the activity is illegal. Indeed, in some cases all may be legal – for example, oil and aid. Sixth, the presence of these potential sources is not by itself enough to cause war. There are peaceful societies which produce and trade in every one of the listed commodities (even drugs). Other factors need to be present to transform the situation into one of war – in particular the more fundamental economic and political causes of war discussed above. Seventh, the illegality of many of these transactions, together with the breakdown in formal trade and banking systems which often occurs in wars or in weak states, means that informal channels dominate, including cultural networks.

Finally, global connections are critically important. First, there has to be a global market – it is consumers outside the country in conflict, mostly in OECD countries, that provide a market for the commodities; second, global restrictions on production and trade are generally responsible for the existence of rents; third, global companies invariably play a role in trade, and often in production. These manifold global connections mean that potentially global policies could reduce, if not eliminate, these sources of war-finance.

The remainder of this section provides brief overviews of each of the sources of finance listed above, and their contribution to war motivation and finance.

Diamonds

The role of diamonds in financing conflict is well-known as a result of effective NGO campaigns. Diamonds are a particularly suitable commodity for conflict-finance as they are high value and portable: 1 kilogram of exports from Sierra Leone, for example, realized $1.15m in 1999. Around 4 per cent of world production, valued at nearly $7.0 billion a year, is estimated to be directly related to conflict-finance. Alluvial diamond deposits are mined by small enterprises employing diggers using simple technology. These are the deposits which are to be found in West and Central Africa, and provide most of the war-finance secured by rebels.

Examples of diamond-financed conflict include:

- Angola, where diamonds financed the independence movement and later the UNITA rebels. UNITA is estimated to have controlled 70 per cent of the country's diamond production, generating $3.7 billion over a seven-year period – much of it purchased by de Beers. (Global Witness 1998).
- Sierra Leone, where both the RUF and government were largely financed by diamonds. One report suggested that 'The point of the war may not be to win it, but to engage in profitable crime under the cover of war. Diamonds, in fact, have fuelled Sierra Leone's conflict for the better part of three decades.'(PAC 2000). The huge discrepancy between Sierra Leone's official diamond exports in 1998 and 1999 (totalling $3.0m) and imports recorded in Belgium ($96.2m) indicate the extent of rebel control over diamonds (Goreux 2001).
- The Congo is a third war-zone where diamonds have played a major role in war-finance. An international company, Oryx, has an agreement with the Congo and Zimbabwe governments for commercial exploitation of major natural resources, involving a $1 billion agreement for diamonds, as well as concessions for other resources including timber (see below).

Global connections are vital for the diamond trade. Global actors are responsible for trade, polishing and, of course, final consumption. The South African company, De Beers, dominates the market, owning 40 per cent of diamond mines, and until the late 1990s regulated the world price by buying up most diamonds and managing a buffer stock. Around half the world's diamond polishing takes place in India, while half the world's diamonds (polished and rough) are traded via Antwerp. A small number of banks specialize in the diamond trade – in Antwerp two banks account for 90 per cent of the financing (Global Witness 2000) Half the value of final consumption is in the US.

Preliminary moves to outlaw 'conflict diamonds' were made by the industry itself in July 2000, in the so-called Kimberley process. The

Kimberley Process Certification Scheme (KPCS) was formally launched in January 2003. This agreement committed participants to certify that shipments of rough diamonds do not include 'conflict' diamonds. Yet a survey in 2004 'show[ed] that the majority of diamond jewellery retailers continue to fail to deliver on repeated promises to stem the trade in conflict diamonds' (Global Witness 2004, p. 3) Supporting legislation by importing countries should help enforce the scheme. For example, the US passed a 'clean diamonds' Act in 2003, aimed at excluding conflict diamonds from international trade.

A notable aspect of the significant progress that has been made in reducing the contribution of conflict-diamonds is the role of NGOs in monitoring the situation, publicizing it, and orchestrating public opinion.

Timber

Logging and the sale of hardwoods has been a major source of war profiteering and finance in Cambodia, Burma, Indonesia, Liberia and Sierra Leone. Hardwoods have a global market and are valuable and easy to acquire, especially in wartime conditions when regulatory systems are weak. Logging companies collaborate with government or rebels according to who controls the area. Government-controlled production may, of course, be perfectly legal (though sometimes illegal activities are sanctioned to allow diversion of profits from the state to private pockets). Rebel sources are generally illegal. Illegal products are estimated to account for as much as half of the EU's timber imports.

Examples of timber-financed conflicts include:

- Cambodia, where the Khmer Rouge used timber sales to finance warfare (and other services) both in government and later when fighting in opposition. The economic survival of the Khmer Rouge was linked to the control of natural resources (Le Billon and Bakker 2001). The July 1997 coup was also financed by timber, secured from regional military units with business support. Logging concessions were subsequently used by the government to reward supporters.
- In Burma, exploitation of timber has been a major source of war revenue for the government during its long civil war. At the same time Thai logging companies have worked with rebel organizations.
- In Liberia, Charles Taylor's National Patriotic Front of Liberia (NPFL) funded the rebellion by exploiting natural resources (timber, iron ore, rubber and diamonds). After gaining power, he used logging concessions to monopolize gains for his supporters, and diverted much revenue to provide funds for arms imports and for support for the RUF in Sierra Leone.

- Zimbabwe's intervention in the war in the Congo was largely motivated by the commercial concessions gained, among which timber is important: one company received the logging rights to 33 million hectares.

Policies to control the timber trade are at a much earlier stage than those towards diamonds, although certification schemes have been initiated, primarily for environmental reasons. Much of the massive illegal logging is for profit, not for supporting conflict. Measures are gradually being adopted to control this trade, but to date they have mainly been ineffective.

Oil

Oil revenue confers large resources on governments via royalties and taxation. Revenues can readily be diverted to personal pockets and/or to arms purchases, thus providing a strong motive to hold onto power and a means of so doing. It is also a contributory motive for SDMs and their suppression, such as those of Biafra, East Timor and Aceh. Since production is highly capital-intensive and requires the participation of large international companies, revenue tends to go to governments rather than rebel movements – who may use it to suppress opposition, although it has been used to underwrite separatist movements. Major examples are:

- Angola, where oil revenue financed government military operations, much revenue apparently disappearing from public budget allocations (Le Billon 2001); about $1.4 billion of state income was unaccounted for in 2000 (Global Witness Press Release, 13 December 2001).
- Sudan: in the late 1990s, control over the oil fields became 'central to the war between government and armed opposition forces, as well as the ongoing conflict between the various militia factions' (Amnesty International, May 2000, quoted in Swanson 2002). Non-Arab minorities in the south were violently displaced to clear the area for oil production. Oil revenues also provided finance for arms. Military expansion almost doubled in the three years after oil revenue began to flow. Again, international companies were involved – this time Talisman, a Canadian company with local partners (*New York Times*, 17 October 2000).
- Burma: two major oil companies (Unocal and TotalFinaElf) developed gas production in contested areas. It has been alleged that Total lent the government helicopters for the fight against minorities in the Tenasserim area. The gas pipeline passes through areas where the Karen and Mons minorities live, and its construction provides further motive and opportunity for suppressing opposition among these peoples.
- In Western Sahara, the granting of prospecting contracts by the Moroccan government to two international firms in territory claimed by the Polisario Front, which is seeking independence, was described as a

'provocation…that worsens an already worrisome situation' (Mohammed Abdelaziz, head of the Polisario movement, quoted by Reuters, 24 October 2001).

Oil companies are necessarily complicit in the use of oil-finance. Yet what they do is generally legal and in collaboration with governments, while fungibility of resources weakens the direct connection between oil-finance and war-finance. NGO and public pressure can, nonetheless, sometimes be at least partially effective – for example, with respect to Shell's operations in Nigeria.

Drugs

The illegality of the drugs trade gives rise to huge rents. For example, it was estimated that if cocaine had been legal in 1990, the street price (broadly reflecting costs of production and trade) would have been one twenty-fifth of the actual US price (Sarmiento 1990). Finance from the production and sale of drugs tends to go to rebels rather than governments, though pro-government militias sometimes benefit, as is the case in Colombia. Non-producers can also gain from drug trading – for example, in Guatemala and the IRA in Northern Ireland. Drug money not only finances arms, but also provides a motive for profiteers to perpetuate conflict. The beneficiaries include small-scale farmers for whom the production of poppies or coca provides a livelihood where there are few alternatives. Attempts to suppress production without providing viable alternative livelihoods thus extends, rather than reduces, support for rebels.

- Afghanistan: poppy production was estimated to have increased twelve-fold from the early 1980s to the mid-1990s. By the mid-1990s, poppies were the country's main export crop, and Afghanistan was estimated to be responsible for 40 per cent of world poppy production (Donini 1996). The value of production was estimated at about ten times 'official' exports (Rubin 1997). Drug revenues provided the major source of foreign exchange for arms (Marsden and Samman 2001). After 1998, the Taliban attempted to suppress production. However, it has revived in the post-Taliban regime.
- Colombia: coca production is the most profitable crop in the Colombian Amazon. Adjustment policies of the IMF and World Bank in the 1980s and 1990s further undermined the profitability of food production, increasing the relative advantages of coca (Avirgan 2002). By the 1990s coca was estimated to cover 150,000 hectares with 300,000 people directly dependent on production, although some decline is reported since then (*Financial Times*, 19 July 2005). Most cultivation is in areas controlled by the rebels who finance their activities by taxing production

> and transport. At the same time, government allied paramilitary groups have been funded by drug trafficking and have been closely linked to drug cartels. In addition, generous US aid (amounting to $3 b. during Plan Colombia) to suppress drug production supports the military activities of the government. (Vargas Meza 1999)

The developed countries, led by the US, have been trying to eliminate production, imports and consumption of drugs for several decades, with very limited impact. Current policies include the use of substantial military force – with finance and equipment from the US – intended to eradicate drug production and often being redirected against the rebels. According to a report by the International Crisis Group, the policy fails to affect the price and availability of illicit drugs in the US, and it also causes severe damage in target countries, undermining efforts to gain civilian control of military forces in Colombia, fomenting unrest and harming the environment (ICG 2005).

An NGOs' manifesto to the UN General Assembly in 1998 argued that the international conventions on control of the drug trade had been ineffective in controlling the drugs trade or consumption, had led to criminalization of producers and traders, and had involved violation of human rights. They proposed that production of drugs by small farmers should not be prosecuted; that small farmers should be offered profitable alternatives; military eradication measures should be stopped; and prosecution of consumers should cease (Manifesto of the International Coalition of NGOs for a Just and Effective Policy of Drugs, Vienna, 15 March 1998 http://www.tni.org/drugs/encod/oasis.htm.)

These proposals provide a basis for policies towards drugs in war. So long as drug production and consumption remains illegal, it will provide an important motive for conflict, since conflict makes it easier to sustain illegal activities and to hide the profits in ways that facilitate war-finance. Legalization would thus help reduce the role of drugs in motivation and war-finance. However, the political prospects for this, particularly in the US, are small.

Aid

In contrast to the illegal drug trade, aid provides a substantial and totally legal source of war-finance, with official aid supporting governments, and rebels receiving some NGO support.

During the cold war, aid from East and West provided the main financial support for those countries fighting wars by proxy. After the cold war such aid diminished and many of the wars by proxy came to an end. Some countries in conflict, however, continued to receive substantial amounts. For example, Israel ($236 per capita, 1998) and Palestine ($208), while significant amounts (between $25 and $66 per head) went to Angola, the Congo Liberia and Uganda. A new form of war by proxy (the War against Terror) developed post 9/11, again associated with enhanced aid flows (for example, to Pakistan, the Philippines, Nepal). Whatever the intentions of aid-givers, indirectly aid (including humanitarian aid) provides resources that governments can use for military activities (see Stewart and Samman 2001).

Studies of Rwanda, Cambodia and the Sudan illustrate the important role which can be played by aid:

- The Rwanda case pre-1994 shows how aid-financed development can be associated with sharply rising inequality, extreme poverty and high levels of exclusion – conditions which provide fertile soil for conflict. Despite sustained growth until the mid-1980s, a skewed pattern of growth had left almost 90 per cent of the population below the poverty line (Uven 2000). There was a huge increase in inequality between 1982 and 1994 (Maton 1994). One study showed that the net result of an IDA-supported rural development project from 1972 to 1984 was:

  > a great increase in inequality between regions, classes, groups and individuals... A small group of people – politicians, civil servants, project employees – managed to obtain most of the advantages of the multi-million dollar project: jobs in and outside of the project, free land for cultivation by family members, rentiers, or political clients. (Uven 2000, p. 70, referring to findings of Lemarchand 1982)

- Cambodia in the 1970s is somewhat similar to Rwanda, when huge amounts of military and economic aid flowed to the Lon Nol government. Meanwhile, state resources (essentially US aid) were diverted to 'a small group of army officers, bureaucrats, and urban commercial elite' which embezzled much of the aid inflows (Le Billon and Bakker 2000, p. 69). Like Rwanda, the aid-supported development process had led to rising inequality, enriched the elite and left the rural peasantry in poverty. As with Rwanda, this generated a social and economic situation which eventually resulted in genocide.
- Sudan received large flows of aid during nearly two decades of war, much of it in the form of food aid. Despite this, there were severe food shortages among some groups. In 1988, 30,000 people died in camps. The food aid was used by the Sudanese government to pursue its war aims: it aimed to prevent any aid reaching the South so as to force people to move into camps, where they suffered from diseases and food shortages and were sometime used as slave labour. When donors tried to circumvent this via a special programme for the South, the Sudanese government attempted to block air flights, bombed airstrips and occasionally attacked

relief personnel. Food aid was diverted to or plundered by the military. Generous financial aid also supported military expenditure indirectly which amounted to almost twice expenditure on health and education combined (Keen 1994; Keen 2001b). Throughout the Darfur crisis, aid has continued to flow to the Sudanese government, even though there is evidence that the government is implicated in the activities of the militias.

Not all aid to countries in conflict, of course, is used to support governments' war aims. In Mozambique, for example, food aid was widely distributed (including to rebel areas) and saved many lives. Yet aid flows are unearned resources, like natural resources, which are readily diverted to war aims, and where the government is an active participant in conflict it is to be expected that it will be used in this way.

Diasporas

Another important global source of support for some SDMs is provided by diasporas. Diasporas not only provide family remittances to their countries of origin but can also influence policy in their host countries. They may also act as a conduit for illegal trade and arms supplies.

Diaspora financing can be important for SDMs where the diaspora is large, is located in areas of the world where earnings are significant and the SDM appeals to perceptions of shared identity.

- The Sri Lankan Tamil diaspora across Western Europe, North America and Australia – estimated at 600–800,000 – was a strong source of support for the separatist LTTE. Diaspora-based LTTE activists are reported to have run a complex international network of fund-raising and arms procurement and conduct a sophisticated lobbying campaign with foreign governments and international organizations (see Venugopal, this volume).
- In Somalia, diaspora remittances were estimated at $338 million in 1985, much of it going to the north. Diaspora remittances provided the main financial support of the Somaliland 'government': according to one estimate, it receives $150m. annually, far in excess of official aid.
- The Irish diaspora dates back to the large migrations in the nineteenth century, mainly to the US and UK. In the US in particular, the diaspora formed a powerful lobby group in support of the Republican movement. Fund-raising was led by Irish Northern Aid (NORAID) which probably constituted the main source of finance to the IRA. Since 11 September fund-raising and lobbying activities by diaspora organizations supporting groups in Northern Ireland which do not respect the Good Friday Agreement have been greatly restricted. Remittances from the Protestant

diaspora in the UK, allied to local right-wing groups, provide a source of funds for the Unionists.

- In Algeria, the *Front de Libération Nationale* organized systematic collections among the migrant population in France for the independence struggle in Algeria. Subsequently, supporters of the *Front Islamique du Salut* sought asylum in countries such as Germany and the UK and became a source of support for the Islamistes. In the 1980s and 1990s many Islamist social welfare organizations were supported by Islamic banks: for example, *Al Taqwa*, which has been linked to the Egyptian Muslim Brotherhood.

Diaspora activism is generally more important as a political platform for SDMs, a method of gaining diplomatic and financial support, rather than for the actual finance or arms that they supply. The clearest example here is that of the Jewish diaspora that eventually succeeded in securing recognition for the state of Israel, which subsequently gained hugely from official flows of aid and arms mainly generated as a result of diaspora pressure. In Northern Ireland, the most important factor sustaining the conflict was the systematic discrimination against the Catholic population. Hence the Macbride principles, aimed at eliminating discrimination, which were adopted in the US as a result of diaspora pressure, represented a crucial intervention. However, in some SDMs, where other sources of finance are limited, diaspora-provided funds can be of critical importance – as seems to have been the case in Northern Ireland and Sri Lanka. Host governments can attempt to restrict such remittances. These restrictions may be quite effective where fund-raising mainly depends on individual contributions, as in the case of Irish organizations in the US. But the leaky nature of global financial controls means that restrictions are unlikely to be effective in most contexts.

Some conclusions on sources of finance

Global sources of finance for conflict are pervasive, as illustrated in Table 2.3. They are also very difficult to control, as is apparent from the discussion above of each individual category. A prime reason for this is that there are strong political and economic interests in continuing most of the trades, so that a reversal can only be achieved by powerful counter forces. To this end, NGO monitoring and campaigning combined with political (and/or consumer) pressure in the consuming countries can be effective, as exemplified in the progress made on diamonds, and occasionally other commodities (for example, oil). In other areas, there has been little progress because of strategic and domestic political interests in the developed countries, for instance, with respect to aid to Israel or the Sudan. In addition, even where trade in conflict commodities becomes illegal, war conditions make it easy

Table 2.3 External Sources of finance for some recent conflicts

Country	*Offical military aid*[a]	*Non-military aid*[a]	*Loans private, for arms and other*[b]	*Natural resources advances*[a]	*Natural resources current sales*[b]	*From diaspora*[c]
Angola	West, S.Africa[b] Cuba[a]	Considerable	Considerable	large, for oil; and diamonds	Oil and diamonds	Little
Afghanistan	USSR[a]; West[b] Pakistan; Saudi Arabia. NGOs; Islamic community	Some	Some	finance for oil pipe line	heroin; smuggling manufactured products; gems	Little
Burma		Limited	Some	No	heroin; timber	Little
Cambodia	some: China, West	Limited	Some	Some	timber	Little
Colombia	US	US aid for drug eradication	Large	No	cocaine	Little
Liberia	West	Limited	Some	concessions to private companies	timber, diamonds, rubber, iron ore	Little
Mozambique	S.Africa; Cuba; West	limited during war; substantial subsequently	Large	No	limited	No

Table 2.3 (Continued)

Country	*Offical military aid*[a]	*Non-military aid*[a]	*Loans private, for arms and other*[b]	*Natural resources advances*[a]	*Natural resources current sales*[b]	*From diaspora*
Nicaragua	Russia; Cuba; US	Some	Large	No	limited	No
Rwanda	some	from West and IFIs [a]	Limited	No	No	Little
Sierra Leone	limited	From West initially; later little	Some	Some	diamonds	Little
Somalia	limited	Limited	Limited	No	little	Significant
Sri Lanka	some[a]; India (1980s)[b]	from West and IFIs – considerable[a]	Some	No	limited	Considerable
Sudan	substantial	substantial, West	Substantial	No	little; oil?	Little
Uganda	limited	Limited	Limited	No	little	little

a. Mainly to government; b. to government and rebels.

to evade national controls, while global liberalization has increased the difficulties of making global controls watertight. The fact that so many of the transactions are illegal and therefore do not appear in the accounts of public companies make them especially difficult to control. The cultural networks that facilitate trade in war zones – for example, drugs in and from Afghanistan and Colombia, diamonds in Sierra Leone or timber in Burma – can readily avoid the rather half-hearted attempts to control them. Drugs and aid provide graphic examples of the difficulties. On the one hand, the flourishing drug trade illustrates how difficult it is to control trade even when the commodity is outlawed everywhere and the most powerful countries in the world are intent on eliminating it. On the other hand, official flows of aid are totally within official control. Yet large flows which directly or indirectly finance conflicts continue to many conflict-countries for strategic or domestic political reasons.

Nevertheless, consumers of the commodities at issue and political movements can put pressure on developed country governments with some success. Groups of consumers have considerable potential power if they can be organized to use it. Moreover, effective controls over financial flows can help enforce constraints over particular commodities, or flows to particular countries, by making it difficult to realize the money acquired through commodity trade – these, and their limitations, are discussed by FitzGerald (this volume).

Global policies to reduce the fundamental causes of conflict

Earlier we identified certain economic developments as likely to raise the risk of violence. These include poverty, economic stagnation, unequal development, particularly inequalities across regions and ethnicities, and a weak state that provides little in the way of social services or human security for its people. The globalizing economy and global conditionalities contributed to some of these developments as evidenced by:

- a global slow down in the rate of growth;
- uneven growth, with many countries suffering low or negative growth;
- rising vertical and horizontal inequality in many countries;
- a declining role of the state in many countries, with falls in tax revenues, cutbacks in services, and a move in service provision away from central governments to local governments or NGOs.
- global pressure for multiparty democracy without appropriate mechanisms for ethnically divided societies.

These trends clearly have not occurred in *all* countries and are not only (or necessarily mainly) the responsibility of global, as against domestic, policy. Yet global policies must consider the failures of globalization as well as the successes if violent conflict is to be limited. Developing a global economy which incorporates all countries and within them most people must be an important element of any policy aimed at reducing conflict.

This is not the place to go into a full analysis of global policies needed to achieve a fairer distribution of world output and a wider spread of the benefits of globalization between and within countries. Below is just a summary of major elements of global policy change likely to help bring about a more peaceful world:[5]

- Improving the world trading system so as to eliminate the current bias against developing countries. This would involve liberalizing developed country trade in agriculture and labour-intensive products (notably textiles). Agreement was reached on both these issues in the Uruguay round, but these have not been put into effect.
- Permitting developing countries to introduce infant industry protection so as to allow them to realize the learning and scale economies essential for international competitiveness.[6]
- Introducing policies to help improve the terms of trade for developing countries, including collective producer taxation of commodities whose demand is inelastic; increasing retained value-added on primary commodities by promoting processing in developing countries; promotion of diversification in primary commodity specialist economies.
- Altering the rules on intellectual property so as eliminate developing country payment on all essential drugs and other basic goods for the poor, and outlawing patenting of natural products from developing countries.
- Raising aggregate aid levels and redirecting aid towards the poor in poor countries.
- Introducing global taxation of global activities (such as the Tobin tax on short-term capital transactions) to support global public goods (including peace-keeping activities; schemes to support essential drugs for the poor).[7]
- Altering conditionalities and the disbursement of aid so as to strengthen governments, by supporting tax increases in countries where tax revenue is low; distributing aid via governments rather than NGOs except in very extreme cases of dysfunctional or one-sided governments.
- Using aid and conditionalities to improve horizontal inequality – by ensuring that all expenditures are fairly distributed across ethnic groups.
- Political conditionality to recognize the need for constrained democracy in divided societies – that is, democracy designed to protect minority rights, ensure inclusive government and respect universal human rights.

Conclusion

Most struggles for self-determination have strong local causes involving a combination of cultural, economic and political factors. Global influences, however, often play a strong role in contributing to the inequalities and deprivations, while they also facilitate the finance of the struggles and provide private incentives for individuals to fight, both among the government and the rebels. Global cultural connections also play a part. On the one hand, diasporas can be an important source of finance for particular groups; on the other, cultural connections facilitate trade and finance, particularly when the trade is illegal.

In summary, while it would be wrong to attribute to global influences major responsibility for all the conflicts in the world today, there is no doubt that the current system of globalization has contributed to the motivation as well as the finance of many of today's conflicts; global policy change could consequently do much to reduce it. Since 11 September, the developed countries have seen the need to have effective controls over finance for terrorist activities, and progress has been made in tightening controls. But there has been much less recognition that it is essential to tackle the more fundamental economic and political causes of such struggles, if violent contests for self-determination are to be avoided. Policies aimed at reducing the finance of conflict alone are unlikely to be effective for two reasons: first, because it is almost certainly impossible to secure comprehensive regulation for both technical and political reasons; second, because so long as the fundamental underlying economic and political causes remain, violent conflicts will continue, financed by exploiting loopholes or evading the regulations, or by resorting to home-grown weapons. Without the more fundamental improvements in underlying economic and political conditions, actions directed at sources of finance alone are likely to have only a small impact.

Notes

1. I am very grateful for comments from participants at a workshop in June 2002, and the rest of our research group for helpful and detailed comments and suggestions.
2. The measure adopted is natural resource production as a share of Gross Domestic Product.
3. Rather complex and unconvincing reasons have been advanced for this peak. Cramer (2001) has criticized the assumptions underlying the Collier and Hoeffler methodology.
4. Data from World Bank, *World Development Report*, 2000/1. Similar conclusions emerge from data on African HIPC countries produced by Murshed (2001).
5. This is drawn from work by the author and others, including Cornia, *et al.* (1986); Stewart (1995a,b); Fitzgerald (2001); Oxfam (2002).
6. As Chang (2002) has pointed out, this was the policy adopted by the industrialized countries in the initial stages of industrialization. This is also true of Korea's development and that of Taiwan. (Wade 1990; Amsden 1989).
7. See ul Haq, M., Kaul, *et al.* (1996).

References

Alexander, J., J. McGregor and T. Ranger (2000) 'Ethnicity and the Politics of Conflict: The Case of Matabeleland' in E. W. Nafziger, S. Frances and R. Väyrynen (eds) *War, Hunger and Displacement: The Origin of Humanitarian Emergencies*. Oxford: OUP.

Amsden, A. (1989) *Asia's Next Giant: South Korea and Late Industrialization*. New York: Oxford University Press.

Avirgan, T. (2002) 'Drugs, Colombia and Globalization', *Guerrilla News Network*. http://www.guerrillanews.com/war_on_drugs/doc379.html.

Barrows, W. (1976) 'Ethnic Diversity and Political Instability in Black Africa', *Comparative Political Studies*, 9 (2), 139–70.

Chang, H-J. (2002) *Kicking Away the Ladder*. London: Anthem Press.

Cohen, A. (1974) *Two-dimensional Man: An Essay on the Anthropology of Power and Symbolism in Complex Society*. Berkeley, CA: University of California Press.

Collier, P. and A. Hoeffler (2000) *Greed and Grievance in Civil War*. Washington, DC: World Bank.

Cornia, G. A. (2004) *Inequality, Growth, and Poverty in an Era of Liberalization and Globalization*. Oxford: OUP.

Cornia, G. A., R. Jolly and F. Stewart (1986) *Adjustment with a Human Face*. Oxford: OUP.

Cornia, G. A. and K. Sampsa (1999) *Trends in Income Distribution in the Post World War II Period: Evidence and Interpretation*. Helsinki: WIDER.

Cramer, C. (2001) *Homo economicus goes to war: methodological individualism, rational choice and the political economy of war*. London: SOAS.

Cramer, C. (2003) 'Does Inequality Cause Conflict', *Journal of International Development*, 15, 397–412.

De Soysa, I. and E. Neumayer (2003) *Natural Resources and Civil War: Another Look with New Data*. London: London School of Economics, Department of Geography and Environment.

Donini, A. (1996) *The Policies of Mercy: UN Coordination in Afghanistan, Mozambique and Rwanda*. Providence: Thomas Watson Jr. Institute for International Studies.

Duffield, M. (2001) *Global Governance and the New Wars*. London: Zed Books.

Ebadawi, I. and N. Sambanis (2002) 'How Much War Will We See? Explaining the Prevalence of Civil War', *Journal of Conflict Resolution*, Vol. 46, No. 3, 307–334 (2002).

Fairhead, J. (2000) 'The Conflict over Natural and Environmental Resources' in E. W. Nafiziger, F. Stewart and R. Vayrynen (eds) *War, Hunger and Displacement: The Origin of Humanitarian Emergencies*. Oxford: OUP.

Fitzgerald, E. V. K. (2001) 'The International Political Economy of Conflicts in Poor Countries' in F. Stewart, E. V. K. FitzGerald *et al.* (eds) *War and Underdevelopment*. Oxford: OUP.

Fleshman, Michael (2001) 'Conflict Diamonds Evade UN Sanctions', *Africa Recovery*, 15(4).

Glazer, N. and D. Moynihan (1975) *Ethnicity, Theory and Experience*. Cambridge, MA: Harvard University Press.

Global Witness (1998) *A Rough Trade: the Role of Companies and Governments in the Angolan Conflict*. London: Global Witness.

Global Witness (2000) *Possibilities for the Identification, Certification and Control of Diamonds*. London: Global Witness.

Global Witness (2002) 'The Logs of War: The Timber Trade and Armed Conflict', Programme for International Cooperation and Conhttp://www.christian-aid.org.uk/indepth/0103suda/sudanoil.htmflict Resolution, Fafo-report 379, http://www.globalwitness.org/reports/show.php/en.00011.html.
Global Witness (2004) 'Summary of UK and US Results of Global Witness and Amnesty International Survey', *Déjà Vu*, October.
Goreux, L. (2001) *Conflict Diamonds*. Washington, DC: World Bank.
Grunberg, I. (1998) 'Double Jeopardy: Globalisation, Liberalisation and the Fiscal Squeeze', *World Development* 26(4), 591–605.
Gurr, T. R. (1993) *Minorities at Risk: A Global View of Ethnopolitical Conflicts*. Washington DC: Institute of Peace Press.
Guttierez, F. S. (2005) 'Criminals and Rebels? A Discussion of Civil War and Criminality from the Colombian Experience', *Politics and Society*, 32(2), 257–85.
Haq, M. E. (2000) *Drugs in South Asia*. London: Palgrave Macmillan.
Hegre, Håvard and Nils Petter Gleditsch (2001) 'Political Institutions, Globalization, and Conflict'. Paper presented at the World Bank Conference 'Economics and Politics of Civil War: Launching a Case-Study Project', Oslo, 11–12 June.
Hirshleifer, J. (1994) 'The Dark Side of the Force', *Economic Inquiry*, XXXII, 1–10.
Horowitz, D. (1985) *Ethnic Groups in Conflict*. Berkeley, CA: University of California Press.
International Crisis Group (ICG) (2005) 'War and Drugs in Colombia', London: International Crisis Group.http://www.globalwitness.org/reports/show.php/en.00011.html.
Kaplan, R. (1994) 'The Coming Anarchy: How Scarcity, Crime Overpopulation and Disease are Threatening the Social Fabric of our Planet', *Atlantic Monthly* (February), 44–74.
Keen, D. (1994) *The Benefits of Famine: a Political Economy of Famine Relief in Southwestern Sudan 1883–1989*. Princeton, NJ: Princeton University Press.
Keen, D. (1998) *The Economic Functions of Violence in Civil Wars*. Oxford: Oxford University Press for the International Institute for Strategic Studies.
Keen, D. (2001a) 'Sierra Leone: War and its Functions' in F. Stewart and V. FitzGerald (eds) *War and Underdevelopment*. Oxford: OUP.
Keen, D. (2001b) 'Sudan: conflict and rationality' in F. Stewart, E. V. K. FitzGerald *et al.* (eds) *War and Underdevelopment, Volume Two, Country Experiences*. Oxford: OUP.
Le Billon, P. and K. Bakker (2000) 'Cambodia: genocide, autocracy, and the overpoliticised state' in E. W. Nafiziger, F. Stewart and R. Väyrynen (eds) *War, Hunger and Displacement: The Origin of Humanitarian Emergencies*. Oxford: OUP.
Le Billon, Philippe (2001) 'Angola's political economy of war: The role of oil and diamonds, 1975–2000', *African Affairs*, 100: 55–80.
Lichbach, M. I. (1989) 'An evaluation of "Does economic inequality breed political conflict?" studies', *World politics* 41(4): 431–70.
Lundberg, M. and L. Squire (2003) 'The simultaneous evolution of growth and inequality', *The Economic Journal*, 113, pp 326–44.
Mancini, L. (2005) 'Horizontal inequalities and communal violence: evidence from Indonesian districts', CRISE Working Paper, 22.
Marsden, P. and E. Samman (2001) 'Afghanistan: the economic and social impact of conflict' in F. Stewart, E. V. K. FitzGerald *et al.* (eds) *War and Underdevelopment, Volume Two: Country Experiences*. Oxford: OUP.
Maton, J. (1994) *Développement Economique et Social au Rwanda entre 1993 et 1993. Le dixième decile en face de l'apocalypse*. Ghent: Faculty of Economics. University of Ghent.

Murshed, S. M. (2001) *Tax competition, globalisation and declining social protection.* Globalisation and Children, Innocenti Research Centre, Florence.

Nafziger, E. W. and J. Auvinen (2000) 'The Economic Causes of Humanitarian Emergencies' in E. W. Nafziger, S. Frances and R. Väyrynen (eds) *War, Hunger and Displacement: The Origin of Humanitarian Emergencies.* Oxford: OUP.

Nafziger, E. W. and J. Auvinen (2002) 'Economic Development, Inequality, War and State Violence', *World Development*, 30(2), 153–63.

Nafziger, E. W., F. Stewart, and R. Väyrynen (2000) *War, Hunger and Displacement: The Origin of Humanitarian Emergencies.* Oxford: OUP.

Østby, G. (2004) *Do Horizontal Inequalities Matter for Civil Conflict?* Oslo: Centre for Study of Civil War (CSCW), International Peace Research Institute (PRIO).

Oxfam (2002) *Rigged Rules and Double Standards: Trade, Globalisation and the Fight Against Poverty.* Oxford: OXFAM.

PAC (2000) *The Heart of the Matter: Sierra Leone, Diamonds and Human Security.* Ottawa: Partnership Africa Canada.

Ranger, T. (1983). 'The Invention of Tradition in Colonial Africa' in E. Hobsbawm and T. Ranger, *The Invention of Tradition.* Cambridge: Canto.

Reno, W. (1998) *Warlord Politics and African states.* Boulder, CO: Lynne Rienner.

Reno, W. (2000) 'Liberia and Sierra Leone: The Competition for Patronage in Resource-Rich Economies' in E. W. Nafziger, S. Frances and R. Väyrynen (eds) *War, Hunger and Displacement: The Origin of Humanitarian Emergencies.* Oxford: OUP.

Reynal-Querol, M. (2001) *Ethnicity, Political Systems and Civil War.* Barcelona: Institut d'Analisis Economic, Campus de la UAB, Bellatera-Barcelona.

Roberts, H. (2001) *Co-opting identity: The Manipulation of Berberism, the Frustration of Democratisation and the Generation of Violence in Algeria.* London: LSE, Crisis States Programme.

Rodriguez, F. and D. Rodrik (1999) 'Trade Policy and Economic Growth: A Skeptic's Guide to the Cross-National Evidence', *NBER Working Paper*, 7081.

Rodrik, D. (1997) *Has Globalization Gone Too Far?* Washington, DC: Institute for International Economics.

Rubin, B. (1997) *Afghanistan: The Last Cold War Conflict, the First Post-Cold War Conflict.* Helsinki: WIDER.

Ruiz, B. (2001) *The Colombian Civil War.* Jefferson, NC: McFarland & Co.

Sachs, J. and A. Warner (1995) 'Economic Reform and the Process of Global Integration', *Brookings Papers on Economic Activity*, **1**, 1–118.

Sarmiento, E. (1990) 'Economia de Narcotrafico', *Desarollo y Sociedad*, 11–40.

Stewart, F. (1995a) *Adjustment and Poverty: Options and Choices.* London: Routledge.

Stewart, F. (1995b) 'Biases in Global Markets: Can the Forces of Inequity and Marginalisation be Modified?' in M. ul Haq, R. Jolly, P. Streeten and K. Haq. (eds) *The UN and the Bretton Woods Institutions: New Challenges for the Twenty-First Century.* London: Macmillan.

Stewart, F. (2001) 'Horizontal Inequalities as a Source of Conflict' in F. Hampson and D. Malone (eds), *From Reaction to Prevention.* London: Lynne Rienner.

Stewart, F. (2002) *Horizontal Inequality: a Neglected Dimension of Development.* Helsinki: WIDER Annual Development Lecture.

Stewart, F. and E. Samman (2001), 'Food Aid During Civil War: Conflicting Conclusions from Alternative Approaches' in F. Stewart, E. V. K. FitzGerald *et al.* (eds) *War and Underdevelopment, Volume One, The Economic and Social Consequences of Conflict.* Oxford: OUP.

Stewart, F., E. V. K. FitzGerald *et al.* (2001) *War and Underdevelopment, Volume One, The Economic and Social Consequences of Conflict*. Oxford: OUP
Swanson, P. (2002) *Fuelling Conflict: The Oil Industry and Armed Conflict*. Oslo: FAFO.
Turton, D. (1997) 'War and Ethnicity: Global Connections and Local Violence in North East Africa and Former Yugoslavia', *Oxford Development Studies*, 25, 77–94.
ul Haq, M., I. Kaul, and I. Grunberg (eds) (1996) *The Tobin Tax: Coping with Financial Volatility*. New York: Oxford University Press.
UN (2001) *Illegal Exploitation of Natural Resources and Other Forms of Wealth in the Republic of Congo*. New York: United Nations.
UNDP (1999) *Human Development Report 1999*. Oxford: OUP.
UNDP (2001) *Human Development Report 2001*. New York: United Nations.
UNDP (2002) *Human Development Report 2002*. New York: United Nations.
Uven, P. (2000) 'Rwanda: The Social Roots of Genocide' in E. W. Nafiziger, F. Stewart and R. Väyrynen (eds) *War, Hunger and Displacement: The Origin of Humanitarian Emergencies, Vol. Two*. Oxford: OUP.
Vargas Meza, R. (1999) *The Revolutionary Armed Forces of Colombia (FARC) and the Illicit Drug Trade*. Washington, DC: Transnational Institute (TNI).
Väyrynen, R. (2000) 'Weak States and Humanitarian Emergencies' in E. W. Nafziger, F. Stewart and R. Väyrynen (eds) *War, Hunger and Displacement: The Origin of Humanitarian Emergencies*. Oxford: OUP.
Wade, R. (1990) *Governing the Market: Economic Theory and the Role of Government in East Asian Industrialization*. Princeton, NJ: Princeton University Press.
Wade, R. (2001) 'Global Inequality: Winners and Losers', *The Economist* (April 28th), 93–7.
Walter, B. (2001) *Explaining the Recurrence of Civil War*. World Bank Workshop on Civil Wars and Post-Conflict Transitions, 18–20, May 2001.
Wang, M. (2001) 'Trade Liberalisation and Income Distribution: The Cross-country Evidence', M.Sc. in Economics for Development, Extended Essay, Queen Elizabeth House, Oxford: University of Oxford.
Willett, S. (2001) 'Structural Conflict in the New Global Disorder', *IDS Bulletin*, 32(2).

3

Global–Local Cultural Links: Diaspora, Transnationalism, Solidarities and the Media

Sandra Dudley[1] *and Cathie Lloyd*

Introduction

There are as many different versions, perceptions and means of interaction with 'global cultural forces' as there are locales and social groups in the world. Central to these are translocal and transnational pathways and their intersections, the routes along which cultural influences travel and operate. These include migration, travel and diaspora; transnational solidarities that cross ethnic, political and religious boundaries (including international non-governmental organisations, INGOS) and the media. In this chapter we explore specific global cultural influences and the pathways along which they operate in the particular contexts of Irish, Kurdish and Islamist self-determination movements (SDMs).

The chapter looks at diaspora, then at some other transnational connections and finally at some of the roles played by new media. Initially, we clarify what we mean by 'identity'. This 'is a problematic term, a catch-all for the political, ethnic, national, cultural, socio-economic, territorial and gender frameworks that give structure and meaning to people's lives' (Dudley 2000). It implies a sense of things in common, a sharing of the legacies of history and of future prospects (De Vos 1995). It is also relational: I am Me because of how I and others define me *in relation to* others. Many different forms of 'identity', a dynamic, fluid conflation of personally, socially, politically and culturally derived perspectives on self and other, are important in analysing SDMs and their cultural components and influences.

Ethnic and other forms of identity

For present purposes, the most predominant form of identity is 'ethnic identity' or 'ethnicity' (which here we treat as synonymous). Sharing or imagining the sharing of an ethnicity with active participants is important for the diffuse support base of many SDMs. Diasporas and those to whom they relate 'back home' by definition consist of groups sharing a sense of identity thought of mainly in ethnic terms. This means belonging to a group with a common name, ancestry, past, culture, link with a homeland and sense of solidarity (Smith 1986). Within ethnic groups who see themselves as denied the right to self-determination, ethnic identity is formed in dialectical relationship to economic, political and cultural processes of exclusion and denial by another significant group or groups. Kurdish identity, for example, given its fragmented geographical position, is formed in relation to aspects of the Iraqis, Turks, Iranians and Syrians (Vali 1994), while Irish identity is formed, in part at least, in opposition to the British. Ethnicity is part of a bundle of multifaceted identities, varying in saliency at different moments in the history of a group. It is essentially a resource rather than a stable state of being. Groups may not always act on their ethnicity but it can be a latent factor, with territorial attachment becoming more important when a group is oppressed *as* an ethnic group or when members of the group migrate and assert themselves in a new context (Rex 1996).

Especially interesting in SDM contexts is the degree to which political aspiration combines with migration, forced displacement or other processes and vehicles that increase and alter engagement with the wider world to strengthen and/or modify senses of ethnic or other identity. Furthermore, as influence of global cultural forces increases, so does the associated awareness of the international political importance of *having* an 'identity' in the first place (Handler and Linnekin 1984). The articulation and re-formation of 'identity', defined in ethnic, religious or other terms, thus becomes a self-conscious and deliberate endeavour.

It is now generally accepted that the genealogy of ethnicity, like that of the nation, has been influenced by colonial states and associated anthropological, historical and other constructions.[2] Nationalism and ethnicity are seen as products of the modern world (Anderson 1991; Gellner 1994), although ethnicity tends not to be prioritized as important in the development of nationalism (Smith [1986, 1994] being a notable exception), at least not until the influence of colonial constructions of ethnicity took hold in many parts of the world. It is now commonplace to describe the totalizing, controlling and categorizing needs of the imperial system as leading to the self-consciousness and politicization of ethnicity and, inevitably, ethnonationalist conflicts and collective violence (Horowitz 1985; Tambiah 1996). Thus in order to understand SDMs and global influences upon them we need to be aware of pre-colonial and colonial (including missionary) systems and their impacts, as well as more recent political contexts such as post-colonial states, the cold war and post-cold war eras, and the war on terrorism. We lack space to discuss them here, but they comprise the overall political and historical context of what follows. Yet however recent may be self-conscious constructions of ethnicity (and 'nation' and other potential objectives of SDMs), and whatever the history of their development, it is a fact that *now* ethnicity *matters* to many groups represented in active SDMs.

That the Karenni, for example, now call themselves 'Karenni' and define it in certain ways, matters in itself (Dudley 2000). So too does the claim by certain Islamist organizations to be representative of 'true' Islam. The 'truth', if it exists, in what 'Karenni' actually means or what 'Islam' is actually about, matters less than the way in which SDMs and their supporters seek to manipulate such claims not only in their relationships with potential members who share their ethnicity or religious identity but also in their response to wider global cultural influences.

Migration and diaspora

'Diaspora' is a 'double facing...social organization...act[ing] as a bridge between the particular and the universal' (Cohen 1997, p. 170). Diaspora can act as a bridge between global cultural influences and SDMs and their constituency populations. Culturally, the movement of people is the most obvious way in which ideas spread and change. Politically and economically, international links between groups sharing ideas of a common identity are important in lobbying and in channelling funds on behalf of specific SDMs.

The idea of diaspora is not new but economic globalization, advanced communications and travel technologies have increased the scale and complexity of movements of people and thus the scope of their potential interactions and separations. Voluntary and forced migrations can bring together in the relatively narrow confines of cities or refugee camps, heterogeneous populations with little or no shared life before migration. Political awareness and activity are often different in diaspora, as is the extent to which migrants and their descendants feel themselves part of wider, (post)modern global networks. Rather than feeling divorced from 'home' those living in diaspora often work creatively to maintain a sense of continuity with the past, with 'home', and with their own self-perception, an identity that is itself defined in relation to 'home' in some way, even for third or later generations of migrants. Ideas of 'home' are central to culturally constituted personal and communal histories and ways of seeing the world (Dudley 2000; Hirschon 2001), and diaspora often provides a context for strengthening and transforming collective identity.

Common views of the problematic nature of the diasporic and/or displaced state are biased in favour of globally dominant norms of settled living and based on assumptions about the rootedness of culture (Clifford 1988; Malkki 1995). Nonetheless, being in diaspora is a cultural experience; to borrow from Muecke 'the experience...is profoundly cultural because it compels [people] to resolve what Max Weber ([1915] 1958) identified as the problem of meaning, the need to affirm "the ultimate explicableness of experience"' (1987, p. 274, cited in Daniel and Knudsen 1995, p. 2).

All social life involves the negotiation of meaning, but in diaspora the added spatial and temporal distance from 'home' means that people need also to maintain a connection between 'here' and 'there', and to mediate a relationship between 'now (that I am here)' and 'then (when I or my antecedents were there)'. There is continual imaginative, cognitive and often physical movement, too, between new and old places, the present and the past. Seeking to maintain a connection with 'home' is part of maintaining an idea of personal and communal continuity through space and time, an important component in identity. So, once Irish migrants had begun to establish themselves in their country of migration it became possible for them to envisage ways of keeping Irish culture alive and maintaining contacts with their homeland.

Pertinent here are ways in which migrants and their descendants organize themselves into groups to maintain connections with 'home' and how these groups relate to SDMs. Research in this area has focused on ethnic minority/immigrant associations and whether they *insulate* members of migrant populations from, or help them to *integrate* into, the wider host society. This has immediate relevance to their relations with homeland politics. In integrating, migrant groups seek to develop the means to become citizens of their new country and perhaps to attempt to have an impact on its policy towards their country of origin through the formation of an ethnic lobby or the occupation of influential political positions. Insulation, on the other hand, ensures that migrant associations remain oriented to their homeland, perhaps in terms of the sending home of remittances or in forming the base of solidarity actions, directly intervening in homeland politics.

Ethnic minority associations have also been shown to be central to the formation of a migrant identity. While acknowledging the fundamental role of the family and wider kinship structures in migrant lives, Rex showed that associations take over some of these roles. They help the migrant by maintaining contact with the homeland and its culture, supporting material needs such as the search for employment, housing and education. By focusing on education, associations combine the goals of extending the range of opportunities open to migrants *and* helping to maintain their culture of origin often through links with the homeland. There is a major overlap between the structure of migrant associations and that of migrant communities which exert a moral influence over the individual and help to define their identity (Rex *et al.* 1987, p. 18) in relation to the dual poles of the 'host' community and the community of origin.

Migrant associations act differently depending on the political culture and structure of the host society. In France, for example, since the reforms of the 1980s[3] immigrants have been active in exercizing the right of association. Associative politics have been described as a 'new citizenship', based on the idea of active political participation, open to people who do not possess formal citizenship rights (Wihtol de Wenden and Leveau 2001). In France, such associations may be political, but they are not given official funding if they have an exclusively *ethnic* or *religious* appeal. In other countries such as the Netherlands and Germany, migrant associations take on more of a cultural, religious or ethnic form, in response to the way in which wider civil society is organized (Kastoryano 1994). The British 'race relations' approach from the 1960s helped to shape patterns of political contention by minority groups, through a racialized system of cultural pluralism (Statham 1999). This was so important that during preparations for the 1991 census Irish community groups pressed to be recognized in the ethnic classification so as to be able to gain access to funding and be considered by policy makers (Lloyd 1995).

Homeland circumstances also help determine the relationship migrant groups may have with authorities in their country of origin. Associations operate within a complex network, relating the personal to the local, national and international. Some countries such as Morocco do not permit the holding of dual nationality, while others, such as Ireland, are more flexible.[4] These attitudes may shift in time: thus Turkey's application to join the EU has helped change attitudes towards dual nationality and human rights, while Ireland's ability to attract massive foreign investment and support from the EU and USA has reversed disparities between North and South.

Migrant associations vary in their access to funding or political resources. Kurdish groups are differentiated by religious or political factors and focus on a particular form of action: cultural, trade union, provision of welfare. Long-established groups like the Irish in Australia or USA are more involved with structures of government, know about sources of funding, and have members who are socially integrated and occupationally mobile.

Feminist research on North Africans in France and on Turkish women in Germany has drawn attention to the opportunities provided by associations for women working as community mediators (Lutz 1993; Bertaux *et al.* 1996; Bouabdillah 1997). Many associations position themselves between the community they serve and the 'host' society, making it possible to act as brokers giving members opportunities to build expertise and increase involvement with the wider society and the country of origin (Lloyd 1999).

In general, migration opens a political space for people to make an impact on international politics:

> Labor [*sic*] migration has greatly increased the scope of nongovernmental contacts between homelands and host societies. Therefore, the control exercised by governments over their bilateral relations has been weakened and a major new foreign policy issue area has emerged. (Miller 1982, p. 57)

In examining ethnic mobilization in relation to homeland politics, the most immediately relevant category is the *mobilized* diaspora that interacts with dominant groups through élite members (Armstrong 1976). We can understand how a group becomes mobilized by examining its internal stratification in terms of both identities and strategies (Bousetta 2000). A group's potential political mobilization may be limited if its élite members are educated within the institutions of the dominant group and if their subsequent aspirations are channelled towards the dominant institutions of society rather than their community of origin (Leifer 1981). Leaders become brokers, political entrepreneurs or, in the case of women, mediators who manage relationships with host society (Rex 1991; Banton 2000). How far a contesting group can formally access resources and institutions, and how vulnerable or receptive the political system is to the group's actions, is important (Fillieule 1993). Similarly, Geddes shows how the activities and effectiveness of migrant interest groups relate to the framework for political action provided by configurations of responsibility in the EU for immigration and asylum policy. These structures which present opportunities for pro-migrant interest group mobilization, have had limited success (Geddes 1998; Danese 1998).

While political refugees may take a more active political role than economic migrants in relation to events in their homelands, it is often impossible to distinguish between them, and in practice political refugees may 'wish to leave political activism behind [and move on] while so-called economic migrants become politicized from afar' (Portes 1999; Landolt *et al.* 1999; Østergaard-Nielson 2001). There are also differences amongst members of any one diaspora community in terms of their involvement in self-determination movements in their homeland relating to differences in class, gender, generation and involvement with the life of their new home. Younger people are often said to be more involved with the political and cultural life of their new country (Østergaard-Nielson 2001, p. 11), yet second or third generation migrants are often those *most* likely to reject the host culture and to become increasingly active in political activities concerning SDMs in and/or concerned with the country of ethnic origin (Eade and Garbin 2002; Lloyd 2002). Diaspora communities in difficult socioeconomic positions in their host countries seem to develop a stronger identification with the cultural and political life of their homeland (Smith 1998).

Some migrants struggle with ideas of 'loyalty' towards their old and new countries. This may lead to intervention by homeland governments in affairs of the diaspora (Sheffer 1986). Homeland religious organizations may set up religious missions, importing ideological and political struggles of the homeland as well as wider issues (as in the context of rich Muslim countries such as Saudi Arabia [Rex 1991, p. 73]), while some foreign governments may also operate to control the migrant group, as in the Iranian authorities' surveillance of students from Iran in the 1970s and 1980s or the similar behaviour of the Apartheid government in South Africa.

Migration may afford a group a wider range of spaces within which to mobilize than they have access to in their country of origin. The changing dynamics of global influences on SDMs among the Irish and the Kurds, are illustrative here.

The Irish

The Irish struggle for self-determination in a united Ireland is at least six centuries old. After 1922, the island of Ireland was partitioned on a temporary basis into a Free State and the six northern counties of East Ulster. The political system set up in the six counties, which remained a contested part of the United Kingdom, gave the Protestant Unionist population permanent political control and economic dominance. Since the establishment of the Free State, later Republic, in the south of Ireland, the self-determination struggle has been focused in the North, where many aspects of life such as place names and the right to public space, are contested across a divide whose definition itself is debated. Even the naming of the opposing groups reflects nuances of political divisions: Nationalists/Republicans/Catholics as opposed to Loyalists/Unionists/Protestants. Recently, the conflict has entered a new and complex phase, with the negotiation of a peace settlement in 1998 and the development of significant cross-border institutions. At the same time, active minorities on both the Unionist and the Nationalist sides resent the way in which the peace settlement was negotiated; among them are groups such as the Real and Continuity IRA, who continue to pursue their goals through violence. Another significant development is a crisis of identity on the part of the Unionist population.

The Irish diaspora has been among the most important external influences on self-determination struggles in Ireland because of its political and economic leverage. The Irish migrated in large numbers due to the distress and famines of the nineteenth century to England, Scotland, North America and Australia where they now form an old and powerful diaspora. The Irish lobby is one of the most effective in Washington, DC, while in Britain, Irish organizations and individuals have been important in the labour movement and in civil rights campaigns related to 'the troubles'.

The two biggest Irish migrant communities are in the USA and in the UK. In both there are recognized structures in civil society for ethnic minority groups to organize and lobby policymakers. The Irish community is one of the most effectively organized in the USA, while in Britain its place as an ethnic minority group has only recently been officially recognized. The term 'Irish community' may be misleading: like any ethnic group, 'the Irish community' is internally differentiated by gender, generation or place of origin. It would be more precise to refer to 'Irish communities', except that elements of the Unionist community would be more likely to identify as citizens of the UK rather than as 'Irish'.

The physical proximity of the Irish community in Britain to Ireland means that many people return regularly for holidays or to live permanently, and it is relatively well informed about developments in Ireland.

Living in Britain, the ex-colonial power, the Irish have experienced serious levels of discrimination and disadvantage especially in health, housing and (un)employment (CRE 1997). Anti-Irish racism has become particularly virulent at key moments such as the 1974 Birmingham bombings (Lloyd 1995, pp. 26–9; Hickman and Walter 1997). Changing political relationships between Britain and Ireland make for a dynamic which incorporates exclusion and inferiorization and confers on the Irish in Britain the status of a 'suspect community' (Hillyard 1993). The introduction of the Prevention of Terrorism Act (PTA) in 1974 was an important landmark in a series of repressive measures against the Irish in Britain (Bunyan 1977). Between 1974–84, 86 per cent of those detained under the PTA were released without charge and the main aim of a high proportion of the arrests appeared to be to gather intelligence about the Irish community (Hillyard 1993, p. 148). Several important miscarriages of justice gave rise to (ultimately successful) campaigns for release from prison, notably the Birmingham Six, Guildford Four and Maguire Seven. The combination of discrimination and harassment created a general feeling of insecurity, while curtailing legitimate political debate about self-determination struggles in Ireland.[5] Many community leaders were obliged to adopt a strategy of quiescence to facilitate integration into British society.

Irish migrants in Britain have sought to affect British policy in Ireland, support the Irish community and influence public opinion. Even before the introduction of voting rights through the European Union, Republic of Ireland citizens had the right to vote and stand for elected office in Britain. One of the most important voluntary organizations has been the Connolly Association, formed in 1938. Its activities were rooted in the labour movement and the anti-imperialist struggle (growing out of Irish involvement in International Brigades in Spain, independence struggles in Kenya in the 1950s and later in Cyprus and Zimbabwe). It played an important role in British trade unions in campaigning against dangerous working conditions on building sites (where many Irish men worked) and, in the 1970s, in the Troops Out Movement, in shows of solidarity with Irish prisoners (particularly during the period of internment) and in campaigns against the PTA, the use of plastic bullets in Northern Ireland and British miscarriages of justice. Recently, groups focusing on the welfare of Irish migrants to Britain have become increasingly self-confident. Successful lobbying, together with increased migration of well-qualified young professionals and a greater visibility of Irish people in the media, not just as entertainers but also in authoritative roles, have resulted in changes in the perception of the Irish in Britain. These changes indicate the opening of a political space for the debate and recognition of a positive Irish identity.

There are debates and connections between home and diaspora communities on the Unionist side, too. Finlay documents a number of studies of renewed sectarian violence on the part of some Unionist communities as the post-1998 peace process progressed (2001). They have shifted from triumphalism to defeat, alienation and resistance, encapsulated in the notion of the 'defeated superiority complex' like other settler communities in the post-colonial period (Clayton 1996; Finlay 2001). The most vulnerable elements of this population are poor, working-class Unionists whose attachments to the United Kingdom were based on their former position of relative privilege and secure employment. Their new insecurity can be seen in the pleas for recognition to the Protestant Ulster diaspora in websites such as that of the Ulster Loyalists[6] which celebrates the achievements of the Ulster Scotch (*sic*).

Distance in time and space between Irish–Americans and Ireland affects the construction of their identity rather differently than that of the Irish in Britain. In the USA, the Irish are one of the oldest and most influential lobbying groups. Irish–American organizations can be traced back to the 1830s when the Ancient Order of Hibernians (AOH), originating in Ireland, was established in the USA. Tracing one's ancestors is important in the USA, and proof of Irish ancestry is necessary for membership of the AOH. For many years, the AOH operated secretly, providing funds for newly arrived migrants and defending the property of the Catholic Church.[7] Today, it is the body which defines the boundaries and characteristics of Irish America. It organizes the annual St Patrick's Day march in New York (and other cities). Its conservative role is illustrated through disputes over the right of newer groups, defined according to sexual identity, to participate in the New York march (Marston 2002).

Irish Americans have been important in funding the nationalist cause in Ireland through cultural and financial links. The operation of diaspora politics depends on how diaspora communities identify with the cultural and political life of their homeland and some Irish in Ireland have difficulties with Irish–American readings of the situation, such as the AOH's rejection of gay Irish people and Irish–American calls for a boycott of British goods including 'British' whisky. The Irish–American community includes 'hard line' elements that have been difficult for the present leadership of Sinn Fein to handle as they have moved towards a broader more democratic strategy.

The Kurds

The territory known as Kurdistan has been in dispute since the collapse of the Ottoman Empire. Under the Treaty of Lausanne in 1923, Kurdistan was divided and distributed between Iran, Iraq, Syria and, mostly, Turkey. Today Kurds comprise about 20 per cent of the population of Turkey, 15 per cent of the population of Iran, 27 per cent of the population of Iraq and less than 10 per cent of the population of Syria with a further 800,000 living abroad, mainly in Europe. The lands to which the Kurds lay claim are in authoritarian states with little scope for the development of civil society.

About half of the Kurdish population (23–28 million) live in Turkey, mostly in the rural and underdeveloped southeast. Kurdish lands were expropriated by the Forced Residency Act of 1930 and a series of revolts followed, most recently the PKK, formed in the 1970s and led by Abdullah Ocalan, while the more moderate PSK (Socialist Party), advocates Kurdish regional status.[8] In Turkey any expression by Kurds of their identity including use of the Kurdish language was illegal until 1991. Attempts to organize politically have been suppressed: Kurdish political parties have been banned and party members imprisoned. The Turkish state deployed some 300,000 troops to the southeast at an annual cost of $8 billion and set up a system of 'village guards', Kurds paid and armed by the Turkish state to keep the PKK guerrillas at bay. If a village refuses to participate, it faces demolition by the Turkish military, while those that comply become targets of the PKK. Between 1984 and 1996 20,000 people had been killed and 3,000 villages were destroyed in an effort to root out PKK sympathizers, resulting in more than 2 million refugees.

Turkey's aspirations to become a member of the European Union have floundered on its human rights record, partly in respect of the Kurds. In August 2002, responding to an earlier EU deadline for human rights reforms, the Turkish parliament legislated to abolish the death penalty, establish language rights for the Kurdish minority and relax prohibitions on public meetings and criticism of military and other state institutions. The measures allow the Kurdish language to be taught but not in state schools. Television and radio broadcasts are permitted in Kurdish provided they do not incite violence. These measures meant that the Kurdish separatist leader, Abdullah Ocalan, captured in 1999, would not be executed.

For a long time the Kurdish struggle was marked by the lack of even the most precarious homeland, until the establishment of the semi-autonomous Iraqi Kurdistan in 1992, where freedom of speech, assembly and association were enjoyed, with unfettered satellite and Internet access which greatly facilitated links with diaspora Kurds (Lawrence 2000; Zanger 2002). It now has regional status. The Kurds gained significant parliamentary representation in the January 2005 elections in Iraq and the PUK leader, Jalal Talabani, was elected President.

In the 1960s Kurds began to arrive in Germany, the Benelux countries, Austria, Switzerland and France as immigrant workers under contracts based on inter-government agreements. Like other economic migrants, they formed associations and joined trade unions. Following the Islamic Revolution in Iran in 1979, the Army *coup d'état* in Turkey in 1980 and the long campaign against the Kurds in Iraq, Kurdish political refugees arrived in Western Europe. This exodus increased with the 1992 campaign of forced evacuation and destruction of Kurdish villages, together with political assassinations of Kurdish elites by Turkish 'death squads' and paramilitary forces, and inter-Kurdish clashes in Iraqi Kurdistan after 1994. These asylum seekers were more politically motivated; they formed associations to assert Kurdish identity and formed the basis of a Kurdish lobby (Rigoni 1998).

The most widely accepted estimates of the number of Kurds sets their number at about 850,000 in Western Europe. The Kurdish intelligentsia were attracted to Sweden for the opportunities for artistic creation. The main concentrations of Kurdish diaspora populations live in Germany and France.[9] While the associative structure set up by early waves of Kurdish migrants was based on construction and textile workers, in the 1970s and 1980s politically active refugees established more overtly political associations: the *Komkar* (Federation of Associations of Kurdish Workers) affiliated to the TKSP[10] and the *Feyka* (Federation of Cultural Associations of the Patriotic Workers of Kurdistan) affiliated to the PKK developed in Germany. Their initial aims were to maintain and recreate Kurdish identity, providing Kurdish language classes for young people. While the *Komkar* adopted a broad diplomatic approach, seeking the support of all political tendencies, acceptance of the *Feyka* has been curtailed by the threat of PKK violent actions (notably in 1993 and 1996) attacking Turkish economic interests in Germany (Rigoni 1998). In response, Turkey has exerted pressure on European governments, especially Germany, to ban the *Feyka* or at least keep them under surveillance.

The political action of the Kurdish diaspora is affected by their access to citizenship rights in the country of immigration. It is easier in France than in Germany to obtain nationality and a large proportion of the Kurdish-origin population has taken French nationality, which they view as an acceptable choice compared to the imposition of Turkish nationality at home.

Kurdish associations vary from the local, community-based association to the national research institute. They offer a base for (mainly but not exclusively) men to meet to drink tea, watch satellite television and read newspapers to keep in touch with home. While their scope for political expression is restricted in Turkey and Iraq, in Europe they have access to more democratic political arenas where members can develop the habitus of the professional political actor: theories, strategies, historical traditions, economic resources and language. *Feyka* associations in Germany and France tend to focus on public street demonstration and the occupation of buildings (Rigoni 1998). Regular collective actions reinforce the community: European meetings of Kurdish networks in Germany enabled the Kurdish diaspora to mobilize following the arrest of Abdullah Ocalan in cultural, economic and political exchanges with fellow Kurds.

The use of public demonstrations and the recourse to violence indicate that Kurds lack political leverage compared with the Irish in the USA. Kurdish diaspora organizations are not wealthy and their structures are maintained by individual contributions and voluntary labour.

Transnational political and religious networks and solidarities

Within migrant associations solidarity operates through the sharing of experience, respect and equality between members of the community, and the provision of opportunities for disadvantaged groups (Hayward 1959; Hechter *et al.* 1982; Rorty 1989; Lambert 1994; Widegren 1997; Patel 1999). Solidarity links diaspora associations with human rights and others with whom they do not share an ethnic or cultural bond. Transnational political and religious connections between members of diasporic networks, for example, can be one element in a 'multiplicity of nodes' (van de Veer 2001, p. 3). The dynamics of specific SDMs that have impacted transnationally can be illuminated by tracing the connections between these nodes. Transnational connections in politics and religion are especially powerful in drawing in those separated by national boundaries.

While the Nationalist/Republican parts of the Irish diaspora in Britain, for example, have historically had a close relationship with the British left, the Unionist/Loyalist relationship is closer to the British state, army and the Royal Ulster Constabulary (now the Police Service of Northern Ireland). There is also a well documented link between the most extreme elements among Loyalists and the British neo-fascist right (McVeigh 1992).[11] *Searchlight* Magazine and *Statewatch* have documented connections between Combat 18 and other racist groups active in football violence and extreme Ulster loyalist groups such as the Loyalist Volunteer Force (LVF). The institutional links between Unionist paramilitaries and the British security services have been investigated by the Stevens enquiry into collusion between loyalist murder gangs and members of the security forces in Northern Ireland.[12] Press reports claim that the British army's Force Research Unit (FRU) employed agents to infiltrate loyalist paramilitary murder gangs and was complicit in some murders, notably that of the Republican solicitor Pat Finucane.[13] It is also thought that FRU records show they used agents to ensure 'proper targeting' of IRA suspects prior to assassination.

Such cross-group bonds may be perceived in terms of religion or political ideology through the identification by one group with some element of in the agenda of another. Temporary alliances and/or unequal sympathies may also comprise wider solidarities that may sometimes impact upon the evolving ideology, strategy and destiny of a SDM as much as, if not more than, explicit diasporic connections. The roots of these wider solidarities may lie in both specific SDMs and diasporas, and in transnational social movements (TSMs): 'the *broad tendencies* that often manifest themselves in...International Non-Governmental Organizations (INGOs) [such as] human rights, women's, peace, labour, green or student movements' (Cohen 1998, p. 1). Cohen claims that by the 1990s these TSMs, together with transnational corporations, were emerging as significant new agents of global change that contradicted a still prevalent state-centric view of global politics (*ibid*). Eighty per cent of the world's people do not live in democracies: for them 'perhaps the most important form of civil society is organizing in alliance with a TSM' (*ibid*: 6). But what is the nature and impact on SDM ideologies and strategies of such alliances? Cohen claims we can class TSMs as transnational communities: their members may not be tied by ethnic or religious bonds, but TSMs nonetheless embody three shifts that 'involve the constitution of "community"' (*ibid*: 7): a switch from emancipatory to identity politics, a demand for more meaningful political participation, and a widening transnational repertoire. For us the most significant of these are the widening transnational repertoire and the switch to identity politics. As TSMs have given an increasing number of people a new sense of responsibility and 'a new practice of self-determination and solidarity' (Hegedus 1989, p. 33, cited in Cohen 1998, p. 8) between themselves and others so 'political conflicts and processes have invaded the private realm where individuals make personal choices concerning identities, lifestyle preferences and everyday relationships' (Cohen 1998, p. 7).

TSMs – NGOs, INGOs and more informal networks – provide valuable transnational networks of support and advocacy for those involved in many SDMs. In particular, 'a much sought after strategy for transnational political networks' is the co-opting of NGOs and INGOs since they 'facilitate contact with levels of policy making which are otherwise difficult to gain access to' (Østergaard-Nielsen 2001, p. 16). Østergaard-Nielsen cites Andean indigenous and Kurdish political organizations who depend upon lobbying of the UN and other international organizations by INGOs such as the Unrepresented People's Organization (UNPO).

TSMs do not just function as conduits, supports and targets for lobbying. They also 'provide a normative frame of reference for those [SDMs] advocating democratization and human rights agendas' (Østergaard-Nielsen 2001, p. 16) and a normative frame of opposition for SDMs advocating rather different agendas. SDMs such as the Burmese pro-democracy movement increasingly absorb and use international human rights rhetoric both to explain their cause to a wider international audience and to attempt to garner additional international support (see Dudley, this volume). Some Kurdish political organizations have similarly progressed from left-wing rhetoric concerning worker freedom to a more international language that privileges Kurdish human rights (Østergaard-Nielsen 2001). Modifying rhetoric thus renders the cause more intelligible to, and gains the sympathy of, a wider audience.

Some roles of media and new media

'(S)omething like a transnational public sphere has . . . rendered any strictly bounded sense of community or locality obsolete' (Gupta and Ferguson 1992, p. 9). If so, the media (especially satellite TV and the Internet), together with increased human mobility, have played a significant role in this process and in the associated growth of translocal understandings and transnational solidarities. New technologies and the Internet in particular play a Janus-faced role in the new global politics of identity: cultural distinctiveness is seen as resilient and as something that can be formalized and strengthened by use of new technologies; yet at the same time these Internet technologies are powerful and global enough to undermine 'traditional' local identities.

Furthermore, while access to new technologies is by no means solely the preserve of those in rich countries, international variations in access are significant. Nonetheless, since the mid-1990s many disparate SDMs and TSMs have been effectively using the Internet to expose grievances and attempt to garner sympathy and support (Dudley, this volume). Particularly successful in this regard has been the Zapatista movement and their mission to inform the wider world about Mexico's Chiapas peoples and Zapatista guerrilla activity (see Castells 1997, Martinez-Torres 2001, Russell 2001).

Cyber-Islam:

'Cyber-Islam' (Lubeck 2000, p. 151) employs 'modern organizational tools and "cell" structures borrowed from western anti-systemic movements' and pursues 'an alternative route to modernity, one that self-consciously intends to "Islamize modernity"'. Indeed, Turner (1994, p. 86) claims that, for a religion that has always had universalist objectives, it is only with the advent of new information and communication technologies (ICTs) such as the Internet, satellite television and cellular telephones that a 'globalization of Islam' has become possible. But the Islam represented through such media is multiple, with no clear, single authoritative version projected around the world. Progressive and critical Islamic scholarship as well as conservative and marginal political moral views, and a multitude of positions in between, are found on different Muslim websites. An increasingly transnational Islam is taking shape in the spaces created by the intersections of new ICTs, Muslim organizations, and mobile sections of diaspora and 'home' Muslim populations, including travelling *imams* (Mandaville 2001).

Migration, travel and ICTs all have an effect on the gaze with which people look beyond themselves; Gardner refers to Bangladeshi migrants to the Middle East and the UK who 'have moved from an Islam based around localised cultures and moulded to the culture and geography of the homelands, to an international Islam of Muslims from many different countries and cultures' (1993, p. 225, cited in Vertovec 2000). ICTs both facilitate anonymous debate amongst Muslims and with others, and provide a platform for marginal groups that might not otherwise reach a wide audience. Elements of political Islam seem to benefit from transnational contexts, perhaps because they are particularly effective in using new opportunities to extend existing networks. Political Islamist movements often attract greater support from abroad than their local political opponents; in Indonesia: 'the neofundamentalists have strong organizational and ideological ties to transnational Islamist movements' whereas their civil democratic opposition tends 'to be grounded in organizations and ideologies distinctive to Indonesia and earlier traditions of Indonesian nationalism' (Hefner 2002, p. 1).

ICTs also facilitate the strengthening of notions of 'community' and its boundedness. Certainly, transnational networks are not unprecedented: earlier migration and structures such as *hawala* money transfer systems mean that Muslims, like many others, had networked, culturally bounded communities (Castells 1996) crossing national borders long before the advent of modern ICTs. Nonetheless, technology has enhanced networking potentialities. In doing so, it has also increased opportunities for developing ideas of 'community' and belonging: ICTs provide an immediate medium through which to spread one version of a particular community's core values and of what it means to belong to and have that community identity. The idea of community so promulgated is still defined by cultural, political and moral values, but is no longer confined by geographical boundaries. In the Arab Gulf, for example:

> [t]raditionalising forms of Islam . . . flourish most clearly in off-shore settings connected by contemporary [ICT] . . . systems, whose technology and management are . . . external to the [Arab Gulf and] beam into the sites from which their funding comes, images of domestic and Islamic community. (Dresch *et al.* 1998, p. 4)

The core community values and criteria of belonging disseminated by a group often include a shared bond of suffering through which the experience of exploitation, discrimination and disenfranchisement is one of the most powerful factors in binding people together (Davis 1992). Such ideas are not new and have been used in Islamic civil society and other networks. ICTs provide a renewed opportunity to strengthen such bonds, enhancing awareness of international contexts and thus of relative deprivation, real or imagined. Surfing the Web and watching satellite TV one does not only develop an idea of what one is missing, but also a better, if partial, idea of the 'world out there', a clearly defined Other against which one can better define oneself and, perhaps, choose to rail.

Bonds of suffering help to mobilize (often politically marginal) elements of communities. Concern over discrimination against Muslims, for example, is limited to neither the Muslim mainstream nor the margins. Yet this is exploited particularly effectively via ICTs by radical, marginal groups. Abu Hamza, leader of the Supporters of Shari'ah (SoS) based at the North London Central Mosque, for example, writes of a 'global conspiracy against Muslims', although the website was closed down by its UK Internet Service Provider (ISP) after 11 September 2001. A similarly radical British Muslim group, Al-Muhajiroun, led by Omar Bakhri and also based in London, in leaflets addressing such topics as 'Islamophobia' on its website described the world's Muslim community as being 'butchered' on a global scale.[14]

SoS, Al-Muhajiroun and others like them have been adept at exploiting notions of Muslim victimhood and suffering. They have associated with each other and with similar groups such as Sakina Security Services (SSS), Society of Converts to Islam, and the Society of Muslim Lawyers, networking at such events as the Second Conference of Islamic Revival Movements (London, 1999), subsequently disseminating joint declarations.[15] They have also distributed other material either through their own websites or via international Islamist websites.[16]

Radical political Islam websites have also served as platforms for practical calls to action ranging from public demonstrations in the UK to travelling to Afghanistan to fight with the Taliban. Al-Muhajiroun frequently advertised demonstrations and talks in different parts of the UK. Furthermore, web-based calls to action have since 11 September 2001 included general urging to support a military *jihad* 'verbally, financially and physically',[17] but also the advertising of military *jihad* training courses 'using live ammunition' run by such organizations as SSS (Cowell 2001). Nonetheless, groups such as these remain small and marginal.

Satellite TV and print media:

Also important, not in terms of direct recruitment but in spreading information and thus potentially shifting opinions amongst grassroot Muslim networks and amongst decision-makers, are relatively independent satellite TV channels such as, in the Arab world, Al-Jazeera, and lesser known channels such as Abu Dhabi TV. As Hudson points out, although Al-Jazeera's audience might fall below that of entertainment-focused satellite channels, 'there seems little doubt that Al-Jazeera has a significant if not predominant presence within its targeted audience of educated, professionally oriented individuals in or near the circles of political influence' (Hudson 2001, p. 5). It is also, he claims, 'thought to have a high degree of saturation among Arab communities of the diaspora, especially in the United States and Europe' (*ibid*). Al-Jazeera has developed a highly interactive relationship with its audience, using polling and requesting email responses to its debate and other opinion programmes, and now having a well-visited website. Indeed, the significance of Al-Jazeera in the aftermath of 11 September 2001 was well recognized by the US Government, not only because of Al-Jazeera's broadcasting of Osama bin Laden's videotape addresses but also its significance to educated, opinion-forming classes in the Middle East and in the Arab diaspora. The USA's attempts initially to control or gag Al-Jazeera and, when it realized that this was not going to be straightforward, its subsequent consideration of using Al-Jazeera to put across its own message (Beers 2001, Campagna 2001), testify to this.

Print media also provide channels of opinion 'at home' and in diaspora. Diaspora newspapers may provide 'alternative' voices, so that in the aftermath of 11 September 2001, for example, the British *Asian Xpress* called for an end to the bombing of Afghanistan and for a willingness to 'put vengeful pride aside' for humanitarian reasons and for Ramadan (editorial, 26 October 2001). The *BRITasian*, conversely, echoed the government's sentiments that 'this is not a war on Islam', and carried patriotic interviews with British Muslims, including a Muslim Royal Navy captain, supporting British involvement in Afghanistan (*BRITasian*, 26 October 2001). The *Eastern Eye* more neutrally stated that while British Muslims were divided about the war on the Taliban and Al Qaeda, British youth who went to fight for the Taliban were 'foolhardy' and that both the Taliban and the events of 11 September 2001 were 'contradictory to the ideals of the faith preached by the Prophet' (editorial, 26 October 2001). All diaspora Asian newspapers carried little on the Israel/Palestine aspects of the 'war on terror', concentrating on impacts on South Asia or on the South Asian diaspora in Britain.

Appadurai's 'diasporic public spheres' (1996) are set up and perpetuated by the role of electronic media in particular in starting 'new conversations between those who move and those who stay' (*ibid*, p. 22), through email, news-lists, and online chat-rooms. Newspapers, ethnic film and TV also have a major role in maintaining connections and perpetuating certain stereotypes between and amongst members of diasporic communities, as in 'Bollywood' films. Such media can provide an outlet and means of political leverage internationally and in diaspora host nations, in addition to public demonstrations or recourse to violence. Yet often these media attempt to cover self-determination disputes 'back home' only to find that outsiders, if not members of the diasporas themselves, suspect their motive. The Kurdish satellite MED-TV broadcast news, discussion and entertainment to 30 million Kurds in the Middle East, Europe, and the Russian Federation. It 'pride[d] itself on its unbiased coverage of all sides in the Kurdistan dispute' (Ryan 1997, p. 98, cited in Karim 1998) and yet was viewed as threatening, especially by Turkey, which lobbied Western European governments to close it down (Karim 1998, p. 10).

Conclusion

In seeking to understand SDMs, we need to understand how they see themselves. Important components of this self-image include the notion of a bond of suffering. The peddling of images of the 'good life' on globally accessible media such as satellite TV and the Internet may give rise to feelings of relative deprivation (Runciman 1966). Such ideas may be as important as local leaders' exploitations of real economic inequalities in providing both the necessary dissatisfaction for a SDM to arise, and in strengthening a shared, communal identity. In diaspora such processes may create a *new* communal identity and 'a hybrid of: past alliances, the re-establishment of relations through the new group, as well as the experiences of negotiating real life in the new country of settlement and interaction with other individuals/groups in that society' (Karim 1998, p. 13).

Because they can exert such a powerful hold over certain individuals and groups, politics and religion play a major part in these processes of identity formation and reformation. They can also have an impact upon how others see and interact with SDMs, and thus ultimately also upon their likely strategy and trajectory. Many Muslim groups get lumped together by others as 'Islamic fundamentalists'. In turn, such fundamentalist identity may be reappropriated and positively embraced by insiders, thus both enhancing an oppositional relationship to those who originally applied it and helping to forge a bond between different groups and causes in some way associated with political Islam.

For diaspora groups, identity constructions are also related to geographical and cognitive relations with the country of origin, and depend on factors such as the circumstances of migration and the frequency of contact with the country of origin. A migrant group with apparently little interest in the affairs of its country of origin may still respond to major political developments. Channels and political opportunities open to migrant groups in the country in which they are living are also important. Central to identity formation in diaspora are the ways in which the host society perceives the migrants. For Irish people living in Britain, as we have seen, being discriminated against and simultaneously having significant lobbying potential and being intimately bound up with social and political issues in the host as well as 'home' country, has significant impact on self-image and political agenda.

It is now commonly accepted that media of various kinds play a crucial role not only in reflecting national and other identities, but also in actually constructing them (Anderson 1991). Certainly, media can play important roles in SDM identity formation and in perceptions of and responses to SDMs as is demonstrated by attempts to harness, manipulate and silence different media sectors. Media also influence commodity marketing and people's knowledge of the world and what is available in it. The degree to which people perceive themselves to have either commodities or more abstract notions such as 'freedom' affects their identity. How this intersects with their economic agenda may affect the emergence and trajectory of SDMs. While 'global diasporas and translocal solidarities continually challenge the nation–state's capacity to mobilize let alone monopolize allegiance and loyalty' (Foster 1999, p. 265), at the same time people

> seem to be promised ever more possibilities for freedom and autonomy through their consumption choices ... global flows of media images incite people living in the most remote villages ... to new and powerful

> fantasies of self-fashioning through consumption. The ideal of personal efficacy achieved through consumption everywhere rivals the ideal of citizens determining their collective existence. (*Ibid*)

Indeed, another way to explore the global cultural impact on SDMs would be to examine the role of commodity marketing and mass consumption in producing political identity, not least because members of some SDM constituency populations, such as Burma's Korean National Progressive Party (KNPP), have not had a chance to be 'citizens' *before* they have found themselves, in exile in a market economy, becoming 'consumers'.

The objectives and processes of SDMs, like that special case of self-determination, nation building, are continually being reworked and negotiated within a global cultural and economic context. Crucial to this are power, education, language, culture, and the control of communication of ideas about identity and purpose (Gellner 1983, Anderson 1991). Political consciousness develops and is controlled unevenly among social groups. Our SDMs may be just another form of Fox's 'nationalist ideologies', a notion he uses to refer to the general 'production of conceptions of peoplehood' for which, unlike 'nationalisms', an independent, bounded state is not necessary (Fox 1990, p. 2). Thus, he suggests, one can talk of similar processes at work not only in a territorially defined 'nation' but also in 'subnationalisms', 'ethnicity' and so forth. All, he argues, are 'cultural productions of identity' (*ibid*, p. 4) as, we suggest, are SDMs. Cultural identity production and global cultural links thus crucially influence the global economic links and networks discussed elsewhere in this volume.

Notes

1. Sandra Dudley acknowledges her debt to her late father, Robert Dudley, and his impassioned arguments on some of the topics discussed in this chapter.
2. In Africa, Malkki notes that 'there is a chilling traffic back and forth between the essentialist constructions of historians, anthropologists, and colonial administrators, and those of Hutu and Tutsi ethnic nationalism' (1995, p. 14).
3. In 1981 the French Government reformed the law which since 1939 had prevented foreigners from leading associations. Before 1981 they had operated through a system of 'borrowed names' by which people with French nationality provided a titular head for legal purposes. This of course did not preclude them from forming *informal* associations.
4. Article 2 of the Constitution of Ireland (1937) states 'the Irish nation cherishes its special affinity with people of Irish ancestry living abroad who share its cultural identity and heritage'.
5. For many years, it was forbidden to broadcast the spoken word of Sinn Fein leaders and actors' voices were used.
6. http://www.ulsterloyalist.co.uk (accessed 15/7/05).
7. http://www.aoh.com (15/7/05).
8. http://www.kurdistan.nu (15/7/05).

9. This section draws on fieldwork undertaken in Paris by Cathie Lloyd for an ESRC-funded project (L213262016) *Civic stratification, exclusion and migratory trajectories in three European states, France, Italy and the United Kingdom.*
10. *Komkar* is now present in eight European countries, the *Feykar* in ten.
11. In particular the National Front, the British National Party and Combat 18.
12. See www.met.police.uk/commissioner/stevens3.htm (15/7/05).
13. *The Guardian* 2/8/2002.
14. http://www.almuhajiroun.com, accessed 3/8/02. Now closed.
15. http://www.ummah.net/jihad/articles/declaration.html, accessed 3/8/02. Now closed.
16. http://www.ummah.net (15/7/05).
17. http://www.almuhajiroun.com/press_releases/07_11_2001.html, accessed 3/8/02. Now closed.

References

Anderson, B. (1991) *Imagined Communities. Reflections on the Origin and Spread of Nationalism*. London: Verso.

Armstrong, J. (1976) 'Mobilized and Proletarian Diasporas', *American Political Science Review*, 70(2), 393–403.

Appadurai, A. (1996), *Modernity at Large: Cultural Dimensions of Globalization*. Minneapolis, MN: University of Minnesota Press.

Asian Xpress (2001) Editorial, 26 October.

Banton, M. (2000) 'Ethnic Conflict', *Sociology* 34(3, August), 481–98.

Beers, C. (2001) 'US Considers Advertising on Al Jazeera TV', *AdAge* 15 (October 2001).

Bertaux, S., Beski, S. and Delcroix, C. (1996), *Les Médiatrices dans les Quartiers Fragilisés*. Paris: La Documentation Française.

Bouabdillah, P. (1997) 'Les Femmes-relais et leur Action' in N. Bentchichou (ed.) *Les Femmes de l'Immigration au Quotidien*. Paris: Licorne/ L'Harmattan, pp. 72–9.

Bousetta, H. (2000) 'Institutional theories of immigrant ethnic mobilisation: relevance and limitations', *Journal of Ethnic and Migration Studies*, 26(2), 229–45.

BRITasian (2001) Editorial, 26 October.

Bunyan, T. (1977) *The History and Practice of the Political Police in Britain*, London: Quartet.

Campagna, J. (2001) 'Between Two Worlds: Qatar's Al-Jazeera Satellite Channel Faces Conflicting Expectations', *CPJ Briefings: Press Freedom Reports*, http://www.cpj.org/Briefings/2001/aljazeera_oct01/aljazeera_oct01.html, accessed 21/7/05.

Castells, M. (1997) *The Power of Identity*. Oxford: Blackwell.

Castells, M. (1996) 'The Net and the Self', *Cultural Anthropology*, 16(1); 9–38.

Clayton, P. (1996) *Enemies and Passing Friends: Settler Ideologies in Twentieth Century Ulster*. London: Pluto Press.

Clifford, J. (1988) *The Predicament of Culture. Twentieth Century Ethnography, Literature and Art*. Cambridge, MA: Harvard University Press.

Cohen, R. (1997) *Global Diasporas: an Introduction*. London: University College London Press.

Cohen, R. (1998) 'Transnational Social Movements: An Assessment', paper presented to the Transnational Communities Programme Seminar, School of Geography, University of Oxford, 19 June 1998, http://www.transcomm.ox.ac.uk/working%20papers/cohen.pdf, accessed 21/7/05.

Cohen, R. (1998) 'Transnational Social Movements: An Assessment', Working Papers on Transnational Communities (WPTC 98-09), www.transcomm.ox.ac.uk

CRE (1997) *The Irish in Britain*. London: Commission for Racial Equality.

Cowell, A. (2001) 'Britain Tracing Trail of One More Jihad Group', *The New York Times on the web*, 4 October 2001, http://www.nytimes.com, accessed 3/8/02.

Danese, G. (1998) 'Transnational Collective Action in Europe: The Case of Migrants in Italy and Spain', *Journal of Ethnic and Migration Studies*, 24(4); 715–34.

Daniel, E.V. and Knudsen, J. (1995) 'Introduction' in E.V. Daniel and J. Knudsen (eds) *Mistrusting Refugees*. Berkeley, CA: University of California Press, pp. 1–12.

Davis, J. (1992) 'The Anthropology of Suffering', *Journal of Refugee Studies*, 5(2); 149–60.

De Vos, G. (1995) 'Ethnic Pluralism: Conflict and Accommodation. The Role of Ethnicity in Social History' in L. Romanucci-Ross and G. De Vos (eds) *Ethnic Identity: Creation, Conflict and Accommodation*. London: Sage, pp. 349–79.

Dresch, P., Piscatori, J. and al-rasheed, M. (1998) 'Connection and Imagery: Transnational Culture Flows and the Arab Gulf', ESRC Transnational Communities Research Programme, http://www.transcomm.ox.ac.uk/wwwroot/dresch.htm#Long%20 Description.

Dudley, S. (2000) 'Displacement and Identity: Karenni Refugees in Thailand', unpublished DPhil thesis, University of Oxford.

Eade, J. and Garbin, D. (2002) 'Changing Narratives of Violence, Struggle and Resistance: Bangladeshis and the Competition for Resources in the Global City', *Oxford Development Studies*, 30(2), 137–50.

Eastern Eye (2001) Editorial, 26 October.

Fillieule, O. (1993) *Sociologie de la Protestation. Les Formes de l'Action Collective dans la France Contemporaine*. Paris: L'Harmattan.

Finlay, A. (2001) 'Defeatism and Northern Protestant "Identity"', *The Global Review of Ethnopolitics*, 1(2), 3–20.

Foster, R. (1999) 'The Commercial Construction of "New Nations"', *Journal of Material Culture*, 4(3), 263–92.

Fox, R. G. (1990) 'Introduction' in R. G. Fox (ed.) *Nationalist Ideologies and the Production of National Cultures*. Washington, D.C.: American Anthropological Association, pp. 1–14.

Gardner, K. (1993) 'Mullahs, Migrants, Miracles: Travel and Transformation in Sylhet', *Contributions to Indian Sociology*, 27(2), 213–35.

Geddes, A. (1998) 'The Representation of "Migrants' Interests" in the European Union', *Journal of Ethnic and Migration Studies*, 24(4), 695–713.

Gellner, E. (1994) *Encounters with Nationalism*. Oxford: Blackwell.

Gellner, E. (1983) *Nations and Nationalism*. Ithaca, NY: Cornell UP.

Gupta, A. and Ferguson, J. (1992) 'Beyond "Culture": Space, Identity, and the Politics of Difference', *Cultural Anthropology*, 7, 6–23.

Handler, R. and Linnekin, J. (1984) 'Tradition, Genuine or Spurious', *Journal of American Folklore*, 97, 273–90.

Hayward, J. (1959) 'Solidarity: the Social History of an Idea in Nineteenth Century France', *International Review of Social History* iv, 261–84.

Hechter, M., Friedman, D. and Appelbaum, M. (1982) 'A Theory of Ethnic Collective Action', *International Migration Review*, 16(2), 412–34.

Hefner, R. (2002) *Civil Islam: Muslims and Democratization in Indonesia*. Princeton, NJ: Princeton University Press.

Hegedus, Z. (1989) 'Social Movements and Social Change in Self-creative Society: New Civil Initiatives in the International Arena', *International Sociology*, 4(1).

Hickman, M. and Walter, B. (1997) *Discrimination and the Irish Community in Britain: A Report of Research Undertaken for the CRE*. London: Commission for Racial Equality.
Hillyard, P. (1993) *Suspect Community*. London: Pluto.
Hirschon, R. (2001) 'Surpassing Nostalgia: Personhood and the Experience of Displacement', 13th Elizabeth Colson Lecture in Forced Migration, Refugee Studies Centre, University of Oxford, June 2001.
Horowitz, D. (1985) *Ethnic Groups in Conflict*. Berkeley, CA: University of California Press.
Hudson, M. (2001) 'Creative Destruction: Information Technology and the Political Culture Revolution in the Arab World,' New Media and Information Technology in the Middle East Working Paper, http://nmit.georgetown.edu/papers/mchudson.htm, accessed 15/7/05.
Karim, K. H. (1998) 'From Ethnic Media to Global Media: Transnational Communication Networks among Diasporic Communities', paper presented to the Transnational Communities Programme Seminar, School of Geography, University of Oxford, June 1998, http://www.transcomm.ox.ac.uk/working%20papers/karim. pdf, accessed 21/7/05.
Karim, K. (2002) 'Globalization, Communication and Diaspora' in P. Attallah and L. Shade (eds) *Mediascapes*. Scarborough: Nelson, pp. 272–90.
Kastoryano, R. (1994) 'The Transnational Migration Network of Non-Europeans within Europe', *Esprit* (3–4): 171–7.
Lambert, J. (1994) *Solidarity and Survival: A Vision for Europe*. Aldershot: Avebury.
Landolt, P., Autler, L. and Baires, S. (1999) 'From Hermano Lejano to Hermano Mayor: The Dialectics of Salvadoran Transnationalism', *Ethnic and Racial Studies*, 22(2), 290–315.
Lawrence, D. (2000) 'Iraq: A Decade of Devastation', *Middle East Report*, Summer, 215.
Leifer, E. (1981) 'Competing Models of Political Mobilization: The Role of Ethnic Ties', *American Journal of Sociology*, 87(1), 23–47.
Lloyd, C. (1995) *The Irish Community in Britain: Discrimination, Disadvantage and Racism: an Annotated Bibliography*. London: University of North London Press.
Lloyd, C. (1999) 'Transnational Mobilisations in Contexts of Violent Conflict, The Case of Solidarity with Women in Algeria', *Contemporary Politics*, 5(4), 365–77.
Lloyd, C. (2002) 'Thinking about the Local and the Global in the Algerian Context', *Oxford Development Studies*, 30(2), 151–63.
Lubeck, P. (2000) 'The Islamic Revival. Antinomies of Islamic Movements under Globalization' in R. Cohen and S. Rai (eds) *Global Social Movements*. London: Athlone Press, pp. 146–64.
Lutz, H. (1993) 'In Between or Bridging Cultural Gaps? Migrant Women from Turkey as Mediators', *New Community*, 19, 485–92.
Malkki, L. (1995) *Purity and Exile: Violence, Memory and National Cosmology Among Hutu Refugees in Tanzania*. London: University of Chicago Press.
Mandaville, P. (1999) 'Digital Islam: Changing the Boundaries of Religious Knowledge?', *ISIM Newsletter*, (2), 48.
Mandaville, P. (2001) *Transnational Muslim Politics: Reimagining the Umma*. London: Routledge.
Marston, S. (2002) 'Making Difference: Conflict over Irish Identity in the New York City St Patrick's Day Parade', *Political Geography* (21): 373–92.
Martinez-Torres, M. (2001) 'Civil society, the Internet, and the Zapatistas', *Peace Review*, 13(3), 347–55.
McVeigh, R. (1992) 'The Specificity of Irish Racism', *Race and Class*, 3(4), 31–45.

Miller, M. (1982) 'The Political Impact of Foreign Labor: A Re-evaluation of the Western European Experience', *International Migration Review*, 16(1), 27–60.
Muecke, M. (1987) 'Resettled Refugees' Reconstruction of Identity: Lao in Seattle', *Urban Anthropology*, 6(3), 273–90.
Østergaard-Nielson, E. (2001) 'The Politics of Migrants' Transnational Political Practices', Paper Presented at Transnational Migration: Comparative Perspectives Conference, Princeton University, July 2001, http://www.transcomm.ox.ac.uk/working%20papes/Levitt.pdf, accessed 38/7/02.
Patel, P. (1999) 'Difficult Alliances: Treading the Minefield of Identity and Solidarity Politics', *Soundings*, (12, Summer), 115–26.
Portes, A. (1999) 'Conclusion: Towards a New World – The Origins and Effects of Transnational Activities', *Ethnic and Racial Studies*, 22(2), 463–77.
Rex, J. (1991) *Ethnic Identity and Ethnic Mobilisation in Britain*. Coventry: Centre for Research in Ethnic Relations.
Rex, J. (1996) *Ethnic Minorities in the Modern Nation State*. Aldershot: Avebury.
Rex, J., Joly, D. and Wilpert, C. (1987) *Immigrant Associations in Europe*. Aldershot: Gower.
Rigoni, I. (1998) 'Les Mobilisations des Kurdes en Europe', *Revue Européenne des Migrations Internationales*, 14(3), 203–23.
Rorty, R. (1989) *Contingency, Irony and Solidarity*. Cambridge: Cambridge University Press.
Runciman, W. G. (1966) *Relative Deprivation and Social Justice: a Study of Attitudes to Social Inequality in Twentieth-century England*. London: Routledge & Kegan Paul.
Russell, A. (2001) 'The Zapatistas Online: Shifting the Discourse of Globalization', *Gazette*, 63(5), 399–413.
Ryan, N. (1997) 'Television nation', *Wired*, (98).
Sheffer, G. (1986) 'Modern Diasporas in International Politics', *Modern Diasporas in International Politics*. Kent: Croom Helm.
Smith, A. (1986) *The Ethnic Origins of Nations*. Oxford: Blackwell.
Smith, A. (1994) 'Ethnic Nationalism and the Plight of Minorities', *Journal of Refugee Studies*, 72/3, 186–98.
Smith, R. (1998) 'Politics of Membership within the Context of Mexico and US Migration' in M. Smith and L. Guarnizo (eds) *Transnationalism from Below*. New Brunswick, NJ: Transaction Publishers, pp. 196–240.
Statham, P. (1999) 'Political Mobilisation by Minorities in Britain: Negative Feedback of "Race Relations"?', *Journal of Ethnic and Migration Studies*, 25(4), 597–26.
Tambiah, S. (1996) *Levelling Crowds: Ethnonationalist Conflicts and Collective Violence in South Asia*. Berkeley, CA: University of California Press.
Turner, B. (1994) *Orientalism, Postmodernism and Globalism*. London: Routledge.
Vali, A. (1994) 'Genese et Structure du Nationalisme Kurde en Iran', *Peuples Méditerranéens*; 68–9, juillet-décembre.
van de Veer, P. (2001) 'Transnational Religion', paper presented at Transnational Migration: Comparative Perspectives Conference, Princeton University, July 2001, http://www.transcomm.ox.ac.uk/working%20papers/WPTC-01–18%20Van%20der%20Veer.pdf, accessed 21/7/05.
Vertovec, S. (2000) 'Religion and Diaspora', paper presented at the 'New landscapes of Religion in the West' conference, School of Geography and the Environment, University of Oxford, September 2000, http://www.transcomm.ox.ac.uk/working%20papers%Vertovec01.pdf, accessed 27/7/02.

Weber, M. (1915/1958) 'The Social Psychology of World Religions' in H. H. Gerth and C. Wright Mills (eds) *From Max Weber*. New York: Oxford University Press.
Widegren, O. (1997) 'Social Solidarity and Social Exchange', *Sociology*, 31(4), 755–71.
Wihtol de Wenden, C. and Leveau, R. (2001) *La Beurgeoisie. Les Trois Ages de la Vie Associative Issue de l'Immigration*. Paris: CNRS Editions.
Zanger, M. (2002) 'The US and the Kurds of Iraq: A Bitter History', *Middle East Report*, Note 104 (August 9).

4

Global Financial Information, Compliance Incentives and Conflict Funding

Valpy FitzGerald

Introduction[1]

Since the attack of 11 September 2001 on the USA, the interdiction of terrorist funds has occupied the attention of international organizations and national governments throughout the world, and has been defined as a central element of the 'war on terror'. During the succeeding twelve months trans-border cooperation on the provision of financial information was strengthened, led by Washington and London in their double role as strategic security allies and regulators of the two major global financial centres. In this period, some 166 countries issued orders blocking the terrorist assets, but only US $112 million of funds were frozen.[2] However, closer examination reveals that it proved very difficult to ensure timely reporting of the financial transactions of targeted individuals or groups, or to deny them access to the international financial system.[3]

Logically, this initiative should affect SDM financing as well as conflict funding more generally – particularly where the inevitable attempts by incumbent states to outlaw such movements are supported by international organizations. A 'self-determination movement' (SDM) in this context is understood to be an organized movement to fundamentally change the nature of a nation–state in order to permit those represented by the movement to gain greater autonomy. This change may take the form of either the creation of a separate geographical entity or the replacement of the existing state by a fundamentally different social order. The former case, of separation, is usually identified with a particular ethnic group that inhabits the region in question, a group that demands separation in order to escape repression by the incumbent state (itself often dominated by a distinct ethnic group, majority or minority). Clear examples of this are East Timor, Northern Ireland, Eritrea and the former Yugoslavia. The latter case of replacement refers to much more than a change of government (albeit by violent means), but rather a change in the social 'constitution' – during much of the twentieth century this involved the construction of socialism (for example, China, Cuba), but was then succeeded by movements to replace communism by capitalism (for example, Poland, Rumania), and dictatorship and military rule by democracy (for example, the Philippines). There are of course cases of ethnic overthrows of whole states (South Africa, Zimbabwe) and the establishment of theocratic states (Iran, Afghanistan) has also become a significant phenomenon.

This definition of the SDM, therefore, implies a widespread support among the social group in question and fundamental change as the objective. It thus excludes violent actions by small groups of activists on the one hand (such as the Weathermen), and attempts to capture the state by military means in order to replace the leadership (for example, Sierra Leone). Terrorism proper is understood to be violent actions by non-state groups against civilian targets for the purpose of achieving political ends. SDMs may or may not engage in terrorism in this strict sense; indeed, most SDMs try to avoid actions against civilians as this would reduce their support. Moreover, non-democratic states may (and often do) engage in illegal repression of civilians that is effectively a form of terrorism.

The incumbent state will logically oppose the attempt to overthrow its fundamental constitution or to separate part of its territory. This usually involves the use of armed force, to which the SDM may respond equally with armed actions. These actions are inevitably termed 'crimes' or 'terrorism' by the state, although of course other states may support the SDM, turning a blind eye to its armed activities or even supporting them as 'freedom fighters'. Indeed, it is very difficult, if not impossible, for an SDM to be sustained without the implicit or explicit support of another state – if only as a safe haven. In consequence, a key objective of the incumbent state and its allies is to define opposition SDMs as international terrorists.

The need for considerable and continuous funding and the need to transfer these funds internationally imposes an effective budget constraint on non-state conflict participant's SDMs as well as on terrorism proper – that can reduce the number and intensity of attacks as effectively as direct police action (Sandler *et al.*, 1983). Further, there are considerable externalities to other states arising from the interdiction of international terrorism or the containment of SDMs in any one territory, while the costs are local, so that there are potential gains from international cooperation in this field and a temptation – particularly for small states – to engage in free-riding (Lee 1988).

Within the limitations of publicly available information,[4] this paper sets out to explore this issue from the viewpoint of the economics of financial regulation. The key issue is the geostrategic need for more information on the identity of transactors and the ability to freeze/expropriate assets and/or gain information on other related activities. However, the regulators' problem is that the large unregulated flows generated by broadly legal activities such as tax avoidance and migrant remittances provide cover for crime-related transactions (Johnson 2001). To the extent that the loss of secrecy and increased reporting requirements involves a loss in efficiency of the market as a whole by increasing transactions costs, this must be set against the less tangible global welfare gain of increased security. The obvious parallel here is with the logic of the trade-off between efficiency and stability in financial markets which brings about the need for prudential regulation to prevent systemic risk and thus the obligation to provide proprietary information to regulators in exchange for the licence to operate (Goodhart *et al.*, 1998).

In economic theory financial intermediaries undertake the task of monitoring the firms to whom they lend on behalf of the households who deposit funds with them (Diamond 1984). These intermediaries enjoy scale and learning economies in this activity, and possess privileged information about their debtors. In consequence they are in a unique position to provide accurate information on their clients to the regulatory authorities without undue cost. Further, financial intermediaries possess considerable information on their creditors, particularly when they provide a wide range of financial services and thus build up a picture of clients' assets and activities. Traditionally, therefore, financial intermediaries in OECD countries have worked closely with national law enforcement authorities in the detection of criminal activities – particularly the transfer of criminal proceeds and the evasion of tax obligations. However, over the last decade the competitive forces associated with financial globalization have tended to undermine this relationship: on the one hand, banks have increasingly moved away from direct lending towards the management of capital market assets, and so there is much less non-financial information available on borrowers; on the other hand, high net worth individuals regard secrecy as a key service, and in the absence of capital controls can move funds rapidly to another jurisdiction if this is not provided.

The demand for secrecy ranges from concealing assets from other family members or business associates, through tax evasion to laundering the proceeds of criminal activities. International law enforcement, however, requires information about depositors and users of financial services. This information asymmetry is precisely the reverse of that analysed in the financial literature, where it is assumed that the lender has insufficient information to properly monitor the borrower (Hiller 1997). Further, in the case of interdiction of cross-border terrorist funds, there is the additional complication that the origin of the funds can be fully legitimate (for example, a scholarship fund) and their use also (for example, hotel bills) until the attack takes place.

First this chapter will examine attempts to detect and interdict illegal financial flows related to the funding of trans-border terrorism, which are built on existing systems of reporting the use of financial systems for illegal purposes. This covers multilateral coordination on financial interdiction, the role of unregulated money transfer networks (MTNs) and the problem of offshore financial centres (OFCs). The limitations of this approach are shown to derive from the bias of economic incentives towards less rather than more disclosure. The next section examines the multilateral and unilateral attempts during the twelve months after the attack of September 2001 to strengthen regulatory controls on international banking and to regulate informal transfer systems. The effect of this effort on self-determination movements is examined in the following section, from which it is clear that SDMs have merely been treated as terrorist organizations according to the definitions of incumbent states. The final section concludes that unless market incentives work with – rather than against – regulatory disclosure, there is little prospect of substantial progress in the interdiction of terrorist funds. A possible policy solution could combine trans-border withholding taxes on transactions with unregulated high-wealth clients, supported by the establishment of a bank-based system for low-cost money transfers by emigrants. However, this would require a clear concept of 'legitimate' SDMs unless they are all to be branded as terrorists by the incumbent state and thus prevented from raising or transferring funds internationally.

Antecedents for the interdiction of financial transfers

Money laundering and the international banking system

Mechanisms to interdict terrorist financing have been built upon the foundations of those already established for the prevention of financial crime including money laundering. Existing multi-lateral regulation bodies such as the Financial Action Task Force (FATF) of the G7, Interpol and the United Nations have long been involved in attempts to coordinate reactions to all forms of trans-border financial crime (Johnson 2001). In the immediate aftermath of September 2001 it thus appeared that that the most effective way to counter this threat was to redirect and intensify the efforts of already existing multilateral monitoring and coordination bodies.

In the 'formal sector' of international banking, the weakest link appears to be the essentially self-regulated international network of correspondent banks. International correspondent banking exists in order that banks may provide a wide range of alternate services for their clients in territories where they have no established branches. This in turn makes these formal financial institutions vulnerable to unwitting collusion in money laundering activities. This problem is most evident when international correspondent banks engage partners domiciled in poorly regulated emerging market countries. These arrangements allow the transfer of both illegally and legally derived money from the unregulated into the regulated financial institutions, thus 'allowing funds in through the backdoor of the regulated institutions to commence or continue the laundering process' (Johnson 2001 p. 130).

For banks, attempts to detect and interdict terrorist financing are dealt with through existing mechanisms to counter money laundering. However, while most money laundering funds derive from other criminal offences, such as the sale of illegal drugs, the sources of terrorist funds are frequently legal. The banking sector is aware that any action which would be able to limit terrorist financing would require cooperation between banks, between governments and between banks and governments. This cooperation would take the form of information sharing and the creation of new mechanisms to track suspicious behaviour. A group of twelve leading international banks agreed to the 'Wolfsberg Principles' for self-regulation in October 2000.[5] These principles were established with assistance from Transparency International (an anti-corruption NGO) and focus on increased due diligence on the part of the banks. In particular, they are expected to be more aware of their customers and their actions. The 'Wolfsberg Group' extended their principles to meet the new concern of terrorist financing, increasing the due diligence expected from their members.

Various United Nations agencies were also previously involved in combating financial crime in general and terrorist funding in particular. Existing UN resolutions, such as the 1999 International Convention for the Suppression of the Financing of Terrorism, were used as a starting point for new action. The perception of new threats gave greater importance to the ratification of existing legislation. Additionally, the UN Security Council and General Assembly have adopted resolutions calling upon all states to act to stop terrorism and its supporters in all ways. The most powerful of these resolutions, detailing measures to be taken to suppress the financing of terrorist acts, is Security Council Resolution 1373. The UN called for increased cooperation from all member states to stop acts of terrorism and the means by which terrorist actions were supported.

Multilateral monitoring and policy proposing organizations such as the FATF were already concerned with financial crime, in particular money laundering. The FATF was founded in 1989 to coordinate policies against the misuse of the financial system by money laundering.[6] Now including 29 member states and several regional affiliated bodies, it monitors the actions of member states in implementing anti-money laundering policy and promoting such policies around the world. Its 'Forty Recommendations' delineate measures for law enforcement agencies, banks and governments. These recommendations are designed to be widely applied, providing flexibility for individual states to apply them in their own jurisdictions. The FATF recommendations are composed of several sections, including the criminalization of laundering money from crime, the requirement of banks to know their clients, and reporting any suspicious transactions to their governments. The FATF not only contributes to monitoring but also provides a platform for information sharing among law enforcement and regulatory officials from member states and international organizations.

At these annual meetings, member regulators discuss advances changes in money laundering and new ways to counteract it.

Informal financial systems

Multilateral bodies such as the FATF, although principally concerned with the integrity of the international banking system, have also expressed considerable concern about global money transfer networks (MTNs), particularly unregulated or 'informal' MTNs such as the *hawala* system. The regulatory problems they raise are complex, both because it is very difficult to trace the activities of these networks accurately, and because it is unclear how to regulate them even in principle. The apparent use of informal MTNs by terrorists has increased the pressure to bring them under regulatory control.[7]

All informal MTNs share a common set of operational characteristics, a 'lack of records, customer identification or regulatory oversight, and the potential for misuse by criminals'.[8] Those most commonly referred to are the Chinese *chit* or *chop* system of East and Southeast Asia, the *black market peso exchange* system of Latin America, and the *hawala* system, with its offshoot the *hundi* system in South Asia. Mirroring established migrant labour patterns, these networks provide unregulated (and thus cheaper) remittance services between developed and developing countries.

Unregulated small-scale money transfer networks are also used to transfer funds between commercial parties both within and across national borders.[9] The final settlement between the associate *hawaladars* may be made through various mechanisms such as bank transfers, reciprocal remittances, manipulation of trade invoices, smuggling of gold or drugs or through the physical movement of cash by trusted couriers. Informal MTNs are often held to be 'archaic' or 'underground' financial systems (Gilligan 2001). However, such networks are better viewed as a structural response to information asymmetries in the financial services market place and a necessary feature of segmented financial systems (Nawaz *et al.*, 2002). This explains why these networks thrive: they are used predominantly by those consumers, particularly the poor, who are not served by formal financial institutions because of cost and risk. Specifically, they provide a rapid, reliable and relatively cheap means for migrant workers to remit cash to poor and illiterate families.

Given that migrant remittances provide the 'base load' for such systems, informal MTNs have two further advantages over the formal financial system. First, they avoid the additional costs imposed by regulation of banks, for prudential as well as policing purposes. The introduction of international codes and standards by the G7 through the Financial Stability Forum, as well as increased consumer protection, has led to increased costs for banks, which are passed on as transactions fees.[10] This makes the international transfer of relatively small sums highly unattractive to banks.

Second, hawala networks circumvent the record keeping that formal banking involves. Thus they provide the highly valued 'financial' service of customer confidentiality similar to that offered by offshore financial centres – particularly for the transactions of wealthy individuals with highly regulated OECD countries. Although hawala networks rely on traditional forms of personal trust rather than written contracts, they also use formal banking systems and continually respond to the ongoing process of financial globalization. For example, they are well suited to new e-commerce platforms and form a key element of international 'cyber-laundering' business along with activities such as gambling (Philippsohn 2001).

Offshore financial centres

International capital mobility makes criminal and terrorist funds transfer easier, particularly since these transactions can be obscured by the quasi-legal flows related to tax evasion, which require a similar degree of secrecy. The role of the tax factor in determining business location gives rise to wasteful tax competition for investment, particularly between small developing countries with a small business sector of their own, for whom the positive externalities of such investment are a significant source of national income, but who do not bear the externalities involved in terms of tax loss to other countries (UNCTAD 1995). The deregulation of cross-border capital flows also reduces or even eliminates the information about investors generated by licensing systems. Liberalization too reduces the transactions cost of the use of off-shore financial centres (OFCs) to channel cross-border capital flows through the incorporation of offshore holding companies. The object here is not so much to attract foreign investment as such, but rather the administration of assets and tax revenue. The use of these schemes is detrimental to both the home and host country through reduced tax revenues and distorted investment inflows (OECD 1998).

The number of double taxation agreements has thus increased rapidly in recent decades, and there are now some two thousand such treaties in existence. The principle of information exchange between national tax authorities has been intrinsic to such treaties since the last century and was central to the draft tax convention prepared by the League of Nations in 1935 (IBFD 1998). These treaties become ineffective if offshore centres are used as transfer pricing points as well as for tax avoidance (JCT 1999). The OECD Multilateral Convention on Mutual Administrative Assistance in Tax Matters established in 1988 ensures that information on such holding is shared between OECD members – but not with non-members. Extensive transfer pricing and tax-induced capital restructuring (for example, intra-firm debt) take place despite the OECD Model Tax Convention and the OECD Transfer Pricing Guidelines (Bartelsman and Beetsma 2000). A significant problem associated with this issue is that of offshore financial centres. By allowing multinationals, through transfer pricing, to declare the majority of their profits in shell companies registered in OFCs, the tax revenues resulting from investment and production in (non-OFC) countries are lost to the hosts. The Financial Stability Forum (FSF 2000) has addressed the issue of OFCs from the point of view of systemic instability in international capital markets. Those centres unable or unwilling to adhere to international supervisory standards of cooperation and transparency pose two serious problems. First, there are prudential concerns for the effective supervision of international financial intermediaries in order to forestall a bank collapse from putting the payments system in danger. Second, there are market integrity concerns relating to the effectiveness of international enforcement efforts in respect of illicit activity and abusive market behaviour.

There are thus substantial global welfare losses from OFCs to be set against the marginal benefits to small economies with no other legal source of high income other than perhaps tourism. These losses are composed of the loss of fiscal revenue to other jurisdictions where firms' and individuals' economic activities take place on the one hand, and the cover that tax evasion flows give to money laundering, narcotics funding – and now terrorist finance – on the other (UN 1998). IMF research on the prudential issues raised suggests that

> OFCs attract funds because they promise anonymity and the possibility of tax avoidance or evasion. A high level of bank secrecy is almost invariably used as a selling point by OFCs, some of which have been (and are) exploited also for activities related to money laundering. (Errico and Musalem 1999, p. 10)

The Financial Action Task Force (OECD 2000) initially defined some thirty-five jurisdictions as 'non-cooperative countries or territories' in key areas of transparency and information exchange required to meet international anti-money laundering standards for – a list which included the Bahamas, Cayman Islands, St. Kitts and Nevis, St Vincent and Grenadines, Dominica and Panama in the region as well as Israel, Lebanon, Liechtenstein, Philippines and Russia. Six, including Bermuda and the Caymans, rapidly made commitments to eliminate harmful practices by the end of 2005. In the wake of global anti-terrorist measures after September 2001, the remaining Caribbean states and UK dependencies (and the Channel Islands) in the region had signed by February 2002, embracing international standards for transparency, exchange of information and fair tax competition (FSF 2000). It remains to be seen, however, how effective the information exchange is in practice, because this would mean that OFCs would lose most of their financial services income.

Interventions in the international financial system during the first year of the 'war on terrorism'

The Financial Action Task Force

Most of the actions taken in the immediate aftermath of September 11 involved the restructuring of existing bodies to meet this new threat. In October 2001, the Financial Action Task Force expanded its mandate from narcotics-related money laundering to include terrorist financing. Its existing mandate apparently made it particularly suitable to prevent the misuses of world financial system by terrorists. Following this, the FATF issued a series of special recommendations to be adopted by member states. These recommendations drew upon the content of the 'Forty Recommendations' but were more closely concerned with terrorist funding. The seven parts of the new FATF guidelines include the criminalization of terrorist funding and connected money laundering, followed by the seizing and confiscating of terrorist assets.[11] States should also increase cooperation, sharing information and assisting others in bringing financial criminals to justice. However, relatively little thought has apparently been given yet to implementation, with decisions instead being left up to individual member states for the time being. The FATF has yet to develop interpretations based on the experience of member states: effectively it is still at the data gathering stage.

The FATF recommendations are intended to separate the legal and necessary actions of remittances and the donation of money to non-profit organizations on the one hand from the illegal acts of financial crime and support of terrorist activities on the other. Unlike more traditional money laundering, in which crime has already taken place before the money is transferred, the origins of terrorist financial support may be completely legal until they enter terrorist financial channels. Informal channels such as hawala are used legally by many to transmit their remittances to their home countries, as well as providing a conduit for terrorist support. As a result, these transactions are both more difficult to track and risk impeding legal financial transfers. Since these transfers are by nature informal, there is no 'paper trail' for investigators to follow. In an attempt to curtail an activity that seems unregulatable, the FATF recommendations suggest promoting alternative means for transferring money and increasing the number of documents kept on transactions. Additionally, wire transfer operators have been asked to keep additional records of transactions and to attach all information of sender and recipient at all points in the transaction.[12] At the same time, the recommendations call upon those who conduct any transactions – including large cash operations such as gambling – to 'know their customers' and to attach this identification material to the transfer. The lack of this information is seen as suspicious and is liable to be reported – but the effectiveness of this measure is likely to be very limited.

The FATF is a monitoring, coordinating multi-lateral organization, but its means are limited to cope with its new mandate. After the 30 October 2001 statement of the Special Principles on Terrorism, the FATF released documents to help states identify suspicious activities. The first step in the FATF monitoring procedure involved a self-assessment questionnaire to all member states, to track their progress in implementing these new guidelines.[13] Subsequently non-member states were also invited to fill out this questionnaire. The questionnaire is designed not only to determine if states have been implementing the guidelines but also to provide case studies for other states to follow in their policy design. Drawing upon the results of some of the questionnaires, the FATF produced guidance notes to help financial institutions to avoid becoming the unwitting conduit for terrorist funds.[14]

Other multilateral action

The G7 itself also took action to increase information sharing and cooperation in broader measures to fight financial crime. While the impetus for these actions is relatively new, it draws upon previous anti-money lending and anti-drug smuggling agreements. At the G8 meeting of 13–14 May 2002 measures were taken to increase cooperation across borders, particularly in electronic communications and e-commerce, in an attempt to stop terrorists from abusing the system.[15]

In November 2001, the wider G20 group of leading developed and developing countries adopted an action plan to increase cooperation among states and with international institutions to adopt measures necessary to limit international terrorist funding. According to this plan, all states would ratify the existing conventions and resolutions dealing with terrorist financing; collectively they would draw up lists of offending groups so that their assets could be frozen and information would be shared to make action possible.[16] Liaising with the FATF and other international actors, common standards limiting terrorist financing were to be implemented. Also, more developed countries promised financial support and assistance to those states that lacked the infrastructure to carry out these missions effectively. Aside from multilateral agreements from groups such as the G7, ASEAN and others, multilateral designations of terrorist suspects remain the most noticeable sign of this cooperation. The United States has used the medium of joint declarations of terrorists and terrorist-supporting groups to promote cooperation in this effort.[17]

Additionally, US officials pointed to the willingness of other states to issue designations of terrorist supporting groups on their own and with US support.[18] These declarations and the negotiation required to agree upon them formed a key part of this cooperation. However, the United States itself did not comply with the first item of the FATF recommendation list: to ratify the 1999 UN Convention on the Suppression of Terrorist Financing.

Indeed, only seven OECD member states had ratified the convention (Austria, Canada, France, Iceland, the Netherlands, Spain and the United Kingdom) by mid-2002.[19] The European Union was quick to support the US-led actions to stop the flow of funds that support terrorist activities and issued three separate lists of designated terrorist supporters whose assets should be blocked by the end of 2001. However, the legal and financial infrastructure appear to be inadequate to implement these decisions, and only the UK froze significant sums.[20]

Meanwhile, informal financial transactions systems such as hawala networks have been the subject of increased regulation and anti-money laundering declarations. While states such as the UAE have not banned hawala, it is important that they are seen to be participating in the international struggle against terrorism. In May 2002 at Abu Dhabi representatives from regional banking and law enforcement agencies called for the application of the FATF regulations to the hawala industry, declaring that 'the international community should continue to work individually and collectively to regulate the hawala system for legitimate commerce and to prevent its exploitation or misuse by criminals and others', and that to this end they should 'designate competent supervisors to monitor and enforce the application of the recommendations of the Financial Action Task Force to hawala dealers and other alternative remittance providers'.[21]The proposals to regulate hawala stems from the positive aspects of this system and the fear that any attempt to eliminate informal channels would merely drive more transactions underground. In May 2002 the Central Bank of the UAE announced that hawala operators in the UAE would be licensed and regulated.[22] Pakistan has launched a scheme to convince its nationals to avoid unofficial channels, including novel incentives such as baggage allowances and preferential treatment at airports.[23]

The campaign to interdict terrorist financing seems to demonstrate the value of intergovernmental cooperation. However, many measures taken recently are commitments rather than action. While it is too soon to determine how successful the adopted measures have been, success seems limited mainly to unilateral action *within* the United States and the United Kingdom. To ensure the wholehearted participation of other member countries of the OECD and of leading emerging market countries would require that they have a more effective share in decision making by international bodies. To the extent that that the proposal for fiscal compliance incentives discussed below were to be implemented, this would also provide a stronger economic motive for governments of small or poor countries to participate more effectively in the suppression of terrorism.

Unilateral Intervention

The US response to terrorist financing was probably the swiftest and most wide ranging. The October 2001 Patriot Act includes several amendments to the bank secrecy act and new anti-money laundering measures.[24] Within the Patriot Act, Title III is the International Money Laundering Abatement and Anti-Terrorist Financing Act of 2001. The Financial Crimes Section of the Department of the Treasury is the government agency responsible for determining policy on terrorist financing. The American Banking Association (ABA) has cooperated with this agency to introduce new practices to reduce money laundering. In February 2002, the ABA announced new procedures to reduce the threat of terrorists misusing the US banking structures, including new checks for the opening of bank accounts.[25] However, the ABA has also challenged certain aspects of the Patriot Act, claiming that new provisions for cooperation between the government and the banks might impinge upon existing agreements of ongoing information sharing.[26] They fear that the creation of new channels might circumvent older ones and even make information sharing more difficult, and that the time restrictions on reporting are unrealistic.

The US Treasury has devoted substantial resources to waging the financial war on terrorism. The initial step was to identify the terrorists and terror-supporting groups and to freeze their assets. The next was the regulation of charities to ensure that money intended for legitimate purposes was not used to support terrorism. US officials leading the fight against terrorist financing thus announced a second phase of attack: informal money transfer systems including hawala and charitable donations. The Secretary of the Treasury announced: ' We are driving the terrorists out of the modern financial infrastructure and into less efficient transfer methods, which are more difficult, slower and more easily intercepted by law enforcement.'[27] The designation of Islamic charities abroad as supporting terrorists and blocking of their resources has also been a US-led initiative, and include the Saudi decision to require charities to report to the foreign ministry about activities abroad, more regulation and increased transparency of charities in Pakistan and greater government supervision of charities in Egypt.[28]

The British government has a substantial history of anti-money laundering and anti-terrorist financing actions, but a new terrorist finance team was set up in November 2001, bringing together different interested agencies.[29] The British Government had begun to take actions against terrorist financing since 1992, but after 11 September the assets of 100 organizations and over 200 individuals were frozen. New anti-terrorist legislation increased the powers of the police to monitor and seize assets of those suspected to be engaged in terrorist activities and increased the requirements of banks to report suspicious activities.[30] According to its own progress report in April 2002 the UK was already compliant with most of the FATF recommendations and was seeking to pass legislation that would satisfy the remaining recommendations. The banks and financial services industry has also taken the initiative to introduce stricter controls over anti-money laundering system. In July 2002 the major UK banks announced that they would identify suspicious accounts established since 1994, before international regulations require.[31]

It would seem, therefore, that unilateral intervention has been more effective than multilateral action. On the one hand, as New York and London are the only truly global financial centres, to deny their use to terrorist groups is a major achievement. On the other hand, most of the rest of the world – non-OECD countries and offshore-centres in particular – are thereby excluded and arguably become more difficult to monitor.

Impact of terrorist interdiction on the funding of self-determination movements

The inclusion of SDMs in the interdiction of terrorist funds

The limited impact of global attempts to curtail terrorist financing has had more effect on SDMs. Many SDMs were placed on a variety of terrorist financing lists compiled by the US, the EU and the UN – although not consistently. Moreover, it is impossible to discern how much effect these indictments have had on self-determination groups and their ability to gain funding. The fact that these initiatives have not had much success against al Qaeda does not necessarily imply less impact on SDMs, because the latter by virtue of their extent and territorial base are easier to detect and thus interdict. The global war against terrorism has resulted in a blurring of the definition between terrorism and self-determination as many countries have sought to brand their domestic and international opposition in acceptable terms. Since the United States seeks the assistance of allies to stop the flows of money that enable terrorism, it has expanded the scope of the mission, which was initially limited closely to al Qaeda and its actions. In all, 208 countries and jurisdictions expressed support for the financial aspect war on terror. Of these, 166 have issued orders freezing assets of terrorist organizations – usually including their domestic armed opposition, if one exists.[32] The global war on terror is to some extent based on inter-state reciprocity, that is, the US seeks the assistance of other states in its fight against al Qaeda and a possible intervention in Iraq. In turn it is willing to support the anti-terrorist actions of other states.

Initially, the placing of names on the 'list' thus concerned al Qaeda and very closely associated groups and individuals. However, when war on terror was expanded US Undersecretary Gurulé insisted in a congressional hearing that 'the president's mandate has been to go after all terrorist groups, not simply Al Qaeda and the Taliban. Our priority has been Al Qaeda, but we have focused as well on other terrorist groups, such as ETA and the IRA.'[33] The US willingness to expand the number of enemies can be seen as a side payment to allies or those whom it sought as allies. As long as those allies were willing to participate in blocking resources and sharing of information, the US was willing to add the names of unrelated groups. In the process many groups connected to a wide variety of SDMs were added to the list.

The US and its European allies had different responses to international terrorist groups. US attempts to use extraterritorial powers to stop terrorist financing have made the FATF and the EU impose stricter policies on the freezing of assets and financial sanctions.[34] Initially the global war on terrorist financing was mainly US-led with little allied involvement. As of April 2002, the US had listed 165 names of groups and individuals out of a total of 192, while Spain had added 21 groups, and the UK, six groups.[35] EU member states were very unwilling to extend the blocking of assets to non-al Qaeda groups – that is, SDMs. EU rules on interdicting terrorist financing require that groups in question be placed on the United Nations list of terrorist organizations, a law that the US has asked its European allies to change.[36]

The interdiction of terrorist financing has clearly had substantial effect on financing of SDMs even though these effects might not have been as focused on international terrorism as was desired. The US Treasury has announced that terrorist fund-raising is now less efficient.[37] However, these groups still find sources of funds to support their actions. In general, indicted groups have been forced to turn to other, often more illegal, sources of funding. Thus instead of appealing to political supporters, they become more involved in other illegal activities such as drug trafficking and smuggling. Seizure of their assets makes them turn increasingly to other ways of transporting their assets. Thus instead of using banks or even informal means of transferring money they are increasingly using diamonds and gold to finance their activities. By being driven more underground, it becomes even more difficult for finances to be checked.

The US maintains four different lists detailing terrorist sponsors. Firstly, the list of states that sponsor terrorist acts. Next, the list of foreign terrorist organizations, which lists 29 of these organizations. While the assets of these groups are frozen and members are likely to be refused entry into the US, the assets of supporters may not be seized.[38] Two new lists, created after 11 September, extend the powers of the previous act. The terrorist-financing list consists of a list of groups, individuals and companies involved in conducting and supporting terrorist activities. The assets of any group or individual on this list are to be frozen but immigration restrictions are under the rubric of another list, the Terrorist Exclusion List. This list forms a part of the Patriot Act and includes suspected terrorist organizations and groups, whose members could be expelled or forbidden from entering the United States.[39]

The impact on SDMs

Paramilitary groups in Northern Ireland were not initially part of the focus of the financial war on terror, even though some of the terrorist groups were previously banned in the US. On 31 October 2001, the US banned the Real IRA;[40] and on 31 December 2001 five Unionist and republican groups were added to the US financial sanctions against terrorist groups. These included Continuity IRA (CIRA), Loyalist Volunteer Force (LVF), Orange Volunteers, Red Hand Defenders (RHD) and the Ulster Defence Association (a.k.a. Ulster Freedom Fighters).[41] Paramilitary groups such as the IRA, Real IRA, UVF, and UDA are increasingly involved in organized crime to fund their activities. These crimes provide a growing bulk of their resources. A House of Commons committee reported that the IRA and the Real IRA are involved in such activity. In particular, up to 80 per cent of the involvement of the Real IRA on the British mainland is organized crime, rather than terrorist activities per se.[42] In its 2002 threat assessment, the UK government claimed significant progress in disrupting terrorist activity in Northern Ireland. This progress, the disruption of 42 out of 79 criminal groups, took the form of arresting members of these groups and successful prosecution.[43] However, the connection between terrorist groups and other organized crime is concerning. It is possible that illegal activities such as drug dealing, money laundering and fuel smuggling are being undertaken by larger groups. Nearly half of all organized crime groups are connected with or controlled by paramilitary organizations.[44] Organized crime provides much of the funding for these groups and there are increasing connections between these groups both within Northern Ireland and around the world.

Initially the LTTE in Sri Lanka were not a part of the US-led global war on terrorism, so they were not included on the new terrorist financing list and not part of the primary focus.[45] The LTTE[46] were listed on 31 October 2001. The Tamil Tigers are believed to get a substantial amount of their funding from the Tamil diaspora; in particular, Tamil charities in Canada have been cited for their funding of such activity. The Sri Lankan Government believed that the Tamil population in Canada was the largest source of funds for the self-determination movement.[47] While the LTTE had been banned in the US from 1997, they were only added to the terrorist list by Canada in November 2001. This freezing of assets may be part of the reason why negotiations were finally progressing in the summer of 2002.

In Burma/Myanmar, the ruling junta used the excuse of terrorism to continue to repress the opposition. They used the rhetoric of the global war on terror to continue to sideline the opposition. With the US emphasis on the war on terrorism, less attention has been paid to the issues of drug production and smuggling.[48] The government remains on the FATF list of non-cooperative countries and territories, which includes states that have refused to comply adequately with the FATF efforts to stop money laundering. [49]But since Myanmar is a member of ASEAN and had accepted the ASEAN joint statement on measures to counteract terrorism, it is likely to play a somewhat larger role in the global fight against terrorist financing, but likely to be using these actions for its own benefit. The United Wa State Army has been funded by exports of methamphetamine and heroin.

The Turkish Government has also used the framework of international terrorism to continue to limit the funding of the Kurdish self-determination movements. Turkey was one of the few states to have had a specific anti-terrorism law prior to September 2001.[50] At the same time, as a part of its EU candidacy, Turkey has changed its laws, eliminating the ban on Kurdish language and protecting the human rights of Kurds. Some Kurdish self-determination groups were already considered to be terrorist groups prior to 11 September and they were some of the first non-al Qaeda groups to be included on the US terrorism list. The PKK earned some of its funding from taxation of drug shipments and the protection of drug traffickers. In October 2001, Dev sol and the PKK were added to the list.[51] Both of these groups had been listed in previous US reports on global terrorism. Additionally, the Eastern Turkistan Islamic Movement (ETIM or ETIP) was added to the US list of terrorist groups on 3 September 2002.[52] In 2002, the PKK changed its name to KADEK and announced that it would reform into a politically oriented group. However, it retained the same leadership and the US government continued to see it as a threat to security and American interests.[53] Thus in December, the US government added three names to the listing of the PKK, the result of cooperation with the Turkish government in other aspects of the war on terrorism and a potential intervention in Iraq. [54]

The Colombian FARC was added to the EU terrorism list in June of 2002, conversely the FARC has been listed as a terrorist organization by the US for many years. The ELN and the FARC were listed on 31 October 2001.[55] These SDMs are involved at least in the protection of drug growers and probably production and trafficking as well, so international illegal activity provides the bulk of their funding. The US has given substantial military aid to the Bogota government because in

> Colombia the drug traffickers, the terrorist groups and the illegal self defense groups, some of which are terrorist organizations themselves, all carry out the most extreme attacks on society. The two major insurgency groups, the FARC and the National Liberation Army or the ELN have divided the territory and they are carrying out acts of violence against the citizens and public officials. Likewise the paramilitary members have raised funds through extortion or by protecting laboratory operations in Northern and Central Colombia.[56]

The attempts at interdiction of terrorist financing and drug trafficking in Colombia originated in 1995 when an Executive Order imposed sanctions on specific narcotics traffickers. Since then this has affected

> over 575 businesses and individuals including 10 drug cartel leaders, 230 businesses, and 335 other individuals. Four of the most notorious Colombian drug cartel leaders were identified in the Executive Order itself... Consequences of sanctions against Colombian drug cartels have been swift, clear and compelling...In May of 2001, more than 60 of these SDNT companies with an estimated annual aggregate income of more than $230 million have been liquidated, or were in the process of liquidation.[57]

There is little evidence to link the SDM of East Timor to 'international terrorism', but this is also due to timing since East Timor was already independent prior to the great push against terrorist financing. Other self-determination movements in Indonesia, in particular Islamic groups, have been connected to the global war on terror. However, the increased security risk has led to greater concern from Indonesia and Australia, a tendency exacerbated by the 2002 attack in Bali. Australia and Indonesia plan to co-host an international conference on terrorist financing. Indeed, the fight against terrorist financing has been a way for many countries to resume closer ties with Indonesia, after they were broken following the conflict in East Timor. In the summer of 2002, for instance, the US agreed to give Indonesia $50 million to support their fight against terrorism.[58]

In sum, most of the significant SDMs currently active have become subject to the new offensive against international terrorism and by strengthened international police action by virtue of their involvement with narcotics. There are some signs that this pressure has been successful in forcing peace negotiations. However, whether lack of access to legitimate (for example, diaspora) sources of support has forced a reliance on narcotics traffic is a serious issue for the future. It should not be forgotten that SDMs previously considered as 'freedom fighters' supported by the US and Europe such as the Mujahideen in Afghanistan, the Khmer Rouge in Cambodia and the Contras in Nicaragua were actively encouraged to finance themselves in this way.

Creating economic incentives for compliance

The evidence presented above demonstrates that systemic features of the international financial system make limiting conflict finances very difficult. The reliance on existing international financial monitoring arrangements seemed logical, but failed to learn from the lessons of past failure. Above all, the proposed interventions failed to create positive economic incentives for compliance in order to counteract the existing disincentives for disclosure experienced by financial intermediaries and regulatory jurisdictions. Moreover, even within highly regulated institutional structures the nature of bank secrecy makes the tracking of transactions difficult. With the growth of the Internet and the increasing impersonalization of the banking industry, banks find it more difficult to detect suspicious transactions. For many offshore banking companies their very comparative advantage is in high secrecy and minimal records. As a result, cooperation faces obstacles from all sides. Indeed, governments are often unwilling to share information with banks, expecting instead that banks will act as a conduit for information to the government.

By definition, attempts to exercise some form of regulatory control over hawala systems imply that these informal networks will become either increasingly formalized or they will cease to exist. Either way, any curtailment of the operations of informal MTNs is likely to have negative collateral impacts, and in particular upon marginalized users of these networks who have little or no access to formal financial services. It would not be desirable to close down these systems – even if it were possible – because they help the poor and the small enterprises that provide the bulk of employment. There are two clearly preferable solutions: to oblige the formal banking system to provide these services at low cost to migrants; or to extend existing micro-credit systems, which reach these clients at the local level in developing countries, to the international level by recognizing them as correspondent banks.

In sum, there is no strong economic incentive for financial intermediaries to comply in reporting dubious transactions, as the probability of conviction is low and fines small. There are strong incentives for non-compliance as the sums of money involved are large and costs of monitoring are substantial – especially as high-wealth clients value secrecy highly. It is thus necessary to internalize the externalities caused by non-compliant institutions and jurisdictions, and make it unprofitable for them to handle these transactions – or at least to make it so expensive that the resources available to criminals and terrorists are significantly reduced thereby.

A logical solution to this problem could be to shift from the present 'blacklist' system such as that administered by the US Office of Foreign Assets Control to an equivalent 'whitelist' system based on persons or firms registered for tax purposes (and thus monitored) in OECD countries and qualified emerging markets. Transactions with compliant jurisdictions (that is, those sharing full information with OECD member countries) made by persons or firms not properly registered for tax purposes would then be subject to a substantial withholding tax.[59] This would create a strong incentive against dealing with unregulated agents. This would have three strong positive effects: first, it would make handling unregistered funds unprofitable – or at worst, cost criminals a great deal to transact, reducing their liquidity and eroding their assets. Second, the process of levying the tax would provide a steady information flow on the pattern of payments not now available. Third, it would mean effective closure of tax havens and a large increase in fiscal resources for both developed countries (to balance increased security expenditure) and developing countries to reduce social disparities. The European Community proposal for the taxation of cross-border interest payments, the 'withholding tax directive', is a precedent that shows that a measure of this nature is politically and administratively feasible (EC 1998).

The concern of OECD members to coordinate measures against tax evasion, avoidance and competition between themselves – and the resultant pressure on offshore centres – has until now been based mainly on concern for their own tax bases. To extend such cooperative measures towards the main emerging markets would be a logical and technically feasible step, particularly since there are strong economic arguments for imposing with-holding taxes in order to reduce the volatility short-term financial flows (Zee 1998). On more general grounds, the leading scholar of international tax economics argues that the time has come for the establishment of a 'world tax organization' that would not impose or collect taxes, but rather support national authorities by exercising surveillance on tax systems worldwide, resolving disputes on tax competition and developing codes of conduct for tax administration (Tanzi 1996). Supporting the interdiction of criminal and terrorist funds would be a powerful additional justification for an overdue international reform.

However, this would leave SDMs in an anomalous position. Clearly incumbent states (and some other regional or international powers) have a vested interest in declaring internal opposition illegal, particularly when armed conflict is involved. If this is automatically ratified internationally, then oppressive regimes are reinforced and genuine self-determination becomes virtually impossible – despite being enshrined in the UN Charter. Some procedure is probably needed for 'recognizing' SDMs in the way that belligerents are recognized in the international law relating to war. There is some precedent for this approach in cases such as the admission of the PLO to observer status at the UN. Until this issue is resolved, self-determination movements will continue to be drawn into international criminal activity.

Notes

1. I am very grateful to Rachel Ziemba of St Antony's College for diligent and expert research assistance, and to the Carnegie Foundation for funding. The detailed information in this chapter refers to the experience of financial interdiction up to the end of 2002. However, the situation analysed here still had not changed substantially by the end of 2005.
2. US Treasury Secretary Paul O'Neill, Remarks to Asia Pacific Economic Cooperation Forum: Policy Dialogue on Combating Terrorist Financing, Los Cabos, Mexico, 5 September 2002 http://www.treas.gov/press.releases/po3392.htm
3. UN Report on Terrorism, Sept 5 2002. www.un.org/terrorism
4. These limitations illuminate the implicit contradiction inherent in this process: Intelligence work is generally conducted in secret, but to restrict terrorist financing

the authorities have to inform the public because interdiction is implemented through the market. While almost all states have accepted this responsibility, they lack the resources or the interest for substantial implementation. Thus, the greatest amount of information can be found on the US Treasury's Financial Crimes website, followed by the UK Treasury. Conversely, other countries, including other members of the G7 such as France, appear much less involved in dissemination.

5. More details about the Wolfsberg Group can be found on http://www.wolfsberg-principles.com.
6. On the FATF, see http://www.fatf-gafi.org/AboutFATF_en.htm
7. 'La technique de l'hawala, méthode de financement de l'internationale terroriste', *Le Monde*, 23 September 2001.
8. FATF-XI Report on Money Laundering Typologies 1999–2000, http://www.fatf-gafi.org/FATDocs_en.htm#Trends.
9. In India as much as half of national economic activity is said to make some use of the hawala system; see 'Trois grands systèmes parallèles de fonds ont été identifiés' *Le Monde*, 2 October 2001.
10. 'Suffering under the Weight' *The Banker*, December 2001.
11. FATF Special Guidelines on Terrorism, http://www.fatf-gafi.org/SRecsTF_en. htm
12. *Ibid.*
13. Self-Assessment Exercise: FATF Special Recommendations on Terrorist Financing, http://www.fatf-gafi.org/SAQTF_en.htm
14. Guidance for Financial Institutions in Detecting Terrorist Financing Activities http://www.fatf-gafi.org/TerFinance_en.htm
15. Christopher Chipello, G-8 Agrees to Step Up Cooperation In Fight Against Terror Financing, *Wall Street Journal*, May 15, 2002, http://online.wsj.com/article/0,,SB1021416029274629600,00.html
16. Action Plan of the G20 on Terrorist Financing, http://www.mof.go.jp/english/if/011118b.htm
17. Deputy US Treasury Secretary Kenneth Dam 'The Financial Front of the War on Terrorism – the Next Phase' speech at the Council on Foreign Relations, New York, 8 June 2002.
18. 'US Terror Fund Drive Stalls' http://news.bbc.co.uk/2/hi/business/2225967.stm
19. OECD Observer, June 2002. http://www.oecdobserver.org/news/fullstory.php/aid/717
20. O'Neill, *op.cit.*
21. Declaration from International Conference on Hawala, 15–16 May 2002. http://www.uaeinteract.com/news
22. http://www.uaeinteract.com/news
23. Julia Wheeler, 'Pakistan Money-laundering Clampdown', 6 October 2001, BBC online http://news.bbc.co.uk/hi/english/world/south_asia/newsid_1583000/1583040.stm
24. On the American Banking Association's efforts to counter money-laundering, see http://www.aba.com/press + room/pr_moneylaunderingissue.htm
25. http://www.aba.com/Press + Room/byrne_testimony_021202.htm
26. http://www.aba.com/NR/rdonlyres/00005432njkvucdfzjiojgef/USAPatriotsec314commetletter2.pdf
27. O'Neill *op. cit.*
28. Testimony of Kenneth Dam, Deputy Secretary of the Treasury before the Senate Committee on Banking, Housing and Urban Affairs, Subcommittee on International Trade and Finance, 1 August 2002, 2, http://www.treas.gov/press/releases/po3315.htm

29. UK Treasury, International Fight against Terrorist Financing-UK progress report, 12 April 2002, http://www.britain-info.org/usaterrorism/xq/asp/SarticleType.1/Article_ID.2283
30. Anti-Terrorism, Crime and Security Act, 2001, www.hmso.gov.uk
31. Ruth Kelly, MP, Speech to the financial services authority (FSA) Money-laundering Conference, 11 July 2002, 3, http://www.hm-treasury.gov.uk/newsroom_and_speeches/speeches/finsecspeech.htm
32. Financial Actions in the War on Terrorism, http://www.whitehouse.gov/response/financialresponse.html
33. 'Hearing to Examine the Efforts of the OSCE to Coordinate Counterterrorism Activities Among its 55 Participating States.' 8 May 2002.
34. Alexander (2002).
35. 'International Response: US and Europe disagree over terrorist funds', Global Security Newswire, 11 April 2002, www.nti.org/d_newswire/issues/2002/4/11/2p.html
36. 'International response' (*ibid*).
37. Mark Huband, 'Funding for Terror Network "Now Less Efficient,"' *Financial Times*, 10 September 2002.
38. AFP, 'US Lists in the war on terrorism', 8 September 2002.
39. 'US Lists' (*ibid*).
40. Executive order, 6.
41. US executive order, 4.
42. AP, 'Ulster paramilitaries raising millions through crime: report', 3 July 2002.
43. Richard Evans, 'Organised crime and terrorist Financing in Northern Ireland' *Jane's Intelligence Review*, http://www.janes.com/security/law_enforcement/news/jir/jir020815_1_n.shtml
44. Organised crime task force, 'Manifestations of Organised Crime in NI, http://www.octf.gov.uk/manifest.cfm
45. Yahoo India News, 'LTTE not in US List', 24 September 2001, http://in.news,yahoo.com/010923/16/15ahn.html
46. US Executive order, 11.
47. BBC online, 'Canada outlaws Tamil Tigers', http://news.bbc.co.uk/2/hi/south_asia/1647172.htm
48. Deutsche Press Agentur 'Southeast Asia comes to terms with post 9/11 America', 3 September 2002.
49. FATF, 'FATF Annual report for 2001–2002 released', www.oecd.org/fatf
50. Herbert Morals, 'Behind the lines in the war on terrorist funding' *International Financial Law Review*, December 2001.
51. US executive order 11, 15.
52. US Executive Order, 5.
53. Harry Dunphy, AP, 9 December 2002.
54. A Bulletin from the Office of Foreign Assets Control – 3 December 2002, http://www.treas.gov/offices/enforcement/ofac/bulletin.txt
55. US executive order, 11.
56. Testimony of Richard Newcomb, Director, U.S. Department of Foreign Assets Control, Hearing of the Senate Judiciary Subcommittee on Technology, Terrorism and Government Information, 13 March 2002.
57. *Ibid*.
58. Matthew Lee, US gives Indonesia 50 million dollars to combat terror groups, AFP, 2 August 2002.
59. At, say, 25 per cent of the gross transaction – which is the retention tax levied presently within the EU for fees paid to non-residents.

References

Alexander, K. (2001) 'The Need for Efficient International Financial Regulation and the Role of a Global Supervisor', *Journal of Money Laundering Control*, 5(1) 52–65.

Alexander, K. (2002) 'Extraterritorial US Banking Regulation and International Terrorism: The Patriot Act and the International Response', *Journal of International Banking Regulation*, 3(4).

Bartelsman, E. C. and R.M.W.J. Beetsma (2000) 'Why Pay More? Corporate Tax Avoidance Through Transfer Pricing in OECD Countries', *CEPR Discussion Paper* 2543. London: Centre for Economic Policy Research.

Diamond, D. W. (1984) 'Financial Intermediation and Delegated Monitoring', *Review of Economic Studies*, 51, 393–414.

EC (1998) 'Proposal for a Council Directive to Ensure a Minimum of Effective Taxation of Savings Income in the Form of Interest Payments within the Community (598PC0295)'. Brussels: European Commission.

Errico, L. and A. Musalem (1999) 'Offshore Banking: an Analysis of Micro- and Macro-prudential Issues', *IMF Working Paper* 99/05. Washington, DC: International Monetary Fund.

FitzGerald, E. V. K. (2002) 'International Tax Cooperation and Capital Mobility', *Oxford Development Studies*, 30(3), 251–66.

FSF (2000) *Report of the Working Group on Offshore Centres*. Basle: Financial Stability Forum.

Gilligan, G. (2001) 'Going Underground – the Not So New Way to Bank', *Journal of Financial Crime*, 9(2), 105–8.

Goodhart, C., P. Hartmann, D. Llewellyn and L. Rojas-Suarez and S. Weisbrod (1998) *Financial Regulation*. London: Routledge.

Hiller, B. (1997) *The Economics of Asymmetric Information*. Basingstoke: Palgrave Macmillan.

IBFD (1998) *Annual Report 1997–1998*. Amsterdam: International Bureau of Fiscal Documentation.

JCT (1999) *Overview of Present-Law Rules and Economic Issues in International Taxation* (JCX-13–99). Washington, DC: US Congress Joint Committee on Taxation.

Johnson, J. (2001) 'In Pursuit of Dirty Money: Identifying Weaknesses in the Global Financial System', *Journal of Money Laundering Control*, 5(2), 126–8.

Lee, D.R. (1988) 'Free Riding and Paid Riding in the Fight against Terrorism', *American Economic Review*, 78(2), 22–6.

Nawaz, S., R. McKinnon and R. Webb (2002) 'The War on South Asia's Hawala Networks: Fighting Financial Crime or Undermining Financial Services for the Poor?' Manchester: Institute for Development Policy Management, Manchester University.

OECD (1998) *Harmful Tax Competition: an Emerging Global Issue*. Paris: Organization for Economic Cooperation and Development.

OECD (2000) *Towards Global Tax Cooperation: Progress in Identifying and Eliminating Harmful Tax Practices*. Paris: Organization for Economic Cooperation and Development.

Philippsohn, S. (2001) 'The Dangers of New Technology – Laundering on the Internet', *Journal of Money Laundering Control*, 5(1), 66–85.

Sandler, T., J. T. Tschirhart and J. Cauley (1983) 'A Theoretical Analysis of Transnational Terrorism', *American Political Science Review*, 77(1), 36–54.

Santomero, A. (1984) 'Modelling the Banking Firm: A Survey', *Journal of Money, Credit and Banking*, 16(4), 576–602.

Stiglitz, J. (2002) 'Information and the Change in the Paradigm in Economics', *American Economic Review*, 92(3), 460–501.
Tanzi, V. (1996) 'Globalization, Tax Competition and the Future of Tax Systems', *IMF Working Paper*, 96(141), Washington, DC: International Monetary Fund.
UN (1998) *Financial Havens, Banking Secrecy and Money Laundering*. Vienna: UN Office for Drug Control and Crime Prevention.
UNCTAD (1995) *Incentives and Foreign Direct Investment*. Geneva: United Nations Conference on Trade and Development.
Zee, H. H. (1998) 'Taxation of Financial Capital in a Globalised Environment: The Role of Withholding Taxes', *National Tax Journal*, 51(3), 587–99.

5

Self-Determination in the Global Context

Rajesh Venugopal[1]

Introduction

One of the central paradoxes of the post-cold war world is the parallel occurrence of tendencies towards greater integration and disintegration. The end of the cold war, the expansion of cross-border economic linkages, migrant and refugee flows, and the rapid growth and diffusion of communication and media technology have created the conditions for an unprecedented global political, economic and cultural integration. But at the same time such processes have also given rise to a number of violent and disintegrative conflicts that have led to the break-up of several large states into smaller, often equally unstable units.

This paradox of integration amid disintegration was vividly apparent, for example, during negotiations for the greater political, economic and social integration of the European Union states under the Maastricht Treaty in 1991, which was being conducted at the very time when a violent disintegration was unfolding on the EU's very doorstep in Yugoslavia. Similarly, the integration of the oil-rich Caucasus and Black Sea regions into the global economy in the early 1990s occurred amidst the painful disintegration of the Soviet economy, as new international political borders abruptly tore up the hitherto contiguous economic geographies of Armenia and Azerbaijan, Georgia and Russia, or Turkmenistan and Uzbekistan. In turn, most of these new states were born with fragile border delineations and have faced pressures for further fragmentation from awkwardly positioned enclaves within them such as Nagorno–Karabakh, South Ossetia, Abkhazia and Chechnya. Other such parallel processes of disintegration amid integration underlie the implosion of formal state institutions during the 1990s in countries such as Afghanistan, Somalia, Liberia, and Sierra Leone, which were replaced with more diffuse forms of political and military authority, often linked to the control of lucrative global economic linkages.

Under these circumstances, the future of the nation–state has been called into question in relation to the pressures it faces from above and below, and to the ways in which movements for self-determination are formulating and asserting alternate forms of socio-political identity and community. This chapter, together with others in this volume, is fundamentally concerned with how these conflict-ridden processes of self-determination can be analysed and understood in the global context.

The significance of introducing the global context here is partly a response to the somewhat lop-sided analytical categories that have emerged in post-cold war conflict studies. At the end of the cold war, theorists of the 'liberal peace' suggested that the triumph of liberal democratic institutions and market economies around the world would spur a new era of global peace based on the rule of law and ties of mutual dependence. In contrast, two influential 'pessimists' of the early 1990s, Samuel Huntington (1993) and Robert Kaplan (1994) have argued that the post-cold war world remained dangerous and unstable. Huntington asserted that with the end of the grand ideological divisions of the cold war, latent cultural differences would resurface as a source of conflict. Kaplan instead described an increasingly chaotic and violence-prone post-cold war world arising from the collapse of formal states, coupled with stresses caused by over-population and environmental degradation.

What is interesting to note is that despite the considerable differences between, and even among them, the post-cold war optimists and pessimists bear a common understanding that *the sources of peace are global, but the sources of conflict are domestic*. Peace is assumed to arise from the adoption of global (liberal) political and economic ideals. Conflict instead is supposed to emanate from ethnic atavism or from a descent into a violent competition for survival.

Indeed, the fact that an increasing number of violent conflicts since the end of the cold war are internal in nature, and often result from the implosion of state institutions has strongly influenced the ways in which they have been explained, both in the culturalist and political economy paradigms. Internal wars are considered *ipso facto* to arise and persist because of overwhelmingly internal causes such as the resurgence of pre-modern identities, poor domestic economic policies, the failure of collective action or even the occurrence of 'greed' among the population. In essence, the fact that the actual military confrontation in these conflicts occurs within certain bounded geographical spaces has led to the misleading assumption that their causation and dynamics are entirely restricted to these same spaces. By logical extension, external political and military interventions into such conflicts are habitually styled as sterile, surgical and even charitable actions untainted by the messy internal causes that give rise to conflict.

Indeed, much of the post-cold war international policy debate on external intervention has analysed the outbreak of internal conflicts around the world not just as the result of internal causes, but due to an *absence* of sufficient external engagement. Within this, there are three distinct categories: political, economic, and cultural/normative. The first is the 'orphaned conflict' argument, which holds that conflicts break out and persist where there is a lack of appropriate international political or military involvement due to indifference or ignorance. The second is related to poverty, and suggests that violent conflict persists in poor countries that are marginalized from the global economy and that thus fail to reap the benefits of globalization. The third is the 'cultural barbarism' argument, which despite being rarely vocalized as such, is the very present sub-text underlying external intervention, suggesting that violent conflict results from an ignorance or defiance of internationally prescribed, or 'universal', norms of socio-political conduct.

This contention that conflicts are the result of internal factors, compounded by global indifference and disengagement has gained in strength and sophistication over the decade that transpired from the early failure of international intervention in Somalia (1992–94) to the apparent later success in East Timor (1999–2002). For example, in the prelude to the invasion of Afghanistan in October 2001, it was widely suggested that the extended humanitarian crisis and civil war that had prevailed there since the Soviet and US withdrawal were the result of apathy and indifference by the outside world. British Prime Minister Tony Blair captured this line of thought following the fall of Kabul in November 2001 when he made a direct pledge to the forgotten people of Afghanistan that: 'this time we will not walk away from you' (Blair, 2001). He subsequently made an almost identical pledge some sixteen months later, as British and American forces embarked on their next military invasion, declaring of the Iraqi people that: 'they've been let down before, my message to them today is we will not let you down' (Blair, 2003).

Clearly, there is a sense of contrition in these comments, reflecting an implicit hint of culpability. But it is important to note that this is not in any sense an admission of any direct culpability of the British or Americans in the genesis of the political or humanitarian catastrophes in Afghanistan or Iraq. Rather, it is an admission of indirect or negligent culpability caused because of the lack of timely intervention. Indeed, the logic and legitimacy of external interventions are critically based on the presumption that the distant tragedies they seek to resolve are the result not of past actions but of past inactions. Similarly, the profusion of academic literature on ethnic conflict, civil war and humanitarian crises in the post-cold war era – written overwhelmingly from the perspective of potential external interveners – has understood their 'global dimensions' in very one-sided terms, focusing on their external consequences, but rarely on their external causation. Inadequate external attention to conflict-prone regions has been argued to have grave repercussions for the rest of the world because of their negative spill-over effects. In the inimitable words of Robert Kaplan:

> Sierra Leone is a microcosm of what is occurring . . . throughout West Africa and much of the underdeveloped world: the withering away of

> central governments, the rise of tribal and regional domains, the unchecked spread of disease, and the growing pervasiveness of war... it is Thomas Malthus, the philosopher of demographic doomsday, who is now the prophet of West Africa's future. And West Africa's future, eventually, will also be that of most of the rest of the world. (Kaplan, 1994)

In other words, if left unchecked, the political disintegration, economic poverty and cultural barbarism of internal wars in poor countries hold the possibility of infecting their neighbours and even the wider world. By highlighting the potential for such negative conflict externalities, it is increasingly suggested that intervention in distant trouble spots is no longer a matter of altruism, but of enlightened self-interest on the part of the outside powers who need to protect themselves against the threat of terrorism or uncontrollable refugee flows (for example, Collier *et al.* 2003). In a process that Mark Duffield has referred to as the extension of global liberal governance (Duffield 2001), international intervention is now a carefully calibrated infusion of military force, humanitarian aid, post-conflict reconstruction, capacity building, and re-education of various kinds by a diverse coalition of international actors. Since conflict is viewed as a process arising from a lack of global engagement, such interventions are necessarily meant to reintegrate conflict-ridden states back closely within the web of international political oversight, the global economy, and global normative standards.

In sum, in a post-cold war world dominated by parallel tendencies towards global integration and local disintegration, violent conflict has been characterized by potential external interveners as having internal causes but international consequences. In contrast, by situating internal conflicts within the global context, it can be argued that their occurrence should be viewed as symptomatic not of their exclusion but their inclusion within a global system characterized by changing forms of political, military, economic, and cultural intercourse and integration. This chapter, together with others in this volume has sought to challenge this exclusive focus on the internal by looking at the global dimensions of violent conflict and self-determination. This should not necessarily be seen as an attempt to dismiss the internal sources or to deny the role of domestic social identities and micro-economic motivations. Indeed, any such categorization that strictly segregates the internal and external, or that looks exclusively at the one or the other, is quite unhelpful in understanding the origins and dynamics of conflict. Rather, the purpose here is to view internal political conflicts within the global context as organic components of a single and increasingly inseparable global system. This would imply viewing conflict not just as the product of some individual economic or cultural peculiarities, but also of systemic problems inherent in the dynamics of a changing global order that they are often swept into.

Self-determination

Self-determination is a somewhat difficult concept to handle. Its heavily politicized usage and its recognition as a category within international law has turned it into a loaded, value-laden term that distorts its descriptive significance and complicates its analytical relevance. At its simplest, self-determination connotes the process by which collectives decide their political status, and by which they participate in the creation of constitutive principles and forms of socio-political organization.

The contemporary usage of the term self-determination dates back to the early twentieth-century debates over the 'national question' in Eastern Europe, with reference to the national minorities groups trapped within and between the imperial domains of Prussia, Austria-Hungary, Turkey and Russia. Following the end of World War I, self-determination was codified for the first time in the 1918 constitution of the Soviet Union and became the principle, if not the exact reality, behind the creation of numerous new borders in Europe. Following the end of World War II, self-determination was written into the charter of the United Nations and was subsequently even recognized as a right in international law. During the period 1945–90, self-determination became virtually cognate with the decolonization process as the administrative borders of numerous colonial territories and the institutions of colonial administration were recast into those of sovereign state entities.

Importantly, many of the states that were created through decolonization remain politically and socially fragile, and suffer from questionable popular legitimacy. Some of the largest states in Asia and Africa such as India, Indonesia, Algeria, Sudan, and Nigeria remain vulnerable to violent political conflicts and even insurgent wars, often from movements based on excluded minorities that have explicitly articulated a demand for self-determination. The enduring instability in the decolonized world has since intersected with a third wave of self-determination that has arisen following the end of the cold war in 1990. As a result, it led not only to the rise of several new state entities in the former USSR and Eastern Europe, but also changed the internal dynamics and stability of a number of fragile states and a number of ongoing movements for self-determination within them.

In the course of this complex journey through the twentieth century, the term self-determination has come to be understood as short-form for national self-determination, with reference to non-self governing peoples held involuntarily within empires or multinational states. However, in this volume the scope of the term has been broadened beyond national self-determination to include all movements that seek to effect a serious reconfiguration of state power in pursuit of well-defined social, cultural or economic objectives. To this extent, it has been used to frame the very diverse political conflicts in Algeria, Somalia, the D.R.Congo, Colombia, Sri Lanka, Burma and East Timor.

This extended definition is unconventional, but not entirely an innovation. For example, it falls well within the concepts elaborated in several authoritative international documents. In article 1 of the International Covenant on Economic, Social and Cultural Rights (1966) self-determination is formally recognized as a right by which a people 'freely determine their political status and freely pursue their economic, social and cultural development'. Worded as such, the operation of this right does not appear to be limited to those held under some form of alien occupation. What is central to the extended definition used here is that it describes a process of quite fundamental transformation in state–society relations. As such, it incorporates processes of national as well as 'civic' self-determination. In both cases, the exercise of self-determination critically involves the process of contesting and reconstituting the existing state institutions in order to effect certain socio-economic and ideo-political transformations in society.

There are important repercussions involved in using this extended definition to describe such a diverse group of political conflicts. Most importantly, self-determination bears distinctly non-neutral connotations since it imparts a degree of legitimacy on those it is used to describe. The significance of this legitimacy can be understood in some ways as the mirror-image of the illegitimacy conveyed by the term 'terrorism'. Indeed, the difficulties encountered in adequately defining self-determination parallel similar difficulties in finding an internationally acceptable definition for terrorism. To some extent both terms have passed beyond objective definition, as their function is primarily to signify a subjective distinction between what their users consider legitimate versus illegitimate.

But additionally the use of the term self-determination retains considerable analytical and even epistemological relevance. Firstly, it conveys the sense that the conflicts that have arisen in its wake should be viewed not just in terms of the chaos and violence they have engendered, but also as manifestations of large-scale social, economic and political transformations being contested – both explicit and implicit, and with verifiable underlying causes.

Secondly, the pre-occupation with international terrorism that has arisen since the mid-1990s, and which has accelerated following the 11 September 2001 attacks has promoted a situation where the one-sided attention to policing and preventing non-state violence on a global scale is obscuring the equally global political and economic processes that underlie this violence. Indeed, the moral outrage evoked by the term 'terrorism' is such that any suggestion that it might have underlying causes deserving of analysis has become tantamount to providing it with justification and legitimacy. Terrorism, in effect, has come to mean that which has no legitimate cause – and as such to categorize a phenomenon or entity as terrorist is to effectively exempt it from any meaningful analysis, and to cast it beyond the pale of knowledge and even knowability.

In parallel to this, the experience of civil war and the rise of violent militia groups in countries with lucrative export products such as diamonds, oil or timber has popularized the notion that such conflicts are caused largely by private economic motivations. This has in turn promoted the rise of entirely de-contextualized rational choice explanations of instrumentalist violence, in which conflict appears to be less the subject matter of political economy than industrial organization. In its most extreme version, the 'greed versus grievance' hypothesis explicitly dismisses political, economic or social grievances as merely a discursive veil behind which avaricious 'rebel leaders' engage in the pursuit of personal gain. In essence, it seeks to characterize political conflict as arising from criminal ambition, with very little to distinguish between armed insurgency and armed robbery.

In summary, despite ambiguities in its definition, the enduring analytical relevance of the term 'self-determination' should be seen in the context of the contemporary policy and academic discourse, within which political conflicts stand in danger of being dismissed as either irrational chaos, unknowable terrorism or rational criminality. This chapter outlines two ways in which self-determination can be understood in the global context. The first mechanism encompasses the possibilities inherent in the global system for the rise and sustenance of self-determination movements. For example, global factors may influence and accentuate group identities, sharpen economic tensions, or provide financial, diplomatic or moral support to the combatants. Elsewhere in this volume, these links have been explored by Stewart in terms of the role of the global economy in exacerbating the structural causes of conflict and in providing conflict finance, and by FitzGerald in terms of the interaction between multilateral regulatory mechanisms and the flow of global financial resources to armed conflicts.

A second, and more indirect, global dimension of self-determination relates to the global construction of statehood in economic, political and normative terms. Statehood implies an internally constitutive political relationship with definite social, economic and political functions. The states that have emerged historically through processes of self-determination have often embodied the ideo-political orientation and socio-economic character of the movements that brought about their existence. For example, the three largest states in Asia – China, India and Indonesia – all of which emerged in the late-1940s, contain important differences between each other that can be traced back to the very different kinds of movements that gave rise to them. Many of these differences persist even after five decades of considerable social upheaval and institutional reform in all three countries.

However, the statehood inherent in the self-determination project is critically fashioned and delimited not just by internal, but by global, factors. One strand of the recent literature that has explored the global construction of statehood has applied sociological institutionalism to international relations theory and has demonstrated, for example, that many otherwise anomalous features of contemporary statehood can be understood as a result of their origins in global cultural forces rather than through domestic endogenous evolution (for example, Meyer *et al.* 1997). The coding of social and political rights within national constitutions, for example with relation to womens' suffrage, has been found to relate less to domestic social realities or the strength of the women's movement in individual countries, but more to the spread of universal suffrage as a norm within global political culture (Boli 1987).

A large number of present-day sovereign states were socialized within international society, the global economy and international normative standards for membership in the state system through the experience of colonialism. In the vast majority of formal decolonizations, starting with India in 1947, what passed for self-determination involved remarkably little institutional change but consisted largely of the accelerated induction of trained natives to higher levels of the colonial government, civil administration, judiciary and military.

Self-determination is in this way moulded by global notions of how statehood can be imagined and by the global normative criteria for membership in the state system. In addition, it is constrained by global political and economic institutions and structures that substantially determine the discretionary bounds of what statehood will practically mean.

To summarize, two mechanisms in which self-determination in the global context can be understood are (i) how global circumstances and developments contribute towards (or inhibit) the rise and sustenance of self-determination movements; (ii) how the actual content and scope of statehood is itself defined, fashioned and constrained globally, and how this in turn, determines the shape and fate of self-determination movements. In this chapter different aspects of these two mechanisms are explored using the examples of Colombia and East Timor. In Colombia the dynamics of a long-standing rural insurgency are illustrated in terms of its links with the global economy and global political–military interventions. In East Timor the discussion concerns the very global construction of self-determination and statehood, focusing particularly on the period of UN administration from 1999–2002.

Colombia

The civil war in Colombia is now entering its fourth decade, although it is in many ways a continuation of a longer pattern of conflict and insurgency that is often traced as far back as the time of Simon Bolivar and the independence wars of the early nineteenth century. At a time in the early 1960s when Latin America became an important zone of cold war contention, the basis of Colombia's rural conflict effected a historic shift from an inter-elite rivalry between the Conservative and Liberal parties, to an overtly inter-class form played out between the state and communist insurgent groups. During the 1990s the main protagonists have been guerrilla groups, chiefly the *Fuerzas Armadas Revolucionarias de Colombia* (FARC), and the *Ejército de Liberacion Nacional* (ELN) against the Colombian armed forces and right-wing paramilitary groups such as the *Autodefensas Unidas de Colombia* (AUC).

This section presents a stylized summary of the dynamics of the conflict within the global context, conceptualized here in terms of two parallel and inter-linked but separate processes. These are (i) the way that the underlying political economy of conflict relates to sources of linkages with the global economy such as coffee, oil and cocaine; (ii) the way in which the domestic political instability that has resulted from this has related to international political paradigms, and has invited external politico-military interventions. This global framework is an essential part of understanding the evolution of the present conflict through the cold war and post-cold war period, and in disaggregating the complex nature of its intersection with the drug-economy, the war on drugs and the subsequent war on terrorism.

The underlying economic causes of the conflict can be traced historically to the incorporation of the Colombian rural hinterland within the global economy, and how this has intersected and contributed to changing patterns and rights of land ownership. One such trajectory relates to the transformation of the hacienda system to capitalist farms and ranches in the mid-twentieth century, and the way that demands for land reform since the 1930s have been subject to heavily contested and unevenly enforced government legislation. Another such trajectory relates to the frontier areas of land colonization where the state presence is weak, and where land rights of small colonist farmers are subject to encroachment by larger farmers (See LeGrand 1989). In other parts of the country, the conflict revolves around the expanding oil industry, which is the subject of ongoing international investment in exploration and production and the construction of oil pipelines. More recently, the spread of coca cultivation across large parts of Colombia has turned the country into the most important source point in the global supply chain of illegal drugs. In sum, the conflict in Colombia and the dynamics of its most violent manifestations has occurred without exception at the locus of its intersection with the global economy. As LeGrand (2003) notes 'regions where new commercial crops and export products have developed over the past forty years are the most violent places in Colombia today'.

As the present conflict came into existence in the early 1960s, its domestic protagonists related to a larger global paradigm for sources of identity and legitimacy as well as for political, financial and military support. The nature of the mechanisms by which these external resources became available played an important part in shaping the internal contours of the conflict by affecting not just the ratio of military forces, but also the ideo-political identity and the perceptions that the protagonists had of themselves and of each other. The main guerrilla groups that emerged in the mid-1960s and early-1970s identified themselves on the basis of prevalent international ideo-political frameworks, variously professing links to the USSR, China or Cuba. The government, in turn, identified itself closely as part of the regional and international anti-communist camp, and maintained a close diplomatic relationship with the United States.

In this way, the domestic struggle over land distribution, fought mostly between political constituencies of landless labourers, or land-poor *minifundistas*, and large landowners, expanded and was reconfigured to conform to the global context of an emerging cold-war ideo-political confrontation between Soviet communism and American anti-communism. In a process that was both voluntary and involuntary, the internal protagonists of the conflict came to be recognized and to recognize themselves as part of this grander global confrontation, with their expanded identities providing important international allies and allowing them to record their disparate actions as part of a globally legitimated cause. The head of the Colombian army's counter-insurgency operations during the mid-1980s, General García Echeverri sought to characterize the conflict, in precisely such terms:

> what happens to us in the region . . . has to be understood at the level of geopolitics, the world is being fought over by two great ideologies . . . [that] of Moscow, which suppresses freedoms and that of the western world which defends the democratic view.[2]

This is not to suggest that the widespread tendency to view Colombia's guerrilla warriors as pawns in the global cold war was itself without consequence or criticism. Colombia's Nobel Prize-winning novelist Gabriel García Márquez pleaded against this prevalent categorization, which, he argued, obscured the genuine domestic origins of the conflict:

> the immeasurable violence and pain of our history are the result of age-old inequities and untold bitterness, and not a conspiracy plotted three thousand leagues from our home. (García Márquez 1982)

But the adoption of this emerging global demarcation had important and real domestic repercussions in Colombia beyond the level of global discourse or perception. In that sense, the international ideo-political paradigm was not just a convenient mask that opportunistic local protagonists seized upon to legitimize their actions. Nor was it merely the lens through which ill-informed outsiders chose to interpret those events. Rather, the effects of the international paradigm in providing financial resources, legitimacy and ideo-political identity considerably influenced and shaped the direction of the evolution of internal socio-political alignments.

The Colombian Army, for example, had long been considered a poorly organized militia force closely linked to the Conservative party and the Catholic Church. But as a result of its international exposure and its increasing participation in US-sponsored training courses, such as in the US Army's School of the Americas, young officers gained professional training in anti-insurgency techniques, received political education on subjects such as international communism, and cultivated direct links with the US military hierarchy and with their Latin American contemporaries. Similarly, the influence of Marxist–Leninist ideological thought and political organization meant that the rural poor were organized politically for the first time under an overtly class-conscious and class-specific form, and as part of an avowedly internationalist movement for emancipation.

With the end of the cold war in 1990, the change in the international environment surrounding the conflict considerably changed the nature and operation of the political and economic imperatives relevant to the protagonists. By the early 1980s Colombia had become the epicentre of the global cocaine industry, with vertically-integrated multi-national drug syndicates such as the Medellin and Cali cartels controlling a large segment of the global cocaine supply chain. From the early 1990s large areas of the country came under coca cultivation. Colombia's role as a supplier of drugs to the US multiplied during the 1980s and 1990s even as, and partly because of, the unprecedented US-led drug interdiction efforts have focused on the region.[3] In the late-1990s, after two decades of US drug-prevention assistance, the US State Department estimated that 90 per cent of the cocaine sold in the US, and up to two-thirds of the heroin in the US East Coast still originated in Colombia (US 2001).

The complex intersection of the continuing guerrilla war with the drug economy, which stretches back to the late-1970s, has been the matter of considerable controversy. Colombian officials began to accuse the FARC of drug involvement in the early 1980s, and by 1984 even leading US officials began to characterize the FARC as 'narco-guerrillas'. To a large extent this was part of an active campaign by the Reagan administration between 1984–6 to conflate two hitherto separate objects of demonology: drug smuggling and communist insurgency, and to repackage domestically controversial foreign policy interventions as more legitimate anti-drug interventions.[4] Indeed, there is little dispute that FARC-controlled territories contain large areas of coca cultivation, and that the FARC receives substantial income from taxes levied on the cultivation and transport of drugs in these regions. But this remains only one of the many points of linkage between drugs and insurgency.

The impact of the drug industry (as with coffee, oil or other such sources of linkages to the global economy) and the guerrilla war can be analysed at two inter-linked levels relating to the economy and politics. These are: (i) the way in which the drug industry and the massive repatriation of drug funds have affected the economy, and hence, the underlying political economy of the conflict; (ii) the way in which the complex intersection of the drugs industry with the insurgency is giving rise to external political and military interventions into the conflict. Colombia's drug exports in the late-1990s were estimated around US$3 billion per year, a figure that places it at a close par with petroleum as the country's leading export and which, if included in official statistics, would account for over 15 per cent of all export earnings.[5] Due to a combination of factors, including the large magnitude of the drug surplus relative to the Colombian economy, the close-knit ownership structure of Colombia's formal sector enterprises, the social origins of the drug entrepreneurs, and international police scrutiny over the industry, this illicit surplus could be reinvested in relatively few places. One outcome of this constraint is that it has turned drug entrepreneurs into the country's largest landowners, who control an estimated four million hectares, or up to 10 per cent of Colombia's agricultural land.[6] The scale of the reinvestment of drug profits into land has been such that it is said to have contributed towards 'counter-land reform' – or an increase in the already high concentration of land ownership that is a central underlying cause behind the guerrilla war.

As a result, the emerging overlap between the ranks of the well-armed drug syndicates and large landlords effectively juxtaposed the growing drug industry within the ambit of the ongoing conflict. As they increased their participation in land ownership, drug syndicates inevitably came into conflict with the guerrillas, who espoused radical land reform and demanded taxes from landlords in their areas of control. This gave rise to a number of violent confrontations between the guerrillas and the drug syndicates in the early 1980s and paved the way for the rise of a new anti-guerrilla coalition formed by drug syndicates, large ranchers and the army's anti-insurgency units – dubbed the 'triangle of terror'. By the late-1980s, this new coalition had come to fruition in the birth of a new and far more violent generation of right-wing paramilitary groups.[7]

A separate axis of interaction between the global economy and the conflict in the 1990s arose because of the combination of agricultural trade liberalization on the one hand, and low commodity prices of coffee and other legal export crops on the other. Effectively the latter affected farmers in the food crop and domestic sector, while the former has affected those producing for the export market – in both cases negatively. In sum, they have been responsible for compressing the incomes of small farmers in Colombia, many of whom have subsequently shifted to coca cultivation as an alternative source of livelihood.[8] Between 1992–2000, coca cultivation in Colombia expanded almost four-fold to 136,000 hectares, and Colombia's multi-national drug enterprises accounted for 90 per cent of the cocaine that ultimately found its way into the US to feed the consumption habits of some three million hard-core addicts and an indeterminate number of casual consumers (US 2001).

There are two main repercussions of this ongoing dynamic in relation to the guerrilla war. Firstly, the absence of viable alternatives is bringing thousands of small farmers in Colombia – the main political support base of the guerrilla groups – within the ambit of the drug industry, giving rise to yet another locus of cooperation and confrontation between the drug industry and the guerrilla war. Secondly, it has positioned these small farmers as the primary target of the US war on drugs, a process that is leading to a blurring of lines between the drug war and the guerrilla war.

As the cold war wound down in the late 1980s, it became evident that the new lens with which the US judged Colombia and other countries in the region was less in terms of their governments' co-operation in containing communism, but more in terms of co-operation in containing the drugs trade. In the late 1980s the drug paradigm was institutionalized into foreign aid and foreign policy with the introduction of the controversial 'certification' process, which has since then become a central feature of US–Latin America relations. Henceforth, all US development assistance to countries such as Colombia, including US votes for multilateral development aid, became subject to one over-riding conditionality – that their governments be 'certified' by the White House as extending their full co-operation with Washington's war on drugs.

Thus the rapid expansion of the international drug economy and the externalization of the US war on drugs set the stage for a new generation of US financial, military and diplomatic assistance to the Colombian government.[9] The US–Colombia drug alliance reached its apogee in July 2000 with the launch of the $1.3 billion 'Plan Colombia', the largest US aid package ever to Latin America that made Colombia the third largest recipient of US aid in the world after Israel and Egypt. But Colombia's role as a supplier of drugs to the US multiplied during the 1990s even as, and partly because of, the unprecedented and ever more militarized US-led drug interdiction efforts in the region.

Importantly, through most of the 1990s, the new US-led alliance has been directed at fighting not the guerrilla war but the drug war. Largely due to domestic pressures, the Clinton administration took great pains to prevent its anti-drug military intervention from being construed as direct involvement in a foreign war.[10] For example, military aid was directed largely at the police rather than the army. Furthermore, the US has sought to retain arms-length military involvement even in the anti-drug operations by 'outsourcing' many military functions in guerrilla-sensitive areas. Pilots for US-funded fumigation programmes were contracted from a private US defence contractor, DynCorp, while military training was given through a Virginia-based company, Military Professional Resources International (MPRI).

However, since the late-1990s, US policy-makers have reacted to the escalation in the Colombian conflict by adopting an increasingly unified view of the drug and guerrilla war. This has essentially meant that the guerrilla groups have been rhetorically located at the nexus of both problems, and that greater resources have been deployed to target the one as a means of targeting the other. This approach, which is partly a reversion to a more cold-war era view of the threat posed by Latin American insurgent groups, began to take shape at least as early as 1997, when the US State Department named the FARC and ELN as international terrorist organizations under the Antiterrorism and Effective Death Penalty Act (US 1997). It has gained greater coherence and impetus since January 2001 under the Bush administration, which rehabilitated a number of controversial cold-war era Latin America 'hawks' such as Otto Reich, Elliot Abrams and John Negroponte to influential posts in the foreign policy and security establishment.

Thus it is possible to start unpacking the globalized dynamic of escalation in the links between the drug war and the guerrilla war in the 1990s by presenting a simplified version of the role of the global economy and global politics. Firstly, economic circumstances relating to Colombia's ongoing integration into the world economy are forcing small farmers to switch from legal crops to coca. The repercussions of this are that it is firstly bringing thousands of small farmers in Colombia – the main political support base of the guerrilla groups – within the ambit of the drug industry, giving rise to yet another locus of cooperation and confrontation between the drug industry and the guerrilla war. Secondly, it has positioned these small farmers as the primary target of a globalized political and military response, in the form of the anti-drug war, and specifically, the US-led crop fumigation programme. It is this process that is leading to a blurring of lines between the drug war and the guerrilla war, and causing the complex matrix of protagonists in each one to be collapsed into a single, larger confrontation between the FARC and the US.

The changing nature of US involvement in Colombia is being ushered in not as one of switching from engagement in the drugs war in favour of the guerrilla war, but rather as taking a unified approach to the hitherto parallel wars on drugs and guerrillas. The FARC has explicitly been identified as a primary target within this rubric, leading to an increasingly direct war of words between the FARC and the US, which was at least partly responsible for the collapse of the Pastrana-era peace-initiative. This process has subsequently accelerated with the onset of the new US-led war against terrorism in September 2001, which coincided with the election of Álvaro Uribe Velez as President in May 2002. In the aftermath of the 11 September 2001 attacks, US Secretary of State Colin Powell referred to the FARC as little different from Osama Bin Laden, and has contributed to their re-classification from narco-guerrilla to narco-terrorist (Brodzinsky 2001). Similarly, the Uribe government has pursued a substantially more military solution to the insurgency at the very time when sentiments in Washington have become more sympathetic and amenable to such requests.

East Timor

On 30 August 1999, a UN-administered 'popular consultation' was held in the Indonesian occupied territory of East Timor, in which eligible voters were asked to choose between special autonomy status within Indonesia or outright separation. Despite a mounting campaign of intimidation and the threat of violence by pro-Indonesian militias, some 98 per cent of the 450,000 registered voters nevertheless emerged to cast their ballots. Four days later, even as most people in East Timor itself remained unaware of the result, UN Secretary General Kofi Annan announced to the Security Council in New York that an unambiguous majority of 78.5 percent had voted in favour of separation.[11]

In the eyes of the international community, the people of East Timor were deemed to have expressed their free will and to have exercised a legitimate and long-delayed act of self-determination. Less than three years later, on 20th May 2002, the final outcome of this exercise took the form of a ceremonial transfer of power by Kofi Annan to former guerrilla commander José Alexandre 'Xanana' Gusmão, now President of the newly created *República Democrática de Timor-Leste*. East Timor was the first newly created state entity of the millennium, and was duly admitted as the 191st member of the UN General Assembly in September 2002.

East Timor's exercise of self determination and subsequent achievement of statehood are the result and embodiment of its complex and tragic history. Some 200,000 people, or more than a quarter of the 1975 population are estimated to have died as a direct or indirect result of the Indonesian occupation – many from dislocation and famine that resulted from anti-insurgency operations in the late 1970s. Resistance to the Indonesian occupation occurred over the entire period 1975–99, and took various forms from outright armed guerrilla warfare to student protest demonstrations and international solidarity activism. The 24-year long occupation, the guerrilla war and the enforced political, social and economic integration into Indonesia brought about a more rapid and intrusive period of social change than had occurred before under several centuries of Portuguese control. Many Timorese sought refuge in religion, perhaps in order to reaffirm their cultural distinctness, and membership in the Catholic church, which stood at around 20 per cent in 1975, had expanded to over 90 per cent by the early 1990s.

In these and numerous other ways the making of a contemporary East Timorese national identity, which remained largely in latent form at the end of the Portuguese era in 1975, subsequently occurred in the course of its lengthy and traumatic denial of self-determination since then. But despite the enormous scale of suffering in East Timor and the persistence of an armed resistance movement for over two decades, the events that led up to the referendum exercise in 1999 did not come about directly because of a domestic political or military breakthrough. Rather, the referendum, and the entire trajectory of self-determination that preceded it, were critically fashioned by events that occurred outside the territory and that were often entirely unconnected to East Timor.

The possibility of independence first came into being abruptly in April 1974, after the overthrow of Portugal's conservative Salazar-Caetano dictatorship in the *Revolução dos Cravas*. This window of opportunity was closed, equally abruptly, by an Indonesian military invasion in December 1975 – and remained closed for the rest of the cold war period, primarily because of the support of Indonesia's powerful international allies. The dwindling international media coverage of the issue during the late 1970s and 1980s began referring to East Timor as a 'lost cause', a 'depressing cause', a 'hidden war', a 'forgotten war', or a place of 'silent suffering'. East Timor became a 'stillborn nation'.[12] But the prospects for independence changed dramatically in the 1990s, linked to outside events such as the end of the cold war, the heightened influence of global media and global civil society in the 1990s, the East Asian financial crisis of 1997–99 that crippled Indonesia and brought an end to the Suharto period.

In a post-cold war world filled with weak states, civil wars, secessionist movements and unrecognized self-governing territories, East Timor still represents one of the very few cases where a movement for self-determination has successfully been translated into internationally recognized sovereign statehood. It is also noteworthy for the extent to which it was intense external pressure that finally forced the Indonesian government to permit the August 1999 referendum. This international recognition and support for self-determination in East Timor is significant for two reasons.

Firstly, it represents a reversal in the role played by many of the same international players, particularly the US and Australia. In 1975 it was with the consent, if not close collusion, of these two powers that Indonesia launched a military invasion and annexation of East Timor. The presence of President Gerald Ford and Secretary of State Henry Kissinger in Jakarta on the day before the invasion of East Timor has raised endless speculation over the extent of US acquiescence or instigation.

Meanwhile, Australia's close knowledge of the invasion was finally revealed in 2000 following the declassification of foreign ministry documents.[13] Subsequently, Australia became the only country in the world to grant official recognition to the takeover, at least partly to facilitate the negotiation of offshore oil rights. Meanwhile, the US continued to view Indonesia as a close cold war ally, and worked diplomatically to defuse any attempts to challenge the takeover at the UN in the late 1970s and early 1980s. But by the late 1990s, the international situation was completely transformed, and it was direct pressure from the US and Australia that forced the economically crippled government of B.J. Habibie to re-open the issue of East Timor in January 1999.[14]

Secondly, international support for East Timor stands in stark contrast to the absence of such support in other very similar sounding nearby cases, such as Aceh, West Papua, Bougainville or the Moros. To some extent this is because East Timor was never part of the Dutch East Indies and Indonesia's annexation was never accorded international recognition. But there is still no comparable international support forthcoming even in cases of very similar legal standing, the most striking anomaly being the case of Western Sahara. Nor are there any signs that several de facto self-governing territories such as Abkhazia and Somaliland will eventually be viewed internationally as having exercised juridically legitimate acts of self-determination, regardless of the extent of their territorial control, political stability, popular legitimacy or adherence to democratic norms.

In sum, the circumstances surrounding the internationally supported process of self-determination in East Timor demonstrate, at the very least, that such support is fickle, rare and inconsistent. Furthermore, the fact that East Timor was a recipient of this privileged dispensation of self-determination from above meant that it would be the international community in the guise of the United Nations, rather than the East Timorese or the leaders of the independence movement, that would remain fully responsible and retain full control of the entire process. In form, the UN organized not just the referendum but subsequently took complete charge of the top–down construction of a new state under the authority of a transitional administration vested with absolutist powers. In content, the new state came into existence under overwhelmingly external inspiration, design, funding and supervision, and represents the product of an internationally co-ordinated exercise whose technocratic appearance belies a strong normative and ideological content. Indeed, despite the symbolic significance of the referendum as an expression of public choice and an affirmation of collective rights, the people of East Timor in reality 'self-determined' very little.

The UN Transitional Administration in East Timor (UNTAET) came into being in October 1999 following the referendum, and was charged with restoring security and tackling the immediate humanitarian crisis while supervising the creation of an administrative and political structure.[15] In terms of the scale and scope of its tasks, UNTAET represented an unprecedented expansion of the traditional UN peace-keeping role, beyond even peace-making and into state-building. In pursuit of these objectives, it was vested with equally unprecedented powers of a pseudo-sovereign entity, considerably exceeding those of prior such UN missions during the 1990s such as Namibia, Somalia, Cambodia or Kosovo. One of its own former officials described the scale of UNTAET's writ as resembling that of a 'pre-constitutional monarch' (Chopra 2000). But rather than monarchy, the analogy that better describes the transitional period in East Timor is that of the paternalistic colonial state. In the period of its 32 month operation, UNTAET spent roughly the first half recreating an absolutist colonial-style authority, and the second half mimicking an orderly process of decolonization. To a large extent, the nature and scale of the UN mission in East Timor was a result of its very cathartic disengagement from Indonesia. In the two weeks following the referendum result, pro-Indonesian militias destroyed most of the physical, economic and administrative infrastructure in the territory. They torched over 70 per cent of all buildings and destroyed most livestock, houses, banks, public utilities and government offices. Over half the population had fled their homes in fear of reprisals and many were kidnapped to Indonesian West Timor while the heavily Indonesian-staffed administration collapsed completely.[16]

But the scale of the relief, rehabilitation and refugee problem that followed the referendum does not entirely explain the creation of such an all-powerful transitional authority. Nor does it explain why the self-determination movement in East Timor, which had fought against the odds at home and abroad for 25 years was effectively relegated to little more than advisory status in the creation of their state. An ex-post assessment of UNTAET's role in local capacity-building noted that for its first year of existence, 'UNTAET's policy was more exclusive and less participatory than that of the previous Indonesian government' (Fox 2002). Indeed, UNTAET's very first act in East Timor was to decree itself in full charge of all executive and legislative powers:

> 1.1 All legislative and executive authority with respect to East Timor, including the administration of the judiciary, is vested in UNTAET and is exercised by the Transitional Administrator. In exercising these functions the Transitional Administrator shall consult and cooperate closely with representatives of the East Timorese people.[17]

The Transitional Administrator vested with such viceregal powers was Brazilian national Sergio Vieira de Mello, a career UN bureaucrat who had hurriedly been redeployed from UNMIK in Kosovo to lead UNTAET, and who was subsequently killed as head of the UN mission in Iraq in August 2003. With an annual budget of US$500 million, Vieira De Mello was in command of a team of 700 international civil servants, 1,300 civilian police and a 7,000 strong military force. Although he was enjoined to 'consult' with the East Timorese leadership in his endeavours and did establish close and cordial working relations with many of them, he was personally charged with full legal control of all decision-making powers. His brief was such that he was not made accountable at any level to any entity in East Timor but instead only to the UN Security Council in New York.

Less than a year into its mandate, East Timorese discontent and frustration with UNTAET became more vocal. UNTAET was criticized both for its failure to adequately involve the East Timorese in the transitional government, and for its heavily expatriate-staffed operation. Even in the instances where they were involved, East Timorese leaders complained that they were powerless figureheads. In December 2000, four East Timorese appointed as cabinet ministers resigned together and declared:

> The East Timorese Cabinet members are caricatures of ministers in the government of a banana republic. They have no power, no duties, no resources to function adequately.[18]

Much of the frustration experienced by the East Timorese resulted from the perceptions in the minds of arriving UN officials that the territory entrusted to their care was in a state of Hobbesian void, and that theirs was a largely technocratic task to reconstruct it completely from scratch. The extent of the post-referendum destruction that confronted them led arriving foreign officials to describe their task as akin to 'landing on a desert island and trying to build a nation from scratch' (Mydans 1999). An assessment of the UN's initial tasks in East Timor reflects this spirit:

> What is required now is nothing less than determining the role, structure, dynamics, and future of the new state, including the configuration of basic pillars of governance and separation of powers. (United Nations 2000)

Some also looked at the apparently 'terra nullis' situation post-referendum as a source of opportunity – East Timor was described as a 'petri dish' upon which international development experts could test out contemporary best practice theories. Describing the sweeping powers available to international policy makers, an October 1999 article in the *Wall Street Journal* remarked, without any hint of irony:

> The world's most powerful economic policy makers will get a chance to show how to do it in East Timor . . . these people will be handed a clean slate. Insulated from the domestic political constraints they typically confront elsewhere, they will have what is perhaps a once-in-a-career opportunity to draft a policy blueprint that is entirely in line with the World Bank's and the IMF's fundamental free-market prescriptions for sustainable development. (Casey 1999)

Indeed, the UNTAET mission was by design tightly enmeshed with other elements of the international aid community, particularly the World Bank, IMF and Asian Development Bank. In addition, bilateral donors such as Portugal, Australia, Japan and numerous international NGOs carved out specific niches for themselves in the relief, reconstruction and institution-building process. UNTAET staff and other international aid workers, many of whom were drawn from prior missions such as Cambodia and Kosovo, and who were destined to find themselves later in Afghanistan, were experts in elections, budgeting, police, local administration, and civil society – but were for the most part quite inexpert on East Timor itself. International donor aid for independent East Timor was placed in trust funds operated by the World Bank and United Nations. Even East Timor's voluminous and impressive National Development Plan, drafted by a freshly appointed Planning Commission and reflecting widespread public consultation, came about primarily to facilitate better donor aid co-ordination.[19]

All this is not to suggest that there was necessarily any malevolent intention, abuse of power or mismanagement either by Vieira De Mello or other individuals in UNTAET or the aid agencies – most of whom discharged their duties with genuine dedication under very difficult circumstances. The problems that arose in the transition period were for the most part structural, and related to the process by which the juggernaut of self-determination descended and unfolded. Chopra (2000) has blamed the failure to incorporate the East Timorese on problems inherent in the hasty inception of the mission amid the worsening humanitarian crisis of September 1999. Suhrke (2001), in a detailed study of UNTAET, suggests that much of its institutional character derived from its origins within the Department of Peace Keeping Operations (DPKO) in the UN secretariat in New York. The rationale of peace-keeping required not only an overwhelmingly foreign presence, but one that sought to keep a clear distance from the locals – whom peace-keepers were trained to regard as potentially dangerous belligerents.

But just as the problems of the transitional period cannot be blamed upon any individual failing, it can equally not be reduced to flaws in mission design or implementation. The absolutist scope of UNTAET's authority, and its turn-key approach to state-building were not the result of bureaucratic bungling as such, but were the conscious products of a deliberately maximalist intervention by a deeply conservative international community. Having granted self-determination with the one hand, they kept an exceptionally tight grip on much of the actual determining that took place with the other, such that they could closely monitor and shape the process by which a future member of their own ranks would come into being.

East Timor was reconstructed using a modular design of state-building, largely developed through cross-country expertise in the 'anti-politics machine' of the international development aid sector. The new Republic has incorporated the very latest in institution design, good governance, poverty reduction, gender sensitivity, fiscal policy, macroeconomic management, and participatory methods of development. The highly technocratic nature of this exercise, the inspiration, identity, and methods employed by its key architects, and even the 'participatory' rhetoric that guided the process have meant that the process of state construction in East Timor has oddly come to resemble the construction of an ambitious donor funded aid project. What it lacks as a result is an adequate sense that the new state is the institutional embodiment of the ideals, politics or socio-economic character of a national liberation movement. Instead, East Timor has a state-of-the-art state designed to plug in seamlessly with existing structures of global governance, aid delivery mechanisms, and external reporting and transparency requirements.

The new East Timorese state inaugurated in May 2002 has an elected 88-member legislature that has drafted and approved a lengthy and carefully drafted constitution. There is a 21-member cabinet, an elected head of state, a devolved domestic administrative apparatus, a national police force, a voluminous and detailed national development plan and various functioning ministries charged with executing it. But largely as a function of the way in which self-determination actually arrived in the territory, neither the people of East Timor nor the East Timor independence movement that had fought at home and abroad for 25 years actually played any significant part in its construction, except where they were permitted to do so in roles created for them by the UN. Independence day in that sense represented the moment when the keys to this pre-fabricated state apparatus were handed over to an elected East Timorese leadership.

The rhetorical significance of self-determination in East Timor appears to be that it represented the successful expression of a long-repressed collective desire for independence. After a long and costly struggle, first against Portugal and later against Indonesia, the people of East Timor were for the first time ever given the opportunity to decide their collective political fate – and this is in no sense insignificant. But the structural context in which it occurred suggests instead that this expression of public choice was very limited in scope. Furthermore, it was embedded within, and even subordinated to, a very different exercise through which a successful applicant for membership in international society was being socialized to operate within specific economic, political and normative standards.

Conclusions

This chapter has argued for the importance of looking at contemporary political conflicts and civil wars not merely in terms of their internal causes in cultural or economic terms, but in the global context, and as part of the dynamics of global change. It has outlined two ways in which the realignment of socio-political identities – as manifest in contemporary self-determination movements – intersects with larger global factors.

Firstly, global factors can create the conditions within which existing forms of political community are de-stabilized, states are weakened, new collective identities are crystallized and self-determination movements are brought into being. Secondly, in a related but distinct process, the global economy, global politics and global normative prescriptions form the bounds within which self-determination movements are able to visualize and create new forms of statehood. The first can be viewed as the global 'fuel' so to speak within which self-determination movements are launched and sustained – while the second refers to how global factors shape the 'target' that they seek to reach. In their change and interaction, these two mechanisms comprise a broad framework within which contemporary conflicts can be viewed in the global context, and vice versa.

Notes

1. Thanks are due to Victoria Brittain, Peter Carey, Valpy FitzGerald, Frances Stewart, and Marcella Vigneri for assistance and comments.
2. Quoted in Pearce (1990), p. 245.
3. In part, this was the perverse consequence of the success of drug interdiction in Bolivia and Peru.
4. See Ryan (1989) or Collett (1988).
5. Cited in Bagley (2001).
6. Estimates vary widely, but are frequently much higher.
7. See Romero (2000) for example.
8. For example, see Mathiason (2001).
9. For an informative critique of US intervention in Colombia during the 1990s, see Tickner (2002).
10. See Tamayo (2001).
11. See Martin (2001).
12. See Ramos-Horta (1987).
13. Joliffe (1978), also Dunn (1983), See Australia (2000).
14. See Scheiner (2000), Nevins (2002).
15. UNSC Resolution no. 1272, 25 October 1999.
16. See Martinkus (2001).
17. UNTAET Regulation 1999/1, 27 November 1999.
18. Joint letter to Sergio Vieira de Mello, reported in the *Sydney Morning Herald*, 5 December 2000.
19. Interviews with staff members of the Planning Commission, May 2002.

References

Australia, Department of Foreign Affairs and Trade (2000) *Australia and the Indonesian Incorporation of Portuguese Timor, 1974–76*. Melbourne: Melbourne University Press.

Bagley, B. (2001) 'Drug Trafficking, Political Violence and US Policy in Colombia in the 1990s', *Colombia in Context conference*, Berkeley, CA: 2001.

Blair, A. (2001) Transcript of Prime Minister's Statement on Afghanistan, 13 November 2001, accessed online from http://www.pm.gov.uk/output/page3851.asp on 19 December 2002.

Blair, A. (2003) Prepared comments to Downing Street press conference, 25 March 2003.

Boli, J. (1987) 'Human Rights or State Expansion? Cross-national Definitions of Constitutional Rights, 1870 1970' in G. Thomas, J. Meyer and F. Ramirez, *Institutional Structure: Constituting State, Society and the Individual*, Newbury Park, CA: Sage Publications.

Brodzinsky, S. (2001) 'Terror Fight May Alter Colombia Relations', *Miami Herald*, 6 November 2001.

Casey, Michael (1999) 'In East Timor, World Policy Makers Must Build an Economy from Scratch', *Wall Street Journal*, 6 October 1999.

Chopra, J. (2000) 'The UN's Kingdom of East Timor', *Survival*, 42(3), 27–39.

Collett, Merrill (1988) 'An International Story: The Myth of the 'Narcoguerrillas', *Nation*, 247(4), 13 August 1988.

Collier, P., V. L. Elliott, H. Hegre, A. Hoeffler, M. Reynal-Querol and N. Sambanis. (2003) *Breaking the Conflict Trap: Civil War and Development Policy*. Washington, D.C: World Bank.

Duffield, M. (2001) *Global Governance and the New Wars*. London: Zed.

Dunn, J. (1983) *Timor: A People Betrayed*. Milton, Qld: Jacaranda Press.

Fox, J. (2002) 'East Timor: Assessing UNTAET's Role in Building Local Capacities for the Future', conference paper, *Comparing Experiences of State-Building in Asia and Europe*, Council for Asia Europe Co-operation (CAEC).

García Márquez, G. 'The Solitude of Latin America', *Nobel Prize Lecture*, 8 December 1982.

Huntington, S. (1993) 'The Clash of Civilizations', *Foreign Affairs*, 72(3), 22–8.

Joliffe, J. (1978) *East Timor: Nationalism and Colonialism*. St. Lucia, Qld: University of Queensland Press.

Kaplan, R. (1994) 'The Coming Anarchy', *The Atlantic Monthly*, 273(2), 44–76.

LeGrand, C. (1989) 'Colonization and Violence in Colombia: Perspectives and Debates', *Canadian Journal of Latin American and Caribbean Studies*, 14(28), 5–29.

LeGrand, C. (2003) 'The Colombian Crisis in Historical Perspective', *Canadian Journal of Latin American and Caribbean Studies*, 27(55), 165–209.

Martin, I. (2001) *Self-Determination in East Timor: the United Nations, the Ballot and International Intervention*. Boulder, CO: Lynne Rienner.

Martinkus, J. (2001) *A Dirty Little War*. Sydney: Random House.

Mathiason, N. (2001) 'Coffee Growers Turn to Cocaine', *The Observer*, 12 August 2001.

Meyer, J. W., J. Boli, G. M. Thomas and F. O. Ramirez (1997) 'World Society and the Nation State', *American Journal of Sociology*, 103(1), 144–81.

Mydans, S. (1999) 'World Bank Begins Task of Rebuilding in East Timor', *The New York Times*, 2 November 1999.

Nevins, J. (2002) 'The Making of "Ground Zero" in East Timor in 1999', *Asian Survey*, 42(4), 623–42.

Pearce, J. (1990) *Colombia: Inside the Labyrinth*. Latin America Bureau., p. 245.

Ramos-Horta, J. (1987) *Funu: The Unfinished Saga of East Timor*. Lawrenceville, NJ: Red Sea Press.

Romero, M. (2000) 'Changing Identities and Contested Settings: Regional Elites and the Paramilitaries in Colombia', *International Journal of Politics, Culture and Society*, 14 (1).

Ryan, Randolph (1989) 'Colombia's Other War', *Boston Globe*, 26 November 1989.

Scheiner, C. (2000) 'The United States: From Complicity to Ambiguity' in P. Hainsworth and S.McCloskey (eds) *The East Timor Question: The Struggle for Independence from Indonesia*, London: I.B.Taurus.

Sydney Morning Herald (2000) 'East Timor Leaders Threaten Mass Resignation', 5 December 2000.

Suhrke, A. (2001) 'Peace-keepers as Nation-builders: Dilemmas of the UN in East Timor', *International Peacekeeping*, 8(4).

Tamayo, J. (2001), 'US Civilians on Frontlines of Drug War in Colombia', *Knight Ridder Newspapers*, 26 February 2001.

Tickner, A. (2002) 'US Foreign Policy in Colombia: Bizarre Side-Effects of the 'War on Drugs' in G. Gallon, C. Welna (eds) *Democracy, Human Rights and Peace in Colombia*. University of Notre Dame Press (Kellogg Series), in press.

United Nations (2000), *Building Blocks for a Nation, UN Common Country Assessment for East Timor*. Dili: United Nations.
US Department of State Fact Sheet, (2001) 'Counternarcotics Efforts in the Andean Region', 23 March 2001.
US State Department (1997), *Patterns of Global Terrorism*, Washington, D.C: http://www.state.gov/www/global/terrorism/1997Report/1997index.html.

6

Why Congo Persists: Sovereignty, Globalization and the Violent Reproduction of a Weak State[1]

Pierre Englebert

A multifaceted paradox

Wherever one looks, many elements conspire to suggest that the Democratic Republic of Congo should have collapsed some time ago under the multiple assaults of its own inadequacies as a state, the extreme heterogeneity and polarization of its populations, and the dislocations of globalization and foreign occupation. Yet Congo has gone on defying such expectations and has continued to display a stunning propensity for resilience. This chapter addresses this paradox.

Precious little is redeeming about the state in Congo. Created as the institutional façade of a foreign enterprise of exploitation of ivory and rubber, it reproduced as the instrument of an extractive colonization system, in turns violent and paternalistic. Once independent, it provided the stage and the reason for five years of sheer chaos combining mutinies, secessions, rebellions, coups and a botched UN intervention, then to 32 years of stifling arbitrary rule, predation and eventual economic ruin. 'Liberation' from the Mobutu regime only compounded the existing arbitrariness and poverty with renewed armed conflict, the collapse of the central administrative apparatus and the marginalization of civil society. Meanwhile, the Congolese have never had a chance to choose freely their leaders or political system.

The catastrophic failure of the Congolese state is worsened by the vast heterogeneity of its people and their intense and frequently violent polarization along regional, ethnic and parochial lines. By one count, Congo has no less than 365 ethnic groups.[2] Some are fiercely antagonistic like the Lunda and Balubakat of Katanga, the Lulua and Luba of Kasai, the Hema and Lendu of the Oriental Province, or the Rwandophones and most other groups from the Kivus. The Congolese have also developed strong provincial identities. Katangans and Kasaians have long-lasting grievances vis-à-vis each other and the state. The Kivu provinces are also intensely particularistic. Furthermore, in each province the Congolese tend to make a strong distinction between 'autochthonous' and 'non-autochthonous' populations based on the alleged precedence of their settlement there. Finally, the geographical distribution of Congolese populations concentrates around boundary zones, making Congo akin to a periphery with no core.

Congo's territorial and economic integrity has also come under the repeated assaults of foreign invasions and the informalization of international trade and investment networks over the last decade. Twice since 1996, Rwanda and Uganda have invaded and set up or encouraged localized rebellions. The economy of eastern Congo is now deeply integrated with that of these two countries and of East Africa. Angola, Namibia and Zimbabwe also occupied large segments of the country from 1998 to 2003, albeit formally on behalf of the Kinshasa government. Zimbabwe attempted to reorient the economies of the Kasai and Katanga provinces, which it controlled, in favour of Zimbabwean interests and towards Southern African markets in general.[3] This compounded an already developing reorientation of Kasaian and Katangan economic activities away from Kinshasa and towards Southern Africa (Nest 2001). Simultaneously, and not unrelatedly, the diminished control of the state over its resources and borders has favoured the informalization, criminalization, and internationalization of the exploitation of Congo's massive natural wealth, mainly composed of diamonds, gold, copper, cobalt, uranium, timber and coltan. In other words, Congo has been penetrated by global networks that operate by and large in the margins of the law and bypass existing state structures.[4]

The failures of the Congolese state, the acute polarization of its society and the poundings of globalization make Congo a prime candidate for violent dislocation and reconfiguration at the hands of 'self-determination movements', whether driven by communal grievances or individual profit motivations. After all, if the Southern Sudanese have fought for decades to escape the exploitative domination of their state, why wouldn't the Katangans? If ethnically homogeneous Somalia has broken down, why wouldn't the more numerous pieces of the Congolese puzzle come undone? And if transnational identities and economic flows have facilitated movements against the state in Sri Lanka, Indonesia or Algeria, why would they not yield similar results in Congo? Many observers had indeed predicted the breakdown of Congo as Mobutu's regime crumbled in 1996, based partly on the relatively lively separatist traditions of Katanga, the Kasais and the Kivus. It was not unreasonable to expect then as now that the simmering contradictions of the Congolese state, which had been kept under lid by the perceived imperatives of the cold war, would finally boil over as international norms of sovereignty came under attack, and as new material conditions began to undermine principles of territoriality.[5]

And yet, Congo endures. Moreover, the Congolese profess a remarkable fervour in their attachment to the state. Paradoxically, where one would expect to observe the formation or the rise to salience of alternative identities, one sees a nearly unanimous profession of loyalty to decrepit Congo, both among elites and commoners. At a January 2002 meeting of Congolese president Joseph Kabila and rebel leaders Jean-Pierre Bemba (*Mouvement de Libération du Congo*) and Adolphe Onusumba (*Rassemblement Congolais pour la Démocratie*-Goma), for example, the three factional leaders responsible for the partition of the country all 'reaffirmed their will to see [Congo] recover its unity' (BERCI 2002). These aspirations for national unity are not only a feature of the political class. Opinion polls systematically reveal massive support for the reunification of the country, and fear of its partition.[6] Statements from politicians and evidence from opinion polls fall well short, however, of conveying the puzzling intensity with which the Congolese affirm their national pride. In numerous interviews with Congolese, one encounters a remarkable uniformity of views on this question. In Kisangani, delegates of women's organizations did not identify their number one priority as feeding their children or living in peace. On the contrary, they stated: 'The first thing is unity of the country. That is the first thing we want. We used to be one.'[7] In the same town, a human rights activist declared 'the Congolese do not want to see their country balkanized. Balkanization is a diabolic plan because the desire of the Congolese people to stay together is unquestionable. It would not serve the interests of the population; just the interests of foreign powers.'[8] In Katanga, André Tshombé, the son of the late president of Katanga, Moïse Tshombé, who deems to be his father's political heir, stated 'there is diversity here but [. . . .] we are also Congolese'.[9] And patterns of shirts and *pagnes* often make reference to territorial integrity and national unity. The Congolese never talk of territorial adjustments, partition or reconfigurations, but always use words such as balkanization or dismemberment ('*dépeçage*') and almost universally see any idea of territorial change as evil, conspiratorial, and the result of foreign – and often US – based machinations to prevent Congo from rising to its natural *grandeur*.

This chapter offers a theory of the reproduction of the weak Congolese state in the era of globalization. It argues that, far from abating with the end of the cold war and the weakening of Congo's empirical statehood, Congo's international sovereignty has been preserved if not reinforced by the Congolese and foreign actors alike. For a large number of Congolese elites, state sovereignty is a paramount force, which allows for the transformation of the weak state into an economic resource and dwarfs the potential returns of alternative agendas of self-determination. Because of several benefits associated with the international recognition of Congo's sovereignty, these elites choose to pursue their profiteering strategies in the context of Congo itself. As a result, violent rebellions revolve around the terms of the rebels' integration in the state rather than over the nature of the state itself. Populations at large, on the other hand, value the continued existence of the state despite its abuses, because it offers a structure of predictability that is not associated with guerillas, warlords or secessionist movements. Grass-root Congolese prefer therefore to voice their local cultural identities in competition with each other for access to local resources, rather than in defiance of the state itself. Far from favouring the dilution of the state in their eyes, globalization offers them uncertain and dangerous alternatives, the risks of which they remain adverse to. Foreign companies also find benefits in continuing to deal with the weak state. While its very weaknesses offer numerous opportunities for rents, its continued sovereignty offers them relative guarantees, such as insurance opportunities not available in deals with non-sovereign entities. Finally, Western powers and international organizations also prefer to replicate the structure of Congolese statehood rather than to facilitate alternative scenarios. All of them fear the unknown and the setting of a precedent in revising colonial boundaries. Maintaining Congo also guarantees the continuation of its international obligations to the West, such as debt servicing. As a result, the incentives of the Congolese and of foreign states and companies collude to keep Congo as Congo. Forces of globalization that are expected to dilute the state and promote the politicization of alternative identities, such as the cultural influences of diasporas or the informalization and occasional criminalization of networks of resource exploitation do not, in the end, measure up to the incentives of sovereign reproduction in the Congolese context.

The weak sovereign state as a resource

In order to understand the ways in which the Congolese state has adjusted to the global economic, political and cultural influences of the last decade, one must first apprehend its very nature and the manner in which it functions. Two elements stand out. First, the very weakness of the state is a resource to many Congolese, which paradoxically contributes to its resilience. Second, the international recognition of Congo's sovereignty as a state is a crucial mechanism which guarantees its reproduction and is also a resource in itself.

The benefits of the weak state

Although it may appear at first as merely dysfunctional, the weak Congolese state actually benefits numerous segments of its population. Ministries, state agencies, provincial administrations and other bureaucratic appendages of the state are maintained by state elites, their employees and citizens in general because they derive private benefits from them irrespective of these institutions' capacity to perform their initial public functions. At the most direct level, people continue to report to work in the hope of receiving their wages or in order to preserve their claim to hypothetical future payments of their wages. Thus, whether in government-controlled or in rebel territory, unpaid civil servants start their day by going to work *'pour rester matriculés'* before heading off to their field or to other survival economic activity. This follows the logic of 'salarization' of society by the state which lies at the core of the African post-colonial social contract (Mbembe 2001). But there is more to the persistence of the state than the expectation of direct payments. The capacity to use the weak state as an instrument of predation is the most crucial element of the logic of its survival and reproduction. At many levels of society, people with parcels of state authority, however limited, can market them and extract resources from their fellow citizens, while others, not directly associated with the state, can also benefit from these practices.[10]

This is particularly true at the apex of the state. Laurent-Désiré Kabila, for example, was a prototypical case of translation of economic interests into a strategy of conquest and reproduction of the state under the veil of a discourse of national liberation. Kabila used such a discourse, together with the image of the nationalist hero and the Lumumbist mystique, as part of his strategy to take over the Mobutuist state and profit from it. Kabila was an entrepreneur for whom taking over the state was a remarkable economic opportunity. He treated Congo as one giant resource available for plunder. His COMIEX company entered several commercial deals under the umbrella of the state after his takeover in 1997.[11] He was also believed to participate in diamond trafficking. The killing by security forces of 11 Lebanese diamond traders in the wake of his assassination militates for the thesis that his physical elimination had more to do with a business vendetta than a political coup.[12] Rebel leaders also find an interest in keeping the state machinery alive in the regions under their control. They do so because they wish to preserve the state as an instrument of patronage, a crucial resource to build support for their quest for power (Tull 2003).

Yet Kabila's corporate presidency was not the strategy of one man or an isolated state elite against a dispossessed population or a voiceless civil society, and the patrimonial uses of state institutions by the rebel leaders are not either specific to them. Many people, starting with Kabila's fellow Balubakat in Katanga, benefited from the late president's 'policies' and provided his system with sufficient foundations to function relatively unchallenged from within, and for the state to remain unaffected by its de facto privatization in the hands of political elites. Rebel leaders do not operate in a vacuum either. Irrespective of their popularity, their desire to maintain the state is widely supported. This is because, at many levels of society, people can derive private benefits from the continuation of Congo's weak state institutions. Judges, for example, charge parties for favourable judgments, and clerks sell on-demand modified versions of judgments and official acts. These 'corrupt' judges and clerks depend on the continuation of state weakness for their income, as do the lawyers who probably collect additional fees for their out-of-court settlements and private arbitrations. Although the parties to a case may *prima facie* be perceived as victims of the system's corruption, their need for official documents as evidence of judgments preserves the demand for these state-sanctioned official legal services. In the state's ghostly universities, professors privately charge fees, which the students willingly pay in exchange for a state-sanctioned degree, irrespective of its current lack of substance. The moribund state-owned copper and cobalt-mining company, Gécamines, also represents a substantial resource to state agents and its 24,000 employees. Although its production has collapsed, it remains the owner of Katanga's considerable mineral deposits and can translate its own legal existence into joint-venture contracts with foreign companies, from which its management and local elites accrue substantial income. The government receives revenue from its participation in them, taxes them and imposes miscellaneous additional fees, although much of the production of these joint ventures is then apparently smuggled out to Zambia for processing.

The logic of this system penetrates even further down the social hierarchy. When driving between Congolese cities, one encounters numerous stretches of deeply deteriorated roads, physical expressions of state decay. At the location of significant potholes or some other major obstacle, it is not uncommon to come across virtual roadblocks of local youth, armed with shovels, and demanding payment for their 'maintenance' of the road. In fact, far from repairing or providing maintenance work on the road, they symbolically throw a shovel of dirt into the hole as the car approaches, guaranteeing over the long run that the road remains in bad repair, as happens with other dimensions of Congo's decayed but enduring statehood. Durably fixing the road would deprive these local youth of the immediate source of revenue which they derive from this quasi-taxation of travellers. Hence, the road *with its potholes* is a resource to them. It is the road's very weakness that allows them to turn it into a resource. As a group and from a longer-term perspective, they would probably benefit from fixing it and encouraging traffic, facilitating thereby their village's insertion in local trade networks. But from a short-term individual perspective, they find greater benefit in turning the decayed public road into a private resource. In all the above-mentioned cases it is the very dysfunctionality and weakness of state or state-controlled institutions which allows the latter to be transformed into private resources. There is thus little incentive among the Congolese to boost state capacity or improve the quality of governance, as this would reduce opportunities for income while promoting at best only distant improvements in the quality of life.

Finally, the weak state is not only an instrumental resource for predatory human relations; it also represents an intrinsic resource to individuals at the bottom of the social hierarchy. For grass-root Congolese, who find themselves systematically on the predated side of Congolese history, the state remains a crucial resource to the extent that it offers a minimum level of certainty about public life, the opportunity to form relatively stable expectations about where power and resources lie, and a modicum of reduction of transaction costs as they go about their lives. Political uncertainty, warlords, insurgencies and the like, on the other hand, blur the cards of politics for common people and complicate, if not endanger, their daily lives. State stability is therefore an intrinsic resource in the lives of people who have to struggle for survival as it represents an anchor in their volatile and vulnerable life.[13]

The benefits of sovereignty

There is more than the mere weakness of the state to transform it into a private resource, however. The international recognition of the sovereignty of Congo's state institutions is a paramount mechanism by which, first, the weak state can be reproduced and its predatory nature maintained and, second, additional resources can accrue to the holders of state power. The impact of international sovereignty on the reproduction of the predatory state is thus twofold: it supports predatory activities; and it is a resource to be exploited *per se*.

The juridical guarantee of the state's existence that is the by-product of international sovereignty reduces pressures for capacity building.[14] By guaranteeing its existence under virtually any set of circumstances, international sovereignty allows the state to enforce itself upon its citizens without having to resort to continuous violence, and without the capacity to truly penetrate society. To refer to Migdal's classic terminology, sovereignty shields political elites from the penalties associated with the 'weak state–strong society' dichotomy (Migdal 1988). It prevents failed institutions from disappearing and allows them to outlive their functional existence.

The second supportive role of sovereignty is further reaching. In their predatory activities, state agents derive domestic power from the evidence of their international legitimacy. Sovereignty, with its international sanction, gives state institutions and personnel, substance, structure and power, and makes them hard to escape for the Congolese. One of its main benefits is to allow governments to present predation as policy, which somewhat shields it from challenges. This was the case, for example, with Mobutu's policy of 'Zaireanization' of foreign-owned assets in 1974, which privately transferred the assets of foreigners to government cronies and their allies, a case of theft masqueraded as policy. It was also the case of the 1981 law that stripped all Rwandophone Congolese of their citizenship, a case of governmental repression of a minority. The capacity to act as sovereign ruler is also what has allowed individuals in the Kinshasa government to engage in what the United Nations has called 'asset stripping'. According to the final report of the UN Panel of Experts on the

Illegal Exploitation of Natural Resources and Other Forms of Wealth of the Democratic Republic of Congo, an 'elite network' of Congolese and Zimbabwean state and military interests 'transferred ownership of at least US$5billion of assets from the State mining sector to private companies under its control in the past three years with no compensation or benefit for the State treasury of the Democratic Republic of Congo (UN 2002)'. In this case, sovereignty is a legal artifice which protects the exploitation of Congo's resources by state elites and their allies. Rebel leaders, deprived of international sovereignty, do not have the same options. In the east of the country, Rwanda and Uganda by and large directly exploit natural resources under their military control, bypassing local rebel organizations and juridical pretenses. Local rebels then try to control and tax the residual production, but are incapable of entering into contractual relations of exploitation or to transfer ownership of local assets to themselves, as they lack the juridical personality to do so.

International sovereignty is not only a domestic currency. It also shields weak governments from outside interference, as they can raise the principle of non-intervention in their domestic affairs against outside attempts to check their excesses. Only in the most outrageous cases of genocide and crimes against humanity is this principle bent in international law, and even then hardly so (as witnessed by the lack of serious intervention on behalf of Rwanda's Tutsis in 1994). When they do in fact end up accused of abuses, governments can still hide behind their sovereignty to dodge the bullet, with the likely sympathy of many other governments (as attested by most of Africa's failure to condemn Zimbabwe's recent predatory policies and electoral frauds). In the words of Congolese government spokesman, Kikaya Bin Karubi, 'The Congolese government is the legitimate government of this country . . . Whatever we do is legitimate.'[15]

Beyond these adjuvant roles to state predation, sovereignty also represents intrinsic value to holders of state power. First and foremost, international sovereignty entitles regimes to official development assistance, which fuels their networks of patronage and funds the transformation of the state into a resource.[16] While they may appear restricted to political elites, aid flows benefit a cross-section of Congolese society, which appropriates them through the government's budget and the clientelistic networks of political elites. Whether aid flows accrue to the state budget or to the private accounts of holders of state authority is a more or less moot distinction in Congo, since most of the budget itself is privatized. Many civil servants and soldiers on payrolls are fictitious. Salaries given to these people actually represent the private conversion of institutional public resources. In addition, the budget (when there is one – there weren't any for the first few years of L.-D. Kabila's rule) is by and large allocated to discretionary funds. In 1992, the Bank of Zaire reported that 95 per cent of the national budget was earmarked for the services of the presidency (65 per cent according to the World Bank) as opposed to 4 per cent for agriculture and 0 per cent for social services.[17] Foreign aid is thus a highly valuable resource for power holders. And it is conditioned by norms of sovereign statehood and territorial integrity, as only recognized countries receive development aid.

International sovereignty also facilitates foreign direct investments, from which local elites benefit. These are often conditional upon guarantees of insurance and arbitration, access to which depends on the sovereign status of the recipient country. The World Bank's Multilateral Investment Guarantee Agency (MIGA) only works with sovereign entities. The United States' Overseas Private Investment Corporation (OPIC) only offers insurance to investors operating in entities recognized by the United States government. As a result, the Kinshasa government is much more likely to attract foreign operators in the regions under its control – and extract resources from them and in conjunction with them – than are rebel authorities in their regions. In fact, there have only been two documented instances of contractual investments between foreign companies and non-state authorities in Congo. In the first case, Anglo–American, a South African mining company, concluded an investment contract worth almost $1bn with Laurent-Désiré Kabila a few months before the latter took over power in Kinshasa. It was, however, only after both Mbuji-Mayi and Lubumbashi had fallen to Kabila's troops in April 1997, and barely a month before the fall of Kinshasa, that Anglo–American embarked on this deal. As Michael Ross notes, therefore, this was an instance of 'future booty' based on the anticipation of Kabila's approaching sovereignty, rather than of pure contracting between rebels and foreign firms (Ross 2002). The second instance occurred in the east of the country, in November 1999, under control of the spin-off rebel group *Rassemblement Congolais pour la Démocratie-Mouvement de Libération* (RCD-ML), and involved a less-than-reputable firm, the First International Bank of Grenada (FIBG), which agreed to spend $16m for the renovation of 15 hospitals and some roads in the *Orientale* province, apparently in exchange for becoming the equivalent of the RCD's central bank and issuing 'a mining-assets backed new currency in the rebel territories'. Had this deal actually gone through, it would have constituted a remarkable case of institutional innovation and an attempt by a rebel organization to take over some of the trappings of sovereignty. The RCD-ML soon fizzled away as a credible organization, however, and seemed to sink the deal with it, though it is unclear whether this arrangement could have become operational even if RCD-ML had survived. FIBG had indeed been previously banned from activities in Canada because of investment frauds, and the US Customs service was investigating it for money laundering allegations.[18] These two exceptions notwithstanding, foreign investments are overwhelmingly limited to zones of international sovereignty.

The preference for nationalism

Functions of the nationalist discourse

The benefits of weak statehood and sovereignty promote the adoption of a nationalist, rather than secessionist or revolutionary, outlook by most Congolese, despite the failures of the state and the multiple polarizations of society. For elites, the nationalist discourse provides the ideological legitimation of their strategy of institutions-as-resources, a tool for reinforcing and reproducing the state, and a means to counteract and disenfranchise the political expression of alternative public identities. For citizens in general, nationalism is the political expression of a preference for established, if dysfunctional, state institutions over unpredictable reconfigurations of power and economic life. The following pages focus mostly on the behavior and rationales of political elites.

The rapidity with which most pre-independence Congolese political elites switched from defending their regional interests to pursuing nationalist agendas illustrates the benefits they found in this ideology for their pursuit of power. At the constitution-making Round-Table of 1960 already, the idea of a unified Congo was removed from the realm of the negotiable. Rejecting a system that would have given more power to the provinces, independence politician Joseph Iléo declared: 'The conference certainly does not have the objective to prepare the explosion [*éclatement*] of Congo.'[19] Most regional leaders then traded off their separatist or federalist demands for positions in the national state. Joseph Kasavubu, who had earlier announced the creation of a Bakongo-based 'Republic of Central Kongo' was offered the presidency by the Belgians partly out of fear of Bakongo separatism (Verhaegen and vanderlinden 1980). In exchange, he buried once and for all any element of Bakongo autonomy or irredentism in his discourse. Moïse Tshombé followed the same logic, although a few years later. After having rejected the national idea and launched the secession of Katanga from 1960 to 1963, he became prime minister of all of Congo in 1964, trading off regional autonomous aspirations for a central position in state power.

The same holds true of contemporary rebel groups whose overwhelming interest in (re)gaining access to state power was illustrated by the power-sharing outcome of the Inter-Congolese Dialogue of 2002–03 (Bouvier 2004). Even the RCD rebellion, despite persistent rumours of its separatist intentions, did not have independence or secession as an objective, but rather the promotion of the interests of Rwandophone populations within Congo. Hence, the use of the nationalistic discourse as an ideological justification for such objectives. In the words of the RCD-Goma Secretary-General Azaryas Ruberwa:

> We want a united Congo. *There are more advantages to a united Congo than a partitioned Congo.* We have never thought of secession. It is impossible to conceive of it... What we do want is to change the mode of management

> in Congo and to have more autonomy for the provinces. We want federalism. We say yes to the unity of Congo but never to unitarism.... Territorial integrity allows us to remain *une puissance en Afrique* [sic] ... Let's create a Congolese nation because it does not exist yet. (Emphasis mine)[20]

In Congo, political violence provides the means to fight for (re)insertion into the system by marginalized and excluded groups. It does not represent attempts to challenge, reform, revolutionize or break away from the state. The association of political violence with a universal nationalist discourse is thus only superficially paradoxical. While competing for state access for the benefit of the particularistic interests of their own group, political elites use a nationalist discourse as platform to build a minimum winning coalition, define others as non-patriotic and keep them on the outside. Competition in the display of nationalism can thus be perceived as competition for power. The nationalist discourse becomes the foundation for the reproduction of the state's otherwise failed and predatory institutions, denying legitimacy to alternative scenarios and confining all other such actions to military factionalism for control of the state itself, or to the non-threatening realm of 'civil society'. By reinforcing the reproduction of the state, it guarantees the predatory potential of its institutions.

Although the country's natural wealth may be concentrated in regions far away from the capital, the limited likelihood that any secessionist movement would be internationally recognized considerably reduces the appeal of local separatist strategies of power in normal times. Secessionist moments in Congo's history have occurred when the sovereignty of the central state was challenged from outside, or when the economic returns to sovereignty depreciated. This happened in the very early years of independence when it was not yet clear how livable postcolonies would be, and when political chaos in the capital led foreign powers to consider other options than backing the state as a whole. It also happened in the 1990s when Mobutu's failure to convincingly democratize and his recourse to violence against students at the University of Lubumbashi led the West to marginalize him and cut off virtually all aid flows to his regime. In times like these, it makes sense for local elites to capitalize on the weakening international status of the state and experiment with local strategies of power and access to resources. This is what explains the secessions of the 1960s and the drives for autonomy of Kasai and Katanga in the 1990s. But the embrace by the West of Kabila's takeover in 1997 (embalmed in nationalist discourse) again put an end to opportunities for local strategies of self-determination and brought the Congolese back around their state. When nationalism prevails, however, local identities fail to find outlets to their cultural specificities. As a result, therefore ethnic clientelism and polarization rise and coexist with a nationalist discourse.

Secessions can thus be expected if the potential return of local resources, in the absence of international recognition, outweighs the potential return of resources associated with control or partial control of the sovereign national state. To the extent that they represent the actions of political elites choosing to capitalize upon local cultural or economic grievances, separatist decisions must therefore be understood as rational calculus of potential costs and benefits. In Congo, the appeal of the state competes with the appeal of local raw materials in the decisions of regional leaders to secede or not. But without international recognition of the sovereignty of public authorities making a claim to these raw materials their physical control is usually not sufficient for their translation into resources.

Self-Determination in Congolese History: Congo's history illustrates the see-saw between nationalism and separatism as a function of the strength and perceived benefits of sovereignty. Movements towards autonomy and secession are attempted either when the sovereignty of the central state is contested from abroad, or when the benefits of institutional enforcement and resource distribution associated with sovereignty are threatened.

Although it was partly a Belgian plot to retain control over the mineral resources of Congo, the Katanga secession of 1960–63 also broadly derived from Congolese dynamics of power, identity differentiation and resource grievances.[21] Above all, it was an opportunistic decision by Moïse Tshombé who bet on the possibility that the Congolese state would not survive the upheavals and mutinies that immediately followed the proclamation of its independence on 30 June 1960, and decided there was more potential for a future in regional rather than in national politics. The Katanga declaration of independence occurred on 12 July, eight days after the beginning of the *Force Publique* mutiny. On 13 July Prime Minister Lumumba broke diplomatic relations with Belgium because of its sympathies with Katanga, inadvertently reducing Congo's international sovereignty in the process. The next day Kasavubu and Lumumba approached the Soviet Union about the possibility of military assistance (Verhaegen and Vanderlinden 1980). Compounded with the two men's incapacity to restore order in their country, this request further weakened the legitimacy of the central state in the eyes of the West in the cold war context, as it weighed the benefits of protecting a fractured newly independent Congo with potentially communist tendencies, against a relatively more peaceful and pro-capitalist Katanga. Tensions then mounted between Kasavubu and Lumumba, who dismissed each other from office and further projected abroad the image of a stillborn state, which in turn gave additional momentum to the secession, predicated as it was upon the uncertainties of state recognition.

After initial hesitations in 1960, during which Tshombé seized his opportunity, the international community rallied behind the sovereignty of Congo and doomed Katanga's chances for successful secession. During the whole period from 1960 to 1963, however, Tshombé continued to negotiate with the Congolese government on the terms of a possible reunification, which is further evidence that Congolese secessions are not so much instances of cultural self-determination as tactical moves for state power. Tellingly, after the defeat of his secession, Tshombé became prime minister of Congo in 1964. Foreign powers by and large guaranteed the reproduction of the Congolese state at this very early stage and provided it with life support, crucially altering the expected payoffs of Tshombé's action and turning Congo from a moribund shell into a worthwhile resource.

The 'Great Mining State of South Kasai' was the other main secessionist movement of that period. In August 1960, after Lumumba had managed to hand over the province's leadership to a Lulua, although the Baluba had won the most seats in the May 1960 elections, Lumumba's troops attacked Mbuji-Mayi in South Kasai and massacred Baluba civilian populations. In response, Albert Kalonji, a Luba from Kasai who was one of Lumumba's main rivals in the *Mouvement National Congolais* (MNC) and was embittered by his failure to secure an influential position in the national government, proclaimed the Mining State, and organized for autonomous rule. More than Tshombé, Kalonji was a political opportunist who seized the occasion of a chaotic central state in Kinshasa to reorient his quest for power on the local stage. The autonomous state functioned relatively well until September 1962 when the central government facilitated a local military revolt to regain control of the province. Again, no country recognized the sovereignty of South Kasai and Kalonji eventually turned his attentions to the national political stage, becoming agriculture minister in the 1964 Tshombé government.

Both Katanga and South Kasai illustrate the extent to which a weakening of the perceived sovereignty of the central state triggered local strategies of power by Congolese regional elites, how these were in turn aborted when the respective sovereignty statuses of central and provincial authorities were clarified, and how the West and the then Western-dominated UN system conditioned these local dynamics with their capacity to grant sovereign status to territorial entities. Following the stabilization of the sovereign status of Congo after 1963, and the display by the international community of its willingness to intervene on behalf of Congo's territorial integrity, challenges to state authority no longer took on separatist dimensions but were limited to violent attempts to wrestle control of the state away from its perceived 'neo-colonialist' regime.

The Mulelist and Simba rebellions of the 1963–67 period illustrate the changing nature of the Congolese political game. Although the state was still weak and armed struggles appeared to be a reasonable means to achieve power, the objective of each of these movements was to take over the entire country rather than to break away from it. This was also the case with the 1977 and 1978 Shaba (ex-Katanga) invasions from Angola and Zambia by the Congo National Liberation Front (FNLC), composed mainly of remnants from Tshombé's secessionist troops. Although its origins derived from the Katanga secession of 1960–63, the FNLC took great pains to differentiate itself from the Katanga secessionist movement and stressed the element of national liberation of Congo in both its name and its stated goal of overthrowing president Mobutu and taking over the entire country. The significance of the Shaba invasions is that formerly secessionist actors, marginalized from the Congolese state, resorted to armed insurrection not so much to carve themselves a new political space but to change the regime at the core of Congo and force their own reintegration in the post-colonial state. This strategy is surprising if one thinks of the southern Katanga populations as somehow primordially separatist. If one considers, however, the political choices of local elites as a function of resource maximization, and the latter as a function of their perception of where sovereignty lies, the FNLC approach was quite rational.

The next section considers to what extent changes that have intervened in the international state system since the early 1990s have contributed to changing the parameters of political action and self-determination in Congo. At the core of this investigation is the question of whether the benefits of sovereignty have been deflated by trends associated with globalization.

Globalization, sovereignty and self-determination

State dilution and strategies of autonomy in the early 1990s

After 1990 the partition of the Soviet Union and the ideological push by the West for the spread of electoral democracy combined to undermine the international legitimacy of the Mobutu regime, which was unwilling to democratize, and cast fresh doubts in the minds of the Congolese as to the solidity of their country's sovereignty. Mobutu's new outcast status was a particularly important factor as it resulted in a dramatic collapse of aid flows to Zaire and turned the national state into a much less appealing stage for the acquisition of resources (Figure 6.1). The perception of changing international norms regarding territorial integrity and the increased inability of the central state to transform its institutions into resources for lack of funding, led to a regain of autonomy-seeking activities by regional political leaders.

Not surprisingly, Katanga authorities were the first to make a significant move. On 15 August 1992 Etienne Tshisekedi of Kasai, a long-time Mobutu opponent, was elected prime minister by the Sovereign National Conference in replacement of Nguza Karl I Bond, a Lunda from Katanga related to Moïse Tshombé, Mobutu client, and president of the *Union des Fédéralistes et Républicains Indépendants* (UFERI). Anti-Kasaian violence unfolded in Katanga the very next day. On 21 August Nguza stated that his province did not recognize the authority of the new prime minister, and that Shaba as a whole was now in opposition to the government. After further violence, the province's governor, Gabriel Kyungu Wa Kumwanza, recommended that people from Kasai living in Shaba be expelled. Refugees were gathered in concentration

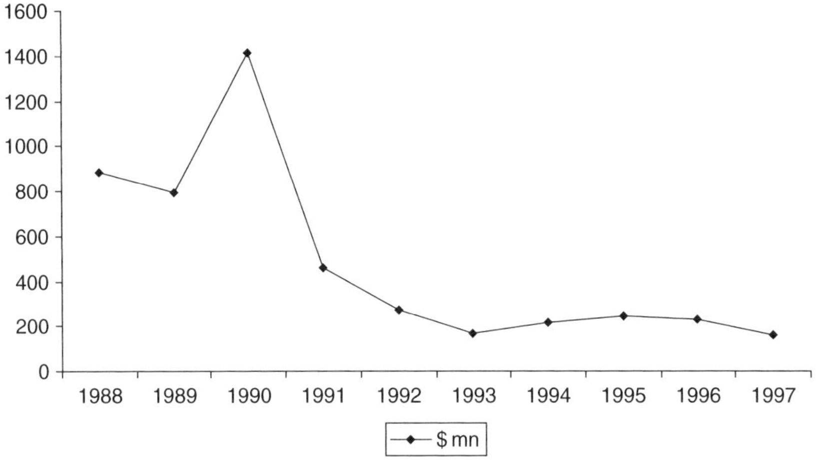

Figure 6.1 DRC: Total aid flows, including UN
Source: OECD, *Geographical Distribution of Financial Flows to Developing Countries*, Paris: OECD, miscellaneous years.

camps, awaiting repatriation to Kasai. Encouraged by Mobutu who wanted to weaken the prime minister appointed by the national conference, Nguza then vowed that there would be no national reconciliation with Katanga under the auspices of the current government and refused to rule out the possibility of secession. In December 1993, Kyungu proclaimed his province's autonomy and announced the imposition of taxes at the borders.

This episode of near provincial self-determination illustrates the extent to which secessionist decisions are mostly predicated upon the strategies of elites, which are in turn conditioned by the international status of the state rather than upon primordial identities. It is indeed often argued that the Lundas of Katanga are secessionist while the Balubakat are nationalist, based on the pattern of the 1960s secession, which was driven by Lunda politicians, while the northern Balubakat, under the leadership of Jason Sendwe, chose a nationalist path behind Lumumba. The events of 1992–93, however, saw an alliance of a Lunda politician, Nguza, with a Mulubakat, Kyungu, in favour of provincial separatism, as a consequence of their similar reading of the national political situation. In the 1960s, the respective leaders of these two communities had made different choices, but these proceeded from their perceived interests rather than from different ethnic outlooks.

The case of Kasai Oriental's autonomy from 1993 to 1996 was more truly an instance of a fairly homogeneous community, the Baluba, erecting their own institutions in the wake of the apparent collapse of the central state. The role of the Shaban ethnic cleansing of 1992–94 was important in getting Kasai started on its own drive for autonomy. With the influx of highly skilled Luba refugees, Mbuji-Mayi began to boom and diamond-mining operations were reinforced by all the former Gécamines engineers. Kasai enjoyed relative prosperity, at least by the standards of the rest of Zaire, and developed its own university and a Conference for the Economic Development of Eastern Kasai (CODEKO), which took over regional development planning. By refusing to recognize new banknotes introduced by the Kinshasa regime, Kasai essentially developed its own currency and exchange rate, and altogether avoided inflation while the rest of the country experienced price rises above 8,000 per cent a year over the same period. By 1996 Kasai had reached such a remarkable level of autonomy that it caught the attention of *The Economist*: 'Eastern Kasai is all but independent of Kinshasa . . . Instead, it responds to two local powers: the bishop and the diamond mine . . . A strong scent of independence hangs in the air.'[22]

These experiments in autonomy came to an end with the rise of the AFDL and the Rwandan invasion of 1996, which restored an internationally recognizable authority in Kinshasa and ironically (given its own border-crossing origins) provided a new boost to Congo's fledgling sovereignty. By supporting Kabila, the international community contributed to putting an end to local movements of self-determination. As a result, local politicians rejoined the fold of national politics and local experiences in state substitution (such as Kasai's) folded in the face of a new imposition of state authority and renewed control by state actors over the mining industry.

The resurrection of the weak state

Since the Kabila takeover of 1997 the Congolese state has successfully resisted all regional, international and global assaults on its existence, and has in fact continued to find resources for its reproduction beyond its own borders. Globalization, as defined by the new patterns of trade, financial and information flows that followed the end of the cold war, has not resulted in an erosion of either the idea of the Congolese state or its international sovereignty. Processes of decision making involving the agencies of the state have continued to be recognized as legitimate (despite their usual neglect of the interests of the Congolese) while those of alternative institutions – whether rebel leaders, non-governmental organizations, church groups or 'traditional' authorities – have been marginalized. Since 1997, the global system has once again come to the rescue of the idea of Congo while all elements on the ground militated for its dissolution. As local dynamics keep on trying to erase Congo, a global logic keeps on bringing it back.

The United Nations has been one of the main instruments in support of Congo's continued sovereignty. It has repeatedly endorsed the territorial integrity and sovereignty of the country and its interventions have reinforced the state, reaffirming its existence against all empirical evidence on the ground. In the 15 UN Security Council resolutions on Congo or the Great

Lakes region passed between 1996 and 2002, respect for territorial integrity was mentioned 31 times. The UN has also demonstrated a presumption that promoting the reach of the state would contribute to curing Congo's ills, despite the evidence that the state fully participates in the exploitation of the country's resources for the private gains of the holders of state power. The UN Panel of Experts on the Illegal Exploitation of Natural Resources in the DRC stated in its October 2002 report that a 'step towards halting the exploitation of natural resources will be the early establishment of an all-inclusive transitional government . . . which would ensure that central government control is reinstated' (p. 28). This statement came in the wake of pages of evidence related to the abuses and exploitation by government officials and rebels alike. How bringing these together in the state would reduce rather than magnify their exploitative behavior was not demonstrated, nor does it make intuitive sense. Finally, the presence of MONUC, the *Mission de l'Organisation des Nations Unies au Congo*, in Kinshasa and across the country has reinforced the perception of validity of the state, no longer a decayed and dying system but now the local counterpart to a significant group of international bureaucrats and military personnel from around the world. MONUC's flights across the frontline (the only ones linking Kinshasa to rebel territories between 1998 and 2003) have also reinforced the idea of the country (and were used by some for arbitrage between the foreign currency markets of Kinshasa and those of Goma and Kisangani).

Foreign aid, both bilateral and multilateral, has also contributed to reinforcing the reproduction of Congo since the late 1990s. While the drying up of aid and its increased diversion towards non-governmental organizations in the first half of the decade led to centrifugal strategies by regional political elites, aid donors and creditors' eagerness to cooperate with new state authorities since 1997 has brought many political actors back around the state, as aid resources underwrite the patron–client relationships which define power relations throughout Congolese society. The incentive for nationalism implied by the quest for access to official development assistance has also been magnified by the very public current preferences for territorial integrity of aid donors themselves. In 2002, for example, pledges of aid by the IMF and Belgium were linked to the successful outcome of the Inter-Congolese Dialogue and the country's reunification.

By and large, therefore, the embrace or rejection of the state is partly a function of the capacity of the sovereign state to deliver the resources of foreign aid to Congolese political elites and their followers. Whereas in the early 1990s the West conditioned this marketability of sovereignty to democratic progress, it is now content to reserve it to those willing to preserve the state. The Congolese adjusted their political strategies accordingly. Table 6.1 illustrates the extent to which self-determination instances, defined as secession attempts or major rebellions, respond to these aid incentives. It shows that aid disbursements since 1960 have been significantly lower on

Table 6.1 Foreign aid, secessions and rebellions

Average annual aid disbursements (in million current US$)	
In years preceding secession attempts or rebellions (n = 14)	257.3
In other years (n = 23)	519.3
t = 2.794; P > t (one-tailed) = 0.0042	

Source: OECD, *Geographical Distribution of Aid Flows . . .*, miscellaneous years. Data missing for 1968.

average in years preceding separatist or rebellious activity than in years preceding instances of social peace, suggesting that Congolese elites adjust their behaviour to the economic returns of sovereignty. The correlation between foreign aid and instances of rebellion and secession lagged by one year is an astounding $r = -.43$.

Similarly to foreign aid, investments are conditional upon territorial integrity if only to the extent that integrity provides sovereignty which in turn opens up avenues of insurance and arbitration for foreign investors (See Reno 2001). Despite all the talk about the informalization, if not criminalization, of international transactions in the wake of globalization, sovereignty has remained a crucial parameter for foreign investors in Congo. Very few agreements were made between foreign companies and the AFDL in the 1996–97 period before the overthrow of Mobutu, and the few that were made occurred at a time when its eventual victory and control of the sovereign state was no longer in doubt. Similarly, hardly any foreign investment has taken place since 1998 in rebel-controlled territories, apart from those of sovereign actors themselves, such as Rwanda, Uganda and the companies linked to their political elites.

The interests of risk-minimizing foreign investors reinforce the incentives for territorial integrity and those for the preservation of international sovereignty faced by the Congolese. While the informalization of trade and investment relations over the last decade has made it easier for foreign investors to strike individual deals with local strongmen and eschew the state and national regulations, they have continued to prefer trading and investing with local counterparts who can avail themselves of the mantel of state sovereignty, because sovereignty mitigates some of the risks they face and compares favourably to the uncertainty associated with dealing with warlords (See Gorus 2000).

More important than private foreign entrepreneurs have been the sovereign foreign investors – mainly Rwanda, Uganda and Zimbabwe – who have operated in rebel- and government-controlled territories since 1998, and have all but economically dismembered the country. Yet they have stopped well short of its political dismemberment because the preservation of the Congolese state has always been an essential component of their profit-maximization strategies. In the case of Rwanda and Uganda the essential feature of their economic exploitation of Congo is its direct nature. The Rwandan Patriotic Army and the Ugandan People Defense Forces operate directly in Congolese territory and their private partners tend to be Rwandan and Ugandan businesses. Both the Congolese state and the rebel authorities are bypassed in these deals. This direct economic exploitation has had two consequences. First, neither Kigali nor Kampala has wished to encourage the institutional development of their respective Congolese rebel counterparts, as their direct exploitation benefits from the absence of capable institutions. A weak Congolese state and weak rebel groups, unable to effectively assert their territorial and administrative controls, provide optimal conditions for the Rwandan and Ugandan economic strategies. As a result, these rebel movements have not taken on the proto-state characteristics typical of self-determination movements, nor have they developed political agendas of state substitution. Second, the direct exploitation of Congo's eastern region by Rwandans and Ugandans has triggered a nationalist reaction by local populations which has made it all but impossible for any rebel authority to develop a separatist agenda.

In the case of the Zimbabwean occupation of the mineral areas of Kasai and Katanga, there has been systematic collaboration with members of the Congolese government in the exploitation of Congo's natural resources. These formal 'joint ventures' between the Congolese state and Zimbabwean entrepreneurs have put a premium on the reproduction of the weak state in these regions. For the Congolese elites, the weak state facilitates the conversion of their formal public functions into private gains. For the Zimbabweans, it provides a seal of legality to their business deals.[23] The economic appetites of Congolese and Zimbabwean political elites account therefore for much of the Congolese institutional rigidity, in contrast to the business informality and criminalization that prevail on the ground.

While the rules of the post-cold war era in Africa have facilitated the violation of boundaries, a once sacrosanct principle of inter-state relations in Africa, they have not promoted a redefinition of nation–states. The cases of Ugandan, Rwandan and Zimbabwean interventions in Congo demonstrate the extent to which the violation of the state's territorial integrity combines with the preservation of its sovereign shell to generate unusually profitable conditions for both invading and invaded political elites. The findings from this section suggest that global political and economic influences have failed to affect the benefits of sovereignty and the subsequent nationalist calculus of Congolese elites. The global norm that whatever political authority inherits the postcolonial African state is automatically imbued with international sovereignty, whereas secessionist governments are not, remains the most important cultural flow in shaping the contours of struggles of self-determination in Congo. It accounts for the paradox that a state as culturally heterogeneous, resource-rich, and grossly malevolent as Congo does not generate credible self-determination movements but produces instead an apparently irrational nationalist fervour. As the previous evidence suggests, the irony of Congolese nationalism and of its anti-partition discourse is that they set the stage and provide the mechanism for the private dismemberment of Congo's assets. Congo is maintained so that it can be emptied of its substance. But then, how does Congo's cultural diversity express itself? Where do sub-national identities find cultural and political outlets?

Why ethnic salience does not translate in ethnic self-determination

Strategies of state-as-resource, whether instrumental or intrinsic, and their attendant nationalist expressions preclude the voicing of local cultural identities, which are then left to find outlets in demands for federalism and in 'tribal' clientelism, differentiation and polarization. The popular 'flow and closure' argument, according to which the uncertainties of globalized flows lead to the reinforcement of local identities as closure mechanisms, does not quite apply in Congo.[24] On the contrary, it is the incentive for the maintenance of the Congolese state, rather than its dilution through global informal markets, that leads to the perpetuation and magnification of parochial identities. Nationalism dialectically generates ethnicity.

For the Congolese, the demand for federalism is an expression of identity differences that remains within the realm of the politically feasible, as opposed to separatism. It represents an attempt to reconcile the existence of Congo with aspirations for emancipation from its domination. As such, federalism is usually popular with public opinion and with opposition politicians (who perceive it as an opportunity to play a local power card without threatening the overall system and losing the benefits associated with sovereignty). Indeed, every time the Congolese have an opportunity to express themselves in relatively non-threatening environments, they voice their desire for federalism. This was the case at the *Table-Ronde* in Brussels in 1960, though colonial influence managed to maintain a dose of unitarism in the system. The Antananarivo Conference of March 1961 resulted in a proposal for a loose confederation in which each province was largely autonomous but under one foreign policy. It happened again in 1964 with the never-implemented Luluabourg Constitution, which created 22 quasi-federated provinces. The 1992 Sovereign National Conference also overwhelmingly approved federalism for Congo.

Yet once in power politicians typically repress such aspirations in order to avoid any dilution of their authority and the rise of independent sources of institutional power, and instead impose unitary structures, usually with the support of western donors. Lumumba in 1960, Mobutu in 1965 and Kabila in 1997 all proceeded from the same logic of power and tried to put an end to democratic expressions of cultural differences in Congo. Popular attitudes adjust to these realities of power. Whereas pro-federalist attitudes are the default among the Congolese, these preferences are usually toned down when central authority is effective or at least able to marginalize any federalist discourse. Since the beginning of the latest war, in 1998, successive Congolese governments have also successfully associated demands for federalism with separatist agendas, with the consequence that outspoken federalists – such as the RCD-Goma and its feared 'provincial assemblies' – are now labeled anti-Congo. As a consequence, pro-federalist sentiments in Kinshasa's public opinion polls have fallen from 41 per cent in May 1998 to 33 per cent in December 2000, and 23 per cent in January 2002.[25] The politically acceptable discourse now, even among opponents and members of civil society, calls for federalism *after* the hypothetical transition from the current regime to a reunified Congo with a democratically elected government, or for a 'unitary but strongly decentralized system', as the expression goes.

The elusiveness of the federal option has stifled the expression of local identities and relegated them to parallel social networks which the nationalist discourse stigmatizes as 'tribalistic' and which, while serving the interests of their members, fail to translate their aspirations into a self-determination project, converting them instead into parochial strategies of access to state power and resources. Such strategies imply either a dynamic process of identity differentiation as justification for claims to participate in the system, or a process of polarization of local groups as they compete for state-controlled resources. Paradoxically, then, the very centralization of the nationalist state triggers local dynamics of ethnic differentiation and polarization that lead to ever narrower definitions of identity.

The Chokwe of Katanga illustrate the logic of ethnic differentiation. The Chokwe, who originate in Angola, spread through the southwestern region of Katanga in the eighteenth century and eventually became geographically and culturally close to the Lunda with whom they have considerable spatial overlap and similar interests (Olson 1996; Kakwata Mwalukesa 1999). Yet while some Chokwe participated with the Lunda in CONAKAT in the 1960s, most of them chose to stay away from the Lunda-dominated party and instead marked their difference by joining the nationalist Balubakat-dominated *Cartel Katangais* as part of ATCAR, the *Alliance des Tshokwé du Congo, Angola et Rhodésie*. Although both the Lunda and the Chokwe are now politically marginalized and suffer from the hegemony of the Balubakat in Katanga, the Chokwe have continued their policy of self-dissociation from the Lunda while the latter, who benefit from greater recognition and whose emperor is a member of parliament, claim to have traditional authority over the Chokwe.[26] It makes sense for the Lunda, who have some limited access to power, to claim representation of the Chokwe so as to increase their demographic weight and consequent demands on state resources. For Chokwe elites, on the other hand, it equally makes sense to reinforce their group's cultural difference so as to seize control of their own representation and bypass the local mediation of the Lunda in their access to state resources.

The current socio-political organization of the Chokwe in Katanga reflects this strategy of ethnic differentiation as a clientelistic organizational principle for access to networks of power and resources. Like many other Congolese groups, the Chokwe are organized in a mutual welfare society, the *Mutuelle Culturelle Kulivwa*. This is a cultural association of modern elites, a lobbying organization for the betterment of mostly urbanized and educated individuals sharing Chokwe cultural identity. Its leadership is composed of a lecturer at the University of Lubumbashi, two managers at Gécamines, a lawyer and former minister of Mines under Mobutu, a retired civil servant, the former director of Katanga's central prison and a former secretary of the Ministry of Interior under Mobutu.[27] In other words, these are either former political elites, sidelined by current power configurations, or economic elites suffering from the marginalization of Katanga's main parastatals. Either way, they are relative outcasts of the system, suffering from a loss of political access. The *Mutuelle* is their organizational response to this loss and it is based on ethnic solidarity and on the reinforcement of the projection of their cultural identity, mostly in the form of differentiation from the Lunda. This organization is essentially clientelistic as the *Mutuelle* structures its members' access to state resource as a group. It negotiates and lobbies for their participation in the system (mostly in the form of public employment) but does not challenge it. Its competition with other regional *mutuelles* for access to the state leads to increased cultural differentiation among these groups and undermines national and provincial identities. As part of this strategy of cultural differentiation, *Kulivwa* has sponsored the writing of a book on the history of the Chokwe people and is planning a Chokwe museum (Kakwata Mwalukesa 1999). The book and the museum project are part of an effort of cultural preservation, a reinvention and imagination of Chokwe identity in today's Congo.

Yet *Kulivwa* does not stand in opposition to the state as an organization of alternative action. It does not promote the political expression of Chokwe identity as a matter of cultural self-determination. On the contrary, its members all individually operate in the margins of state power. Rather than affirming their existence as a group *vis-à-vis* the state, as would a self-determination movement, they do so *vis-à-vis* other local groups in order to single out the merits of their claims to association with the state. For the Chokwe the main competitors are the Lunda, who are often believed to be an umbrella group exerting authority over them. The writing of its history by the Chokwe is an exercise in denying this assimilation. 'The way history was written before is like a type of repression', complain the members of *Kulivwa*. 'Our history is always drowned in that of the Lunda.'[28] The book stresses that the Chokwe are not under the authority of the Lunda's Mwaant Yav and recounts how, in 1885, they even captured the Mwaant Yav's capital city. It also offers a chronology of the Chokwe chiefs and attempts to belittle the reach of Lunda authority by arguing that Angola's Lunda are in fact a different group (another instance of self-differentiation as the Chokwe themselves originated in Angola).

This pattern of cultural self-affirmation aimed at other groups rather than at the state simultaneously reinforces the continued existence of the weak state and promotes parochial polarization. Tribalism and the state are thus reproduced at the same time. The Chokwe are but one example of this phenomenon. Across Congo, *mutuelles* are the expressions of the clientelistic dimension of *tribalisme*, its institutionalized façade, as they offer their support to politicians in exchange for the redistribution of state resources to their members. According to Maurice Etukomalu, chair of the Topoke's *Isonga–Songa Mutuelle* in *Orientale* Province, 'Any politician who wants a solid foundation has to go through us.' Just as *Kulivwa* is complacent *vis-à-vis* the state, *Isonga–Songa* does not challenge the rule of the RCD-Goma in Kisangani. On the contrary, they see the rebels as their pathway to the spoils of power and simply ask to be taken into account: 'We are a force capable of giving a foundation to the RCD.'[29]

In other instances, however, ethnic identities lead to more violent polarization. This is usually the case when scarcities are more pronounced, as in the Kivu regions where demographic pressures were compounded by refugee flows from Rwanda in the 1990s. Rapid population growth led to difficult issues of land allocation, particularly critical in this agricultural region. The identity problem in Eastern Congo has already been well researched.[30] The questions to be addressed here are the relationship between the reproduction of the national state and ethnic violence in the Kivus and the degree to which this ethnic violence can be associated with attempts at political self-determination.

Although identity relations in Eastern Congo are very complex and cannot be collapsed into a single explanatory framework, political violence in the Kivus is at least partly about access to state power, and less about cultural self-determination than may appear at first. The Congolese Tutsi from South Kivu, known as the Banyamulenge, are fighting for their reinsertion into the Congolese political system, from which they were originally outcast under the Mobutu regime. While the Congolese authorities' attitude towards the Banyamulenge derive in large part from regional politics, and particularly from Congo's relations with Rwanda and Uganda, the Banyamulenge's own agenda remains overwhelmingly domestic and parallels but does not equate the struggle of the Rwandan Tutsi against the remnants of the Hutu-based Habyarimana regime. Transnational linkages and cultural similarities do not translate into irredentism or other forms of attempts at self-determination for the Congolese Tutsi. Rather, the appeal of the state remains the prevalent motivation, focusing their struggle on the question of citizenship and linking local violence with moments of power redistribution in Kinshasa. The dispossession by the Congolese state of their status as participants in its system, a blatant case of horizontal inequality, has not resulted in a will to escape the system but rather in repeated desperate attempts to rejoin it. Transnational spaces with Rwanda and the overflow of the latter's ethnic conflict into Congo have created a temporary congruence of objectives but not a common identity between Rwandan and Congolese Tutsis. For sure, political dynamics in Rwanda have changed political dynamics in Kivu, particularly as they have led to the polarization of Hutu and Tutsi communities among the Banyarwanda. Yet they have led to an increasingly narrow definition of political identities and an increasingly complex pattern of political violence in the region, rather than to the transnational aggregation of identities in a challenge to the established order.

The weakening of the Congolese state in the 1990s and the continued denial of the federalist option by the Congolese ruling elites created the conditions for a rise in both the clientelistic and violent expressions of ethnic competition. Despite the weakness of the state, however, ethnic politics in Congo has remained a struggle for access to the resources of power. Identity has been instrumental in fighting for state resources, but has rarely conferred the fundamental motivation for political emancipation from the state.

Is Congo different?

The logic of the sovereign state as private resource triggers paradoxical outcomes in Congo. In light of its institutional weakness and its social heterogeneity, Congo would have been expected to fall apart in the era of globalized economic and cultural flows. Congo betrays expectations that link the rise of local identity politics to globalization, as a parochial reaction to global standardization, an expression of the need for local closure in the face of globalized flows (Meyer and Geschiere 1999). What Congo suggests, instead, is that there are alternative coalitions of global forces and domestic factors which promote national identities and repress local ones.

How different is Congo, then, and can anything be learned from it with comparative relevance? While possibly more extreme in its deviances, Congo is not as different from other African states as it may seem. Young and Beissinger have highlighted that, compared to those of post-Soviet Eurasia, for example, African conflicts are generally much more about control of the state than about territorial control. They muse for the whole continent when they notice that 'particularly striking in the large zones of disorder in contemporary Africa is the relative absence of ethnic self-determination'.[31] There are two prima facie explanations for this. First, as suggested by Beissinger and Young, few African states are based on ethno-national project, deriving instead their national identity from territorially defined states. As a result, the status of minority is rarely lived as one of domination at the hands of someone else's state. Rather, the state is neutrally defined as postcolonial territory and is up for grabs by any group capable of doing so. Second, the sheer poverty of Africa makes state sovereignty one of the prime resources everywhere, and dwarfs the relative returns of alternatives to the state. This is not necessarily true in more industrial countries where competing sources of revenues exist for the leaders of potential self-determination movements, which may affect their cost–benefit analysis of rebellion.

Furthermore, among the few actual contemporary cases of self-proclaimed self-determination movements in Africa, several belong to the realm of posturing more than to that of actual challenge of the state. Barotseland secessionists in Zambia or Casamance separatists in Senegal no longer truly harbour ambitions of breaking away from the state but maintain this discourse as part of their strategies of renegotiating their allegiance to the state or as the justifying discourse of mostly criminal – and no longer political – activities.

Most cases of political violence in Africa are therefore by and large consistent with the Congolese story. Neither the Liberian nor the Sierra Leonean wars, for example, resulted in self-determination movements, pitting instead factions for control of the state.

The only clear-cut cases of self-determination in Sub-Saharan Africa are a handful: Eritrea, Somaliland, Southern Sudan. They suggest that challenges to the postcolonial African social contract may take place either when there is a historical claim for separate colonial existence (as in Eritrea or Somaliland),[32] where there are reinforcing cleavages that magnify grievances and truly create a sense of minority at risk (as is the case in Southern Sudan where race, religion and resource distribution overlap) or where culturally specific diasporas reproduce and crystallize sub-national identities and provide the means for their local political expression (as is the case with Somaliland, or Sri Lanka outside of Africa). In other circumstances the Congolese model, for all its paradoxical idiosyncracies, may well provide the blueprint of the stifling of self-determination in Africa.

Notes

1. This chapter was written in early 2003. A substantially longer version is available as Queen Elizabeth House Working Paper WPS 95, February 2003, (http://www2.qeh.ox.ac.uk/pdf/qehwp/qehwps95.pdf). It benefited from the superb research and editorial assistance of Rebecca Hummel, Lisa Mueller and Stacy Tarango, and from the insightful comments of Francesca Bomboko, Paule Bouvier, Abdul Raufu Mustapha, Denis Tull and Crawford Young.
2. Ndaywel è Nziem (1998):256–7.
3. See Global Witness (2002) UN (2002).
4. See UN (2002), and the transcripts of the ongoing Great Lakes Commission of Enquiry of the Senate of Belgium (www.senat.be). See also IPIS (2002).
5. On the systematic rescuing of the Congolese/Zairean state by its Western partners during the Cold War, see Schatzberg (1991).

6. See the very consistent results on this question of the multiple polls of the Bureau d'Etudes et de Recherches Consulting International (BERCI, Kinshasa) since the late 1990s.
7. Interview with women's NGOs, Kisangani, November 2001.
8. Interview with civic-oriented NGOs, Kisangani, November 2001.
9. Interview with André Tshombé, Lubumbashi, April 2002.
10. See Chabal and Daloz (1998)'s idea of 'instrumentalization' of dysfunctionality in Africa.
11. See, for example, *Africa Research Bulletin: Economic, Financial and Technical Series*, September–October 2001, 14928.
12. See Observatoire de l'Afrique Centrale, Volume 5, No 42, 14–20 October 2002 [www.obsac.com/OBSV5N43-ProcessMzee1021.html].
13. I am grateful to Alice Sindzingre to whom I owe this point. See also Nest (2002).
14. See Jackson and Rosberg (1982) for the original statement of this thesis.
15. 'DR Congo Plunder Denied,' BBC News [http://news.bbc.co.uk/1/hi/world/Africa/2349631.stm].
16. See Clapham (1996).
17. Cited in Reno (1998) pp.151–2.
18. *Africa Research Bulletin*, December 1999–January 2000, 14162–14163.
19. Gérard-Libois (1963) p. 41.
20. Interview with Azarias Ruberwa, Goma, November 2001.
21. See J. Gérard-Libois (1963) p. 8.
22. 'Zaire: A Provincial Gem.' *The Economist*, 27 April 1996. See also Howard French (1996) 'A Neglected Region Loosens Ties to Zaire.' *New York Times*, 18 September 1996:A1, A4.
23. With great irony and a profound understanding of the benefits of sovereignty, the company set up by the Zimbabwean armed forces to represent its commercial operations in Congo is called Operation Sovereign Legitimacy (OSLEG).
24. Although De Boek identifies such an effect among the diamond-trading Lunda astride Congo and Angola, in Meyer and Geschiere (1999).
25. BERCI reports, May 1998, December 2000 and January 2002.
26. Interview with Mwaant Yaav, Lubumbashi, April 2002.
27. Group interview with Chokwe *Mutuelle*, Lubumbashi, April 2002.
28. Group interview with Chokwe *Mutuelle*, Lubumbashi, April 2002.
29. Interview with Maurice Etukomalu, Chair of Isonga-Songa *Mutuelle*, Kisangani, November 2001.
30. On the identity question in Eastern Congo (which is linked to the Great Lakes conflicts) see, among others, Mamdani (2001), Lemarchand (1997), Willame (1997), Doom and Gorus (2000); and Mararo (1997).
31. Beissinger and Young (2002), p. 479.
32. This will affect not so much the intensity of the local grievances but the likelihood of success, since the case of past sovereignty can be made, and will lower therefore the threshold of violent political action, *ceteris paribus*. The colonial distinctiveness argument has also been used, but without success, by Casamance rebels and by Katanga secessionists.

References

Africa Research Bulletin, December 1999–January 2000.
Africa Research Bulletin: Economic, Financial and Technical Series, September–October 2001, 14928.

Beissinger, M. and C. Young (2002) 'The Effective State in Postcolonial Africa and Post-Soviet Eurasia: Hopeless Chimera or Possible Dream?' in Beissinger and Young (eds) *Beyond State Crisis: Postcolonial Africa and Post-Soviet Eurasia in Comparative Perspective*. Washington, DC: Woodrow Wilson Center Press.

BERCI reports, May 1998, December 2000 and January 2002.

Bouvier, P. (2004) *Le Dialogue Intercongolais: Chronique d'une Négociation à la Lisière du Chaos*. Paris: L'Harmattan.

Chabal, P. and J.-P. Daloz (1998) *Africa Works: The Instrumentalization of Disorder*. Bloomington, IN: Indiana University Press.

Clapham, C. (1996) *Africa and the International System: The Politics of State Survival*. Cambridge: Cambridge University Press.

Doom, R. and J. Gorus (2000) *Politics of Identity and Economic Conflict in the Great Lakes Region*. Brussels: VUB University Press.

Gérard-Libois, J. (1963) *La Sécession katangaise*. Brussels: CRISP.

Global Witness (2002) *Branching Out: Zimbabwe's Resource Colonialism in Democratic Republic of Congo*. London: Global Witness.

Gorus, J. (2000) 'Violence in Katanga' in D. Goyvaerts (ed.) *Conflict and Ethnicity in Central Africa*. Tokyo: Tokyo University of Foreign Studies.

IPIS (2002) *Supporting the War Economy in the DRC: European Companies and the Coltan Trade. Five Case Studies*. January 2002.

Jackson, R. H. and C. G. Rosberg (1982), 'Why Africa's Weak States Persist: The Empirical and the Juridical in Statehood', *World Politics*, 1, 1–24.

Kakwata Mwalukesa, Jean-Félix (1999) *Histoire du Peuple Tshokwe*. Lubumbashi, May 1999. Unpublished Manuscript.

Lemarchand, R. (1997) 'Patterns of State Collapse and Reconstruction in Central Africa: Reflections on the Crisis in the Great Lakes Region', *Afrika Spectrum*, 1997, 32(2), 173–93.

Mamdani, M. (2001) *When Victims Become Killers*. Princeton, NJ: Princeton University Press.

Mararo, B. (1997) 'Land, Power and Ethnic Conflict in Masisi, 1940s–1994', *International Journal of African Historical Studies*, 30, 503–37.

Mbembe, A. (2001) *On the Postcolony*. Berkeley, CA: University of California Press.

Meyer, B. and P. Geschiere (eds) (1999) *Globalization and Identity: Dialectics of Flow and Closure*. Oxford: Blackwell.

Migdal, J. (1988) *Strong Societies and Weak States: State–Society Relations and State Capabilities in the Third World*. Princeton, NJ: Princeton University Press.

Ndaywel è Nziem, I. (1998) *Histoire Générale du Congo: De l'Héritage Ancien à la République Démocratique*. Paris: Duculot.

Nest, M. (2001) 'Ambitions, Profits and Loss: Zimbabwean Economic Involvement in the Democratic Republic of Congo', *African Affairs* 100, 479.

Nest, M. (2002) *The Evolution of a Fragmented State: The Case of the Democratic Republic of Congo*. Unpublished PhD dissertation, New York University.

Observatoire de l'Afrique Centrale (2002) Volume 5, No 42, 14–20 October 2002 www.obsac.com/OBSV5N43-ProcessMzee1021.html.

Olson, J.S. (1996) *The Peoples of Africa: An Ethnohistorical Dictionary*. Westport, CT: Greenwood Press.

Reno, W. (1998) *Warlord Politics and African States*. Boulder, CO.: Lynne Rienner.

Reno, W. (2001) 'How Sovereignty Matters: International Markets and the Political Economy of Local Politics in Weak States' in T. Callaghy, R. Kassimir and R. Latham (eds). *Intervention and Transnationalism in Africa: Global–Local Networks of Power*. Cambridge: Cambridge University Press.

Ross, M. (2002) 'Booty Futures: Africa's Civil Wars and the Futures Market for Natural Resources', UCLA Department of Political Science, Working Paper, December 2002.
Schatzberg, M. (1991) *Mobutu or Chaos? The United States and Zaire, 1960–1990*. Lanham, MD: University Press of America.
Tull, D. (2003) 'A Reconfiguration of Political Order? The State of the State in North Kivu (DR Congo)', *African Affairs*, 102(408), 429–46.
UN (2002) *Final Report of the Panel of Experts on the Illegal Exploitation of Natural Resources and Other Forms of Wealth of the Democratic Republic of Congo*. New York: United Nations Security Council, S/2002/1146, 16 October 2002.
Verhaegen, B. and J. Vanderlinden (1980) 'La Politique' in J. Vanderlinden (ed.) *Du Congo au Zaire 1960–1980: Essai de bilan*. Brussels: CRISP.
Willame, J-C. (1997) *Banyarwanda et Banyamulenge: Violences Ethniques et Gestion de l'Identitaire au Kivu*. Paris: L'Harmattan.

7
Somalia: State Failure and Self-Determination in the Shadow of the Global Economy

William Reno

Introduction

Somalia was one of Africa's few real nation–states, with a shared language and single ethnic culture. The five points of the star on its flag were meant as a call to 'lost' Somalis in Kenya, Ethiopia, and Djibouti left out in 1960 when independence led to the union of British Somaliland and the UN trust territory under Italian administration, a cause for which Siyyad Barre's regime (1969–91) attacked Ethiopia in 1977–78. Yet in 1991 Somalia's capital, Mogadishu, hosted 40 distinct armed groups (Peterson 2000, p. 21). Shortly before, the dying regime killed 50,000 fellow Somalis in a failed attempt to repress rebellion in the north (Africa Watch 1990, p. 218). At the start of 2005, the closest thing to a central government in Mogadishu had been evicted from a Nairobi hotel and then faced rioters when its officials ventured into the old capital.

Hargeisa, the main city in Somalia's north, celebrated Somaliland's declaration of independence on 18 May 1991. Heads of clans transformed themselves into a national assembly. Its government has ministries, issues currency, keeps order with a new police force, and collects revenues to provide citizens with basic public services. But officials in Somaliland contend with an international community that does not recognize their authority. The United Nation's 1960 Declaration on the Granting of Independence to Colonial Countries and Peoples (Resolution 1514) accepted self-determination only within the context of ex-colonial boundaries. Resolution 1514 declared that 'any attempt aimed at the partial or total disruption of the national unity and territorial integrity of a country is incompatible with the purposes and principles of the Charter of the United Nations', a sentiment reinforced in Organization of African Unity condemnations of separatist movements.[1] Moreover, many scholars are sceptical about the viability of new state-building projects. They argue that foreign aid, clandestine rackets and overseas remittances enable militia leaders and armed gangs to bypass dealing with local people to get resources to buy weapons and maintain their armies.[2] The key argument in this chapter, however, is that community leaders in Somaliland have forced armed groups to do just that. Together, they built polities – state-like authorities – outside the old framework of decolonization and have done so amidst all of the international economic forces that are seen as inimical to any indigenous attempt to create order in places like Somalia.

What explains radically different responses of similar societies to global strategic marginality and state administrative collapse? Why do people create (or fail to create) new administrations and identities amidst greater global economic integration that diasporas and clandestine trades bring? Are Somaliland's rulers simply unreconstructed clan politicians, their power undermined by the demise of the old Somalia, abandoned by global economic and strategic interests, leaving them to preside over isolated, contentious clan-based enclaves? Or did Somalia's collapse create in the north a reordered authority that accepts the social power of clan-based organizations, but also finds new, sustainable ways to configure internal politics and relations with a world economy?

Somaliland society built new political authority around three axes. The first involves a shift toward greater reliance on solidarity groups such as clans, sub-clans and lineages that claim people's loyalties and resources. This organizing force in Somali society interacts with other social factors in a fluid process that responds to political and economic exigencies of collapsing central state authority. A second axis incorporates clandestine and informal economic channels in conflict. It is not always true that collapsing state control empowers self-interested predators who grab valuable resources and not all who exercise coercion do so for personal economic gain.[3] Some who turn their backs on immediate economic gains survive and successfully encourage others to cooperate with them, even amidst threats from predatory rivals. Indeed, some Somali militia leaders forego easy predatory gains, while others use violence even where gains are marginal.

Shifts in global economic norms and practices since the 1970s constitute a third axis. Some changes reinforce connections between state collapse, marginality and continuing conflict. Other changes give some social networks space to reconfigure economic ties to their advantage. This outcome suggests that the contemporary world economy and state system permit greater heterogeneity in strategies of engagement from the periphery than normally supposed. Where this occurs, it is central to understanding how globalization affects the construction of identity and the formation of political authority on the margins of world economic and diplomatic transactions.

I argue that the nature of politics in the 1970s and 1980s, especially the distribution of social control over violence and markets, unintentionally left some northern leaders with more social raw material to reconstruct a single polity after 1991 – to 'self-determine' – compared to southern counterparts. Northerners had more flexibility to experiment, to tie commerce to the interests of central authority and order and exploit norms in international commercial and diplomatic practice. Lessons of Somaliland apply wherever communally based solidarities (in Central Asia, the Caucasus, and southern Nigeria) connect people to global economic networks in a context of weak or absent state administrations. Subsequent political arrangements in Somaliland differ significantly from state-building models that privilege clear distinctions between public and private spheres of activity and geographically centralized bureaucratic hierarchies. Somaliland authorities preside over a hybrid organization which is state-like in the basic sense of preserving order. It functions as a pole around which citizens establish a shared identity and manage the community's conduct of relations with outsiders – all integral elements of self-determination.

Political and institutional variation occurs despite the fact that people in Somaliland shared with other Somalis similar economic constraints and historical experiences of state rule. All older Somalis experienced cold war era nationalist policies, including the irredentist project in the 1970s. All fell victim to the dramatic weakening of state agencies and faced fear, uncertainties and predations of political entrepreneurs attending the collapse of the state administration during the 1980s. Each region faced risks of fragmentation such as grievances and intermingled communal settlements, factors with the potential to create opportunities for political entrepreneurs. In fact, the self-declared Republic of Somaliland historically has been more marginal to world strategic and formal commercial concerns than the south and experienced greater violence in the late 1980s. Distant from the capital, it was short-changed in earlier efforts to build state institutions, both in colonial and nationalist periods. Colonial administration had a disruptive impact upon local social organization everywhere. Taken together, these factors make the emergence of an autonomous Somaliland capable of defining a political community and organizing its relations with the rest of the world even more baffling.

Instrumentalist and rational choice approaches to conflict have a hard time explaining this outcome. One could attribute good sense and foresight to political actors, but that glosses over highly unpredictable, violent and threatening environments and erratic decision-making processes that all share. All who live on the margins of the world economy, whether they fight or peaceably reorganize their communities, contend with the breakdown of old economies, erratic aid from former colonial powers or superpower patrons. Those with fighting nearby face the risk of contagion of disorder and fear. Moreover, Somaliland's diaspora represents a larger percentage of total population and contributes more to local incomes compared to elsewhere in Somalia. According to Collier this manner of economic and social externalization should lead to a greater likelihood of conflict (Collier 2001). In fact, it is compatible with, and even plays a key role in, the opposite outcome.

Divergent outcomes in Somalia are explained here in an institutional framework shaping the calculus of opportunities. Evidence shows that actors try to maximize their personal political or material gains. The institutions at hand are not limited to clans or remnants of the old state. They include novel commercial and legal arrangements in the wider world economy, contacts with overseas Somalis and new alliances with non-state international agencies. They may or may not be rooted in custom and tradition, but are central to regulating who gets resources, who is considered legitimate and who exercises coercion.

Four observations incorporate this modified institutional approach to explain divergent experiences with conflict and order in the wake of state collapse in the cases examined below. First, local community responses to economic marginality and political exclusion in pre-conflict periods can emerge as mediating institutions that defuse local confrontations and violence once widespread conflict breaks out. These can become institutionalized even in clandestine economies that elsewhere fuel violence. Second, the local notables who had been most marginalized in pre-conflict periods are the most likely to emerge during conflicts with enough local legitimacy and leverage over other local actors to act as organizers of order once violence threatens to become widespread or to revive order in conflict zones. Third, outside aid resources and offers to mediate conflicts can offer new niches to violent political entrepreneurs and weaken local strategies for maintaining order. Fourth, if these conditions for local order are met, otherwise unrecognized authorities are in a good position to manipulate international norms and practices to pursue their aims of self-determination and get outsiders to at least tolerate their accomplishment.

Clan and lineage clearly play important roles in Somali politics and are crucial units of analysis. One scholar, for example, identifies six major clans and at least 67 sub-clans that have become involved in conflict in the 1990s (Mansur 1995). Yet if social structures play important roles in shaping conflicts, rigid assumptions about their impacts do not explain why some groups are able to contain entrepreneurs of violence in their midst while others cooperate with them, and still others become victims. If, as I propose below, people in these communities can tailor their own organizations, procedures and solutions to concrete circumstances, then it is more useful to look at clan and lineage structures through the lens of political and economic institutions, both formal and informal. In that case, colonial rule emerges as an important influence on social organization and social control of resources used in warfare in the 1990s. Differences in pre-conflict rule and local responses are also a good place to start to explain contemporary variations in the political orders of northern and southern Somalia.

State collapse and violent fragmentation in the south

Italian administrators brought a tight connection between state policy and commerce in 1919 with the establishment of the Societa Agricola Italo Somala

(SAIS) in the fertile river valleys of southern Somalia. But concession holders discovered that they could not attract workers, as smallholders were reluctant to leave their farms for wages and weaken the social reciprocities and protections of family and lineage that it would entail. Local elders also discouraged young men from accepting paid labour that would undermine their control over marriage, through which they exercised power, adjudicated local political concerns about family alliances and redress for past wrongs or losses (Menkhaus 1989, pp. 247–8).

The Italian invasion of Ethiopia in 1935 and the conscription of 40,000 Somali troops gave Italian officials the means to forcibly remove local farmers from their land. This shift in labour in southern river valleys also disrupted local food production and forced more people to seek labour contracts, some of which provided food as compensation. Some young men discovered what elders feared; that employment on plantations growing bananas for the Italian market freed them from constraints of local custom. Employers also recruited young women to provide workers with wives from outside the area to convince their workers to settle on plantations (Hess 1996). This change increased matrimonial options for young men and undermined elders' uses of matrimony in constructing flexible, cross-cutting ties between local lineages (Iye n.d.).

State subsidies for commercial farms also initiated a pattern of drawing powerful actors from the capital into southern economic and political affairs. Investment was intended to uproot local producers' control over land and force them to engage fully within a national economy. By the mid 1930s SAIS became Italy's main banana supplier and Somalia's largest commercial agricultural enterprise with help from import tariffs and subsidies. An export quota survived the collapse of the Somali state under the Lomé Conventions that protected Somali banana exports to the European Union up to 1999. Colonial policy thus segued into later policies of 'national self-sufficiency' that masked capital-based elites' manipulation of state economic policies for personal enrichment and weakened regional power bases of rival politicians. This political allocation of economic opportunities drew outsiders into the region to control land and monopolize access to economic opportunities with help from the coercive force of the state. When conflict increased in the 1980s, these elites could call upon distant ethnic kinsmen who, once freed of the social restraints on violence that their home communities would impose, had become particularly effective fighters.

Thus economic growth and government revenue in Italian Somalia and the independent Somali state relied on coercion and privileged connections to political authority in the capital. Colonial officials needed this strategy to bolster a formal economy export market that could provide revenues to the state. Despite the eventual diminishment of formal state control over transactions, colonial policy resembled later practice in that beneficiaries relied upon the support of key officials – later, patronage bosses – who used coercion and public assets to ensure commercial success. For example, 1955 banana exports to Italy provided $7.6 million of the colony's total exports of $10.8 million only because SAIS enjoyed tariff exemptions and state-regulated pricing in Italy (IBRD 1957, p. 63). SAIS also produced textiles, soap and sugar for local consumption at 40 per cent above world prices, again with the benefit of tariff protection and privileged access to state credits. A focus on external markets and state support for large-scale enterprises continued long after achieving independence in 1960 and expanded with large-scale aid projects that boosted commercial agriculture to about 20 per cent of all farming land in southern Somalia's river valleys (Menkhaus and Craven 1996, p. 166).

Italian Somalia entered the 1950s heavily reliant upon subsidies from Rome. From 1951 to 1957, the colony generated average annual revenues of only $5.4 million, requiring a subsidy averaging $9 million.[4] 'The hard facts', wrote investigators, 'are that the traditional sectors of the economy offer little prospect for rapid expansion, while European agriculture has grown up on a largely artificial basis' (IBRD 1957, p. 91). This did not deter multilateral creditors and foreign donors during the 1960s and 1970s from supporting a large expansion of plantation agriculture. From 1960 to 1981, 18 per cent of remaining smallholders in the Jubba River Valley faced forcible expropriations for state farms, most without compensation. The impact on local communities was more dramatic than those figures suggest, since water diversions to large irrigation schemes left additional land infertile (Menkhaus 1989, p. 166).

Foreign aid reinforced the place of commercial farms in elite political strategies. Foreign support for the three largest farms in Jubba from 1976 to the late 1980s totaled at least $325 million, while direct state aid exceeded $50 million annually, a considerable sum given the country's GDP of $1.7 billion in 1987.[5] Privatization of enterprises, begun in 1981, further tightened ties between political power and one of the country's primary economic assets. A 1975 land tenure law gave legal sanction to civil servants and businessmen who could get government backing to claim village lands. Registering titles became 'a political rather than an economic process' reported a foreign technical expert. 'The successful individual is one that has contacts in the bureaucracy, knowledge of how to "work the system", clan and personal ties with high government officials' at the expense of smallholders who held land on the basis of custom and lineage ties solidified through marriage (Hoben 1988, p. 216). The land grab in southern areas alienated a further 6,000 ha in addition to the 16,000 ha lost to plantations, increasing the importance of this region as a source of political patronage beyond its value as a recipient of foreign aid. This also reinforced the control of powerful outsiders with close ties to the political elite in the capital over the region's economy (Roth 1987; Gunn 1987).

Merging political networks and official economic policies destroyed local customary authorities' control over resources. This helped shape conflict in the 1990s, since it drew into the region outside elites of mixed origins, some of whom became important political actors in the river valleys through their positions in the hierarchy of the dictatorship in the capital that tied their economic power to state coercion. As state control diminished in the 1980s, they exercised this power for themselves to recruit and field armed forces. The significance of colonial and nationalist policies lay in providing these actors with tools to become violent entrepreneurs as these policies weakened local capacity to resist this process.

Control over major plantations in the south played key roles in the strategies of two major militia leaders in the early 1990s. General Mohammed Aydeed, who had held positions in the government in the 1980s, and his backers provided land in the river valleys on which disaffected *mooryaan* ('dispossessed ones') could settle. Aydeed used the attractions of this region to recruit followers from his own Habr Gidir clan to join his faction of the United Somali Congress (USC). Other strongmen from Barre's time saw a strategy of survival in southern farms. Aydeed's principal backer, Mogadishu-based businessman Usman Ato, organized the looting of farm equipment, then helped set up militia-controlled plantations. Ato already had a base in the area, since he had been allocated a farm in the 1980s that his sister ran.[6] Barre's former defence minister, Adan Abdullahi Nur 'Gabeeyow' also used southern farming lands as patronage on his own to attract and organize fighters, first after teaming up with Col Omar Jess, and continuing after he switched to the side of General Mohammed Said Hersi 'Morgan', another Barre crony and head of the Somali National Front (SNF).

Continued exports of bananas to Europe provided hard currency incomes to entrepreneurs, about $26 million in 1990, and in the range of $6 to $8 million in 1994.[7] These resources and opportunities drew in *mooryaan* from other regions seeking refuge, employment and food. Col. Omar Jess, for example, used the southern region as a base for displaced members of his Ogadeen clansmen once Jess recognized in 1990 that his presidential patron was failing. The report of an aid worker in 1995 reflected the presence of large numbers of armed outsiders:

> In lower Jubba, the district commanders and militia are the only structure of authority...There is no civilian administration. Osman Ato's farm is where the main commander is based.[8]

Despite the collapse of state administration, the merging of economic and coercive power shrank the social space for indigenous resistance. Defensive groups of local farmers from the Shebelle and Jubba valleys such as the Somali African Muki Organization (SAMO) remained weak because they lacked access to hard currency with which to buy weapons and to recruit their own *mooryaan* from outside the region.

This organization of conflict is not a result of clan politics *per se*. Instead, it follows from earlier state policies that undermined local customary contract arrangements and political institutions based upon elders' control of marriage and land allocation. As outsiders disrupted local matrimonial customs and seized local farms, local people lost control of resources to oppose these interlopers. Indigenous people and newcomers alike became 'stabilized' around rigid lineage identities as a consequence of the coercion, then outright violence of economic policies that created security dilemmas for entire communities. Denied means or incentives to make local political accommodations, newcomers petitioned patrons in the capital to hold onto their assets and positions. Eventually they had to seek protection from clan militias that also served the same entrepreneurial purpose, except now in more outwardly violent ways.

Indigenous inhabitants had fewer choices. If they lacked weapons, they had to seek protection as subordinates to local armed groups, or take their chances in poorly armed home guard militias. These rigidified lines of conflict fit the expectations of scholars that political entrepreneurs will exploit these security dilemmas to get control of local resources. This was especially true among new arrivals who were outsiders and who could call upon distant kinsmen to tip the balance of power. The nature of violence in southern regions illustrates the proposition that outsider elites who had benefited from privileged access to the political networks of the crumbling state fit expectations that state collapse and violent exploitation of resources will lead to long-term conflict, rigidified ethnic defensive groups and will undermine alternative political communities. Economic globalization in this setting adds resources to the battles of political entrepreneurs and thus creates formidable obstacles to organizing stable political authority.

Northern marginality

While Italian Somalia depended upon subsidies to underwrite exports and maintain state agencies, officials in British Somaliland insisted that the colony remain 'undisturbed' and get by with a tiny state apparatus. British administrative responses to the anti-colonial resistance of Sayyid Mohamed Abdille Hussan, the 'Mad Mullah of Somaliland', whose fighters held off British forces for twenty years from 1900 to 1920, explains some of this caution. 'The expatriate administration', wrote Lewis, 'consequently received stern admonitions from London that nothing was ever to be done again that could possibly provoke the Somalis' (Lewis 1994, p. 4). Thus Somali regions experienced very different legacies of colonial rule, depending on whether they were included in Italian or British realms.

Differences in style, however, did not translate into dramatic variation in levels of colonial intrusion in local societies. British officers probably thought that direct rule and economic intervention of the Italian sort would lead to local resistance, would be too costly and would weaken the willingness of local leaders to collaborate with, or at least tolerate, colonial rule. As elsewhere in

Africa, the legal and administrative goal in Somaliland was to stabilize social organization, as understood by British officials. This meant that while Italian officials were trying to destroy lineage control over potential workers, British authorities recognized *diya*-paying groups as basic political institutions. These groups pledged to pay blood money to the families of victims of violence to resolve feuds, an element of customary law that regulates social interactions. Lewis takes these groups as integral to local society and stresses the minimal impact of colonial rule on local society, and even asserts 'during the colonial period, hardly any attempt was made to artificially erect a system of Indirect Rule' (Lewis 1994, p. 23). This view was at odds with British payments of stipends to headmen who used their role in British colonial administration as a tool for fighting their rivals or for self-enrichment.[9]

Colonial rule actually did change social structures in Northern Somalia. Recognizing *diya*-paying groups gave local headmen a stake in enforcing colonial ordinances, since transgressions netted them a portion of fines. It was in British colonial administrative interests to support headmen, since *diya* gave justification to British ordinances prescribing collective punishment for infractions in lieu of a large and expensive bureaucracy.[10] Headmen wanted to rigidify these boundaries to make sure that individuals and families did not reinterpret their lineage to escape obligations incurred by people unknown or distant from them. This rigidity reinforced the colonial legal notion of blood group solidarity and recruited blood groups to control 'members' to avoid liability for their actions (Kittermaster 1927, pp. 329–37). Thus British, like Italian, administration laid foundations for less flexible definitions of clanship that helped aggravate group security dilemmas and provided platforms for political entrepreneurs in conflicts of the 1980s and 1990s.

The British north, however, lacked the Italian south's history of state appropriation of economic assets on behalf of outsiders. This condition continued into Barre's regime and became a major factor in shaping the local development of social regulation of violence in the 1990s and 2000s, examined below. Colonial authorities levied no head taxes, using taxes on trade to pay for administration (Young 1994, p. 133), and expressed their hostility to economic development. An official from London charged with charting a development plan for the colony in the 1950s complained that, taking fears of disorder to heart, local administrators feared social disruption and 'modern' social pressures. To avoid these evils, they defied directives from London that local officers considered imprudent (Hunt 1951). 'As a result', reported Lewis, 'the traditional attitudes of pastoral Somali society were even more strongly entrenched in the north, while the south, by contrast, appeared in many respects more modernist in outlook' (Lewis 1988, p. 169). Local society may have seemed 'traditional' to some scholars (Lewis 1994, p. 23) although administrative intervention in local social categories suggests otherwise.

Given these similarities, it is even more baffling that armed entrepreneurs in the south failed to build a stable political order after 1991 while armed northern leaders found ways to manage conflict, build cross-cutting alliances, and rein in violence without the aid of outside force or subsidies. As evidence below shows, colonial experiences were not decisive in shaping contemporary identity and political organization, though they are important for influencing social categories and the distribution of resources. The key variable shaping these outcomes lies in the nature of rule in post-colonial Somalia, specifically the extent to which local elites either joined or were excluded from political networks dominating commerce.

Patronage politics, foreign aid and creeping state collapse

The 1960 unification of British Somaliland and Italian Somalia as an independent state did not result in a reduction of external financial support. Though they attracted little foreign investment, Somalia's rulers discovered that they could use their state's sovereignty to attract other resources. They perfected the art of playing to the diplomatic and strategic interests of former colonial rulers, superpowers and others willing to exchange aid for ideological allegiance, diplomatic alignment, or access to military bases (David 1991). Politicians used these resources to attract domestic support and manage rivals. As southern Somali agricultural projects showed, capital-based rulers used foreign aid to build political networks that later provided key agents of violence and armed groups of followers when central control over this network collapsed. Thus the strategies for building a state and political community on the margins of the global economy after 1960 also lay at the heart of state collapse and violent community fragmentation after 1990.

This political strategy intensified after the coup of General Mohamed Siyyad Barre on 21 October 1969. Initially he appeared to support a state-building project. Barre announced that speakers of the Somali language should be unified in a single state and supported crash literacy programmes to propagate a new Somali script. In 1970 he unveiled a 'Scientific Socialist' ideology and invited the Soviet navy to lease the port of Berbera in former British Somaliland. Barre took ideological cues and foreigners' cash where he could find them, but he pursued a consistent strategy of centralizing his political command over Somali society. This extended to an irredentist project for which he gave official support to the Northern Frontier District Liberation Front in Kenya and the Front de Libération de la Côte des Somalis in neighbouring French Somaliland and infiltration of Ogadeeni clan fighters of the Somali–Abo Liberation Front (SALF) and the Western Somalia Liberation Front (WSLF) to 'reclaim' ethnic Somali territory in Ethiopia's Ogaden.[11] SALF and WSLF ties to the Somali government were tight.[12] By March 1978, however, Ethiopian counter-attacks reached Somali territory after Soviet officials decided to aid Ethiopia's new Marxist regime. Barre's attack on Ethiopia had later consequences as Ethiopian leaders concluded that keeping Somalia divided after Barre's fall in 1991 was integral to their own security.

Barre managed to find a new external source of income. Through the 1980s the US government provided more than $800 million in aid. A quarter of this was devoted to military expenditures. Italy was more generous and was willing to include local politicians in insider deals in providing over a billion dollars in the 1980s for more than 100 projects, which contributed to Barre's role as a distributor of largesse to his informal political network of associates, both inside government and in 'private' (but politically well connected) business. Outside aid generated $2.8 billion for Somalia between 1972 and 1989, making that country Africa's greatest beneficiary of aid on a per capita basis (Sommer 1994, p. 7). The geographic and political distribution of aid, however, shows that it became a major source of corruption. The extreme dependence on foreign aid for 90 per cent of development spending reinforced Barre's centrality in all avenues of economic life as manager of formal state allocations and as patron to political allies. Barre's domination of these economic channels entrenched his power in the institutional frameworks of communities targeted for development spending. He also used these initiatives to overlay his own political network over old informal local networks. The consequence later would be that informal mediating institutions and the authority of 'traditional' leaders would be weakest in these areas once sustained conflict broke out in the late 1980s. When examined in its patrimonial context, it also provides a guide for predicting which communities would organize their own responses to state collapse and which ones would not, and how each would respond to economic opportunities in the 1990s and 2000s.

Meanwhile, agricultural projects absorbed 22 per cent of development spending in the 1980s, with 90 per cent of that allocated to large-scale commercial farming. Politically favoured groups benefited from the construction of dams, irrigation and plantation farming in the south and received the bulk of this spending (World Bank 1991). Foreign experts complained that Somali policy excluded more numerous pastoralists, especially those in northern areas, even though agricultural support rose as a proportion of development spending during this period.[13] Further accentuating the social differentiation that development spending promoted, social service expenditures fell from 6.3 per cent of official budgets in 1975 to less than one per cent in 1989. By the 1980s even this small amount was reserved in large part to provide housing for faculty and staff at the National University in Mogadishu (World Bank 1991, p. 124).

Likewise, policy failure coupled with a steady flow of foreign aid helped civil servants migrate into regime-sanctioned clandestine channels. By 1989 civil servants were paid only three to four per cent of the real value of their

1975 salaries and had to support themselves through corruption, bribes and kickbacks. As salaries declined, Barre increased civil service employment from about 20,000 in 1969 to over 56,000 in 1983. This made association with foreign financed development projects a vital part of the survival strategies of civil servants and turned these projects into an even more valuable political resource for Barre. A foreign consultant observed, however, that the civil service lost many educated employees, particularly those who came from the north and whom Barre regarded as less desirable as political clients (Gregory 1990, p. 12). As shown below, politically marginalized communities in the north were forced to become more adept at exploiting the economic opportunities of clandestine markets and overseas employment on their own, often in defiance of the regime and in conflict with clandestine rackets that regime favourites ran.

Even when Barre's irredentist adventure and economic management brought widespread insecurity, foreign relief aid offered him political resources to plough back into his 'official' clandestine economy. UN officials, for example, in the report published in the early 1980s, complained that $100 million in relief aid to refugees of the 1977–78 war was distributed on the basis of clan leadership loyalties to Barre, and was used to reinforce the control of regime strongmen who oversaw the distribution of relief aid. Aid workers testified that food was pilfered from convoys and sold in local markets with the connivance of local officials. UN officials used similar complaints of pilferage to justify intervention in the early 1990s. It is no coincidence that the same individuals and armed groups were responsible for this use of violence in both periods, though prior to 1990 they were part of regime policy. One aid worker estimated that three quarters of all supplies were stolen, with some going directly to militias that attacked clans that Barre believed opposed his rule (Tucker 1984, p. 22). Massive over-counting of refugees, 1.5 million by Somali government estimate versus the 650,000 count of aid agencies, also aimed to generate resources for patronage (Gersony 1989).

Clandestine markets, political entrepreneurs and the destruction of southern elite autonomy

The failure of the Ogaden invasion posed a serious challenge to Barre's authority. He could no longer mobilize a broad-based coalition on the basis of a vague socialist ideology (or visible evidence of general economic development), nor could he unify his country in a regional state-building campaign. He shifted toward more exclusive reliance on manipulating markets and directing the violent predations of strongmen who were allied with his regime. This strategy, already seen in southern farming areas, shaped the physical and social distribution of insider beneficiaries and outsiders to Barre's rule. Ironically, those who were left out – usually against their will – gained social tools that they used later to impose order and build defensive networks against local predation and disruptive elements of the world economy. Thus this analysis locates the primary cause of Somalia's disruption as a consequence of the internal configuration of patronage politics and state collapse. Economic globalization contributed to this process insofar as resources and opportunities were channelled in ways that undermined social cohesion, which was precisely the aim of Barre's patrimonial strategy, along with securing those resources for him to distribute at his personal discretion to his supporters. Likewise, global economic transactions became the key either to later fragmentation or consolidation of communities, depending upon how those communities allocated those resources after the central state collapsed.

Barre's patrimonial strategy was not always successful and even engendered an attempted overthrow in 1978 by one of his own Daarood clansmen, Colonel Abdulahi Yusuf. This alerted Barre to the dangers of delegating too much responsibility to his subordinates, especially those who controlled coercive force and resources in their own right. Yet the war with Ethiopia entailed increasing the army from 22,000 well-armed soldiers in 1977 to over 50,000 troops in 1981 once Barre's adversary acquired Soviet aid and advice. Many of these hastily mobilized soldiers owed more allegiance to commanders who recruited them than to Barre's nationalist vision or his authority. By 1990 numbers reached 60,000 through forced conscription (Pérouse de Montclos 2001, p. 35). Barre's dependence on these regional strongmen within his own political network seriously limited his capacity to mobilize people in this way.

Somalia's increasing dependence on outsiders for aid eased Barre's switch from a bureaucratic state-building project to a patronage network rooted in violent control over economic channels as an alternative strategy of rule. His manipulation of access to economic opportunity made segments of the country's elite beholden to Barre for personal wealth and security. This neutralized the ability of clan elders to control resources to resolve local conflicts, since official favour equipped local strongmen with means to appropriate resources for themselves and their followers. Those beholden to Barre's network still could patronize their own clan's kinsmen. This was Barre's intention, too, since this gave him more leeway to use proxies to manipulate tensions between and within clans to divide not only his opposition, but also ensure that his allies never could mount a direct challenge to his rule. Moreover, Barre chose his associates according to this calculus of clan competition for favour. This arrangement gave the president excellent bases to sharpen and exploit competing security dilemmas within his own political clique. Local power and access to wealth, even in clandestine economies, increasingly came from membership in the capital-based clique, an arrangement designed to harness the ambitions and violent strategies of political entrepreneurs in Barre's divide-and-rule network.

Barre also armed Ogadeeni refugees to fight Isaaq communities in the north who he thought might be inclined to cooperate with his other enemies. Supplied with government arms, Barre used his patronage of Ogadeeni refugees to revive old conflicts over pasturage in Ethiopia with their Isaaq neighbours dating from the 1950s. WSLF fighters also sought to exploit this grievance but could not join with Isaaqs to address this problem if the key to patronage from the capital for Ogadeenis lay in getting guns from Barre's allies to attack other Somalis. Fighting mobilized personal interests in the framework of clan politics, as Lewis observed when he visited the region in the late 1980s:

> Male Ogadeeni refugees [of the Daarood clan] have been encouraged to take over the remains of Isaaq shops and houses in what are now ghost towns. Thus those who were received as refugee guests have supplanted their Isaaq hosts, many of whom – in this bitterly ironic turn of fate – are now refugees in the Ogaden. (Lewis 1990, p. 59)

Through selective arming of Daarood Ogadeenis to target Daarood sub-clans, Barre deflected armed opposition and undermined prospects for coordinated challenge to his rule.

Barre also promoted supporters from among Oromo and Ogadeeni refugees to official positions in the north. State office gave Barre's appointees positions from which to skim humanitarian aid for themselves. Their exemption from enforcement of other laws and economic regulations gave these people privileged commercial positions from which to use their loot in the country's clandestine economy in, for example, smuggling operations. Barre and his associates then could manipulate violence for the benefit of the state through tapping into other informal sectors of the economy. Young men who sought access to clandestine economic opportunities quickly discovered that their best chance of improving their situation lay in joining a regime-approved patron who would supply them with guns, protection and access to economic opportunity on this basis of manipulated inter-clan tensions. This allowed the president to exploit what a UN agency observed as a 'synergy between two forces – increasing economic exclusion and social disintegration' (UNICEF 1995, p. 8). Barre turned violence that might otherwise be directed against his regime into a controlled political space with armed groups preying upon other citizens, leaving victim and predator unable to construct an alternative stable political order.

Chronic instability created some opportunities for northern political entrepreneurs too. Many Isaaq who faced 'official' predation and who wanted to get their pasturage back sided with an armed Isaaq group within the WSLF, the 'Fourth Regiment' that Barre's regime supplied with weapons. They fought Barre's other allies, ensuring that none became so strong that any could repeat the 1978 coup attempt. Meanwhile, inter and intra-clan fighting over pastures in Ethiopia left Barre's Ethiopian enemies with turmoil in their own neighbourhood. Nor could Ethiopians provide too much support to Barre's enemies, lest their Somali clients use this aid to reclaim parts of Ethiopia's Ogaden for themselves. Their 1984 arrest of Abdulahi Yusuf and persistent meddling in the internal politics of the Isaaq opposition fractured these groups, even those that later became the core of the Somaliland administration. Thus parochial politics and Barre's political strategy overwhelmed even the façade of twentieth-century liberation politics.

The political economy of social autonomy in the north

At the start of this turmoil in 1977, foreign donors and creditors pressured Barre's government to undertake economic reform and deregulate exchange rates. They negotiated with Somali officials what was called the *franco valuta* system for local businessmen to convert foreign remittances from Somalia's estimated 250,000 overseas migrant workers earning $1.5 billion annually (Miller 1981, p. 5) at open market rates. The official aim of the policy was to redirect illicit imports of hard currency estimated to top $350 million into legal channels that could benefit the country's depleted treasury (Marchal 1996, p. 35). By 1985 remittances to Somalia totaled an estimated $338 million, about fifteen times the entire wage bill for the country's formal sector (Jamal 1988, p. 239). Northerners contributed disproportionately to these remittances, reflecting the tendency of politically marginalized people to search for work in the Persian Gulf and elsewhere. They did this rather than engage in difficult efforts to get incorporated into the country's increasingly pervasive patronage politics that was reserved for more politically favoured Somalis (Ahmed 2000, pp. 380–1). Isaaq formed the core of a West European-based diaspora among those who worked in Britain's merchant navy after the end of the Second World War. Isaaq migration to Britain followed in the 1960s and 1970s when political aspirants and would-be entrepreneurs lost out in patronage politics after independence, then more so after Barre's 1969 coup.

Instead of deregulating economic exchange, Barre's manipulation of *franco valuta* did the reverse. He retained control over import licensing, distributing it on the basis of political calculations. Those already entrenched in clandestine commerce and diversions of aid were especially well-placed to benefit, since they could channel this capital into what were regime-approved smuggling operations. Barre used uncertainty to enhance his personal control over exchanges, 'canceling' *franco valuta* in 1982 (though application of this 'cancellation' was at Barre's personal discretion) only to revive it in 1984.

Retention of other regulations also gave Barre's regime tools to allow favoured entrepreneurs to undervalue imports, increasing the value of their *franco valuta* profits *vis-à-vis* competitors. These manipulations reinforced the political nature of Somalia's clandestine market as an instrument in Barre's exercise of power. Meanwhile, politically marginalized groups continued to rely upon local solidarities to protect their transactions against inconsistent enforcement of laws and competition from the president's business allies. For example, Ali Mahdi, a big landowner in the south, then later a militia financier, translated his presidential favour in the 1980s into a *franco valuta*-assisted business empire. Ali Mahdi owed his position to Barre's protection rather than his kin. This gave him geographic and social flexibility, defined by Barre's political network rather than on claims he might make on his kinsmen by virtue of custom. This left Ali Mahdi vulnerable to Barre's machinations, and he was jailed in the early 1980s on suspicion of supporting a coup plot. But he was rehabilitated in 1984 in time to profit from *franco valuta*. Ali Mahdi then became a major figure in Mogadishu business circles, largely through managing the Barre regime's ties to Italian businesses, including those that offered access to sophisticated arms.[14] Ali Mahdi made an ideal associate for Barre, since his reliance on the president meant that he would not have any real independent base of support. The social context of Ali Mahdi's power was reflected in his 1991 bid after Barre's flight to get recognized as 'interim president' on the basis of Italian diplomatic support and his ability to arm fighters, not as a representative of a particular group of people or community. These ties and their connection to arms acquisition reinforced the disruptive character of this new elite attached to a centralized and violent patronage network, then courted by foreigners in the 1990s.

Usman Ato, later a financier of Mohammed Aydeed, also consolidated his business position in the 1980s without having to face much of the burden of customary demands or constraints of clan networks from his home community. Like Ali Mahdi, Usman Ato helped organize arms acquisitions for Barre's government. Usman Ato shared 'official' clandestine commercial ties to Aydeed, who had been exiled and then returned to Barre's fold as a defence minister and organizer of arms acquisitions in the 1980s. Like Ali Mahdi, Barre punished, and later rehabilitated both these men by permitting them to exploit new clandestine commercial networks, thus cementing their dependence upon him. These men and their associates still became patrons to kinsmen, but fateful for future conflict, they did not owe their control over resources and business opportunities to approval from clan authorities or conformity to local social conventions.

These men were the people best able to equip fighters, either young clansmen who came to cities to find jobs, or simply the adventurous, ambitious or desperate. As junior members (or aspiring members) of centralized networks, these young men sought relief from insecurity through finding some place in the businesses associated with Barre's patronage networks. Their best chances for relief from poverty came through affiliating with strongmen who could arm them as political muscle or as enforcers in the favoured channels of the clandestine economy. Like their patrons, 'these bands were constituted more according to personal affinities during the last years of Siyaad Barre, and defined by the same types of activities, or by habitation in the same parts of the capital' (Marchal 1993, p. 307). This was not clan warfare in any primordial sense. Instead, it is a good illustration of a security dilemma conducive to forcing would-be victims to find a protector, often kinsmen, to mitigate threats or to share in loot. Barre's political strategy shows that he recognized that this was especially true if fighters and patrons were in 'foreign' territory where the defensive moves of local communities would seem especially threatening to outsiders who, like them, were free from the social bonds of customary means of mitigating conflict. Likewise, 'foreigners' who are outside one's social networks are easier to loot. In this sense, conflict in the 1990s was an intensification of Barre's informal techniques of rule through patronage and regime imposed insecurity.[15]

Once Barre fled Mogadishu in 1991, business kingpins continued to attract young men to fight. In regions where these strongmen could recruit and where their business enterprises generated income, clan elders: 'found themselves attempting to negotiate with young militiamen and bandits from distant clans rather than with "peer" elders', a situation which one scholar blamed for the failure of customary conflict resolution strategies in the south (Menkhaus 2000, p. 191). This pointed to ways that mobility and allegiance to new elites based in appropriation of informal markets and state assets undermined the social control that customary authorities and social obligations once ensured.

Some northern businessmen viewed Barre's *franco valuta* cancellation in 1982 and again in 1985 as an effort to single them out for punishment and to strengthen political control over patronage and clandestine businesses. Some businessmen in the northeast from the Majerteen community complained that few in this region could take advantage of *franco valuta* in the first place because businessmen were subject to predations of private militias that exacted collective punishment in the 1980s after the appearance of Abdulahi Yusuf's SSDF challenge to Barre.[16] Northern economic fortunes suffered further harm from Barre's regime, but in ways that increased their future autonomy from Mogadishu. In 1981, for example, the government imposed a 50 per cent tariff on the north's growing livestock trade to Saudi Arabia, forcing local exporters to rely more heavily upon kinship networks to guarantee transactions across international borders outside the state's regulatory reach (Samatar *et al.* 1988, pp. 92–4). This trade was estimated to have generated several tens of millions of dollars annually through the early 1980s (Samatar 1985). A northern delegation that went to Mogadishu to petition Barre to remove these charges returned home when they were threatened with arrest.[17] Meanwhile, this tariff benefited the inefficient Trans-Juba Livestock Project, funded with Italian and World Bank finance that supported this new source of patronage positions and payouts to regime favourites (Mohamoud 1983, pp. 7–11).

This political and economic marginalization led northern businessmen to seek local protection from predatory exactions from officials. Clan solidarities offered them the best prospects for shielding commerce from harm. Clan based credit systems already existed to manage business networks that remained outside Barre's political grip. These informal credit arrangements enabled local businessmen to tap into locally organized informal remittance systems in which overseas senders and local recipients relied upon customary clan authorities to guarantee contracts, protect members, and adjudicate disputes outside state bureaucracies and the informal patronage institutions that had become increasingly inaccessible to them. Several scholars estimate that 90 per cent of foreign exchange from commerce in 1981 (as distinct from foreign aid to refugees and to Mogadishu) was generated through this trade in livestock, much of which was organized through clan authorities in coordination with remittance flows.[18]

Self-identification as political outsiders appeared as local businessmen compared themselves to Greek, Lebanese and Indian commercial diasporas that have relied upon tight-knit families and community self-help organizations to survive hostile political environments. Northern commerce also made use of the geographic proximity to Djibouti, which became independent of France after 1977. Djibouti's government offered its territory as a low tax entrepôt for trans-shipment of smuggled goods in and out of adjacent Somali territory to benefit from the need of northern entrepreneurs to find a secure environment from which to organize their transactions. This enabled the Djibouti business community and the country's treasury to benefit from their neighbours and clan kinsmen to profit from the smuggling trade in livestock and other goods (Miller 1981, pp. 8–10). Prior to technological developments in telecommunications, Djibouti also harboured trusted Somali financial intermediaries beyond the reach of Barre's government or patronage network who would handle cash for migrants and businessmen and provide credit for those frozen out of Somalia's formal sector and politically allocated *franco valuta* financial markets.

Commercial exclusion from Barre's patronage networks also shaped the organization of armed opposition in the north from the early 1980s. The 1981 founding of the Isaaq-dominated Somali National Movement (SNM), for example, owed much to the financial resources of the Isaaq diaspora community in Britain. The role of clan elders in guaranteeing transactions of these migrants also ensured that clan elders on the whole exercised greater control over the finances and political processes of this group, compared to others involved in Somalia's conflicts (Compagnon 1998, p. 84). This was the result of circumstances, not northern virtue. Moreover, the SNM had to form in exile to escape Barre's wrath. Based in Ethiopia during its 1981–8 exile, it remained under tight control of Ethiopia's President Mengistu. Unlike southern-based militias after 1989, SNM's Ethiopian patron did not allow it to receive foreign aid from a single major donor, lest this give the group the autonomy to defy Mengistu in coordination with Isaaq herders to settle grievances about access to Ethiopian pasture or revive Barre's irredentist dream. Mengistu also interfered in SMN's internal affairs and had early leaders arrested to hinder the SNM's utility as a vehicle for personal ambitions of political entrepreneurs (Adam 1993).

By the time Mengistu forced the SNM to return to Somalia in 1988, the group could not easily finance itself through predation because it never could develop its own source of funding, ether from a generous patron or through looting local communities. Ultimately it had to raise funds through deals with commercial intermediaries within the system constructed outside of Barre's control. Dahab Shiil, later one of Somaliland's largest financial and telecom companies, got its start as an SNM financier. Isaaq financiers based in the Ethiopian town of Dire Dawa intervened in the organization's affairs as they used SNM's radios to transfer money to fighters.[19] This alliance enabled the SNM to tap into migrants' remittances to finance armed struggle, but not in ways that made business enterprises an adjunct to their own organization. This arrangement had a different outcome in the south where militia leaders also were the principal business operators in their region. For their part the private commercial partners in these transactions used this alliance to consolidate their market role in telecoms and financial services in the 1990s, the two services upon which the remittance system depends.

This relationship continued to influence the organization of the SNM when its Ethiopian patrons forced it to return to Hargeisa in 1988. While Barre assigned loyal strongmen the task of attacking Isaaq communities, they were free to support themselves with loot. SNM fighters, on the other hand, could not loot local communities that provided critical income from remittances and which were the bases of the commercial organizations essential to the militia's continued survival. Likewise, this lack of local leverage for armed groups undermined prospects for political entrepreneurs in the organization who entertained notions of fighting their way to power in Mogadishu. Their initial dependence on businessmen who were outside Barre's old networks meant that these men were not as free to loot their home communities as their southern colleagues were doing to pursue ambitions in Mogadishu and the periodic foreign-sponsored peace conferences that gave seats to those whose predations made them difficult to ignore.

This did not mean that the north was free of predation. Brigadier General Omar Jess, the Ogadeeni commander of the refugee militia after the 1978 war, then commander of a militia in the south, used his position in Barre's patronage network to loot. As his patron's fortunes declined, Jess pursued his own ambitions, but this did not require that he shift his strategy for getting resources since he already had built his own commercial networks by virtue of his privileged ties to the president. By the time Barre perceived that Jess was becoming a powerful figure in his own right in the 1988 attack on Hargeisa and the SNM, Jess controlled enough resources to defy Barre's order to leave his military post. An analyst observed that Jess' strength 'comes from having some 8,000 troops, nearly all Ogadeeni, under his direct command'.[20] Clan identity played a major role in this conflict. More important, however, was Jess' ability to sustain his organization through predation, since he did not derive his main income as a consequence of his on-going relationship with powerful members of a particular community. He owed this 'strength' more to his position in a crumbling centralized patronage network and its violent appropriation of clandestine economies and state assets, and less through customary standing as head of a clan.

Controlling political entrepreneurs

Political entrepreneurs still posed a danger to the formation of a separate Somaliland polity outside the predatory framework of the collapse of Barre's patronage networks. Northern politicians were not immune to the allures of competition over the spoils of predation. Abdirahmaan Ali Tuur, an Isaaq and the first president of Somaliland, joined the SNM shortly after its founding in 1981. Tuur's supporters fought in the northern port city of Berbera in February 1992 where they emptied local banks and sacked several NGOs. Conflicts over the integration of clan-based units into a Somaliland national army led to fighting in 1991–2 before clan elders brokered a peace agreement. They criticized Tuur for his close friendship with Aydeed and for his participation in peace conferences organized by the UN and Egyptians. Tuur claimed those seats in negotiations on the basis of his importance as a commander of fighters. That gave him additional incentives to battle others and loot local communities, lest he be left out of any externally brokered settlement that promised control over the whole state – including clandestine and predatory economic opportunities – to the fortunate winners of the mediation effort. Tuur's manoeuvre also informed local notables' criticisms of foreign-organized peace conferences in general. They threaten internal stability through diluting local control over the control of resources since they raise the stakes of struggle to the control the state. This is not a situation easily dealt with in customary law when the locus of that struggle is distant from the social context of its focus.

The majority of the remaining militia commanders were dependent upon local clan elders for recruitment and to maintain loyalty within the ranks since their inability to establish 'liberated zones' in Ethiopian refuges (before their eviction in 1988 after incessant Ethiopian manipulation of leadership politics) led them to turn to Isaaq clan elders to recruit and maintain fighters. Tuur's fighters, on the other hand, found it easier to loot and abuse the local population, since they could escape social consequences of their behaviour. While in Somaliland, Tuur relied upon ties with Mohamed Aydeed for resources and to support him in conflicts with rivals within the SNM in Somaliland. But when local commanders were able to control fighters enough to consolidate forces to oppose him, Tuur's ambition took him from Somaliland to Mogadishu to contend for a role in externally supported peace negotiations. Meanwhile, his associate Jaama Mahamed Ghalib Yare, defeated in the May 1993 presidential elections, helped promote fighting in Burao and Hargeisa in 1994–95, reportedly with the help of bribes, variously reported to be from Aydeed and other southern politicians who resisted Somaliland separatism (Compagnon 1988, pp. 84–5).

Northerners might have been expected to be more susceptible to Barre's strategy of divide-and-rule than their more privileged and better-connected southern neighbours. They were the ones who faced the most vicious initial attacks, bereft of the resources that their southern rivals controlled by virtue of their ties to the old president. But political disfavour and the marginality to clandestine economic opportunities turned out to create organizational means for northern authorities to resist outside interference once conflict started. Marginality was translated into autonomous economic channels even before Barre's rise to power. Then exclusion from the benefits of southern agricultural projects, lack of access to subsidized credit, the fruits of privatization or the benefits of *franco valuta* manipulation in the 1980s forced more northerners abroad in search of work to support themselves and their families.

Overseas work attracted youth from all over Somalia, but by 1987 the majority of the estimated 375,000 migrants in Gulf States were northerners (Ahmed 2000, pp. 380–9). The International Labour Organization estimated in 1985 that 165,000 to 200,000 Somalis lived in the Middle East and remitted approximately 30 per cent of their $700 million annual earnings, resources that contributed to northern elite autonomy and dependence upon local community business structures, rather than to predation.

The behaviour of young fighters in Somalia's north reflected similar elements of local versus outsider control over the distribution of resources. At first it appeared that Northerners faced the problem of self-interested armed young men on the prowl for loot. Gerard Prunier described his visit to Somaliland in 1989: 'The danger while traveling, comes rather from the SNM "auxiliaries", armed youngsters who drift around pretending to be 'Mujahiddins' but without being really attached to any regiment' (Prunier 1991, p. 108). But Prunier observed that these fighters limited their predations to looting aid shipments. He noted 'the difficulty of shooting young apprentice-shiftas because their clan and family backgrounds have to be taken into account, and the same holds for any person they might kill' (*ibid*, p. 109).

Marginality and a new Somaliland identity

The self-declared Republic of Somaliland, however, does not enjoy global recognition as a distinct political community. This reluctance of other states to recognize its sovereignty means that enterprises there face difficulties obtaining access to international institutions and norms that regulate economic opportunities, such as insurance contracts.[21] The absence of international recognition, observes an official of the Somaliland Chamber of Commerce, 'means we cannot enter into formal trade agreements; we cannot even contact the outside world through direct postal services, as we are not a member of the postal union'.[22] Transacting parties have no recourse to a basic international commercial law infrastructure or to conventional international venues for adjudicating commercial disputes such as the American Association of Arbiters, the International Chamber of Commerce, the London Court of International Arbitration or the World Bank's International Center for Settlement of Investment Disputes. The dominance of Anglo-Saxon common law as the standard framework for international commercial arbitration also limits their access to international commercial institutions, as it ties firms to a globally dominant legal system tied to decisions of US District Courts to deny standing to litigants who base claims on laws of entities whose sovereignty is not recognized by the US Government (Nash 1996, pp. 262–5).

The consequence is that the majority of cross-border transactions and foreign investments in Somaliland are best conducted through personal networks. This is where the defensive measures developed during the Barre regime become valuable tools for organizing Somaliland's relations with the global economy while promoting Somaliland's stability. While the legal infrastructure of international commerce keeps larger firms at bay, small Somali entrepreneurs with family ties to the region are able to use practices such as clan-based customs to guarantee contracts and manage risk. This also means that Somali entrepreneurs run nearly all businesses in Somaliland and most have significant connections to the diaspora community and its capital.

This social complexion of commerce gives local authorities a stake in protecting entrepreneurs, most of whom have family ties in the region. Not only does this protect entrepreneurs from competition from larger foreign rivals, it also binds the social control of violence that developed in the 1980s and 1990s to the protection of a local business class and the collection of revenues. Adjudication of business disputes and protection of contracts is an extension of the negotiation process that local authorities were able to impose on militia leaders from the late 1980s. This also gives local authorities the means to keep out entrepreneurs whom they determine might disrupt local order. Their denial of protection keeps resources away from political entrepreneurs who might otherwise use this wealth to raise a militia to contend for power in Mogadishu or make themselves powerful enough that foreign peace brokers will have to include them in negotiations. This arrangement also explains why members of Somaliland's diaspora do not become financiers of armed groups like diasporas from the south where legitimate local authorities do not exercise social control over sources of wealth and coercion. Local authorities' control over the Security Forces of Somaliland, a 7,000-man army of paid soldiers financed through an official budget, along with control over customary adjudication ensures that those who lack their protection will not fare well.

Mogadishu's commerce is not as well regulated through these informal institutions. Militias proliferated again in 2001–2002 as an internationally backed transitional government sought to assert control. UN investigators reported that 'some leading businessmen have outflanked militia leaders from their own clans and have started buying the backing of individual militia fighters' (United Nations Security Council 2002, para. 32). This they attributed to 'part of the competition between Somali groups in advance of the anticipated conference of concerned parties in Nairobi under the auspices of IGAD (Intergovernmental Authority on Development) peace negotiations' (United Nations Security Council 2002, para. 28). This commercial independence also enabled entrepreneurs to use militias to improve their economic fortunes. An attack on the home of the Interior Minister in March 2002 and again in May appeared to stem from a dispute concerning the minister's business operations in the Middle Shabelle Region where he controlled farms (United Nations Security Council 2002, para. 12). Likewise, splits within the Rahanwein Resistance Army (RRA), a southern-based militia, revealed a similar connection between business, political fragmentation and disorder. After declaring a 'South-Western Regional State of Somalia' in April 2002, fighting broke out in July between an RRA commander – a former Barre-era National Security Service Commander – and his deputies over the right to tax trucks passing through Baidoa. Since elders exercise little leverage over militia members who have come from other parts of Somalia, it is entrepreneurs who determine how coercion is used, not local customary authorities.

Somaliland businesses still encounter trouble in organizing transactions with non-Somali partners. Thus businesses that actually conduct operations in Somaliland use off-shore 'home offices' in the globally recognized Djibouti, and now in more internationally connected venues in the United Arab Emirates (UAE), much as the business associates of the SNM in the late 1980s and local entrepreneurs throughout the Barre era 'borrowed' their Ethiopian and Djibouti neighbours' sovereignty to avoid predators within Somalia. During Barre's time this was a defensive measure. Now these ties, reinforced through diaspora connections, are deployed to seek out new economic opportunities, a demonstration of the transformation and reinforcement of an old *ad hoc* practice put to the service of a new task. For example, Somaliland's largest of three airlines, Daallo Airline, is based in Djibouti 'to ensure neutrality, flexibility and independence'. An official in the firm also notes that this arrangement enables underwriters to write policies to insure the company's aircraft. Daallo's venue also is critical for managing inter-airline agreements with foreign carriers, for gaining access to the Gabriel, Galileo and Amadeus global reservation systems, and organizing financial services to collect fares via electronic payments and internet-based systems, all of which require mutually agreeable venues for resolving possible commercial problems.[23]

The advent of the internet mitigates some of these difficulties, since this allows firms to conduct immediate transactions in 'cyber-space'.[24] In practical terms, this gives firms access to the laws and norms of the geographic space in which a server is located. These technical advances favour financial intermediaries such as Dahab Shiil, which was noted above for playing an important role in facilitating the finances of the SNM. This firm formed a telecom subsidiary in Burao, Somtel, to handle directly the growing business in private remittances from migrants. Somtel has also helped address the Chamber of Commerce's complaint about an absence of a postal union agreement though simply organizing a private postal system via an agreement with Ethiopia's state post office. With 1,000 workers, Somtel claims to be Somaliland's largest private employer. Other financial and telecom firms play important roles in organizing a central bank. President Egal (who died on 3 May 2002 and was replaced by Dahir Riyale Kahin) admitted that his regime's currency reserves reside in the State Bank of Ethiopia and that the instant communications of Somaliland's efficient telecom and financial services make this unusual arrangement feasible.[25]

Somaliland's government is forced to rely on business intermediaries that remain offshore at arm's length. Though it is reliant on these businesses for revenue, authorities are forced to take into account business interests in promoting economically efficient policies and in limiting commercial risk within Somaliland. Thus, unlike southern political actors, Somaliland's authorities have an immediate interest in imposing uniform order and controlling coercion. These interests complicate any effort of political figures to subordinate business to a patronage network in Barre's fashion. Somaliland emerges as a remarkable exception for appearing to have solved this serious obstacle to building effective and legitimate polities in the African context. It has done so through adapting to an unconventional international status, and as a response to marginality that in the eyes of many scholars ought to have condemned this community to violence and fragmentation. This relationship of commerce, customary authority and government represents a hybrid 're-traditionalization' of power in that it recovers some of the flexibility of customary authority figures and practices to adjudicate disputes and distribute resources, much like the customary guarantees of contracts in pre-colonial Somalia described earlier in this work. Only now, this social process takes account of a broader global context in which this flexibility becomes advantageous.

In a similar way Somaliland's diaspora, linked to its two million inhabitants and their remittances, forces local authorities to adapt flexible methods to get access to their resources, while also limiting the power of these authorities. While it is difficult to determine what portion are northerners, northern migrants had the advantage of arriving at already established 'beachhead' groups overseas that consolidated, and benefited from, kinship connections and reverse migration (Gundel 2002; Pérouse de Montclos 2002).

Remittances are difficult to quantify. Net estimates for all of Somalia range from $140 million to $800 million annually (UNDP 2001, pp. 64–5). This overshadows the $115 million in donor assistance to all of Somalia in 2000, of which 42 per cent went to Somaliland and Puntland (UN 2001, para. 48). An analyst ventures an estimate of $150 million annually for Somaliland.[26] Somaliland's Ministry of Planning estimated $97 million for remittances in 1997 (Ministry of National Planning and Coordination 1999, p. 12). All of these estimates overshadow government budgets, which in 1999 stood at $26 million to provide for 6,000 civil employees.[27] Remittances also compete with local returns from the export of livestock, which amounted to about $125 million in 2000. Saudi claims of detection of Rift Valley Fever in Somali cattle, coupled with their subsequent ban on Somali cattle imports, prompted a collapse of this source of income and increased local reliance on remittances from overseas. This is thought to have increased the influence of clan elders who pressure overseas communities to send money home (Kibble 2001, p. 16). This income has a substantial impact on local consumption, especially in Hargeisa where remittances are estimated to constitute about 40 per cent of household income (UNDP 2001, p. 105).

Somaliland's diaspora stands at arm's length from the Somaliland government, yet is critical to the viability of a separate Somaliland polity. This relationship, along with the paucity of foreign aid, ensures that resources do not become concentrated in the hands of a single faction, nor in the dispersion and channels of resources do they present an easy target for predatory political entrepreneurs. This conclusion contradicts the findings of recent research that diasporas are more susceptible to extremist appeals because they do not suffer the consequences of subsequent violence (Collier 2001). In fact, Somalia and Somaliland show that, like arguments linking natural resources with predation, this argument misses the variable nature of the underlying political economy of informal and clandestine economies – the main focus of this study – that are responsible for the different organizational outcomes of conflict.

Marginality may promote order in Somaliland. This is not the marginality that preserves pristine local customs, as in the imagination of British colonial officers. Instead it spurs innovation. That Somaliland does not possess global recognition of its sovereignty nor receives much foreign aid forces its government to make deals with powerful groups, especially elders, who control access to overseas resources. Since local firms are forced to locate offices in places like Djibouti and the UAE where they are able to get access to insurance, arbitration and easier access to capital, Hargeisa officials have to rely upon the confidence of elders and families who have connections to diasporas to attract contractors willing to provide services and utilities and collect revenues. Some interpret this as a free market success story (Del Buono and Mubarak 1999). It is more accurate to describe it as a success of institutionalizing a 'clandestine' economy under the social control of clan elders to create order and fend off political entrepreneurs who would otherwise have incentives to prey upon local communities.

Somaliland's persistent lack of global diplomatic recognition, however, remains problematic. Somaliland officials fit their political community within the confines of the former British Somaliland in the hopes that foreigners will recognize their state as they did Eritrea, as a final act of decolonization. In terms of international law, Somaliland's case is stronger, for example, than that for Bosnia (Carroll and Rajagopal 1993, p. 653). Unlike Eritrea, however, Somaliland's army did not capture the capital of the state from which it separated, nor did it secure an agreement from its old capital for separation. More important, continued international efforts to mediate Somalia's conflict do not accept the principle of partition as a solution to conflict. Taiwan provides a better parallel. While much of the rest of the world recognizes Beijing's claims to sovereignty over Taiwan, at least in principle, Taiwan's business families straddle international borders, using bases in Vancouver, Hong Kong and Singapore. Like Taiwan, Somaliland authorities for their part conduct what looks like diplomacy masquerading as business in conjunction with a huge commercial diaspora. Whether it is recognized or not, the end result is that Somaliland's authorities assert self-determination through strategies of gaining control over the exercise of violence and negotiating with productive groups in society for support and revenues to increase the capacity and legitimacy of the political organization. In this regard Somaliland is more state-like in a classical sense than most *de jure* sovereign states in Africa.

Self-determination in the shadow of globalization

This analysis shows the importance of differences in the social control of violence for explaining divergent political outcomes in northern and southern Somalia. The most important element has been the relationship of local elites to economies, whether clandestine, patronage-based or international. Where they have been tied to a centralized patronage network their armed groups turn into predatory gangs. Politically marginal elites, on the other hand, find more incentives to organize armed groups as autonomous protective organizations. These elites also preserve and extend their power to settle disputes, protect people, enforce contracts and ultimately tax those who they protect. In all instances, leaders of militias and local strongmen may look and speak alike and may feel very strongly about obligations to serve the interests of kin. Their differences derive from distinctive styles for managing resources and organized violence.

Somaliland provides a vantage point from which to view the relevance of this difference for contemporary political organization in peripheral areas of the world economy. This process of controlling violence shows that the tumultuous dissolution of political networks in collapsed states into 'network wars' is not inevitable. The contemporary world economy permits local experimentation in forms bearing some resemblance to classic processes of state formation as a consequence of reciprocal relations between 'predators' and 'victims' in which the former gains interests in the security and productivity of the latter. Internal institutional structures and norms, including informal ones, still influence how violence is distributed and controlled, and the options available to ambitious people. This in turn affects the efficiency and organization of economic exchange in a process that permits a diversity of outcomes, including broader social control over the exercise of coercion. This focus highlights how wielders of force participate in the economy and conversely, how economic exchange affects those who manage force (Tilly 1992).

At the start of this chapter, I highlighted four observations that help explain this variation, and by extension the formation of new polities as vehicles for self-determination in the contemporary Somali space. They also provide a basis for drawing out broader implications for self-determination in the contemporary world in the context of state failure, violence and economic marginality. Throughout Somalia unofficial and non-state institutions have played key roles in building new authorities. Inter and intra clan norms, clandestine markets and informal political networks tied to Barre's patrimonial rule all were more important than formal institutions of the Somali state, especially after the collapse of the irredentist state-building project in the late 1970s. Barre and his cronies manipulated laws in the service of patronage and clandestine deals that kept political networks together. Likewise, international aid provided more resources for this social construction of violence and accumulation in the 1980s.

The second observation, however, provides a lens for distinguishing the variable impact of these informal networks for the destruction and reconstitution of authority and the control of coercion. The variety of experiences in the Somali space shows that when formal and informal institutional frameworks favour old networks of elites with greater ties to local communities, the scope for intervention of disruptive political entrepreneurs is reduced. This shows how marginality in the period of patrimonial politics gave incentives to some local authorities to build defensive arrangements. These later turned into social resources that gave clan elders the means to mediate conflict, control coercion and most importantly, regulate the social use of wealth to prevent enterprising strongmen from recruiting young men to loot local communities and rush to bargaining tables in distant cities to assert a claim to rule Somalia.

A major implication of this observation is that activities that governments, international agencies and activists define as fuel for conflict and appropriate targets for suppression – 'conflict diamonds', smuggling rackets and the like – may play important roles in mitigating conflict and underwriting self-determination. It is not the illegal nature of the transactions that features in this analysis. Instead, the social context of these transactions determines the *local* legitimacy of this activity. The major policy implication for this observation is that wanton international suppression of 'illicit' or 'wartime' commerce can increase the risk of violence and undermine successful efforts at promoting order.

Third, where elites who adapt informal institutions – in clandestine commerce in the case of Somaliland – face competition from new institutions and outside resources, the risk of fragmentation is higher. During Barre's regime, the president attracted followers through offering resources that were autonomous of the social control of the communities from which these men hailed. Violence was more prolonged when predators with outside sources of income attacked. The difference in the north was that legitimate local authorities, especially clan elders, could regulate sources of income for local strongmen and recruit them for fighting off interlopers. Later events demonstrated the same principle. Indeed, Ethiopian authorities recognize that endless 'peace conferences' are a good way to keep Somalia fragmented to ensure it never poses an irredentist threat or that Somali groups develop effective ties to Ethiopia's own separatists. The broad policy implications for this finding are that round-tables, conferences, NGO aid and other 'conflict prevention' measures can intensify conflict and promote fragmentation if they are sought without consideration of the nature of local social control over resources and coercion. Peace talks, for example, can attract militia leaders to Mogadishu, resulting in an increase in fighting that overwhelms local mechanisms that elders use to control conflict (UN 2002, para. 6).

Finally, if local actors can regulate access to resources, and control how those resources are used in order to mitigate freelance exercise of coercion without pressure from outsiders with enticements that give enterprising freelancers other alternatives, they can organize their societies to exploit opportunities in the international economy. The world economy is not favourable to places like Somaliland. On the one hand they remain highly dependent upon diaspora remittances, and they are not attractive places for investment by people who do not share the cultural ties and understandings that are integral to the regulation (and success) of business there. On the other hand, this condition may exempt local people from some of the more disruptive aspects of the world economy such as large foreign firms that have more leverage to defy local interests and priorities. Somaliland citizens may lament the poor state of their economy. But strong ties between their diaspora and the informal regulatory power of local authorities seem to offer at least the possibility of following the paths of UAE, Singapore, Hong Kong, and Lebanon – examples of successful integration into the world economy on the basis of transnational family and clan cultural networks rather than the centralizing administrative projects that scholars of early modern European state-building describe. Moreover, state collapse is not a permanent condition. Otherwise where would states have come from in the first place?

Notes

1. Resolution 1514 in United Nations, http://www.unhchr.ch/html/menu3/b/c_coloni.htm, OAU resolutions in Brownlie (1971).
2. For example, Bayart *et al.* (1999).
3. This contrasts with the analysis of Collier (2000).
4. Karp (1960), p.147. A $14 million annual budget ($65 million in 2005 prices) highlights the tiny capacity of the colonial state.
5. Figures from Adam and Ford (1986), Ministry of Jubba Valley Development (1989). GDP from World Bank (1989), p. 221.
6. Interview with UN official, New York, 8 March 2002.
7. The 1990 figure is from 'Banana Wars in Somalia', *Review of African Political Economy*, 64 (1995), 274. The 1994 figure is from *Maanta* [Mogadishu based UN newspaper], 17 November 1994, 2. See also Menkhaus and Prendergast (1995).
8. Human Rights Watch, *Somalia Faces the Future: Human Rights in a Fragmented Society*, (New York: HRW, April 1995), 40.
9. Colonial Office Peace Handbooks (1920), Drake-Brockman (1912), pp. 125–8.
10. *Laws of the Somaliland Protectorate* (1923).
11. On official support for irredentist groups, see Markakis (1987) pp.169–201.
12. *Bulletin of Somali Liberation Fronts*.
13. Somali Ministry of National Planning (1987) p.10. Foreign consultants and advisors often wrote ministry reports evaluating project development.
14. 'Somalia: Power Struggle', *Indian Ocean Newsletter*, 2 February 1991, 1–2.
15. On structural aspects of commitment, see Feardon (1998) pp.107–27.
16. Interviews, 29 January and 5 February 2002.
17. Interview, 12 March 2002.
18. Samatar, Salisbury and Bascom (1988) pp.81–97. See also Lewis (1962) pp.365–85.
19. Interview, 5 March 2002.
20. 'Somalia: The Rise of the Ogadeni', *Africa Confidential*, 26 January 1989, 3.
21. A complaint in multiple interviews.
22. E-mail correspondence, 19 December 2001.
23. E-mail from an agent of Daallo Airlines, 4 April 2002.
24. E-mail from Hargeisa importer, 26 March 2002.
25. 'The Nation Nobody Knows', *The Economist*, 12 April 2001. A UN employee also notes that private firms collects 'official' financial sector statistics. Interview with UNDP officer, 9 January 2002.
26. 'Somaliland's Economy Survives', *Africa Research Bulletin*, May–June 2001, 14791.
27. Economist Intelligence Unit, *Somalia*, May 2000, 33.

References

'Hunting for Oil in Somaliland', *Indian Ocean Newsletter*, 21 April 2001.
'Somaliland's Economy Survives', *Africa Research Bulletin*, May–June 2001, 14791.
'Somalia: Power Struggle', *Indian Ocean Newsletter*, 2 February 1991, 1–2.
Economist Intelligence Unit, *Somalia*, May 2000.

'Somalia: The Rise of the Ogadeni', *Africa Confidential*, 26 January 1989.
'The Nation Nobody Knows', *The Economist*, 12 April 2001.
Adam, H. (1993) 'Militarism and Warlordism: Rethinking the Somali Experience'. Boston, MA: Boston University African Studies Center Working Papers.
Adam, H. and R. Ford, (1986) 'Somalia: Toward a Revised Rural Development Strategy'. Mogadishu: Ministry of Interior.
Africa Watch (1990) *Somalia, a Government at War with Its Own People*. New York: Africa Watch.
Ahmed, I. (2000) 'Remittances and Their Economic Impact in Post-war Somalia', *Disasters*, 24:4.
Bayart, J-F., S.Ellis and B. Hibou (1999) *The Criminalization of the State in Africa*. London: James Currey.
Brownlie, I. (1971) *Basic Documents on African Affairs*. Oxford: Clarendon Press.
Bulletin of Somali Liberation Fronts (in the author's possession).
Carroll, A. and B. Rajagopal (1993) 'The Case for the Independent Statehood of Somaliland', *American University Journal of International Law and Politics*, 8.
Collier, P. (2000) 'Rebellion as a Quasi-Criminal Activity', *Journal of Conflict Resolution*, 44(6), (December).
Collier, P. (2001) 'Economic Causes of Civil Conflict and their Implications for Policy' in C. Crocker and F. O. Hampson (eds) *Managing Global Chaos*. Washington, DC: United States Institute for Peace.
Colonial Office Peace Handbooks (1920) *British Somaliland* (London: HMSO).
Compagnon, D. (1988) 'Somali Armed Movements: The Interplay of Political Entrepreneurship and Clan-Based Factions' in C. Clapham (ed.), *African Guerrillas*, Oxford: James Currey.
David, S. (1991) *Choosing Sides: Alignment and Realignment in the Third World*. Baltimore, MD: Johns Hopkins University Press.
Del Buono, M. and Mubarak, J. (1999) 'The Macroeconomy of Somalia: A Conceptual View'. Nairobi: United Nations Office for Somalia, March.
Drake-Brockman, R. (1912) *British Somaliland*. London: Hurst & Blackett.
Ertman, T. (1997) *Birth of the Leviathan: Building States and Regimes in Early Modern Europe*. New York: Cambridge University Press.
Feardon, J. (1998) 'Commitment Problems and the Spread of Ethnic Conflict' in D. Lake and D. Rothchild (eds) *The International Spread of Ethnic Conflict, Fear, Diffusion, and Escalation*. Princeton, NJ: Princeton University Press.
Gersony, R. (1989) *Why Somalis Flee*. Washington, DC: US Department of State, Bureau of Refugees.
Gregory, P. (1990) 'Somali Civil Service Reform', Mogadishu: USAID mimeo.
Gundel, J. (2002) 'The Migration-Development Links Study: The Somali Case'. Copenhagen: Centre for Development Studies, March 2002.
Gunn, S. (1987) 'Somalia' in J. Powelson and R. Stock (eds) *The Peasant Betrayed: Agriculture and Land Reform in the Third World* (Boston, MA: OGH).
Hess, R. (1966) *Italian Colonialism in Somalia*. Chicago, IL: University of Chicago Press.
Hoben, A. (1988) 'The Political Economy of Land Tenure in Somalia' in R.E. Downs and S.P. Reyna (eds) *Land and Society in Contemporary Africa*. Hanover, NH: University Press of New England.
Human Rights Watch (1995) *Somalia Faces the Future: Human Rights in a Fragmented Society*. New York: HRW, April 1995.
Hunt, J. (1951) *A General Survey of the Somaliland Protectorate, 1944–1950*. London: Crown Agents for the Colonies.

International Bank for Reconstruction and Development (1957) *The Economy of the Trust Territory of Somaliland*. Washington, DC: IBRD.
Iye, A.M. (no date) *Le Verdict de l'Arbe: le Xeer Issa*, Dubai: International Printing Press.
Jamal, V. (1988) 'Somalia: Understanding and Unconventional Economy', *Development and Change*, 19:2.
Karp, M. (1960) *The Economics of Trusteeship in Somalia*. Boston, MA: Boston University Press.
Kibble, S. (2001) 'Somaliland: Surviving Without Recognition; Somalia: Recognised but Failing?', *International Relations*, 15(5), (August 2001).
Kittermaster, H. B. (1927) 'British Somaliland', *Journal of the Africa Society*, 27(108).
Laws of the Somaliland Protectorate. London: Stevens, 1923.
Lewis, I. M. (1962) 'Lineage, Continuity and Modern Commerce in Northern Somaliland' in P. Bohanan, and G. Dalton (eds) *Markets in Africa*. Evanston, IL: Northwestern University Press.
Lewis, I. M. (1988) *A Modern History of Somalia*. Boulder, Co: Westview.
Lewis, I. M. (1990) 'The Ogaden and the Fragility of Somali Segmentary Nationalism', *Horn of Africa*, 13.
Lewis, I. M. (1994) *Blood and Bone: The Call of Kinship in Somali Society*. Lawrenceville, NJ: The Red Sea Press.
Mansur, A.O. (1995) 'The Nature of the Somali Clan System' in A. J. Ahmed (ed.), *The Invention of Somalia*. Lawrenceville, NJ: The Red Sea Press.
Marchal, R. (1993) 'Les *Mooryaan* de Mogadiscio: Formes de la Violence dans un Espace Urbain en Guerre', *Cahiers d'Etudes africaines*, 130(33).
Marchal, R. (1996) *The Post Civil War Somali Business Class*. Paris: EHESS.
Marchal, R. (1997) *Lower Shabelle: Study on Governance*. Nairobi: United Nations Development Office for Somalia, November 1997.
Markakis, J. (1987) *National and Class Conflict in the Horn of Africa*. Cambridge: Cambridge University Press.
Menkhaus, K. and J. Prendergast (1995) 'Political Economy of Post-Intervention Somalia', Somalia Task Force Report #3, April 1995.
Menkhaus, K. and K. Craven (1996) 'Land Alienation and the Imposition of State Farms in the Lower Jubba Valley' in C. Besteman and L. Cassanelli (eds), *The Struggle for Land in Southern Somalia: The War Behind the War*. London: HAAN Publishing, 1996.
Menkhaus, K. (1989) *Rural Transformation and the Roots of Underdevelopment in Somalia's Lower Jubba Valley*. PhD dissertation, Department of Government and International Studies, University of South Carolina.
Menkhaus, K. (2000) 'Traditional Conflict Management in Contemporary Somalia' in I.W. Zartmen, (2000) *Traditional Cures for Modern Conflicts*. Boulder, CO: Lynne Rienner.
Miller, N. (1981) 'The Other Somalia: Illicit Trade and the Hidden Economy'. Hanover, NH: American Universities Field Staff.
Ministry of Jubba Valley Development (1989) *Final Evaluation Report, Jubba Development Analytical Studies Project*. Mogadishu: Ministry of Jubba Valley Development.
Ministry of National Planning and Coordination (1999) *Plan of Action for Repatriation, Rehabilitation and Reintegration*. Hargeisa, photocopy, July 1999.
Mohamoud, O. (1983) 'Crisis and Decay in an Authoritarian Regime', *Horn of Africa*, 4(3).
Mubarak, J.A. (1996) *From Bad Policy to Chaos in Somalia*. Westport, CT: Praeger.
Nash, M. (1996) 'Contemporary Practices of the United States Relating to International Law – Unrecognized Governments Access to US Courts', *American Journal of International Law*, 90(263), 262–5.

North, D. (1990) *Institutions, Institutional Change and Economic Performance*. New York: Cambridge University Press.

Pérouse de Montclos, M.-A. (2001) *Interprétations d'un Conflit: le Cas de la Somalie*. Bordeaux: CEAN.

Pérouse de Montclos, M.-A. (2002) 'A Refugee Diaspora: When the Somali Goes West' in K. Koser (ed.), *New African Diasporas*. London: Routledge.

Peterson, S. (2000) *Me Against My Brother*. New York: Routledge, 2000.

Protectorate of Somaliland *[various years] Somaliland: Reports*. London: HMSO, 1955–1960.

Prunier, G. (1991) 'A Candid View of the Somali National Front', *Horn of Africa*, 14(1–4).

Roth, M. (1987) *An Analysis of Land Tenure and Water Allocation Issues in the Shalambood Irrigation Zone, Somalia*. Madison, WI: University of Wisconsin Land Tenure Center.

Samatar, A. (1985) 'The State, Peasants, and Pastoralists: Agrarian Change and Rural Development in Northern Somalia, 1884–1984', PhD thesis, Berkeley, CA: University of California.

Samatar, A., L. Salisbury, J. Bascom (1988) 'The Political Economy of Livestock Marketing in Northern Somalia', *African Economic History*, 17.

Somali Ministry of National Planning (1987) *Report on the First Meeting of the Joint Coordination Group for Somalia*. Mogadishu: Somali Ministry of National Planning.

Sommer, J. (1994) 'Hope Restored? Humanitarian Aid in Somalia, 1990–1994', Washington, DC: Refugee Policy Group.

Spruyt, H. (1994) *The Sovereign State and Its Competitors*. Princeton, NJ: Princeton University Press.

Tilly, C. (1992) *Coercion, Capital, and European States, AD 990–1992*. Cambridge, MA: Blackwell.

Tucker, J. (1984) 'The Politics of Refugees in Somalia', *Horn of Africa*, 5(3).

UNICEF (1995) *'Year 2050', The Situation of the World's Children*. New York: UNICEF.

United Nations (2001) *Report of the Secretary-General on the Situation in Somalia*. S/2001/963, 11 October 2001.

United Nations (2002) *Report of the Secretary-General on the Situation in Somalia*. S/2002/189, 21 February 2002.

United Nations Development Program (2001) *Human Development Report: Somalia 2001*. New York: UNDP.

United Nations Security Council (2002) *Report of the Team of Experts Appointed Pursuant to Security Council Resolution 1407 (2002), Paragraph 1, Concerning Somalia*. New York: UN, 3 July 2002.

World Bank (1989) *Sub-Saharan Africa: From Crisis to Sustained Development*. Washington, DC: World Bank.

World Bank (1991) *Somalia: Crisis in Public Expenditure Management*. Washington, DC: World Bank Report 8727-SO.

Yager, T. (2002) 'Djibouti, Eritrea, Ethiopia, and Somalia' in US Geological Survey Minerals Yearbook – 2001. Washington, DC: Department of Energy.

Young, C. (1994) *The African Colonial State in Comparative Perspective*. New Haven, CT: Yale University Press.

8
Multiple Causes of Conflict in Algeria: National Identity, Inequality and Political Islam

Cathie Lloyd

During the 1990s the civil conflict in Algeria cost the lives of some 200,000 people and displaced more than one million, increasing pressure on towns and cities (Norwegian Refugee Council 2004). Political leaders, intellectuals and ordinary people, many living in remote villages, lost their lives and the whole population lived in fear and insecurity. At one level the conflict was between radical Islamists and the existing authorities, but if we probe deeper it becomes clear that the conflict was over political legitimacy, exacerbated by mounting social inequalities. In part, then, the conflict has been about people's efforts to make sense of their identities, gain control over their lives and the direction of their society. Challenges to authority and questions of identity have deep roots in Algerian history but they have become acute in the post-cold war period, precipitated by the economic failure of successive governments and hastily imposed economic liberalization and rapid democratization.

This chapter focuses on violent post-colonial conflicts in Algeria. I seek to establish the relationship between locally constructed identities and global cultural forces and to determine what socio-economic factors lie behind these cultural reasons for conflict. A third area of enquiry is the extent to which global cultural links have framed the source, nature and quantity of political and economic resources received by the various parties to the struggle.

In the first part of this chapter I briefly provide historical contextual material which leads into an account of the years of violence, attempts to build a peace process and the extension of the conflict with the recent uprising in Kabylie. The second part looks at how economic and cultural global flows impact on the conflict, focusing on the growth of inequalities, the role of the diaspora, the new media and radical political Islam as a global force.

Historical background

A major problem in writing about conflict is deciding at what point to locate its origins; indeed, as with all histories, that decision alone can lead to different interpretations. I have chosen a long-term perspective. Algeria experienced an extremely violent colonization, and the post-independence settlement failed to provide any closure on the conflicts which had arisen during this period. Algeria has had a particularly turbulent history: colonized during the second millennium BC by the Phoenicians and Romans, invaded in the seventh century by Arab armies carrying the message of Islam when it became part of the Islamic empire which extended to Spain and Portugal by 711. Algerians still look back with nostalgia to the enlightenment of Islamic Andalusia (Ouahnon 1998). To counter the influence of the Catholic kingdoms in Europe in the fifteenth century, the region became a vassal state of the Turkish Ottoman Empire in the early 1500s. Under Turkish rule, the Arabs and Berbers of Algeria were excluded from government, Turkish became the official language and the country was controlled by a Turkish Dey who divided the country under the rule of *Caids*, usually tribal leaders.

During three centuries of Ottoman rule, the region's economy was integrated into the permeable, mobile society of the Mediterranean. French colonial rule after 1830 brought fundamental changes in government. During decades of resistance and economic hardship, the Algerian Muslim population stagnated at around 3 m and the French military and settlers expanded across the coastal cities and into the hinterlands of Saharan Algeria. Algeria was a French colony between 1830–48, fully assimilated as three departments of France from 1848 until independence in 1962. Colonial settlement deprived the original population of their lands and denied them any rights. The European population grew from 833,000 in 1926 to 984,000 in 1954 forming 13 per cent of the population by the 1950s compared with 6–8 per cent in neighbouring Tunisia and Morocco. By the mid-1950s 79 per cent of this population had been born in Algeria (Stora 1991a).

The war of independence (1954–62) was violent and protracted (Horne 1987; Stora 2002). After independence there was no process of reconciliation, or even recognition of the brutality which had taken place on both sides. In the 1950s only a few accounts of the torture used against Algerian nationalists by the French escaped censorship (Alleg 1958; Sartre 1956; Vidal-Naquet 1962). The responsibility of the French state for colonial violence before and during the war of independence remains controversial. Recent memoirs have documented the atrocities committed against Algerian nationalists, including rape and torture of women (Ighilahriz 2001). Only in 1999 did the French government officially recognize the war (which it had previously described as 'operations' or 'events'.[1] In the following year the newspapers *Le Monde* and *L'Humanité* published the *Appel des Douze* signed by distinguished historians, human rights activists and opponents of the war in the 1950s calling for both sides to accept that atrocities had taken place during the war, and for the French authorities to recognize its use of torture.[2]

Stora points out that the uprising of 1 November 1954[3] emerged from a much older political tendency with its roots in the migrant working class. The short-lived *Etoile Nord-Africaine* (ENA) began a process of reclaiming of Algerian identity and a demand for self-determination (Stora 1994). At independence the erasure of the historic origins of Algerian nationalism in favour of a monolithic construction enabled the *Front Islamique du Salut* (FIS) to pose as the inheritors of the *Front de Libération Nationale* (FLN) in the 1990s and in its turn to deny the legitimacy of a pluralist opposition:

> In Algeria the word 'revolution' is used to characterise this period... But it's a faceless revolution because the names of the main actors of Algerian nationalism have been erased: the image given is that of an anonymous people, standing unanimously behind the FLN, relying on an army which has been militarily victorious. (Stora 1991b)[4]

In order to defuse incipient power struggles the newly independent government awarded generous pensions and other privileges to the heroes of the Revolution, containing class conflict by providing social services such as free medical care, education and subsidized food (El-Kenz 1991; Entelis and Naylor 1992; Moussaoui 1994). According to Moussaoui:

> The population conceived its relationship with the State through a tacit contract. It 'gave' the state its oil, for which it had paid the high price of the blood of its martyrs, it expected to be looked after, for nothing. The state could dispose of its oil as long as it could guarantee in return the redistribution of its revenue in political wages and other gratuities. (Moussaoui 1994)

The majority of Algerians are Sunni Muslims, divided between a puritanical Islam and that of the *mrabtin* and the Sufi orders. Maraboutic Islam was a major support of Algerian resistance to the French in 1830–71, but many active within the FLN at independence were inspired by the austere *salafiyya* movement in the Middle East (Roberts 1993). The constitution provided for Islam to be the state religion but 'it had really implied... the subordination of Algeria's religious leaders to the nation–state' (*ibid*).

Control over Algeria's oil fields was an important aspect of the post-war settlement. Oil was nationalized in 1971 and it grew from a relatively small initial base to become 'the core of the government's energy policy and international relations'(Aissaoui 2001). In the first four-year national economic plan (1970–73) hydrocarbons were used to trigger rapid state-led industrialization, which gave rise to substantial migration to the towns.

Agrarian reform involved considerable struggle. Following independence most of the French colons left and their lands were occupied by agricultural workers, largely pre-empting plans to restructure land tenure according to Islamic convention. Algeria's agricultural resources were concentrated in some 1.5 million hectares, about 13 per cent of which produced cereal, wine and citrus fruits and employed some 80,000 agricultural workers geared to export to France (Adamson 1998). A massive agrarian reform was announced in 1971 and the state seized estates owned by absentees and redistributed 50 per cent of arable land. By 1973 an estimated 3 per cent of landowners still owned 25 per cent of the land. Local landowners were supported by conservative religious groups especially in the eastern area around Constantine (Rouadjia 1990). Small investments in agriculture contrasted with the priority given to industrial growth, and agricultural decline placed strain on the family and its generational hierarchies, disrupting 'traditional' sources of authority (Lawless 1984).

During the 1980s mounting social problems were compounded by economic crisis linked to the falling price of oil, the impact of structural adjustment and political upheavals associated with democratization (International Crisis Group 2001). A strict *sharia*-based Family Code was enacted to placate conservative Islamic interests in 1984. By 1985 increasing unemployment, exacerbated by migration from the countryside, housing shortages and stretched educational resources contributed to disillusionment, especially among the young. Open questioning of the system grew, particularly of the economic reforms which aimed to transform the economy into a diversified and market-oriented system (Aissaoui 2001). In fact the opening up of the private sector led to speculation, misappropriation of resources and social inequality.

There are two dimensions to the dynamic behind this inequality: the growing prosperity of an elite linked to the FLN and the development of a parallel economy. After independence a small bourgeoisie began to form from the remnants of the pre-colonial merchant class, descendants of the tribal nobility and the religious *ulama* and those members of the peasantry who had benefited from a French education (Roberts 1983). This regionally divided class operated through a combination of patron–client relations and clan struggles. Roberts points out that the FLN did not control this class – its influence was mainly through its mass organizations of trade unionists, peasants, youth and women.

The second dimension was the growth of a parallel trading economy, depending on official protection:

> There are few parallels in the rentier world...to the wide-scale conversion of army officers and high ranking cadres into pseudo-private entrepreneurs and predators through privatisation, deregulation of importing, liquidation of local public companies and joint ventures between multinationals and the remnants of state companies. (Dillman 2000)

As chaos and inequality mounted, the government attempted to accommodate conservative interest groups wanting to return to an 'authentic' Islamo–Arabic society[5] while yielding to pressures for democratization and liberalisation. An increasingly tense political climate involved growing industrial unrest, violence and state repression. In this context radical political Islam[6] began to garner support.

Women were the first group to experience the new puritanical climate, which accompanied the rise of radical political Islam. Violence was deployed against women whenever they moved outside their allotted sphere (Lloyd 2005). From the early 1970s women had been targeted in this way – female employees of state-owned factories in *Sidi Bel Abes* were prevented from going to work by men throwing stones. Women living alone were particular targets; in June 1989 a divorced woman living with her children in the southern town of Ouargla was stoned by a mob and her house burned down. The following year women in university halls of residence were harassed by FIS militia who imposed a curfew on them and 'corrected' those who challenged this with the aid of a whip or bicycle chain.

Violence against women was symptomatic of the Islamist challenge to modernity. Women's appearance in public, educated and aspiring to employment was interpreted by Islamists as 'westernization' and during the civil war of the 1990s this developed into mass abduction, rape and killing of women.

The years of violence

In this section I sketch the main events in order to begin to indicate how the conflict of the 1990s took such a complex form with different causes of conflict coming to the fore at various stages.

The population of independent Algeria grew from 10m in 1962 to 30m by 2004, with 60 per cent now under the age of twenty. In the 1960s and 1970s the government kept employment high by absorbing labour into the public sector. The fall in oil prices after 1983, which accelerated after 1986, marked the end of the rentier economy. The government attempted to deal with the crisis though privatization and austerity measures, which involved a catastrophic fall in purchasing power.

Unemployment rose from 16 per cent in 1983 to 19.2 per cent in 1987, and 30 per cent in the 1990s; this was mainly caused by loss of jobs in the public and manufacturing sector. Urban youth was particularly affected. Their main employment was wryly expressed in Algerian Arabic as *hittisme*, or the 'employment' of propping up walls. It was among these young people with frustrated ambitions that the regime's main critics were recruited.

On 5 October 1988 riots broke out in Algiers and rapidly spread through the country. It was essentially an uprising of excluded urban youth, those who wanted work, decent housing and services. The youth were joined by organized labour: the *Union Générale des Travailleurs Algériens* (UGTA) held strikes in the postal services and automobile factories. Contemporary accounts compared the *hittistes* with the youth of the Palestinian *intifada* of 1987 – their youth, their defencelessness compared with the well-equipped police and military who confronted them and the way in which radical political Islamists made political capital out of their demands.

The government reacted with a massive military deployment. Several demonstrations (increasingly led by Islamists) were dispersed, initially with water cannon and tear gas, later with live ammunition. More than 500 protestors were killed and thousands sent to camps in the Sahara (Amnesty International 1993; Entelis 1992b). The political response to these events involved opening up the political arena. A referendum approved a programme of reforms and a new constitution followed in February 1989. This formalized the separation of the FLN from the state apparatus, allowed for the creation of political parties and associations, proportional representation, strengthened executive powers and limited the role of the military in politics.

Two years of fevered political activity followed, independent newspapers were launched and associations permitted. Analysts enthused:

> Only in Algeria has there been a serious commitment to political pluralism... Islamic, civic, secular, feminist, student, labour and farmer groups within civil society have had increasing opportunities to attract a following, develop an organizational structure and formulate policy alternatives. (Entelis 1992a)

In less than two years, fifty new political parties emerged, the most successful being the *Front Islamique du Salut* (FIS). The FIS was established in 1989 as a federation of organizations ranging from charitable organizations to trade unions, professional organizations and *jihadist* groups. They organized through the 'independent' mosques which escaped official control by means of a loophole in the regulations. Ali Behadj was reported as saying: 'We control them all. They are worth ten TV channels, a hundred radio stations... They enable us to reach the real people' (Devoluy 1994).

In June 1990 the FIS won 54 per cent of the vote in local elections (the FLN, 33 per cent) and won control of over 1,265 municipal authorities (1,520 remained with the FLN). The experience of FIS rule has not been thoroughly documented and there are contradictory versions. It focused on cultural questions: clamping down on the use of TV satellite dishes and popular music, cancelling funding for the Oran rai music festival in 1990, and in the following year campaigning against all public performances during Ramadan – culminating in the burning down of a concert hall. There were crackdowns on the use of beaches and alcohol. In some areas women were removed from public employment and banners proclaiming the Islamic republic replaced the national flag (Saadi 1991). Commentators judge the FIS to have been conservative in its attitude to social mores and radical in its attitude to political opposition (Joffe 1998).

The FLN was exhausted as a political force; Ghazi Hidouci (an ex-FLN minister) described it as 'a meeting place of vacuity, artifice and incompetence' (Hidouci 1995). Only the FIS and the FFS (Front des Forces Socialistes) spoke in clear and pragmatic terms and mobilized at popular level. Civil society was highly mobilized, many women participated in demonstrations for and against the imposition of the *sharia* through the Family Code (Amrane-Minne 1999).

Yet the FIS failed to build a broad alliance of social classes that could provide a consensus for lasting social change. Gilles Kepel argues that while the Iranian revolution had succeeded in appealing to the key sectors of unemployed youth, the religious and commercial bourgeoisie and the intelligentsia, in Algeria support for the FIS tended to come almost exclusively from unemployed youth and its electoral support was more of a protest vote (Kepel 2000). This failure may partly account for the intimidation recorded by the *Financial Times* in 1989:

> A climate of increasing 'social terrorism' is being unleashed as FIS militants and their shady *shorta Islamiya* (Islamic police) take the law into their own hands. They have threatened journalists, beaten up women... they have also smashed the windows of bars serving wine and questioned university lecturers about the content of what they teach in history and literature. The courts dare not react. (*Financial Times* 28 November 1989)

Once Islamist parties were recognized as legitimate they could draw on international resources, notably from Iran, Saudi Arabia and Islamic banks which funded social welfare activities (Martinez 1999). Welfare structures were established in the municipalities under FIS control, organizing the sale of cheap foodstuffs and encouraging the building of squatter camps.

On 25 May 1991 the FIS called an indefinite general strike, which although not universally supported, managed to paralyze the streets of the main towns with large demonstrations. Armed Afghan FIS supporters[7] built barricades and organized parallel power structures in some neighbourhoods (Issami 2001). The government announced a state of siege and the strike ended officially on 7 June, although symbolic confrontations continued. By the end of the month thousands of protestors had been arrested including the two senior FIS leaders, Abbasi Madani and Ali Benhadj.

The FIS pushed for early legislative elections and the first round took place on 26 December 1991. The FIS vote[8] was large enough to make it possible to achieve a 2/3 majority in the National Assembly, enough to vote Constitutional reforms. Just before the second round, on 11 January 1992, President Chadli Bendjid resigned; the military stepped in and cancelled the elections. A state of emergency was proclaimed and a *Haut Comité d'État* was set up, presided over by Mohamed Boudiaf, a respected elder statesman who had returned from exile in Morocco.

Accounts of these events differ. Opponents of the regime argue that the shadowy military power led by Major General Khaled Nezzar forced Chadli to resign and cancel the elections, probably at the behest of France:

> According to Hubert Vedrine, Mitterand wanted to help Chadli until the end, hoping that he could escape from the hard-liners without having to ally himself with the fundamentalists. Thereafter, French policy was silent, because the President thought that France would have little if any influence in Algeria or any right to a voice. (Friend 1998)

An alternative Algerian version stresses that part of civil society was broadly in favour of stopping the electoral process. Yahia Zoubir writes: 'a segment of civil society encouraged the military to annul the second round of the legislative elections in January 1992 because of the fears the radical Islamists provoked among many Algerians' (Zoubir 1999). Thousands demonstrated in Algiers on 2 January against the FIS and its concept of an Islamist state (Boudjedra 2002).

In the following weeks the FIS organized large demonstrations but Islamist political activity around mosques was banned and activists were arrested and tried by military tribunals: some 12,000 were interned in prison camps in the Sahara or forced underground (Amnesty International 1997).

Ending elections was controversial, drawing attention to key dilemmas of democratization. Some commentators suggested that while 'controlled' democratization may not be democratic in itself, the outcome might be the establishment of a democratic order (Bouandel and Zoubir 1998). It could also be argued that while Algerian civil society was gradually accepting a plurality of political opinions, the state was not concerned with respect for individual human rights. Those responsible for halting the electoral process claimed that the FIS were committed to undemocratic constitutional changes. The FIS was more like a social movement than a democratic party, it never published a comprehensive manifesto, its members were not allowed to resign. It held that other secular or more moderate Islamic parties should be disbanded (Issami 2001). Ali Benhaj is reported as saying that democracy was 'heresy' and 'as for the secularists, pseudo-democrats, atheists, feminists, francophones and other evil doers, the day when we gain power, we'll put boats at their disposal which will take them to their motherland, France' (Amirouche 1998). He stated 'we did not go to the ballot boxes for democracy'(Roberts 1993). International reactions were mixed. There had been concern about what stance a FIS government might take towards the Gulf War. In January 1991 Ali Benhadj, wearing army uniform, demonstrated at the head of thousands of supporters for the government to arm and transport them to Iraq to defend Saddam Hussein (Amirouche 1998).

US advisers reported that in power, the FIS 'would be unpredictable and dependant on political context' possibly leading to conflict with its neighbours (Fuller 1996). There were fears that Islamist support would spread to the rest of the Maghreb: both Morocco and Tunisia closed their borders and the French anticipated a wave of Algerian refugees. Before the halting of the election the British press reported Iraqi and Chinese support for an Algerian nuclear programme and referred to Algeria as a 'second Iran'. The prospect of such a neighbour on the southern rim of the Mediterranean was alarming for western governments; criticism of the cancellation of the elections was muted.

A period of financial uncertainty followed, during which government officials sought support from Western Europe and the Middle East. By the end of February 1992 agreements were concluded with a group of international banks led by the *Crédit Lyonnais*, and the European Community guaranteed loans.[9]

It is important to acknowledge that the FIS was in harmony with a political logic which had been present within the FLN during the Algerian revolution. This current had promoted the idea of an Arab/Islamic nation while rejecting those Algerian revolutionaries who had attempted to turn the democratic principles of the French revolution against the colonizer. For them Algeria was divided into 'authentic' Algerians and those they saw as apostates (Arab Socialists, Nasserians, Baathists and 'democrats'). They equated the Francophone with Francophilia. The FIS was thus able to portray itself as the legitimate anti-colonial inheritor of the FLN, capitalizing on anti-western feeling following the first Gulf war, and rejecting those aspects of democracy which were perceived as western.

Doubts over the FIS commitment to democracy were reinforced by its links with authoritarian Islamic regimes which were encouraging political Islam:

> The FIS has long had good ties with Saudi Arabia and received a great deal of Saudi funding until recent years when the FIS adopted – rather belatedly – a pro-Saddam position in the Gulf War in keeping with the general mood of the population. (Fuller 1996)

While receiving support from Iran they continued to receive funds from private Saudi benefactors and wealthy businessmen who wanted to stake their money on an Islamic future (Anderson 1998).

Although the interrupted democratization appeared to be an internal Algerian affair, global factors were of crucial importance:

> The political developments of the late 1980s and early 1990s cannot be separated from their international and regional contexts, even though there were no apparent causal connections between the major political

> events in other parts of the world with those in Algeria. The collapse of single-party and single-ideology systems, the discrediting of socialist models, the weakening of nationalist and progressive forces in the Arab world, and the resurgence of 'political Islam' in the Middle East, all of these combined to offer a favourable environment which set in motion the widespread rejection of the FLN's rule and the assertion of long-suppressed ideological, cultural-linguistic and political currents. (Aissaoui 2001)

After the cancellation of the elections the situation became polarized. The two biggest political parties, the FLN and the FFS, allied to defend what remained of the democratic process and to oppose the FIS. But the depth of the crisis became evident when President Boudiaf was assassinated by a member of his bodyguard while giving a speech in Annaba on 29 June.

The imprisonment of its leaders gave rise to a power vacuum within the FIS, filled by radicals backed by armed radical Islamists, many of whom had seen active service in Afghanistan and had experience of guerrilla warfare, the ideas of the Taliban and access to international *jihadist* networks (Kepel 2000). The most powerful of these new armed groups was the *Groupe Islamiste Armé* (GIA), formed in 1992 with the slogan 'No dialogue, no truce, no peace.'

It is thought that initially there were links between the FIS and the GIA, as they cooperated in the bombing of Algiers airport and the offices of foreign airlines in August 1992 (Issami 2001). Like the FIS the GIA operated on cultural and political levels, imposing its vision of a 'pure' Islamic society by violently eliminating Western influences. Its initial targets were the forces of law and order, government officials at all levels or intellectuals (journalists,[10] artists, writers, actors, musicians) who could be associated with the government or with western values (Amnesty International 1997; Haroun 2001–2). Between 1993–5 it targeted state education, sabotaging some 700 schools and murdering more than 200 teachers, calling for a national boycott of schools at the beginning of the 1994 academic year. Its failure was an early indication of the movement of public opinion. The terror extended to people who did not observe the Islamists' dress code: men who were clean-shaven or who wore ties, women without *hijab*.[11] As the insurgents were driven out of the major cities, the conflict moved to the countryside where there were several extremely serious massacres at Rais, Beni Messous and Bentala, peaking towards the end of Ramadan 1997 (Amnesty International 1997). Women were abducted and sexually assaulted, prompting the displacement of many families living in isolated areas (Lloyd 2004; Norwegian Refugee Council 2004).

As the more extreme elements won control of the Islamist opposition, they attempted to isolate Algeria. In 1994 a *fatwa* ordered all foreigners to leave the country by the end of the year. They attempted to internationalize the conflict: in December 1994, an Air France airbus was hijacked at Algiers airport and flown to France, threatening to crash the plane into the centre of Paris. It was diverted to Marseilles and the hijackers were overpowered but lives were lost (Ryane 1997). The following summer a series of bombings in the Paris metro killed eight people and wounded 200.[12]

A silence or an opacity which for many years has surrounded the highest spheres of the Algerian authorities has prevented the decoding of the situation and encouraged rumours (Stora 2001). This gave rise to speculation, expressed in a debate on *qui tue qui* (who is killing whom). The killings were reported in the Algerian and international press without any explanation or political context, compounding confusion. The extent of the massacres contrasted bleakly with government assurances that the situation was 'under control' and that they were defeating Islamist terrorism.

The Islamist militias were not disciplined soldiers and it has been suggested that many of the massacres were attempts to intimidate populations (Martinez 1998). Allegations of government involvement persist, notably by the *Mouvement algérien des officiers libres* (MAOL) and by individuals claiming personal experience of the massacres (Nesroullah 2000; Souaida 2001). They claim that the GIA was created by the Algerian security services with help from the French, but other observers have not confirmed this.[13]

Another possibility was that some of the 5,000 self-defence groups set up to support the armed forces committed violence against the civilian population. They were not subject to rigorous discipline and their loyalty to the authorities uncertain (United Nations 1998).

New/old sites of conflict: Kabylie

Approximately 17 per cent of the population of Algeria are Berbers, more are of mixed Arab and Berber parentage. The long-standing political and cultural project of the Berberist movement promotes the Tamazight language and culture, which had been sidelined at independence in favour of the official definition of Algeria as an Arab–Muslim nation. These cultural issues unified the Kabyle bourgeoisie because Arabization threatened their role in the public sector (Roberts 1980; Lorcin 1995).

The banning of a lecture by Mouloud Mammeri on Berber poetry precipitated the protests of the Berber Spring in 1980. The whole region mobilized: factory workers, village populations, university and school students demanded official recognition of Tamazight. In April 2001 a new uprising took place in the region, following the death in police custody of a young man, Massinissa Guermah. Since then there has been a cycle of protests and violent repression by the authorities, which in turn have given rise to future protests. Both main political parties in the region, the FFS and RCD, were outflanked as their pleas for calm were ignored and their offices burnt down by demonstrators. A constitutional amendment now includes *Amazighite* as one of the three basic components of Algerian identity and it is broadcast on the national radio and television.[14]

Although cultural demands were a prominent factor, the underlying cause of the Kabylie uprisings was a rejection of *la hogra*, the disdain with which the authorities treated ordinary people, combined with social injustice. These issues bind the different elements of the conflict together (Roberts 2001).

The impact of economic and cultural global flows

In the first part of this section I focus on the recent economic situation before examining the most significant linkages between Algeria and the rest of the world. The second and third parts survey the key cultural elements of diaspora and new media. In the final part I examine the impact of radical political Islam.

Hydrocarbons (oil and natural gas) represent 97 per cent of Algeria's exports, 30 per cent of its GDP and 65 per cent of the national budget. The state-owned *Sonatrach* controls the industry although some privatization is being negotiated. Despite these resources the Algerian economy is not robust. Between 1990–5 Algeria's GDP fell by 7.9 per cent and per capita national income virtually halved, from $2860 in 1987 to $1520 in 1997. Borrowing to fund investment, consumption and long-term debt rose to nearly 50 per cent of GDP in 2000. In the mid-1990s Algeria's debt was twice rescheduled through the IMF, World Bank and the EU, on condition that there were major economic reforms and a reduced role of the state (Aissaoui 2001; European Commission 2001). The programme involved the devaluation of the Algerian *dinar* by 40 per cent, abolition of basic food subsidies and privatization. Between 1994 and 1998 nearly 1,000 public enterprises were dissolved and 60 per cent of the public sector workforce lost their jobs (Bouandel 2002). Unemployment nearly doubled during the 1990s; about three-quarters of the unemployed were under the age of 25 (Joffe 2002). Algeria has also become a country of insecure employment: legislation ended permanent employment and introduced fixed term contracts throughout the public sector.[15]

About 14 per cent of Algerians (especially those living in the countryside) live below the official poverty line. Consumer prices have risen by 66 per cent since 1995, while wages have only risen by 45 per cent (UNDP 2002). Public investment has fallen in the social sectors: expenditure on state education as a percentage of GNP fell from 9.8 per cent in 1985–7 to 5.1 per cent in 1995–7 and on health from 3.09 per cent in 1996 to 3.1 in 1999–2001(UNDP 2004). Housing occupation is dense, with a deficit of 1,300,000 housing units. An average of 7.54 people per household in 1987 fell to 6.82 in 20001 (CNES 2003). Despite these problems infant mortality, life expectancy and literacy rates are gradually improving.[16]

Some sectors of society have profited: the rescheduling measures enabled the military to recruit and upgrade its equipment: military expenditure rose from 1.5 per cent in 1990 to 3.7 per cent of GDP in 2001. Before privatization, the state ignored the involvement of public employees in private commercial activities. Algerian migrants could import goods and contributed to a parallel trade based on smuggled goods known as *trabendo*. Privatization has facilitated a parallel economy where payments are made to *submariners*, clandestine entrepreneurs linked to the army and the state.

The civil conflict also benefited leaders of the self-defence groups, created by the government after 1995. They have become a new elite, controlling people and resources in areas where the state had lost control (Martinez 1999). Even some of the Islamist emirs developed their own enterprises from the wreckage of companies they had forced to close down (notably in haulage).

By the early years of the new century, the economic situation seems to have stabilized although the 2002 report of the *Conseil National Economique et Social* (CNES) shows Algeria's growth rate at 2.5 per cent, well below that envisaged to maintain current levels of unemployment. The country does depend, however, on international support.

International linkages

In 1994 eight opposition parties including the FIS participated in a peace conference in Rome, facilitated by the Saint Egidio community and agreed a common platform calling for the 'progressive return of civil peace'. They proposed the re-legalization of the FIS and the freeing of imprisoned activists in return for a gradual end to violence in favour of democratic processes, a transitional government prior to multiparty elections and investigation into human rights abuses (Maddy-Weitzman 1997).

The Algerian government rejected the Rome Platform and President Zeroual focused on secret negotiations with FIS leaders and formalistic exercises such as the drafting of a new constitution and electoral laws (Quandt 1998). This gave rise to a military truce in the summer of 1997 and by 1999 some of the 15,200 militias had surrendered and 6,386 were amnestied. Many of the 150,000 strong self-defence groups joined the regular army to fight the GIA/GSPC. Following the election of President Bouteflika in 1999 a *Concorde Civile* was agreed by referendum.[17] It provided for an amnesty for people who had belonged to proscribed organizations (even those who had killed) but who had surrendered arms and information to the authorities.[18] Their civil rights were suspended for a probationary period of ten years.

Although the FFS and FIS have sometimes made appeals, there has been little enthusiasm in Algeria for international intervention. Delegations from the UN High Commission for Human Rights and the European Parliament have visited since 1998 and recommended the maintenance of dialogue with Algerian deputies (United Nations 1998). This paved the way for Algeria's signature of the Barcelona Declaration and involvement in the Euromed process.[19] Despite continued tensions arising from the colonial period,[20] France is Algeria's closest trading partner, accounting for about one-fifth of export/imports, and collaborating closely on the exploitation of petro-chemicals. France continued to support the authorities under successive governments especially after the *Concorde Civile* in 1999 when they led the way in reopening embassies and resumption of regular flights.

Trade with other European countries, particularly Italy and Spain is becoming increasingly important. In April 2002 Algeria became an associate state of the European Union and the EU now accounts for 62.7 per cent of its exports and 58 per cent of its imports.

Although the USA claims limited influence in Algeria it has been involved in construction since the 1970s, when Algeria wanted to reduce dependence on France. US involvement under President Clinton was cautious: the ex-ambassador to Algeria reminded a congressional committee of Algeria's role in the Iran hostage crisis and its continuing support of Iraq:

> The challenge is for the Algerian Government and people to attain their own goals. Algeria is a country of great promise in the throes of a long crisis. Any action we take is meant to be supportive and in the direction of greater political openness, respect for human rights, marginalization of extremism, elimination of terrorism and political violence, of market reform and of hope for the citizens of Algeria.[21]

With the opening up of hydrocarbons to foreign investment, US involvement has increased, particularly in exploration involving major companies such as ARCO, Exxon, Oryx, Mobil, Sun Oil, Andarko and El Paso. Andarko recently discovered twelve new fields with 2.8 billion barrels of oil in the Sahara,[22] and Bechtel built a 600km pipeline for the BP-Sonatrach partnership. Military aid has also grown; in 1997 the US government approved a $32 m contract for Gulfstream Aerospace to sell radar-surveillance aircraft for use against Islamist militias. In November 2002 the US Export–Import bank approved further guarantees for similar purposes.

The diaspora

Algerians have been migrating in considerable numbers since the 1950s, especially to France, and there have been several waves of political exiles. The divisions within this population are reflected in its attitudes towards their country of origin.

On the eve of independence (1962) there were 410,000 Algerians living in France, and this migration continued in a regulated form during the 1960s as Algerians were recruited into the automobile industry (Samers 1997).

The new government encouraged this migration to earn foreign exchange and alleviate unemployment. A culture of immigration developed as immigration helped to meet individual aspirations and subsidized the family back home. From the early 1970s more and more families were reunited and by 1999 there were some 700,000 Algerians living in France, together with some 1m French citizens of Maghrebi origin and another estimated 300,000 North African Jews (Lanier 1991; Morin 1991). Widespread public hostility towards Algerians has frequently caused tension between the two countries, notably in 1973 when a wave of racism prompted the Algerian government to suspend immigration.

Algerian migrants provided an important resource for the nationalist revolution. They supported Messali Hadj's MNA until 1956 when the newly ascendant FLN became the dominant party (Ali 1986; Meynier 2002). The FLN raised funds through a system of donations and fines for non-respect of their proscription of tobacco, alcohol, patronage of French cafes, non-respect of Ramadan, marriages or circumcisions which had not been sanctioned by the FLN (Ali 1986). There was no well-organized system to support any of the political forces in Algeria during the conflict of the 1990s. The diaspora offered informal support to a range of political movements. Most of the major Algerian parties have offices in France and they are present at major political events. The Algerian government provides for 680,000 registered voters in France and consulates in most countries with Algerian populations open polling booths during legislative and presidential elections (Collyer 2003/4).[23]

The diaspora in France maintains cultural ties, while itself embodying an ambiguous attitude to both Algeria and France. Questions of identity have been important especially for young people of Algerian origin: Adil Jazouli has studied their dilemma:

> We don't consider ourselves completely Algerian or completely French...Our parents are Arabs. We were born in France (and only visited Algeria a few times). So what are we? French? Arab? In the eyes of the French we are Arabs...but when we visit Algeria some people call us emigrants and say we've rejected our culture. We've even had stones thrown at us. (Jazouli 1982)

Research shows that the younger age group identifies as Arabs and Muslims in France in differing ways. Some adapt their religious and cultural practices to the secular French context, while others are drawn to radical forms of Islam. Self-affirmation as a militant Muslim attracts young people who are already subject to social exclusion (Wihtol de Wenden and Leveau 2001). The older generation (especially women) are most active in maintaining family obligations and convey economic and cultural resources back and forth across the Mediterranean. Official remittances for Algerians are low compared to migrants from other countries of the Maghreb.

According to the World Bank's development indicators of 2001 Algerians remittances as a percentage of imports of goods and services increased from 2.79 in 1980 to 8.58 in 1995, during the conflict, falling slightly in 1999 to 7.54. Social remittances are also important: that is, exchanges in goods or services which play an important part in relations between the diaspora and the country of origin (Al-Ali, *et al.* 2001; Lloyd 2006 in press).

The new media

Use of new forms of communication through independent radio, satellite television, mobile phones and the internet have transformed contact between the diaspora and their families and friends in Algeria. Much of this exchange took place through an assertion of a pluralistic interpretation of Algerian culture:

> The diaspora experience . . . is defined, not be essence or purity, but by the recognition of a necessary heterogeneity and diversity: by a conception of 'identity' which lives with and through, not despite, difference, by hybridity. (Gross *et al.* 1994)

Music plays a symbolic and rallying role in bringing generations of the Algerian community together to promote the image of 'a contemporary, relaxed, sophisticated, tolerant, urban Algeria' (Gross *et al.* 1994). At the same time, satellite television and increasingly the internet are crucial to diaspora communications. The expansion of these resources was a key part of the processes of democratization and has begun to break down the uniformity of the state-controlled media (the ENTV).

One of the most striking developments of the 1980s was the emergence of a national independent press. The *Algérie Press Service* (APS) was re-launched, linked to new daily newspapers, weeklies and other magazines all with their own websites. Although these independent newspapers are subject to limited state control, it is relatively rare for newspapers to be banned, although the authorities operate a policy of attrition against those who overstep boundaries either through the courts or by calling in payments for the supply of newsprint.

At independence the government prioritized broadcast rather than print media because of low literacy levels. The French introduced radio in 1926 and in 1947 two radio channels in Arabic and Berber were added. The numbers of radio and television receivers have doubled from 244 per 1,000 population in 1997 to 258 in 1992 and the number of television sets from 112 per thousand in 1997 to 210 in 2000.[24]

The use of radio was well illustrated during the 1988 uprising in Algeria. The Paris-based radio station *Beur FM* mounted a 24-hour news service, using telephoned eyewitnesses accounts. This generated solidarity activities, including the collection of medical and other relief supplies (Radio Beur 1988). Algerian associations in France mobilized through neighbourhoods, cultural groups and political parties. As violence increased, exiles became involved in solidarity movements, aiding new arrivals, agitating for a more open visa policy towards Algerians and for a fairer media coverage. Beur FM now broadcasts regularly to North Africa, claiming 500,000 listeners in France and 10,000 in the Maghreb (more than half of which are in Algeria) and has recently set up a television channel, *Beur TV*. Satellite television is of growing importance, especially in the north, where often home-made satellite dishes can capture French and Arabic channels which challenge the official ENTV (Lloyd 2002).

During the 1980s and 1990s radical Islamists made use of videos and audio cassettes to distribute their message, although as we have already noted, their control of the mosques was a major strategic advantage.

Radical political Islam as a global cultural force

Islam defines a conceptual space as well as a religious belief. The majority of Algerians were practising Muslims and their beliefs coexisted with traditions of tolerance in Algerian society. After independence, austere conservative groups began to emerge. The first was the *Association el Qiyam* (1963) inspired by the work of Hassen el Benna, Quotb and Mawdoudi (Issami 2001). A current group close to the Egyptian Muslim Brotherhood emerged during the 1960s, which despite government repression remained active throughout the 1970s and 1980s, occasionally surfacing to protest. They organized vigilante groups ('commandos for the enforcement of good and the pursuit of evil') who attacked delinquents, threw acid at girls not wearing the *hijab* and tried to ban mixed groups of men and women at university and even in family gatherings.

President Chadli Bendjid acted against these groups and limited their activities to publications, discussion and education meetings based in mosques. In the early 1980s many young men linked to these groups left Algeria to train to support the struggle against the Soviet occupation of Afghanistan.

During the 1990s many people who had been involved in Islamist activities fled Algeria seeking asylum in Western Europe and North America, in some cases forming the basis for activist networks. Afghan veterans had become active within the FIS, playing a leading role in the 1991 insurrection. In the mid-1990s their links with disaffected youth in the diaspora was highlighted with the arrests of important networks, especially in France. Such groups are not hierarchical organizations but have a fluid structure, and they may have been infiltrated by criminal gangs and even the Algerian security services (Quandt 1999).

By the late 1990s a new group, thought to have links to al-Quaida, emerged, the *Groupe salafiste pour la prédication et le combat* (GSPC). It is thought to have been funded largely through the laundering of funds raised through protection and extortion rackets and composed of the more extreme elements of the GIA and even deserters from the armed forces (Salgon 2001). This group had roots in marginal elements of the Algerian diaspora, in Spain, France and the Netherlands where 'educational' videos were circulated of how to manufacture car bombs and kill people using knives.[25] Algeria still views the UK as a base for such groups, and calls for their extradition. It is difficult to document international support for the Islamists: in the early 1990s it was thought that a FIS victory in Algeria was inevitable and in 1993 American diplomats began discreet talks with the FIS leadership through the president of its parliament in exile, Anwar Haddam, based in Washington (Phillips 1995). While the US was apparently unconcerned about an Islamist government in Algeria, the French worried about the conflict spilling over into Maghrebi communities in Europe. The turning point for international public opinion was the outbreak of terror in the summer of 1995, the killing of Trappist monks the following May and the al-Qaeda attacks in Kenya and Tanzania in 1998 and New York in September 2001.

Conclusions

The case of Algeria confirms a multi-causal view of conflict in which global cultural and economic flows are strongly involved. This account demonstrates how economic, cultural and political influences have interacted to produce the recent violence in Algeria. These developments have occurred in a context of global cultural forces – political Islam on the one hand, the attractions of western consumerism on the other. We should bear in mind that global cultural and economic forces do not act in one direction, Algerians are inventing their own syntheses.

Struggles over identity have been an important dimension of the conflict, opening social fissures around different interpretations of history, views about the role of religion in society, linguistic questions and Algeria's relationship with its neighbours to the North, South and East. This chapter aimed to address a number of questions about these struggles for self-determination.

While identities may be constructed or accentuated by local leaders they may also be heavily influenced by global cultural forces. This is particularly true of Algeria, located at the confluence of Mediterranean, Arabic and African influences. These cultural links of affinity take 'Algeria's roots . . . far beyond its geographical frontiers. That is why when we speak of it, our lexicon oscillates between Algeria, Maghreb, Adalusia, Mediterranean' (Gonzalez 1998).

In the post-cold war period new axes of conflict have opened up between the West and Muslim societies. The first Gulf war was a defining moment, as the people of Algeria reacted strongly to the arrival of US troops on Saudi soil and the Holy Places. This event together with the continuing conflict in the Occupied Territories of Palestine, has compounded the sense of injustice expressed in different forms of anti-westernism (Ait-Chaalal 2000). Similar dynamics have been enacted with respect to Bosnia, Chechneya, Afghanistan and the 'war against terrorism' since September 2001. At the same time, the Algerian government cooperated with the Bush government as they had done in the 1970s and 1980s over the US hostages in Teheran. Ties with the EU are also growing in importance through the Euro-Med agreements of 1995 and the Association agreement of 2002.

These multiple historical, cultural and economic ties have profoundly influenced the present conflict. In particular, Algeria's search for a post-colonial, post-cold war identity and the tensions this has engendered can only be understood by reference to global cultural forces.

Important socio-economic factors lie behind the cultural reasons for the conflict. While culture, identity and ideology (especially gender relations, language and religion) define the main contested arenas in the conflict, the legitimacy of the regime would not have been contested so profoundly had there not been widespread popular disillusionment based on mass unemployment and deterioration of social and economic conditions.

Global cultural links may also frame the source, nature and quantity of political and economic resources received by groups supporting or opposing the struggles. The single most important global cultural force shaping the Algerian conflict has been radical political Islam, specifically the influences emanating from Saudi Arabia, Iran and Afghanistan. While the Algerian government received support from countries of the European Union and the USA, the Islamists had well-established sources of funding such as Islamic banks. The third side of the triangle, the democratic opposition, receives little if any funding although they did benefit from political support from abroad, especially from the diaspora.

Migration is an important global cultural and political resource for Algeria. For many years it acted as a safety valve to moderate the rise of unemployment. Migrant communities in France were able to sustain their families at home. Yet it is a divided community: the exile of an important part of the Algerian intelligentsia during the 1990s has increased the ability of the diaspora to distribute information about the country, making increasing use of new media. Radical Islam remains a potent form of protest among disaffected unemployed youth, especially in France.

Algeria is well connected to the Francophone and Arabophone world, and increasingly to Africa through the African Union. But it has been relatively insulated from the Anglophone circuits, which dominate many globalized networks. International NGOS have tended to display myopia to anything other than the conflict between the authoritarian government and Islamist groups. In particular the cancellation of the elections in 1992 tended to obscure the many signs of democratic life which were articulating a new political programme.

The early pluralism of the Algerian nationalist movement of the 1950s was destroyed during the struggle for independence. Neither the French nor the Algerians have fully confronted the implications of this violent struggle. Economic problems since the 1980s created new social pressures to which the authorities failed to respond.

Democratization saw the first signs of a plural civil society which was overshadowed by the emergence of a single political force: the FIS, which many viewed as anti-democratic. In the circumstances of a profoundly divided society the key question was not so much why the 1991 elections were cancelled as why they were planned in the first place. Slowly Algeria is beginning to confront the problem of how to move towards greater participation, accountability and an equitable distribution of national resources. A key aspect is the development of a civil society based on historical precedents suited to Algerian society, which many see not in the identity politics of Berber separatism but in the movement for social justice in Kabylie that has the potential of reaching a wider public. Global cultural forces such as the diaspora, new communications and the wider aspirations of young people can also influence these local aspects positively, but they could equally be undermined by a new generation of *jihadists* returning from the current conflict in Iraq.

Notes

1. Loi adoptée par l'Assemblée Nationale relative à la substitution de l'expression 'aux opérations effectuées en Afrique du Nord' par l'expression 'à la guerre d'Algérie et aux combats en Tunisie et au Maroc' http://www.assemblee-nat.fr/2/2textes-html juin 1999, accessed 25/1/06.
2. Appel des Douze à la condamnation de la torture durant la guerre d'Algérie *L'Humanité* 31 octobre 2000. It was hoped that this official French recognition of the war would enable Algerians to confront their history.
3. This is the date normally given to the formation of the FLN and their first bombing campaign in major Algerian cities.
4. All translations from the French are my own.
5. La *loi no 91-05 du 16 janvier 1991 portant généralisation de l'utilisation de la langue arabe* has since been modified, notably by the recognition of the Berber language by the constitutional revision of 9 April 2002. Article 3 now reads: 'tamazight is also a national language and the State will work for its promotion and development through all its forms of expression and uses in the national territory', www.cg.gov.dz/nouveaute2.htm, accessed 25/1/06.
6. The terminology surrounding Islamic fundamentalism is problematic. Alternatives such as religious activism, integrisme, conservatism, traditionalism or orthodoxy are inadequate and I favour the term radical political Islam which helps to focus on its objectives.
7. Some 3–4,000 Algerians who had fought in Afghanistan during the 1980s were known as Afghans.
8. Most commentators now think that FIS support had peaked: they gained 47 per cent of the votes, but abstention levels were up to 41 per cent. The FFS won all 25 seats in the Kabyle region.

9. *Financial Times* 27 February 1992.
10. The International Federation of Journalists documented 90 killings between 1992–99. Independent newspapers were grouped together in a large building in the centre of Algiers 'la maison de la presse' for safety, although this did not prevent bomb attacks.
11. Amnesty International reported two early cases, a 20-year-old secretary, Karima Belhadj, at the office for national security and 17-year old student Katia Bengana, both shot dead for not wearing the hijab.
12. The GIA claimed responsibility for this attack (*Guardian* 2 October 2002).
13. The French press tends to take a sensationalist line on developments in Algeria, for instance *Paris Match* 9 octobre 1997 on the 'land mafia' and *Liberation* 23 décembre 2002 on alleged involvement of the Algerian army in the slaughter of Trappist monks in 1996.
14. *Loi n° 02-03 du 27 Moharram 1423 correspondant au 10 avril 2002 portant révision constitutionnelle.*
15. Loi 90–11, 11 avril 2000.
16. Fertility rates have fallen from 7.4 in 1970–5 to 2.8 in 2000–05; infant mortality (per 1,000 live births) from 143 to 39 between 1970–2002 and life expectancy at birth risen from 54.5 in 1970–75 to 69.7 in 2000–05 UNDP 2004 'Human Development Report 2004. Cultural liberty in today's diverse world', New York: UNDP.
17. *Loi no 98–08 du 29 Rabie El Aouel 1420 (correspondant au 13 juillet 1999) relative au rétablissement de la concorde civile* http://www.el-mouradia.dz/francais/algerie/histoire/loi_sur_la_concorde_civile.htm, accessed June 29, 2005.
18. Amnesty International reported that about 5,500 armed militia had surrendered. Amnesty International (2000) 'Algeria. Truth and Justice obscured by the shadow of impunity' London: Amnesty International.
19. http://europa.eu.int/comm/external_relations/euromed/bd.htm, accessed 25/1/06.
20. The French loi no 2005–158 du 23 février 2005 which called for the positive achievements of French colonialism (especially in North Africa) gave rise to a major diplomatic incident on the eve of the signature of a Friendship Treaty with Algeria.
21. R. E. Neumann 'Algeria's Turmoil', Subcommittee on Africa of the Committee on International Relations, House of Representatives 105th Congress Second Session, 5 February 1998, http://commdocs.house.gov/committees/intrel/hfa47503.000/hfa47503_0htm, accessed 25/1/06.
22. www.anadarko.com, accessed 25/1/06.
23. Algerian exiles and refugees are now widely spread throughout Western Europe: there are communities in Germany (approx 17,500) Belgium (10,000) Spain (25,128) the United Kingdom (10,672) Switzerland and Italy. Collyer, M. 2003/4 'Algerians in the UK' *Navigation Guide*, London: Information Centre about Asylum and Refugees in the UK.
24. www.earthtrends.wri.org, accessed 25/1/06.
25. *Le Monde* 1 octobre 2001.

References

Adamson, K. (1998) *Algeria. A Study in Competing Ideologies*. London: Cassel.
Aissaoui, A. (2001) *The Political Economy of Oil and Gas*. Oxford: Oxford University Press.

Ait-Chaalal (2000) *L'Algérie, Les Etats-Unis et la France: des Discours à l'Action*. Paris: Publisud.
Al-Ali, N., Black, R. and Koser, K. (2001) 'The Limits to Transnationalism: Bosnian and Eritrean Refugees in Europe as Emerging Transnational Communities', *Ethnic and Racial Studies* 24(4): 578–600.
Ali, H. (1986) *La Septième Wilaya. La guerre du FLN en France 1954–1962*. Paris: Le Seuil.
Alleg, H. (1958) *La Question*. Paris: Editions de Minuit.
Amirouche, H. (1998) 'Algeria's Islamist Revolution: The People Versus Democracy?', *Middle East Policy* V(4, January).
Amnesty International (1993) *Algeria, Deteriorating Human Rights under the State of Emergency*. New York: Amnesty International.
——(1997) *Algeria: Civilian Population Caught in a Spirial of Violence*. London: Amnesty International.
——(2000) 'Algeria. Truth and Justice Obscured by the Shadow of Impunity'. London: Amnesty International.
Amrane-Minne, D. (1999) 'Women and Politics in Algeria from the War of Independence to Our Day', *Research in African Literature* 30(3, fall), 62–77.
Anderson, D. (1998) 'Democratization and Foreign Policy in the Arab World: The Domestic Origins of the Jordanian and Algerian Alliances in the 1991 Gulf War' in M. Kahler (ed.) *Liberalisation and Foreign Policy*. New York: Columbia University Press.
Bouandel, Y. (2002) 'Bouteflika's Reforms and the Question of Human Rights in Algeria', *Journal of North African Studies*, 7(2), 23–42.
Bouandel, Y. and Zoubir, Y. (1998) 'Algeria's Elections and the Prelude for Democratization', *Third World Quarterly*, 19(2, June), 177–90.
Boudjedra, R. (2002) 'L'honneur de l'armée Algérienne', *Le Monde*, Paris.
CNES (2003) '4ème Rapport National Sur le Développement Humain (2002)', Alger: Conseil National Economique et Social.
Collyer, M. (2003/4) 'Algerians in the UK' *Navigation Guide*. London: Information Centre about Asylum and Refugees in the UK.
Devoluy, P. (1994) *La Poudrière algérienne: Histoire Secrète d'une République sous Influence*. Paris: Calmann-Levy.
Dillman, B. (2000) *State and Private Sector in Algeria: The Politics of Rent-Seeking and Failed Development*. Boulder CO: Westview.
El-Kenz, A. (1991) *Algerian Reflections on Arab Crises*. Austin TX: Center for Middle Eastern Studies, University of Texas.
Entelis, J. P. (1992a) 'Algeria in Turmoil: Islam, Democracy and the State', *Middle East Policy*, 1(2), 23–35.
——(1992b) 'The Crisis of Authoritarianism in North Africa: The Case of Algeria', *Problems of Communism*, 41(3), 71–81.
Entelis, J. P. and Naylor, P. C. (1992) *State and society in Algeria*, Boulder CO: Westview Press.
European Commission (2001) 'Relationship between Algeria and the EU', Brussels: European Commission, External Relations DG (unit F4).
Friend, J. (1998) *The Long Presidency. France in the Mitterand Years 1981–95*. Boulder CO: Westview.
Fuller, G. (1996) *Algeria: the next fundamentalist state?* Arroyo Center, Santa Monica, CA: Rand Corporation.
Gonzalez, J.-J. *et al.* (1998) *2000 ans d'Algérie*. Biarritz: Atlantica Editions.
Gross, J., McMurray, D. and Swedenburg, T. (1994) 'Arab Noise and Ramadan Nights; Rai, Rap and Franco-Maghrebi Identity', *Diaspora*, 3(1), 3–40.

Haroun, A. (2001–2) 'Algérie, décembre 1991 "Il Fallait Arrêter le Processus Électorale" ', *Confluences Méditerranée*(40, hiver 2001–2).

Hidouci, G. (1995) *Algérie, la libération inachevée*. Paris: La Découverte.

Horne, A. (1987, first published in 1977) *A Savage War of Peace*. London: Macmillan.

Ighilahriz, L. (2001) *Algérienne*. Paris: Fayard/Calmann-Lévy.

International Crisis Group (2001) 'Algeria's Economy: The Vicious Circle of Oil and Violence'. Brussels: ICG.

Issami, M. (2001) *Le FIS et le Terrorisme. Au Coeur de l'Enfer*. Alger: Le Matin.

Jazouli, A. (1982) *La Nouvelle Génération de l'Immigration Maghrébine: Essai d'Analyse Sociologique*. Paris: CIEMI.

Joffe, G. (1998) 'Algeria in Crisis', London: Royal Institute of International Affairs, Briefing Paper No 48, June.

——(2002) 'The Role of Violence within the Algerian Economy', *Journal of North African Studies*, 7(1, spring).

Kepel, G. (2000) *Jihad. L'Expansion et Déclin de l'Islamisme*. Paris: Gallimard.

Lanier, P. (1991) *Les Nouveaux Visages de l'Immigration*. Lyon: Chronique Sociale.

Lawless, R. (1984) 'Algeria: The Contradictions of Rapid Industrialisation' in R. Lawless and A. Findlay (eds) *North Africa: contemporary politics and economic development*. New York: St Martin's Press.

Lloyd, C. (2002) 'Thinking about the local and the global in the Algerian context', *Oxford Development Studies*, 30(2), 151–63.

——(2004) 'Women in Algeria: Dimensions of a Crisis and of a Resistance' in M. Saad and M. Majundar (eds) *Algeria into the New Millennium: Transitions and Challenges*. London: Intellect.

——(2006) 'From Taboo to Political Issue: Mobilisation against Violence against Women in Algeria and the Diaspora', *Women's Studies International Forum* 28.

——(2006 in press) 'Solidarité des Migrants Algériens en France: une Perspective sur leurs Raports avec leur Pays d'Origine', *Actes du Colloque sur l'état des Savoirs sur l'Algérie*, Institut de Sociologie, Université d'Alger, 19–21 septembre 2004.

Lorcin, P. (1995) *Imperial Identities: Stereotyping, Prejudices and Race in Colonial Algeria*. London: Taurus.

Maddy-Weitzman, B. (1997) 'The Islamic Challenge in North Africa', *Middle East Review of International Affairs*, 1(2).

Martinez, L. (1998) *La Guerre Civile en Algérie: 1990–1998*. Paris: Karthala.

——(1999) 'Guerre Civile et Oeuvres Pies en Algérie', *Critique Internationale* (4, été): 127–37.

Meynier, G. (2002) *L'Histoire Intérieure du FLN*. Paris: Fayard.

Morin, G. (1991) 'Le Mosaïque des Français du Maghreb et des Maghrébins de France' in L. C and Y. Lacoste (eds) *L'Etat du Maghreb*. Paris: La Découverte, pp. 533–7.

Moussaoui, A. (1994) 'De la Violence au Djihad', *Annales HSS* (6, novembre–décembre).

Nesroullah, Y. (2000) *Qui a tué à Bentalha? Algérie, Chronique d'un Massacre Annoncé*. Paris: La Découverte et Syros.

Norwegian Refugee Council (2004) 'Profile of Internal Displacement: Algeria', Geneva: Norwegian Refugee Council, Global IDP.

Ouahnon, Y. (1998) 'L'Esprit de Cordoue' in J.-J. Gonzalez *et al.* (eds) *2000 Ans de l'Algérie*. Biarritz: Carnets Seguier, pp. 151–8.

Phillips, J. (1995) 'The Rising Threat of Revolutionary Islam in Algeria', Washington, DC: The Heritage Foundation.

Quandt, W. (1998) *Between Ballots and Bullets: Algeria's Transition from Authoritarianism*. Washington, DC: Brookings Institution.

——(1999) 'Brookings–Sadat Forum: Algeria', *Middle East Policy*, VI (3, February).

Radio Beur (1988) *Octobre à Alger*. Paris: Seuil.
Roberts, H. (1980) 'Towards an Understanding of the Kabyle Question in Contemporary Algeria', *The Maghreb Review* 5–6 (September–December): 115–24.
——(1983) 'The Algerian Bureaucracy' in T. Asad and R. Owen (eds) *Sociology of Developing Societies: The Middle East*. London: Macmillan, pp. 95–114.
——(1993) 'From Radical Mission to Equivocal Ambition: The Expansion and Manipulation of Algerian Islam 1979–1992' in M. E. Marty and R. S. Appelby (eds) *Fundamentalism Project: Accounting for Fundamentalisms*. University of Chicago Press: Fundamentalism Project, Accounting for Fundamentalisms, pp. 428–9.
——(2001) 'Co-opting Identity: The Manipulation of Berberism, the Frustration of Democratization and the Generation of Violence in Algeria'. London: LSE, Crisis States Programme.
Rouadjia, A. (1990) *Les Frères et la Mosquée: Enquête sur le Mouvement Islamiste en Algérie*. Paris: Eds Karthala.
Ryane, M. (1997) 'Chronique de l'Impure', *L'Algérie Littérature/Action* (7–8).
Saadi, N. (1991) *La Femme et la Loi en Algérie*. Alger: UNU/Wider, Eds Bouchene.
Salgon, J.-M. (2001) 'Le Groupe Salafite pour la Prédication et le Combat (GSPC)', *Les Cahiers de l'Orient*,(62).
Samers, M. (1997) 'The Production of Diaspora: Algerian Emigration from Colonialism to Neo-colonialism 1840–1970', *Antipode*, 29 (1), 32–64.
Sartre, J.-P. (1957) 'Le Colonialisme est un Système', *Les Temps Modernes* (mars–avril 1371–1386).
Souaida, H. (2001) *La Sale Guerre – le Témoignage d'un Ancien Officier des Forces Spéciales de l'Armée Algérienne 1992–2000*. Paris: La Découverte.
Stora, B. (1991a) *Histoire de l'Algérie Coloniale 1830–1954*. Paris: La Découverte.
——(1991b) *La Gangrène et l'oubli. La mémoire de la guerre d'Algérie*. Paris: La Découverte.
——(1994) *Histoire de l'Algérie depuis l'indépendance*. Paris: La Découverte.
——(2001) *La Guerre invisible, Algérie années 1990*. Paris: Presses de Sciences-Po.
——(2002, first published 1993) *Histoire de la guerre d'Algérie*. Paris: La Découverte.
UNDP (2002) *Deepening Democracy in a Fragmented World: Human Development Report*. New York/Oxford: Oxford University Press.
——(2004) 'Human Development Report 2004. Cultural Liberty in Today's Diverse World'. New York: UNDP.
United Nations (1998) 'Report of Panel Appointed by the Secretary General to Gather Information on the Situation in Algeria in Order to Provide the International Comunity with Greater Clarity on that Situation'. New York: United Nations.
Vidal-Naquet, P. (1962) *La Raison d'État*. Paris: Minuit.
Wihtol de Wenden, C. and Leveau, R. (2001) *La Beurgeoisie. Les Trois Âges de la Vie Associative Issue de l'Immigration*. Paris: CNRS Editions.
Zoubir, Y. (1999) *North Africa in Transition: State, Society and Economic Transformation in the 1990s*. Gainesville, FL: University Press of Florida.

9

'External' Aspects of Self-Determination Movements in Burma[1]

Sandra Dudley[2]

Introduction

Burma is beautiful. It has the largest land area in mainland Southeast Asia, mountains and pagodas aplenty, an ethnically diverse population of around forty-five millions,[3] a rich array of natural resources including teak, oil, gas, and precious and semi-precious stones, and before the Second World War was so agriculturally productive as to have been known as the rice-bowl of Asia.

Burma is also troubled. Given United Nations Least Developed Country (LDC) Status in 1987, it now struggles to feed all its people. Numerous ethnic struggles have been ongoing since independence from Britain in 1948, particularly in mountainous areas around the perimeter. There is also a continuing struggle for democracy and for the fall of the military regime in Rangoon. The pro-democracy struggle, its leader Daw Aung San Suu Kyi, and the military regime's generally abysmal human rights record have been internationally well known since 1988, when mass demonstrations were brutally put down by the army. Ethnic issues are less familiar abroad, however, as is the extent to which human rights abuses are often specifically targeted at Burma's non-Burman ethnic groups.

This chapter explores some of the 'external' factors involved in struggles for self-determination in Burma, drawing in cultural, economic and political aspects.[4] The various ethnic struggles are numerous and varied in political objective, but generally have a new secessionist state or membership of a truly federal Burma as their aim. In the pro-democracy movement, there is a struggle for a major change in the values and organization of society. The pro-democracy struggle has been largely peaceable on the pro-democracy side, but not on the part of the military regime.[5] Ethnic struggles, in contrast, have comprised ongoing guerrilla warfare and direct armed conflict on both sides lasting, in some cases, over fifty years.

Trying to separate 'external' from 'internal' factors is artificial and arbitrary. An 'external' factor such as an international non-governmental organization (INGO) working inside Burma, for example, is and remains 'external' in so far as its core personnel, objectives, values and financial backing come from 'outside' and are likely to be in step with many 'international' attitudes concerning human rights, human development, and so forth. But the relationship between this INGO and 'insiders', be they HIV-infected villagers, local military officers or senior officials in Rangoon, is neither unidirectional nor momentary. The 'external' resources, values and core experience that stem from contact with the INGO are not received impassively and neutrally: 'internal' responses, attitudes and values not only play a huge part in how external influence is perceived and reacted to, but also feed back to the 'external', perpetuating a complex, fluid relationship in which influence is mutual.

Background

Burma gained independence in 1948.[6] Since 1962, despite various changes in leadership, the government has been military.[7] The population is highly diverse, and *Ethnologue* lists 109 languages.[8] The ethnic majority consists, just, of Burmans, but other groups are numerous in Burman areas and, mostly, in the mountainous regions around the Burman centre.

In 1988, after years of isolationist government, Burma was at an economic low point. The Burmese army, the *Tatmadaw*, responded brutally to pro-democracy demonstrations led by students and Buddhist monks; perhaps 10,000 people were killed.[9] International coverage was slight compared to reporting of the later Tiananmen Square massacre in China, but sufficient to cause outrage. Meanwhile, inside Burma one repressive military regime was replaced with another, the State Law and Order Restoration Council (SLORC). In 1990, the SLORC held a general election in which a landslide victory was won by the National League for Democracy (NLD), led by Daw Aung San Suu Kyi. The NLD's victory was internationally recognized and various resolutions of UN General Assembly mandated senior UN officials to maintain dialogue with Daw Aung San Suu Kyi and the NLD as well as with the SLORC, but the election result was never honoured by the military regime.

The new government – that in 1997 transmogrified into the State Peace and Development Council (SPDC) – was little better on human rights, but it did attempt to modify Burma's economic isolationism. It intended to open up areas of the economy to the private sector which would in turn, it was hoped, lead to some economic opening up to the outside world. Taylor suggests that there was an intention inside Burma to facilitate Western investment from that point but that this was quashed by the political and economic isolation imposed on Burma by the USA, Japan and most of the

European Union (EU) in response to 1988's events: 'Ironically, the end of Burma's self-imposed isolation led to a new isolation, imposed from the outside in an attempt to force from office the new military government' (Taylor 2001c, p. 5).

However, as Steinberg points out, failure to open up Burma's economy was due too to fundamental Burmese mistrust of the private sector, and the fact that for so long and in colonial times especially, the economy and especially the private sector was dominated by outsiders (Indian, British, Chinese): 'political and economic xenophobia feed each other' (Steinberg 2001, p. 45).

Economic and humanitarian problems

It is impossible to write about Burma's economy without an apparently endless series of caveats. As Steinberg explains:

> many statistics are politically correct though lacking in objectivity, some are inaccurate, many are plans that often are simply hopes, some use the official and unrealistic exchange rate, and there are enormous gaps in the data. (Steinberg 2001, p. 44)

By 2000, per capita GDP at the realistic unofficial exchange rate was US$118, and US$1,200 in terms of purchasing power parity (*ibid*, p. 45).[10] Burma's economy has minimal formal activity beyond agriculture, 34.4 per cent of GDP in 2000. Other sectors are stagnant, and all are 'constrained by political instability, a lack of access to capital, poor physical and social infrastructure and the deteriorating macroeconomic environment' (Burma Economic Watch June 2001). In 2001 economic growth 'measured in inflation-adjusted international dollars, became negative' and this was prior to the more recent crisis in the Burmese banking and financial sector (Bradford 2004).[11] Overall, continued growth is unlikely 'without substantial and far more comprehensive economic reforms and foreign assistance' (World Bank 2000). But international support for economic reform is unlikely while foreign debt arrears are so large and without significant political reform (the responses of Japan being a major exception). Furthermore, Collignon estimates that drug revenues to the regime and its allies reach more than half a billion dollars, or US$13 per capita. At market exchange rates this is approximately 20 per cent of official GDP, and over twice the Burmese regime's declared revenue in 1996–7 (Collignon 2001, p. 86).

Other indicators demonstrate the extent of Burma's humanitarian problems. Average life expectancy at birth is 55 (compared with 69 in the East Asia and Pacific region overall); 40 per cent of the population have no access to healthcare, clean water or sanitation; 70 per cent of children do not complete primary school and mortality rates are among the worst in Southeast Asia (infant mortality: 94/1,000 live births; under-five mortality: 147/1,000 live births; maternal mortality: 232/100,000 deliveries).[12]

Burma's human rights record is also appalling; the regime is regularly indicted by international organizations as one of the world's most repressive regimes, with its failure to recognize freedom of speech, its extensive use of forced labour, its closure of universities in order to minimize dissent and the widespread occurrences of political persecution, imprisonment without trial, summary execution, rape and so forth. Meanwhile, HIV/AIDS and other health issues have become increasingly urgent. In, and mostly from, the ethnic areas there are also large numbers of internally displaced persons (IDPs) and refugees. Refugees and migrants now outside Burma include over 250,000 'Rohingyas' (minority Muslims who fled in 1991–2 from Burma's Arakan [Rakhine] State to Bangladesh and whom the UNHCR has since been attempting to resettle in Burma),[13] plus, by July 2001, there were over 136,000 Karen and Karenni refugees and up to 750,000 illegal immigrants in Thailand (BurmaNet 2001).

The ethnic groups

Ethnic diversity combined with the colonial legacy is variously interpreted (Taylor 1987; Gravers 1993; Smith 1991/1999) as a major factor in the struggles ongoing since 1948 in Burma's non-Burman areas. The extent of armed ethnic opposition in Burma has been said to surpass 'even a Lebanon, Yugoslavia or Afghanistan in its complexity' (Smith 2001, p. 32; see also Smith 1991/9). Loss of central control (or the illusion thereof) is intolerable to the military regime, and while a large number of groups have now reached ceasefire agreements with the Burmese, others fight on, using weapons from various sources (particularly Cambodia) paid for by teak and other smuggling revenue. However, the ethnic groups now have significantly less money, partly because of loss of territory to the Burmese army in and since 1997, and partly because on both sides of the border insurgent groups have been increasingly squeezed by Burmese political activity and, in the case of the Thai–Burma border groups, by a reduction in official Thai sympathy to their cause.[14]

Of those groups that have reached ceasefire agreements, among the most sizeable and significant are the Kachin Independence Army (KIA), the New Mon State Party (NMSP) and the Shan State Army (SSA). Areas affected by ceasefires have to a limited degree opened or are in the process of opening up to outsiders, including INGOs. This has made ethnic ceasefire groups reluctant publicly to support the NLD. But ceasefires have not spread all over country, and progress even in ceasefire areas is slow.

Ethnic parties and organizations consider it is the non-Burmans who 'have always paid the highest price for the political volatility in the country at large' (*ibid*), as evidenced by internal displacement and outpouring of refugees on a massive scale particularly after 1988. Nonetheless, internationally, ethnic hardships and struggles have received less coverage and sympathy than has the general pro-democracy cause. Perhaps this is because the ethnic situation is or appears to be so much more complex and entrenched, or perhaps it has less obvious appeal to simplistic ideas of right and wrong. Whatever its cause, it is a relative neglect that the ethnic groups feel sorely.

Narcotics

Some Shan and Wa groups are involved in major narcotic production and sale.[15] Until the late 1990s, Burma was the world's largest opium producer, and in 2001 it regained this title, after the Taliban's success in eliminating 75 per cent of opium production in Afghanistan (*FEER* 2001). Burma probably produces well over 2,000 tonnes of opium a year, supplying most of the heroin consumed in the USA and a large proportion of that used in Europe, together with a large amount of that destined for China.[16] There is insufficient evidence to prove the military government's involvement in narcotics (although see *The Nation* 2001b) but without doubt its local agencies benefit.

Macro-political and macro-economic external factors: an overview

International views: the West

Since 1988, international views have ranged from a Western human rights perspective in which Burma symbolizes a good-versus-evil fight for democracy, to the more opportunistic stance taken by some private companies and governments. The appointment in 1992 of a UN Special Rapporteur on Human Rights in Myanmar was a sign of the level of continuing international concern (Lallah 1998). A major investigation into forced labour practices in Burma was also begun by the International Labour Organization (ILO), which reported in 1998 (Smith 2001, p. 20).[17]

An increasingly strong movement in the West has been lobbying for recognition of the 1990 election result and for general democratic change. This movement comprises both Burmese exiles and foreign activists. It has been strongest and most successful in the USA, partly because a greater number of exiles have sought refuge there, partly because the US government can take a strong human rights line as it has little strategic interest in Burma (except perhaps as a minor stage for playing out wider US–China issues),[18] and partly because of the effectiveness of technological tools such as the Internet.

Activist groups based in the USA and elsewhere have drawn an analogy between Burma and South Africa in their attempt to convince Western governments that trade sanctions would be effective against the Rangoon regime. They also have an articulate, powerful figurehead in Daw Aung San Suu Kyi, and both she and the South Africa analogy have been used as powerful symbols in whipping up popular opinion and the anti-SLORC/SPDC lobby in the West. Yet since 1988, not much has changed for the better inside Burma. Despite

> the opening of the door after 1988, Burma remains . . . very isolated and inward-looking . . . international points of contact and leverage have been

> relatively few. The reality is that military rule has continued, despite the groundswell of foreign support for the pro-democracy movement. Indeed, among postcolonial states in Asia, Burma stands out as a country where international expectations have been most confounded. (Smith 2001, p. 19)

China and South and Southeast Asia

China remains of great significance to Burma. Their cross-border trade reached US$2 billion in 1999 (Kynge and Kazim 2001). China is also the SLORC/SPDC's largest arms supplier: between 1989 and 1996, China provided Burma with military hardware worth US$1.4–2 billion (Rüland 2001, p. 142). As Steinberg suggests, China's support for Rangoon is probably due to a number of factors, including

> China's internal economic liberalization policy, and the strategic importance of Burma, especially to south-west China, as a potential market, supplier of raw materials, an access to the Bay of Bengal, and as a buffer state on the still unsettled and disputed north-east Indian border. (Steinberg 2001, p. 49)

There are also many Chinese immigrants in Burma, and they constitute 20 per cent of the population of Mandalay.

China's support for Rangoon has had a number of influences on other countries in the region. India's concern about China's use of Burma, together with the increasing and associated influence of Pakistan, must, for example, be a major reason for the softening in India's tone towards the Burmese regime. Further east, China's involvement was undermining Thailand's virtual monopoly of border smuggling into and out of Burma. Moreover, ASEAN in general is anxious about Chinese influence in Burma (Munro 1994), fearing that isolating Burma would drive it further into China's arms, although ASEAN's 'constructive engagement' policies have, it is argued, hardened the Burmese position as much as, if not more than, the West's confrontational policies (Rüland 2001).

Meanwhile, Burma's military regime's following the 'Indonesian [Suharto] model' of government has allowed them to survive in power. Indeed, just as to many of their neighbours, this model seemed attractive 'as a means by which economic development can take place in a riven society such as that of Indonesia or Myanmar...without threatening the ongoing basis of military dominance over the state' (Taylor 2001c, p. 11). This approach is unacceptable to western governments but not to China and most ASEAN nations. Thus Burma's post-1988 attempt to overcome isolation, while it may not have succeeded in the West, did so nearer to home. Its joining of ASEAN in 1997 was seen as a considerable success both for Burma and for the pre-existing members of ASEAN.

Nonetheless, frictions with Burma's neighbours, especially Thailand, remain. Since 1997 there has been an increased number of border disputes between the two countries. Furthermore, Thai anxieties about Burmese refugees have heightened. Both the Thais and the United Nations High Commissioner for Refugees (UNHCR involved from 1998 onwards) have been talking hypothetically for years about repatriating them. In 2001 it was reported that Thailand was attempting to persuade Unocal and the Petrol Authority of Thailand (PTT), amongst others, to help set up jobs in Burma to which refugees could return (*The Nation* 2001a). Thai anxieties about illegal Burmese immigrants have also increased, especially since Thailand's financial crisis of 1998. There is also greater resentment of Burmese migrants for the diseases (malaria, HIV/AIDS) they are perceived as spreading.

The Thai military has at times been supportive of its Burmese counterpart in and since 1988. This has been opportunistic: the Thai logging ban in 1989 (due to increasing deforestation in teak forests) meant a need for new teak sources for Thai logging firms, most of which were said to be close to the Thai military. This has also meant a negative change in Thai military and official attitudes towards Burma's ethnic opposition armies, now seen as impediments to the trade of teak and other goods. Meanwhile, other ASEAN countries have been concerned to balance Thai dominance in mainland Southeast Asia. Singapore, for example, has been keen to boost its contacts with Burma, and in the 1990s became one of the regime's main arms suppliers and the second largest foreign investor.

The external and the internal (i): inside looking out

A crucial element in the lack of impact on Burma of external factors is the regime's self-image and views of its country and the outside world. The regime portrays Burma as the 'Yugoslavia of Asia', with all that implies about the 'potential for "Balkanization" and political break-up after the [ethnic] violence that erupted after independence' (Smith 2001, p. 21). It has also been claimed that officially becoming a LDC in 1987, ranked alongside the poorest African countries, was 'a major blow to national pride and self-esteem' (Taylor 2001c, p. 7). However, the military regime actively lobbied for LDC status in order to receive debt relief and lower interest rates, despite their adult literacy rate technically being too high for them to qualify (Steinberg 2001, p. 42). Meanwhile, the numbers in the Burmese military have doubled to 400,000, so that Burma now has 'the largest standing army in South-East Asia' (*ibid*, p. 41). In general, while foreigners may dismiss the pronouncements of the regime as mere, often laughable, propaganda: 'it is... likely... given the insularity of the leadership... that the senior levels actually believe themselves to be under siege and the state in danger of disintegrating' (*ibid*, p. 43).

Indeed, it is the regime's paranoia that perhaps plays the greatest role in its reaction to external factors. The regime's difficulties in dealing with criticism, both internal and external, are admitted privately by anonymous government officials themselves. In the context of criticising the approach of the NLD, for example:

> [w]hat such people warned is that if you confront – even through the tactics of non-violence – a military government that is trained to act according to military principles, then it will always react this way. Confront it, and then it will confront you back...the state of siege mentality is maintained. (Smith 2001, p. 28)

One might add that the international lobby for change has not always recognized the regime's sensitivity and has contributed to the confrontational and non-dialogical nature of most exchanges inside, and concerning, Burma. Furthermore, foreign governments and activists as well as elements within the Burmese opposition itself have not always recognized or acknowledged the extent to which the military regime, while still abhorrent in a great many respects, has moved in some new directions since 1988 (for more on these new directions, good and bad, see Smith and others in Taylor 2001a; see also Fink 2001). Indeed, some have argued that international condemnations of Burma over a period of years have made things worse:

> In a world in which the army saw the country as beleaguered and friendless, and where within the country itself there were perceived to be political and military forces allied with hostile external forces, the extreme of suspicion this generated led to an inability to consider alternative forms of political behaviour other than armed force, and solidarity within the officer corps took precedence over any other consideration. (Taylor 2001c, p. 9)

Suspicion of the West and of outside criticism and 'interference' generally is also related to a more culturally entrenched Burmese nationalism, even xenophobia. Daw Aung San Suu Kyi, for example, has been repeatedly denounced since 1988 in the government-controlled press and threatened with deportation because of her marriage not only to a foreigner, but to a citizen of the former colonial power. Steinberg alleges that the SLORC/SPDC have deliberately exaggerated the xenophobia that already existed in Burma, partly in response to foreign condemnation of the military government, partly in order further to vilify Daw Aung San Suu Kyi and her foreign support, and partly further to condemn the external contacts of many of the ethnic opposition groups. The end result is a paradox: the SPDC is trying to encourage tourism and foreign investment, yet simultaneously it puts much effort into denouncing foreign influences 'seen to be destructive of what the authorities believe to be Burmese (read Burman) culture' (*ibid*). Yet, ironically, foreign economic and other leverage is actually very limited.

Daw Aung San Suu Kyi was awarded the Nobel Peace Prize in 1991, further enhancing an impressive international reputation that she has used effectively as a lobby instrument outside Burma. She has been regularly interviewed by foreign journalists, diplomats and others (between often very long periods of restrictive house arrest) and in the past has routinely requested international trade sanctions, no aid or investment, and no foreign tourism. But this use of her influence on Western governments and public opinion has been controversial within the Burmese opposition. Her position was formerly that any aid or investment would strengthen the Burmese army, but others felt perhaps it would hasten a rise in living standards and thus facilitate social and political change. Ma Thanegi, for example, a former political prisoner and member of the NLD, wanted Daw Aung San Suu Kyi to use her influence 'to win Western aid and, through such a process, begin dialogue with the government over the greater issues of transition' (Smith 2001, p. 28; see also Ma Thanegi 1998). At least one Western diplomat in Rangoon suggested in 1999 that the increasing difficulties and lack of progress inside Burma were placing Daw Aung San Suu Kyi in a difficult position in terms of her relationship with the international community; the more some elements within the NLD pushed for compromise and dialogue with the military regime, the more Daw Aung San Suu Kyi might worry 'that diminishing her demands might diminish her international status and Gandhi-esque aura and the whole impetus of her movement might be damaged' (anonymous diplomat quoted in the *Bangkok Post*, 7 May 1999, cited in Smith 2001, p. 30). More recently, however, Daw Aung San Suu Kyi has been claimed from some quarters to have been projecting a neutral stance on sanctions (Anon. 2002).

On the humanitarian side, compared to Burma's needs 'involvement by UN agencies and INGOs has been relatively small' (Tegenfeldt 2001, p. 114) partly because of concern not to bolster the military's hold on Burma, and partly because of the government's own xenophobic unwillingness to encourage foreign NGOs.

Nonetheless, as the 1990s progressed, Burma became more open to 'humanitarian and development programmes at... community level' (Smith 2001, p. 23). UN agencies have gained greater access, especially in areas such as HIV/AIDS education, anti-narcotics programmes, reforestation, water and sanitation. Post-1993, other groups like Médécins Sans Frontières (MSF) and World Vision were also allowed back into the country (*ibid*).[19] Most agencies involved inside Burma work in health-related areas. Their position is difficult: they receive both international criticism for being involved in Burma in the first place, and obstruction from officials inside Burma. They have also been heavily criticized by Daw Aung San Suu Kyi, who has argued that their assistance programmes help only a relative few.[20]

In general, views inside Burma have stemmed from fixed positions on *all* sides. In 1998–9, for example, the possibility was mooted of a joint UN-International Monetary Fund (IMF) initiative 'to develop a strategy for the future economic development of the country, coupled with a degree of political reconciliation' (Taylor 2001b, pp. 3–4). This initiative was rejected almost instantly, however, by both the military regime and the NLD. So what prognosis is there for Burma? Taylor suggests it is unlikely to change in the way recently witnessed in Indonesia. Not least among the reasons for this is the economy. The Indonesian economy is:

> deeply imbedded [sic] in the structures of the global economy and the ability of its financial institutions to resume economic growth and development are dependent upon support from the International Monetary Fund, the Asian Development Bank, and Western governments and financial institutions, thus ensuring that these bodies have a degree of leverage on events in Jakarta. (Taylor 2001c, p. 13)

But in Burma's case, no similar leverage exists. Meanwhile, according to Taylor, as

> those with the means in the West refuse to engage themselves in Myanmar's affairs at levels more effective than the rhetorical, Myanmar's neighbours are temporarily unable to assist the process of change to any significant degree [as a result of the economic crashes of the 1990s]...Being shunned by the West costs the regime little, but denies the society the capacity to develop and change. (*ibid*)

Steinberg, however, considers that despite the Burmese xenophobia manipulated and magnified by the regime, the real potential dangers to the country are not external: 'rather, they may emanate from the xenophobia that could be directed at internal foreigners should there be any major economic crisis' (2001, p. 51), particularly Burma's Chinese community. He suggests that, as in Indonesia, the regime may try to direct dissatisfaction towards resident Chinese. Economically, foreign investment has lessened since the late 1990s, not least because the Asian financial crisis made it increasingly hard for ASEAN countries to maintain their earlier levels of investment.[21] At the same time, the attitudes of the international community continue to be ineffective and contradictory. Radical positions on human rights such as the stance taken by the USA make gradual, incremental progress difficult, as Steinberg says: 'continually calling for the recognition of the results of the May 1990 elections that resulted in the overwhelming NLD victory' means the USA

> has de facto recognized the NLD as the legitimate government. [Furthermore], by continually and stridently advocating the amelioration

> of the plight, however tragic, of Aung San Suu Kyi, and attempting to secure her future role in a new administration, [the USA] has personalized its foreign policy. (Steinberg 2001, p. 55)

This personalization is unhelpful, as historically and traditionally power in Burma has been in any case a highly individualized phenomenon based on personal charisma, and historically there has been 'a strong tendency for alliances to collapse as authority becomes focused on a leader or small group' (Steinberg 2001, p. 56).

Furthermore, the USA's stance has divorced it from ASEAN on this issue, although admittedly Burma remains a relatively low priority for nations on all sides of the argument (with the exception of Thailand). Nonetheless, the fact remains that USA policy, driven by a core group of congressmen and an effective lobby of Burmese exiles and American activists, is unlikely to change until there is a change of government in Rangoon. But this, as Steinberg admits, seems unlikely without a major uprising on the streets of Burma, which presently seems a remote possibility (Steinberg 2001, p. 57). Foreign investment or sanctions seem unlikely alone to bring about transition to democracy in Burma, but so too do the confrontational stances taken by Western governments and by sections of the political opposition in Burma and abroad. Indeed, such stances may contribute only to an increased divide both between the Burmese regime and foreign governments and agencies, and between Burmese people inside Burma and those living in exile beyond Burma's borders.

The external and the internal (ii): outside looking in

'Outside looking in' includes various exiled communities; foreign and foreign-influenced non-governmental organizations (NGOs) and foundations in Burma, on its borders and beyond; international activist, academic and journalistic communities; the Internet and other media; flows of capital, arms, drugs and consumer goods to and from both the military regime in Rangoon and those groups in opposition to it. It also includes large-scale assistance programmes, policy and action (or lack thereof) on trade with, and economic sanctions against, the Burmese regime; the roles of the UN and other international organizations, and specific regional concerns. Only some of these outside factors, particularly those concerning exiles, activists and the Internet, are explored here.

The role of new media

The most potent means by which exiles, non-Burmese NGOs, interested foreign individuals and others are drawn into closer entanglements not only with each other but also with wider external factors, is computer mediated communication (CMC),[22] which includes email, the world-wide web, bulletin boards and Internet newsgroups. Nowadays, such phenomena are hardly new or strange to many people around the world, and the CMC concerned with the subject of Burma generally provides little exception. One specific factor, however, is that Internet access is virtually impossible for almost everyone inside Burma. The private ownership of a modem (and even a fax machine) requires a special licence that very few are granted (violation of this requirement is punishable by 15 years imprisonment; see Fink 1997) and other, public means of accessing the information superhighway are virtually non-existent.[23]

The CMC discussed here is thus very much an external factor. It is primarily a tool central to the work of NGOs, activists, academics, journalists and others. Indeed, it could be argued that CMC provides the locus for a virtual community of those originally from, or at least interested in, Burma. This in itself has significant impact on those who are *outside* Burma but trying to have an influence on what is happening *inside*. Indirectly, therefore, CMC may have some impact on what happens inside Burma, insofar as it may influence other, non-CMC-based actions and alliances of dissidents, activists, NGOs and others in the world beyond Burma's borders. Directly, however, 'the inside' is both little influenced and poorly represented by CMC. Exceptions include Internet postings by sections and agencies of the Burmese government, particularly its embassy in Canada, and regular inclusion in news bulletins not only of reports carried by foreign news media but also of items in the *New Light of Myanmar*, the Burmese government's own English language newspaper published in Rangoon. Furthermore, 'old media' in the form of radio stations such as the Burmese language services of the BBC World Service, Voice of America, Radio Free Asia and the Norway-based Democratic Voice of Burma, do translate and feed back into Burma news stories and occasionally opinions thereon to have come out of Burma, picked up from Internet reporting as well as from telephone and face-to-face interviews. Nonetheless, the fact remains that for the vast majority of 'ordinary' people inside Burma, be they members of ethnic groups, participants in the pro-democracy struggle, members of the army, or anyone else, 'new media' such as the Internet have little if any impact.

The nature of Burma-focused CMC: content and objectives

That CMC is here primarily an external phenomenon does not mean it is without major significance. CMC is the main means by which disparate, globally spread individuals and groups outside Burma, Burmese or foreign, keep themselves informed, educate others, maintain contacts with each other and, in some cases, organize political opposition activities.[24] There is personal, daily use of email, plus various Burma-focused websites and, perhaps most widely used and significant of all, BurmaNet,[25] a list-server sending out daily news bulletins to subscribers all around the world, its moderator based in Bangkok but its funding American (the Burma Project of George Soros's Open Society Institute [OSI]). BurmaNet was formerly associated with a website, Orchestra Burma, 'dedicated to representing organizations working for democracy and human rights inside Burma' (http://www.orchestraburma.org).[26] Orchestra Burma devoted itself to providing information and links relevant primarily to indigenous organizations; it did not carry information about foreign activist groups or NGOs. The vast archive that is the Online Burma Library (OBL; http://www.burmalibrary.org/) has, along with its other coverage, now largely taken over the role of providing access to ethnic groups' material and views.[27] Other websites more significant than Orchestra Burma include the Free Burma Coalition (FBC; http://www.freeburmacoalition.org), the OSI's Burma Project (http://www.burmaproject.org), and the Burma Fund (http://www.burmafund.org).[28]

These last three cover subjects ranging from political opposition views, human rights abuses in Burma and other news, activism, programmes and scholarships in the USA or elsewhere open to exiled Burmese students, and cultural and economic information concerning Burma and her peoples. All are USA-based and, probably, exiles-in-the-USA-dominated in terms of both adding information to and using the sites. BurmaNet and all the websites mentioned oppose the military regime in Rangoon, though specific objectives, approaches, styles and balance vary. Although still opposed to the regime, the Burma Fund and Burma Project websites and BurmaNet are more neutral in tone than the FBC website, especially with regard to different views within the exiled opposition. BurmaNet aims to disseminate news and information, including that put out by military sources in Rangoon, although it does also occasionally provide its own editorial commentary on certain news stories or articles, especially if they are critical of Daw Aung San Suu Kyi herself or the mainstream democratic opposition in general. That is, BurmaNet will always carry a story critical of Daw Aung San Suu Kyi and/or the NLD – be it one originating with the regime or with some foreign journalist's or academic's critical assessment – but will often add its own opinion. As a result, BurmaNet usually gives the impression of being a relatively objective news vehicle, but occasionally voices opinions that demonstrate an underlying concern to support, and minimize criticism of, opposition orthodoxy centred around Daw Aung San Suu Kyi (albeit that much of that orthodoxy is, unlike Daw Aung San Suu Kyi herself, based abroad). The Burma Fund and Burma Project websites also aim to disseminate information of various kinds, especially news of events inside Burma and reports on human rights abuses perpetrated by the regime. They too have largely supported the opposition orthodoxy, although usually less explicitly than BurmaNet's occasional, defensive editorials. Both the Burma Fund and Burma Project websites provide a large number of links to other organizations' sites, and information and links concerning culture, history and so on as well as news. Both also provide extensive bibliographies. Thus both demonstrate a concern to appeal not only to Burmese exiles and activists, but also to journalistic and academic researchers, and other interested users.

The FBC site has much in common with the Burma Fund and Burma Project, but it also has a particular style and set of objectives of its own. Its main aim, beyond general dissemination of information about the political and human rights situation in Burma, is the encouragement and organization of activism. The site provides ample explanation of the problems inside Burma, particularly those that can be characterized as human rights abuses, and includes documentation of such abuses in the form of interviews and photographs, mostly provided by indigenous groups themselves. This documentation serves both to encourage activism and to provide existing activists with evidence to bolster campaigns. Until late 2003 campaigns included agitating for general trade sanctions and, in the USA, for selective purchasing laws to penalize companies that still invested in/did business with Burma, as well as pressurizing particular companies to withdraw from Burma (for example, Premier Oil, Total-Fina-Elf) and discouraging tourist travel to Burma. Burmese exiles, particularly in the USA, have been heavily involved in such campaigns, but so too have campus-based student groups effectively targeted by the FBC site. FBC has provided information on tapping into international student and other activist networks, and given advice on how to take part in campaigns.

BurmaNet and the three websites discussed all include material specific to the political and humanitarian situations of Burma's ethnic groups. Nonetheless, the heaviest emphasis is still on the struggle for democracy. This follows the Daw Aung San Suu Kyi/NLD orthodoxy that first must come democracy, and only then can the particular concerns of the ethnic groups be addressed. On a nationwide scale, this is understandable: from an NLD perspective, ethnic concerns often seem of only local import whereas democracy is for all. From the perspective of the ethnic opposition parties, however, it seems their concerns are given less weight in the international arena of news and activism and, while they are by no means neglected on BurmaNet and websites, the primary emphasis placed on the struggle for democracy confirms ethnic doubts about their relative level of international support. Having said this, one objective sometimes articulated is the hope that the WWW might enhance inter-group understanding, politically and culturally, although the influence inside Burma is likely to be slight at best.

Using Burma-focused CMC

Subscribers to BurmaNet include individual Burmese living outside Burma, Burmese political opposition (including ethnic) organizations, foreign and – to a lesser extent – Burmese governmental agencies and embassies, NGOs, activists (both foreign and Burmese in exile), academics and journalists. BurmaNet's provision of regular daily news reports of events inside Burma and of relevant events outside it, including coverage of refugee and border issues, comprises reports drawn from Asian English-language newspapers, other foreign media and Burmese state newspapers. It also carries press statements and human rights reports released by various dissident Burmese organizations and – in the case of press statements at least – the Burmese government.[29] Much of the news coverage, especially of events inside Burma and particularly in rural ethnic areas, is of enormous value in itself as it is impossible for foreign journalists to travel to many of these areas; however, this also means that independent verification is impossible. The value of news and dissemination is also more generalized: many exiled Burmese, foreign activists, scholars and other users of BurmaNet are based in North America and Europe, where reading of all the Asian media reports included on BurmaNet would be precluded both by the practical difficulties of accessing Asian newspapers and by the time such a daily exercise would take. To this end, BurmaNet is indispensable to all Burma watchers. Nonetheless, its detailed contents take time to read, and it is unlikely to be greatly engaged with by the casual Burma follower: as 'Strider' (BurmaNet's Bangkok-based moderator) admitted in 1996, the volume of material carried by BurmaNet demands quite a commitment – it is really for the specialist user, whereas websites such as those discussed above are better as more general sources for less involved Burma watchers (Neumann 1996).

There is a small, long-standing Burmese diaspora in Britain, the USA and elsewhere, many members of which are apolitical or even pro-Rangoon. The majority of committed, exiled BurmaNet users, however, are individuals who fled Burma during or after the brutal events of 1988. Many were university students before they left and, now in their thirties, have been enabled by scholarships to return to study at universities in the West. These student exiles in particular find themselves in a situation that facilitates fast learning of computer and Internet use, which then enables and encourages them to use and add to email- and web-based sources of information and news on Burma. Equally, the more CMC is used by the Burmese community in the West, the more the exiled Burmese community in Thailand and India is encouraged to improve its own CMC skills and levels of usage.[30] CMC accessibility is nowhere near the level of every refugee camp along the Thai–Burma border having a computer hooked up to the Internet; but most if not all ethnic political party offices have a computer, a modem and the knowledge to use them.[31] They can use the web and distribute their own news, statements and so forth. In practice, however, input by ethnic groups into BurmaNet and websites is patchy.

Virtual communities?[32]

CMC is a facility of considerable power. Indeed, it seems to confirm now common claims about the Internet enabling the creation of 'virtual communities'. Here, an exile and activist community seems to be informed and brought together by mutual use of information technology.[33] A diverse set is *created* through technology, its members' bonds stemming from their shared involvement in a single issue: Burma and the situation therein. As Strider put it, 'it was the Net...that helped mobilize activists on college campuses and elsewhere in their opposition to investment in Burma' (quoted in Neumann 1996). As Danitz and Strobel identify (1997), the Internet also played a major role in the successful campaign for a bill passed by the state of Massachusetts to impose sanctions on companies investing in Burma, although Massachusetts has no sizeable Burmese population. This, it is claimed, 'illustrates how the Internet can be used to create geographically dispersed networks for non-violent action, even when there is no locally concentrated constituency' (*ibid*). More generally, as Strider has pointed out, 'there are few Burmese in the States, and relatively few people who even know where Burma is. But those who care are organized and effective, and it's because of the Internet' (Neumann 1996).

Certainly, Burma activists are well organized, though relatively few in number, and certainly they use CMC effectively. Indeed, grand claims are made by some observers, for example:

> Burma may be the first international movement for non-violent change in which the Internet has been the movement's tool of choice for those organizing outside of the Southeast Asian nation. The Internet has allowed them to establish a virtual community intent on engaging in cyberdiplomacy to nonviolently pressure the current military regime...to step down and allow the democratically elected officials to take office. The Internet was originally used, and continues to be used today, like a crowbar to pry open the very closed, highly secretive and tightly controlled nation by creating an information-rich highway to the world. The road may have four lanes out of Burma and only one narrow lane in, but it has allowed the global community a glimpse into the real events and happenings inside of Burma and occasionally allowed information to leak back into the country. (Danitz and Strobel 1997)

Such a characterization is, however, problematic. Information circulated on BurmaNet and elsewhere does not, for a start, all emanate inside Burma, and even that which does comes largely from the pronouncements of the NLD and ethnic opposition groups; it does not comprise objective reporting of the situation inside Burma, and there most certainly are not 'four lanes out'.[34]

More broadly, it is deeply questionable how, if at all, CMC really has an impact on the inside. But this may simply demonstrate that the conventional inside/outside distinction is limited in its usefulness: the combination of diaspora and CMC means that struggles are not constrained within borders; nonetheless, we tend still to be principally interested in the outside's impact on the inside. One could argue, however, that, from the perspective of those on the outside who are participating in it, what happens on the outside is as much a part of the whole struggle in its own right as is what happens on the inside. But of course for those on the inside who are perhaps unaware of the struggles on the outside, this is not necessarily so. The net result is an increasing and problematic divergence between inside and outside.

Be they ethnic group members or pro-democracy Burmans, exiles may be more outsiders than they are not, and certainly more so than they consider themselves to be. That is, while on one level CMC and other networking tools create a virtual community, a 'computer-mediated diasporic sphere' (Stubbs 1999) and 'politicised interpolation of 'homeland' across geographical boundaries' (*ibid*) in which the 'idea of the nation flourishes transnationally' (Appadurai 1996, p. 172) it does so in Burma's case in a way that does not include the inside and indeed diverges increasingly from it. The 'long-distance nationalist' (Stubbs 1999; see also Anderson 1992) in exile has both little impact on what happens inside the nation and little (further) price to pay for the possible effects of his or her actions. But this does not necessarily mean the outside is not also an important part of the struggle, or, perhaps, occasionally a separate struggle. Outsiders consider that they too are engaged in struggle; they also, ultimately, construct their own reality. As Stubbs puts it:

> The existence of computer-mediated diasporic public spheres deepens the understanding of what have been termed transnational and postnational imaginings since, as complex discursive and historical fields they represent particular constructions of the national space from diverse global sites, which become, effectively, a unified imagined place or homeland. (Stubbs 1999)

I am not claiming that the outside is just as important as the inside, but analytically we still need to recognize that it has reality and significance for those involved.

Nonetheless, one cannot overstate the significance of the distances, literal and metaphorical, that have opened up between those inside and those outside. Exiles could be said to be forming a new elite – in comparison to those who remain inside – characterized, like all elites, by greater levels of access to education and technology, greater opportunities and skills to manipulate language and technology, and increasing distance from the non-elite. Furthermore, the tiny degree to which CMC has influence on events inside Burma demonstrates the inaccuracy of claims that the Internet contributes to the dialogic process. Certainly, there are Burmese government responses to BurmaNet: the regime now has its own news/discussion group, 'Myanmar-list', which distributes SPDC information sheets and criticism of the pro-democracy movement and of the non-ceasefire ethnic groups.

Activists, both Burmese and foreign, in turn respond critically and sometimes manage to spark a dialogue that happens nowhere else (Fink 1997). Furthermore, in 1997 the SPDC, as well as setting up with the help of an American PR company its own home page, http://www.myanmar.com,[35] 'allegedly hired a former Burmese embassy official to engage in cyberdebate on behalf of the government. But [it] cannot stop the debate and information flows on Burma now circling the globe. All it can do is add its voice to the debate' (Danitz and Strobel 1997). Nonetheless, dialogue is still limited and based on the outside, with little impact inside.

Concluding remarks

This chapter has shown that the views, reactions and experiences inside Burma of outside influences are as important in determining outcomes as are the outside influences themselves. Crucial to the impact of external factors is both the military regime's self-image and view of the outside world, and the type of approach by the international community. The combination of the regime's deliberate fostering of xenophobia (albeit in conflict with attempts to open up the economy) and the confrontational human rights-oriented approaches by certain international elements, has contributed to the ongoing combative and non-dialogic nature of most exchanges inside and concerning Burma. At the same time, the 'constructive engagement' approach of ASEAN and other Asian countries has also served merely to strengthen the Rangoon regime.

Powerful lobbies in the West have been pushing hard for change in Burma and for such change to be brought about by pressure of economic sanctions and political isolation. On the sociological micro-level, the Internet is especially important in this. But pressure exerted by the West has been largely unsuccessful in forcing change inside Burma, because of insufficient economic and political leverage. Nonetheless, to some degree CMC has been successful in the creation of a strong and vibrant international lobbying community of Burmese exiles and foreign activists. Yet CMC is very much an external factor: for the vast majority of 'ordinary' people inside Burma, 'new media' such as the Internet have little if any impact, direct or otherwise.

Furthermore, contrary to some claims, it is unlikely that CMC contributes significantly to ongoing dialogue *inside* Burma. Indeed, it seems more likely that CMC has been one important factor in an increasing divergence between inside and outside. But this does not mean that the lobbying activity outside Burma is without significance: it has changed opinion in some Western governments and boardrooms and it has created its own reality, providing meaning in daily life for many exiles and activists. It has also encouraged the development of language, technological and political skills amongst Burmese exiles. 'Cultural' factors such as CMC draw real, virtual and imaginary connections between different sites and the actors who inhabit them.

Notes

1. I use 'Burma', not 'Myanmar'; the former preferred by my field informants and others opposing the current regime.
2. I am grateful for insightful comments made upon earlier versions by David Arnott, Vicky Bowman, Martin Smith, David Steinberg, and Robert Taylor.
3. World Bank 2000.
4. There is unfortunately insufficient space for the chapter also to examine issues concerning refugee communities and other living in the borderlands between Burma and the world beyond. For more on the Karenni, one such refugee group, see Dudley 2000 and Dudley 2006.
5. As well as killing demonstrators in 1988, as has been widely documented, the military regime has been guilty of widespread human rights abuses since.
6. On colonialism and independence, see Bless 1990, Tinker 1983. On ethnic resistance, see Ghosh 1999.
7. On postcolonial politics in Burma, see Steinberg 1982, Maung Maung Gyi 1983, Taylor 1987, Carey 1997.
8. http://www.sil.org/ethnologue/myan.html. Accessed 21/7/05.
9. Smith 1991, p. 16; see also Lintner 1989, Carey 1997, Anon. 1998, Houtman 1999.
10. The official exchange rate in 2000 was 6.53 Kyat to US$1, while the market rate for the same period was over 500 Kyat/US$ (Burma Economic Watch 2001).
11. On the recent financial crisis, see Turnell and Vicary 2003, Turnell 2004.
12. Tegenfeldt 2001, p. 112; see also Ministry of Health and UNICEF 1995.
13. See AI 1992.
14. Thai authorities' support and sympathy for the struggles of the Burmese ethnic opposition groups on their border has withered as Chinese, Bangladeshi and Indian sympathy and tolerance had already done. For an example of the now toughened attitude of Thai authorities to Burmese refugees, see AFP 2001.
15. The Lahu and the Akha, also traditionally have been and continue to be producers of opium.
16. See Fabre 1999.
17. The full ILO report, http://www.ilo.org/public/english/standards/relm/gb/docs/gb273/myanmar.htm. Accessed 21/7/05.
18. Rajesh Venugopal, personal communication, 2002.
19. For a discussion of some of the implications for Burmese civil society of greater foreign NGO involvement, see Burma Center Netherlands and Transnational Institute 1999.
20. Although c.f. 'We have always said that assistance to Burma should depend on accountability, transparency, and independent monitoring, which is to say that assistance projects, aid projects must be opened to scrutiny . . . to ensure that the right assistance is getting to the right people in the right way . . . that our people are really benefiting', message from Daw Aung San Suu Kyi, 19 July 2002, quoted in Burma UN Service Office 2003.
21. David Arnott (personal communication 2003) argues that 'It is the absence of the rule of (commercial) law, the high degree of corruption and the desire of the military to retain control of the key area of the economy that have been the main disincentives to investment in Burma.'

22. Stubbs 1999.
23. Such restrictions are but one aspect of government control of communications. The state controls TV, radio and print media; telephone tapping and mail opening are routine. Foreign news is also strictly controlled, and to be caught listening to the BBC or similar radio stations can incur a prison sentence. A very few organizations (principally foreign businesses and NGOs) and individuals (senior members of the regime) have access to email providers 'which call to systems outside the country to upload and download mail once a day' (Fink 1997), although even these users are not permitted to access *BurmaNet* or similar sources likely to be critical of the regime (Fink 2001).
24. For a historical overview up to 2000, particularly of the Free Burma movement and the Internet, see Zarni 2000.
25. General and subscribing information, together with current and archived news, is provided at http://www.burmanet.org (accessed 21/7/05). Another important newsgroup is soc.cult.burma. During the 1990s, the main vehicle for Burma CMC was reg-burma, the archive of which is searchable via the OBL at http://www.burmalibrary.org/reg.burma/ (websites accessed 21/7/05).
26. Accessed 1/4/01. The website ceased to exist later that year.
27. David Arnott, personal communication, 2003. Website accessed 21/7/05.
28. All accessed 21/7/05.
29. For further description of *BurmaNet*, see Anon. 1996.
30. Fink 1997.
31. Grants for equipment have been provided by the OSI, amongst other sources. Computers are also used by refugee communities for such purposes as producing educational materials for camp schools.
32. C.f. Rheingold's formulation of 'virtual communities': '[they] are social aggregations that emerge from the Net when enough people carry on . . . public discussions . . . to form webs of personal relationships in cyberspace' (1993, p. 5; see Stubbs 1998 and 1999 for critique).
33. Zarni (2000) writes that '[a]ctivists shared narratives on the Internet, and the excitement and enthusiasm they generated proved contagious. The Internet created a virtual space where the flow of these activist energies was kept alive and re-channeled for ongoing political actions . . .'.
34. Although c.f. Krebs 2001.
35. Accessed 21/7/05.

References

AFP (Associated Free Press) (2001) 'Thai Official Blasts UN over Stance on Myanmar Illegal Immigrants'. Distributed on *BurmaNet*, 19 August 2001.

AI (Amnesty International) (1992) *Human Rights Violations against Muslims in the Rakhine (Arakan) State*. London: Amnesty International.

Anderson, B. (1992) 'The New World Disorder', *New Left Review*, 193, 3–13.

Anon. (1996) 'Arachnophilia (Use of Burmanet on the Internet by the Junta Opposition)', *The Economist*, 340 (August 10 1996), 28.

Anon. (1998) *Burma: Prospects for a Democratic Future*. Cambridge, MA: The World Peace Foundation and Harvard Institute for International Development: Brookings Institute Press.

Anon. (2002) 'Suu Kyi Tells EU she is Neutral on Myanmar Sanctions', Agence France-Presse, 10 September 2002. Distributed on *BurmaNet News*, 10 September 2002, Issue 2084.

Appadurai, A. (1996) *Modernity at Large: Cultural Dimensions of Globalization*. Minneapolis, MN: University of Minnesota Press.

Bless, R. (1990) *'Divide et impera'? Britische Minderheitenpolitik in Burma, 1917–1948*. Stuttgart: Franz Steiner Verlag.

Bradford, W. (2004) 'BEW [Burma Economic Watch] Update, November 2004', http://www.ibiblio.org/obl/docs/BEW_update-11–2004. Accessed 21/7/05.

Burma Center Netherlands and Transnational Institute (ed.) (1999) *Strengthening Civil Society in Burma: Possibilities and Dilemmas for International NGOs*. Chiang Mai: Silkworm Books.

Burma Economic Watch (2001) 'Tables and Data', *Burma Economic Watch*, June 2001, http://www.ibiblio.org/obl/docs/Tables%20and%20Data.htm. Accessed 21/7/05.

BurmaNet (2001) 'Official Refugee Population in Thailand Tops 136,000', *BurmaNet*, August 19, 2001.

Burma UN Service Office (2003) 'Humanitarian Assistance to Burma', http://www.ibiblio.org/obl/docs/Humanitarian-Assistance_Dec2.htm. Accessed 21/7/05.

Carey, P. (ed.) (1997) *Burma: the Challenge of Change in a Divided Society*. Basingstoke: Macmillan.

Collignon, S. (2001) 'Human Rights and the Economy in Burma' in R. H. Taylor (ed.) *Burma: Political Economy under Military Rule*. London: C. Hurst & Co.

Danitz, T. and W. P. Strobel (1997) 'The Internet and Burma: A New Tool for Nonviolent Change', http://www.usip.org/oc/vd/vdpresents/danitzstrobel.html. Accessed 2/11/01.

Dudley, S. (2000) 'Displacement and Identity: Karenni Refugees in Thailand'. Unpublished D Phil thesis, University of Oxford.

Dudley, S. (2006) 'Re-shaping Karenni-ness in Exile: Education, Nationalism and Being in the Wider World' in M. Gravers (ed.) *Ethnic Diversity in Burma*. Leiden: NIAS, University of Leiden Press.

Fabre, G. (1999) *Les Prospérités du Crime*. Paris: UNESCO.

FEER (Far Eastern Economic Review) (2001) 'Taliban Success Opens Door to Burma', *Far Eastern Economic Review*, 5 July 2001.

Fink, C. (1997) 'Burma: Constructive Engagement in Cyberspace?' *Cultural Survival Quarterly*, 21, 4: no page numbers online, http://www.cs.org. Accessed 21/7/05.

Fink, C. (2001) *Living Silence: Burma under Military Rule*. London: Zed Books.

Ghosh, P. (1999) *Brave Men of the Hills: Resistance and Rebellion in Burma, 1825–1932*. Honolulu: University of Hawai'i Press.

Gravers, M. (1993) *Nationalism as Political Paranoia in Burma*. Copenhagen: Nordic Institute of Asian Studies.

Houtman, G. (1999) *Mental Culture in Burmese Crisis Politics: Aung San Suu Kyi and the National League for Democracy*. Tokyo: Tokyo University of Foreign Studies.

Krebs, V. (2001) 'The Impact of the Internet on Myanmar', http://www.firstmonday.dk/issues/issue6_5/krebs/. Accessed 1/4/05.

Kynge, J. and A. Kazim (2001) 'A Tussle for Asia', *Financial Times*, 26 June 2001.

Lallah, R. (1998) *Situation of Human Rights in Myanmar: Report of Special Rapporteur, Mr Rajsoomer Lallah*. Geneva: UN Commission on Human Rights.

Lintner, B. (1989) *Outrage. Burma's Struggle for Democracy*. London: White Lotus.

Ma Thanegi (1998) 'The Burmese Fairy Tale', *Far Eastern Economic Review*, 18 February 1988.

Maung Maung Gyi (1983) *Burmese Political Values: The Socio-Political Roots of Authoritarianism*. New York: Praeger.

Munro, R. H. (1994) 'China's Waxing Spheres of Influence', *Orbis*, 38(4), 585–605.

Neumann, A. Lin. (1996) 'The Resistance Network', *Wired*, 4(1), no page numbers, http://www.wired.com/wired/archive/4.01/countrynet.html. Accessed 21/7/05.

Rheingold, H. (1993) *The Virtual Community: Homesteading on the Electronic Frontier*. Reading: Addison-Wesley.
Rüland, J. (2001) 'Burma Ten Years after the Uprising: The Regional Dimension' in R. H. Taylor (ed.) *Burma: Political Economy under Military Rule*. London: C. Hurst & Co.
Smith, M. (1991/9) *Burma*. London: Zed Books.
Smith, M. (2001) 'Burmese Politics after 1988: An Era of New and Uncertain Change' in R. H. Taylor (ed.) *Burma: Political Economy under Military Rule*. London: C. Hurst & Co.
Steinberg, D. (1982) *Burma: A Socialist Nation of Southeast Asia*. Boulder, CO: Westview Press.
Steinberg, D. (2001) 'The Burmese Conundrum: Approaching Reformation of the Political Economy' in R. H. Taylor (ed.) *Burma: Political Economy under Military Rule*. London: C. Hurst & Co.
Stubbs, P. (1998) 'Conflict and Co-operation in the Virtual Community?: eMail and the Wars of the Yugoslav Succession', *Sociological Research Online*, 3(3) no page numbers, http://www.socresonline.org.uk/socresonline/3/3/7.html. Accessed 1/12/01.
Stubbs, P. (1999) 'Virtual Diaspora? Imagining Croatia On-line', *Sociological Research Online*, 4(2), no page numbers, http://www.socresonline.org.uk/socresonline/4/2/stubbs.html. Accessed 1/12/01.
Taylor, R. H. (1987) *The State in Burma*. Honolulu: University of Hawai'i Press.
Taylor, R. H. (ed.) (2001a) *Burma: Political Economy under Military Rule*. London: C. Hurst & Co.
Taylor, R. H. (2001b) 'Introduction: Stagnation and Stalemate' in R. H. Taylor (ed.) *Burma: Political Economy under Military Rule*. London: C. Hurst & Co.
Taylor, R. H. (2001c) 'Stifling Change: The Army Remains in Command' in R. H. Taylor (ed.) *Burma: Political Economy under Military Rule*. London: C. Hurst & Co.
Tegenfeldt, D. (2001) 'International Non-governmental Organizations in Burma' in R. H. Taylor (ed.) *Burma: Political Economy under Military Rule*. London: C. Hurst & Co.
The Nation (2001a) 'Refugees to Gain from Foreign Minister's Idea', *The Nation*, 26 June 2001.
The Nation (2001b) 'TV Crew Fingers Junta', *The Nation*, 26 June 2001.
Tinker, H. (ed.) (1983) *Burma: The Struggle for Independence*. 2 vols. London: Her Majesty's Stationery Office (HMSO).
Turnell, S. (2004) 'Some Further Developments in Burma's Financial Sector', *Burma Economic Watch* 2004, issue 2. http://www.econ.mq.edu.au/BurmaEconomicWatch/BEWNo2–04.pdf. Accessed 21/7/05.
Turnell, S. and A. Vicary (2003) 'Burma's Banking Crisis: a Commentary', *Burma Economic Watch*, 6 March 2003. http://www.ibiblio.org/obl/docs/BEW2003–03.htm. Accessed 21/7/05.
World Bank (2000) 'Myanmar at a Glance', http://www.worldbank.org/cgi-bin/sendoff.cgi?page=%2Fdata%2Fcountrydata%2Faag%2Fmmr_aag.pdf. Accessed 21/7/05.
Zarni (2000) 'Resistance and cybercommunities' in A. De Vaney, S. Gance and Yan Ma (eds) *Digital Communications and New Coalitions Around the World*. New York: Peter Lang.

10
Sri Lanka: The Global Dimensions of Conflict

Rajesh Venugopal[1]

Introduction

For almost two decades from 1983–2001, Sri Lanka was embroiled in a bitter civil war that comprised a number of different phases and even different protagonists.[2] Over this period, the war claimed over 65,000 lives, and had a particularly devastating effect on the civilian population of the north-east, most of whom lived through extended periods of acute physical and economic insecurity, and suffered repeated episodes of dislocation. At its peak in the late-1990s almost a million people, amounting to one-third of the total north-east population, were living as internal refugees, while as many as a quarter of all Sri Lankan Tamils had left the country altogether. Despite the fact that most of southern Sri Lanka did not experience the war in direct form, it had nevertheless also suffered heavily from a violent campaign of insurgency and counter-insurgency between 1987–90 that claimed as many as 60,000 dead or 'disappeared'. In addition, the south also suffered constant spillover effects of the war in the north-east and was subject to a regular stream of devastating bomb explosions, suicide attacks, and assassinations that maintained a constant atmosphere of tension and fear.

Over time, the nature of the war changed considerably, evolving from a small and localized separatist insurgency in the early 1980s, to an expansive conventional war by the 1990s. In 1987 the war took a complex and unexpected turn when Indian military forces inducted as peace-keepers into the north-east themselves became embroiled in violent conflict with the dominant insurgent group, the Liberation Tigers of Tamil Eelam (LTTE). After the Indian withdrawal in 1990, the LTTE gained control of large parts of the north-east for the first time, where they developed a parallel state apparatus to govern a sizeable civilian population. In December 1995 a major military offensive by the Sri Lankan army forced the LTTE to evacuate from Jaffna. In doing so, the LTTE encouraged several hundred thousand civilians to join them out in an unprecedented refugee exodus. During 1997–99 the LTTE effectively defeated the government's largest ever military offensive, and advanced towards the Jaffna peninsula while retaining control of large tracts of the Vanni region.

But despite the enormous costs that it has incurred and the complex and unexpected directions that the war has taken over the years, the domestic political and military dynamics of the conflict remained surprisingly little different on the eve of the December 2001 ceasefire from what it had been at its onset in July 1983. In political terms, the LTTE fought for the separation of the island's Tamil-dominated north and coastal east as an independent state of 'Tamil Eelam'. Successive governments in Colombo meanwhile rejected this outright and were prepared to consider little more than varying degrees of regional devolution. In the course of the prolonged and overlapping processes of war and peace neither side appeared to have made any substantial compromise on their respective political positions. In the run-up to a new set of peace negotiations in April 2002, LTTE leader V. Prabakharan set out his organization's political demands as the exact same four-point programme that had been advanced in the first set of peace talks held 17 years earlier in August 1985. On the other side, the structure of Sri Lankan party politics made it virtually impossible for any government to offer the minimal political concessions on devolution that were deemed necessary to reach any compromise agreement.

Although several prior rounds of negotiations were held in 1985, 1987, 1990 and 1995, none was successfully converted into a durable settlement, and each one collapsed after a few months with hostilities resuming on more acrimonious terms. In lieu of any such rapprochement, each side ultimately hoped to force through a favourable solution upon the other on the basis of military advantage. But the prospects for any military solution to emerge have steadily weakened over the years as the war has become ever more intractable. Over the 1990–96 period, government forces managed to gain and strengthen their control of most of the populated urban and peri-urban areas of the north-east including Vavuniya, Trincomalee, Batticaloa and Jaffna. But much of the rural hinterland connecting these urban enclaves remained under LTTE control. Conversely, the LTTE itself became increasingly restricted to pockets of sparsely populated and densely forested territory across the north-east, and found it untenable to retain control of large urban areas.

In sum, the internal dimensions of the conflict had been locked in a multi-dimensional stalemate; no political compromise was forthcoming, and no military solution was possible. This internal stalemate has caused the Sri Lankan conflict to become the object of considerable attention by various external actors, who have assumed that some combination of external financial, diplomatic and even military pressure can help to ease the internal deadlock and open the path to peace. As a result, these external interventions, as well as various other external contextual factors entirely unrelated to Sri Lanka have over time become intricately drawn into the dynamics of the conflict, and have come to affect its trajectory in unpredictable ways.

It is of course very difficult to draw sharp lines of distinction between the internal and external, particularly in the case of Sri Lanka, a small island state that has relatively recently emerged from four centuries of domination by a succession of foreign powers, and that is separated by a thin strip of water from a giant neighbour with which it shares close cultural and historical links. The distinctions that stand in reference to the country's present political borders do not necessarily correspond to current or historical geographies of national, cultural, linguistic or economic significance; much of what appears very internal and indigenous to the island contains the clear imprint of prior waves of engagement with various parts of the outside world.

Indeed, this distinction is not intended to form the basis for an alternate explanation of the causation and dynamics of the war – and this paper does not purport to suggest that the political conflict or civil war in Sri Lanka resulted from external rather than internal factors.[3] Nor is there any intent to minimize the agency or culpability of internal protagonists, or indeed the critical responsibility they bear in finding a political solution to the conflict. Instead, this chapter seeks to unravel some aspects of the complex, multi-layered external context within which Sri Lanka's internal conflict has unfolded. The external context is conceptualized here primarily in terms of two parallel and closely linked processes, economic and political. In economic terms, the underlying political economy of the conflict is traced to the nature of Sri Lanka's changing relationship with the global economy since independence. In political terms, the conflict has taken shape with respect to evolving external ideo-political paradigms and geo-political contentions.

Much of the existing literature that explicitly deals with the external dimensions of the Sri Lankan conflict has arisen within the framework of international relations and security studies. Bullion (1995), Kadian (1990), Muni (1993) and De Silva (1998), among others, have studied the internationalization of the conflict in terms of India's heavy involvement in the 1980s. In contrast, during the 1990s the external dimensions of the conflict have been explored with respect not to international relations, but rather international terrorism. For example, Gunaratna (1997) is directed at alerting foreign governments to the international security threat posed by the LTTE. A quite different strand of literature examines the intersection of the conflict with the outside world not in terms of international relations, but the political economy of development. The major preoccupations of this literature have been to examine the relationship between structural adjustment and conflict,[4] and the role of aid organizations in conflict reduction and post-conflict reconstruction.[5] This chapter attempts to weave together many of these different strands in a way that allows some coherent and generalizable inferences to be drawn out and developed.

Economic transformations, 1948–83

In very broad terms, the development of the ethnic conflict in Sri Lanka can be framed within a period of rapid socio-economic transformations designed to change the relationship of the Sri Lankan economy to the global economy. At independence in 1948, Ceylon's highly dualistic economy consisted of a prosperous export plantation sector that coexisted uneasily with an ailing peasant agriculture sector. Over the century from the 1830s to the 1930s, plantation crops such as coffee, and later, tea and rubber, had grown rapidly to occupy over one quarter of all agricultural land and one third of all employment. In contrast, the peasant agriculture sector remained impoverished with poor investment and low levels of productivity, supplying only a fraction of the island's total food requirements. With virtually no manufacturing industry, Ceylon's economy was heavily dependent on the outside world not just for exports of commodity products, but also for imports of basic staples such as rice and textiles.

The introduction of electoral politics in 1931 magnified and extended the effects of Ceylon's external economic vulnerability into the domestic political arena. Post-independence Ceylon suffered its first period of serious political instability in 1953 when the collapse of the commodity boom caused by the end of the Korean War forced the government to withdraw popular welfare subsidies. The domestic political repercussions of the subsidy withdrawal were so grave that it ultimately brought about the resignation of the Prime Minister and catalyzed a substantial transformation in the structure of national politics. Most importantly, the chain of events unleashed by the crisis of 1953 led to the ascendance of a new political force in the form of Sinhala–Buddhist nationalism. By 1956, the transformation of post-colonial politics was marked by the stunning election victory of the Sri Lanka Freedom Party (SLFP), an explicitly Sinhala–Buddhist nationalist party that promised to institute Sinhala as the sole official language of the country.

The significance of the nationalist ascendancy in domestic politics during this period was two-fold. First, it encompassed a typically economic form of nationalism, in that it gave rise to a policy regime that sought to protect domestic entrepreneurs and domestic markets through heavy regulation and taxation of foreign capital and trade. In practice, this meant that Sri Lanka adopted a variant of the dominant economic model of the period across South Asia, Latin America and Africa of import-substitution industrialization and the growth of the public sector. Consequently, there was a massive expansion of the public sector in this period, and the state itself became increasingly central to economic opportunities of various kinds from private sector permits and contracts to formal sector employment.

Secondly, the fact that this was an ethno-linguistic-religious nationalism of the majority community meant that in addition to being vaguely anti-imperialist in character, it was also directed against Sri Lanka's principal ethno-linguistic minority, the Tamils. The polarization of politics along Tamil–Sinhala lines took shape and became accentuated in this period, as the expanding state disbursed its patronage in ways that reflected the Sinhalese demographic and political dominance. This was evident in the access to public sector employment opportunities, the location of labour-intensive public sector industries, the nature of dry-zone irrigation and resettlement projects and by the early 1970s, in the allocation of university places.

This period of economic development ultimately came to an end within two decades under the weight of recurrent internal crisis fuelled paradoxically by increasingly unfavourable external economic factors. Between 1955–75, Sri Lanka's terms of trade dropped by 70 per cent causing a worsening balance of payments and fiscal problem that subsequently reached crisis proportions following the effects of the 1973 global commodity price shock. Within these conditions, the Tamil–Sinhala conflict escalated through two decades of growing political discontent, aggravated by high overall levels of unemployment and inflation that generated increasingly desperate state interventions. Indeed, as Herring (1994) remarks, 'The irony is that for all the political costs of "closing" the economy [under import-substitution], in fact it remained in a critical sense open to external shocks.' Many of these interventions, whether political, economic or cultural were demonstratively designed to generate and capitalize on majoritarian Sinhala sentiment, a factor that grew in importance as other sources of legitimacy and popular support for the government came into question. But with the spread of Tamil–Sinhala sectarian consciousness through the 1960s and 1970s, even state interventions that had no such sectarian content – or economic circumstances such as unemployment that affected all communities more or less equally – came to be increasingly interpreted and channelled in ways that magnified this divide.

The second major period of post-colonial economic transition in Sri Lanka was in the 1977–83 period. This began with the 1977 elections that brought an abrupt end to import-substitution policies, which were quickly replaced with a sweeping programme of market reforms, including trade liberalization, private sector deregulation, and the dismantling of many welfare provisions. As one of the first countries to engage in what would later be known as a structural adjustment programme, Sri Lanka won the considerable support of the aid donor community which was anxious to ensure that it should serve as a successful role model for other developing countries. As a result, Sri Lanka, which had effected a simultaneous shift in foreign policy towards Washington, was rewarded with a massive wave of foreign aid-sponsored public sector investment projects in the post-1977 period largely intended to cushion the domestic economic and political repercussions of the reforms.[6]

Reform protagonists hoped that a reduction in the role of the state, rapid economic growth and an expansion in employment would help to defuse the underlying causes of the conflict. But the political conflict instead worsened very sharply in this very period and took an increasingly violent form, escalating to civil war by 1983. Indeed, the actual impact of the market reforms was far more complex and ambiguous than might otherwise be assumed, and the mechanisms of linkage to the ethnic conflict need to be unravelled very carefully. For example, the increasing role of the private sector brought about by the reforms did not actually correspond to a diminished role for the state. Due to the unprecedented levels of foreign aid that accompanied the reforms, the state sector actually expanded significantly, increasing the scale of various forms of discretionary patronage distribution (Herring 1994; Dunham and Jayasuriya 2001).

The reforms also predictably had a disproportionate impact between Tamils and Sinhalese. Gunasinghe (1984) argues that the reforms hurt Sinhalese businesses and small industrialists that had previously benefited from import tariffs and preferential access to the state. Tamil businesses, on the other hand, whose lack of state access had restricted them to commerce rather than industry, gained handsomely from the market reforms and liberalized foreign trade environment. In terms of agriculture, Jaffna farmers who concentrated on domestic food products such as onions and chillies did well under the import restrictions of the early to mid-1970s but were hurt badly by trade liberalization which triggered an influx of cheap food items (Moore 1985; Shastri 1990; Samarasinghe 1996).

In general, then, the reforms had no uniform impact across ethnic groups per se – as their abrupt consequences hurt Jaffna Tamil farmers but benefited Colombo Tamil merchants. Nevertheless, the frustrations that arose from the abrupt and unequal impact of the reforms were frequently channelled along the Sinhala–Tamil axis, and to some extent deliberately so. In addition, the conflict was also aggravated by the authoritarian and violent implementation of the reforms in which the government undermined democratic norms and promoted the rise of political violence against opponents of all stripes.[7]

In sum, domestic politics in Sri Lanka evolved during the post-colonial period in close relation to the changing nature of the Sri Lankan economy and its linkages to the global economy. The present political conflict emerged during the transition from a plantation-export based economy to a public-sector driven import substitution industrialization model of development. It accelerated and assumed violent form at a time when the state was dismantling welfare subsidies and import-substitution policies, replacing them rapidly with a private-sector driven export-oriented industrialization model.

India and Tamil Nadu

In the 1970s and early 1980s, developments in the subcontinent played an important and multi-faceted role, both active and passive, in the genesis of the conflict. In the early 1970s, as Sri Lankan Tamil politics stood at a critical transitory phase, the political geography of the South Asian region was substantially altered following the break-up of Pakistan's two constituent wings. The civil war that erupted in the former East Pakistan in March 1971 and that ended following the India–Pakistan war of December 1971 remains the most significant event in South Asia's post-colonial geo-politics. It also created a precedent in international law, as existing UN conventions on self-determination were intended to apply only in the case of colonialism, and were worded so as not to encourage the rise of post-colonial secessionist movements. Within these limiting conditions, Bangladesh became the world's first successful post-colonial secessionist state and set a precedent that appeared to signify a new and more permissive atmosphere that might be of benefit for other aspiring self-determination movements.

But more important than the legal precedent it set was that created by the very circumstances in which Bangladesh was created, and the repercussions it held regionally. At a time when Sri Lankan Tamil politics stood at the threshold between federalism and separatism, Indian military intervention in East Pakistan suddenly created the possibility that similar assistance might be forthcoming in carving out a Tamil state in the north-east. Indeed, Jaffna was jubilant at the Indian victory, and leading Tamil politicians made provocative speeches congratulating Indira Gandhi and asking for a similar deliverance for themselves. Despite the fact that India did not offer any such support to Tamil separatism in this period, the perception that such support could be forthcoming formed an implicit if not explicit part of the rationale in advancing a separatist platform, which actually materialized in the immediate aftermath of the separation of Bangladesh, over the 1972–75 period.

Sri Lankan Tamils have historically close links of language, culture and religion with the fifty million Tamils of the Indian state of Tamil Nadu just across the Palk Straits. In the weeks following the anti-Tamil riots of July 1983, during which an estimated 3,000 people were killed, over a hundred thousand Tamils from around the island fled as refugees to India. In Tamil Nadu itself, the vivid press coverage of the riots, followed by the sudden arrival of boat loads of refugees, evoked a massive outpouring of sympathy and outrage; Tamil Nadu quickly became transformed into the most important external mass base of political support for the Eelam movement.

Internal developments in Tamil Nadu itself over the prior decades had also created an environment that was particularly predisposed to supporting the Sri Lankan Tamil cause. Since the late-1960s, Tamil Nadu had been governed by two different Tamil nationalist parties of the 'Dravida' movement that had some obvious similarities and natural affinities with Tamil nationalism in Sri Lanka. Both the Dravida and Eelam movements had gained strength and popularity in championing Tamil language rights during the 1950s and 1960s. In its early years the Dravida movement had also advocated the secession of India's southern states into an independent 'Dravidistan', although this demand was abandoned in the early 1960s.

However, beyond these superficial similarities in post-colonial Tamil politics in India and Sri Lanka, the links between Eelam and Dravida nationalisms were in reality quite weak, the two having developed under substantially different historical and socio-economic circumstances, and virtually opposite political trajectories (Krishna 1997). But by the late 1970s, the increasingly violent escalation of the 'ethnic problem' in Sri Lanka forced the two to relate to one another much closer as the Eelam issue was effectively injected into Dravida politics. Following the July 1983 riots, public opinion in Tamil Nadu was inflamed to the extent that local political parties and personalities competed and sought to outbid one another in their support for the Sri Lankan Tamil cause. The two rival Dravida parties in particular were in the forefront of the Eelam solidarity campaign, providing assistance both to refugees and the militant groups, and exhorting New Delhi to take a more aggressive attitude towards Colombo. Thus between 1983–87, as the locus of Sri Lankan Tamil politics had at least partially been displaced onto Tamil Nadu, it began to interact much more closely with Tamil Nadu politics and subsequently even mapped onto its existing rivalries. At one point the then ruling party in Tamil Nadu, and the state's Chief Minister M. G. Ramachandran, came to be closely linked with the LTTE, while the main opposition party and its leader M. Karunanidhi became associated with one of the LTTE's main rivals, the Tamil Eelam Liberation Organisation (TELO).

But the impact of political developments in Tamil Nadu during the post-colonial period must be seen not just in terms of Sri Lankan Tamils, but of the entire dialectic of Sinhala–Tamil relations, and in the parallel development of both Tamil and Sinhala nationalisms. Despite the fact that they form a large majority, Sinhala nationalism has fed on the notion of the Sinhalese as an encircled minority *vis-à-vis* a monolithic, pan-Tamil 'other' comprising northern Sri Lanka and nearby Tamil Nadu who together outnumber the Sinhalese by a ratio of almost five to one.[8] As a Sinhalese parliamentarian declaimed:

> In this country the problem of the Tamils is not a minority problem. The Sinhalese are a minority in Dravidastan. We are carrying on a struggle for our national existence against the Dravidastan majority.[9]

Sinhala–Buddhist nationalist historiography casts the pre-colonial history of the island in terms of an enduring and persistent conflict between the indigenous Sinhalese and invading Tamil armies from India. Emblematic of this encounter is the widely known and highly mythologized story of the battle in the second century BC between the Sinhalese prince Duttugemunu and the Tamil king Elara contained in the sixth century chronicle, the *Mahavamsa*. It is in this sense that political developments in India during the 1950s–1970s were of significance to Sinhala as much as Tamil nationalism in

Sri Lanka. Indeed, the growth of a secessionist and militant-sounding Tamil nationalist movement in India during the 1950s and 1960s had a relatively minor impact on the conservative Sri Lankan Tamil politics at the time. But the spectre of Tamil Nadu and the Dravida movement served an important function in the construction of Sinhala–Buddhist nationalism, representing as it did the volatile resurgence of a historical nemesis. The Dravida movement was viewed as a dangerous threat that had the ability to destabilize Sri Lanka by inflaming Sri Lankan Tamils to rebellion and secession.

In summary, Sri Lankan Tamil separatism gained critical mass in the 1970s in the immediate aftermath of Bangladesh's independence, and began to form links with a like-minded tradition of Tamil nationalism that held state power at the regional level. At the same time, this very nexus of Dravida–Eelam interaction, which existed more in the realm of rhetoric than reality until the early-1980s, was, combined with India's increasing regional assertiveness, an important factor that fed into some of the most fundamental concerns of Sinhala–Buddhist nationalist sentiment.

The Indian central government's support for the Tamil militants was based on a coincidence of quite separate internal and external compulsions. The internal component was in response to the considerable domestic pressures from Tamil Nadu to intervene in Sri Lanka, although this was also subject to New Delhi's concerns about stirring dormant separatist sentiment in Tamil Nadu itself. Externally, India's policy towards the conflict in Sri Lanka was guided by the cold war context and by strong compulsions to preserve and strengthen India's status as the dominant regional power.

Relations between India and Sri Lanka had been relatively cordial during the 1970s, but worsened significantly in the early 1980s for reasons only partially related to Sri Lanka's growing Tamil insurgency. Following the Soviet invasion of Afghanistan in 1979 and the consequent US military build-up on India's western borders with Pakistan, Sri Lankan President J. R. Jayawardene's strong pro-US foreign policy stance heightened concerns in New Delhi that India was slowly being encircled by hostile forces. The eruption of Sri Lanka's ethnic crisis in 1983 occurred within this context and presented a source of opportunity and danger for India. Above all, India sought to prevent outside powers, particularly the US, from using the conflict as an entry point for further intervention into India's self-declared sphere of influence, and also to ensure that the conflict, while it lasted long enough to punish Sri Lanka, was settled quickly on terms favourable to India.

The Indian government's direct sponsorship of virtually all the different militant groups also emanated from this coincidence of external and internal factors. It was envisaged that as each remained overwhelmingly dependent on Indian patronage, with training camps in India and their leaders resident in Madras, they would all remain under New Delhi's control and would not seek to cultivate other state patrons. Furthermore, the existence of a multiplicity of Sri Lankan Tamil militant groups dependent on Indian patronage meant that New Delhi could pick and choose between them, selectively rewarding the more pliable ones.

Finally, in addition to supporting and arming the Tamil militant groups, India also realized that a drawn-out war would become counter-productive to the extent that it would inevitably attract unwelcome external peace-making attention. As a result, India also sought to retain tight control over any possible political settlement of the conflict. As Indian intelligence agencies trained and armed the militant groups, a succession of Indian foreign ministry officials shuttled between New Delhi, Madras and Colombo to convince the exiled Tamil leadership and the Sri Lankan government to arrive at a negotiated political settlement of the conflict.

In sum, following the events of July 1983, the strong coincidence of internal and external compulsions for New Delhi meant that the escalation to civil war also triggered a parallel escalation of India's role in the war, both as war-maker and peace-maker. In an increasingly desperate attempt to counter India, the Sri Lankan government sought financial, military and diplomatic support from various other countries including Pakistan, China, Israel, the US and the UK. However, most of these countries actually avoided offering much support during this period, at least partly to avoid antagonizing India. The Sri Lankan crisis did not give rise to any overwhelming strategic concern, either in the economic sense such as oil or in terms of the cold war political calculus, of an extent that warranted risking a major diplomatic confrontation with New Delhi. In addition, international media coverage of the 1983 riots, reports by international human rights NGOs, and the arrival of thousands of Tamil refugees in Europe and North America helped to publicize the Sri Lankan Tamil case internationally and made it more complicated internally for many governments to openly support Colombo, which came to be viewed as guilty of promoting genocidal policies towards its minorities.

Consequently, Sri Lanka's cold war allies, many of whom were also its aid donors, and who were also now becoming host to increasing numbers of Tamil refugees, did not rush to either embrace or isolate Sri Lanka politically once the civil war started. Even countries such as the US and Britain, which wished to offer military support to Sri Lanka, decided to do so at an arms-length basis, using semi-official and secret channels. In response to urgent requests for military support after 1983, Sri Lanka was directed by the US to the Israeli secret agencies, and by the British to 'Keeny Meeny Services', an offshore mercenary firm (Muni 1993, p. 53; Bullion 1995).

In effect, despite the efforts of the Sri Lankan government to internationalize the conflict in a way that it could find beneficial, the external dimensions of both war and peace during Eelam War I remained tightly anchored to India. The Indian government's interventions with respect to the conflict were calibrated to ensure that New Delhi's own interests prevailed with respect to a multitude of different parties including the Tamil Nadu electorate, the various Sri Lankan Tamil groups, the Sri Lankan government, and global cold war era geo-politics. Indian support played a critical part in the ability of the militant groups to escalate the insurgency campaign into full-fledged civil war by late-1983. But at the same time, this meant that New Delhi (with varying degrees of success) gained control of the various insurgent groups, influencing their political orientation and altering the balance of inter-group political and military strength. Similarly, India's energetic diplomacy formed the basis for political negotiations between the Sri Lankan government and the various Tamil groups throughout the 1983–87 period. But again, this meant that the form and content of these negotiations was one that was ultimately subordinate to New Delhi's own interests and ambitions.

In this way, the entire trajectory of the conflict, particularly after 1983, became subject to a larger logic that the protagonists themselves had little to do with. India contributed to the destabilization of Sri Lanka in the 1980s strictly to the extent that this could provide the basis upon which a more pliant Sri Lanka could be quickly re-stabilized. India viewed the conflict in Sri Lanka within the lens of its own strategic ambitions as an instrument towards achieving this end, and for a brief period in mid-1987, appeared to have succeeded entirely.

India's two-track policy during 1983–87 of sponsoring both Tamil militancy and peace talks appeared to have reached its crowning glory in a political settlement reached in July 1987 that finally brought Eelam War I to an end. Under the terms of the Indo–Sri Lanka Accord, the Sri Lankan government agreed to make various concessions as a compromise solution short of secession. They also agreed to the induction of an Indian Peace Keeping Force (IPKF) to the north-east who would guarantee the implementation of the terms and the disarmament of the militant groups. None of the militant groups were actually party to the Accord, but it was assumed that India, as their patron, would prevail upon them to accept it and disarm. This, however, proved to be a fatal flaw, as the one dominant militant group, the LTTE, effectively rejected the terms of the Accord. By October 1987 a sequence of controversial events, including the capture and suicide of a group of LTTE militants by the Sri Lankan security forces and a series of massacres of Sinhalese villagers, sparked a new war between the IPKF and the LTTE that marked the most complex reversal in the island's armed conflict.

Although it was widely expected that the LTTE would soon either compromise or crumble in the face of one of the world's largest armies, this proved not to be the case. Instead, the stand-off between the LTTE and IPKF quickly evolved into a bitter military confrontation that lasted two-and-a-half years, ending with the IPKF's unceremonious withdrawal from Sri Lanka in March 1990. Not only did the IPKF's presence fail to enforce the political settlement in the north, but it also induced a serious political destabilization in the south, where widespread opposition to the Indian military presence precipitated the rise of a violent anti-government insurgency. In its campaign against the LTTE, the IPKF quickly lost the support of the Sri Lankan Tamil population that they had ostensibly come to protect, and came to be accused of the same kinds of atrocities against Tamil civilians with which India had earlier charged the Sri Lankan government.

Ultimately, the IPKF's withdrawal at the Sri Lankan government's request brought an end to what was viewed as a humiliating, self-inflicted disaster for India, who appeared incapable of defeating the small guerrilla group that they had themselves only recently trained, armed and presumed to control. As officials in New Delhi drew the conclusion that their entire Sri Lanka policy had disastrously backfired, the IPKF's withdrawal from Sri Lanka came to be symbolic of a much broader Indian withdrawal from the central role it played in the island for the entire decade of the 1980s. As a result, India's multi-faceted role as the central external dimension of the Sri Lankan conflict also came to an end in early 1990.

With the abrupt reversal in its relationship with India between 1987–91, the LTTE had suddenly lost not just a powerful ally, but also rear bases, a logistical support network and supply lines that had been built up across southern India. With the loss of 1,200 IPKF soldiers in Sri Lanka and Rajiv Gandhi's assassination in May 1991, presumedly by the LTTE, India's attitude towards the LTTE had turned from one of ill-concealed support in the early 1980s to open, but restrained, hostility by the early 1990s. Through the 1990s, there were still around 150,000 Sri Lankan Tamils in India, including 65,000 in refugee camps, and there remains substantial humanitarian concern and sympathy for the plight of Sri Lankan Tamils living amid war-time distress. But popular sympathy for the Sri Lankan Tamil cause, even in Tamil Nadu, substantially evaporated during the IPKF period, and even more so after Rajiv Gandhi's assassination. It is under these complex circumstances that the Sri Lankan Tamil refugee diaspora has emerged in the 1990s as the nucleus around which the external political dimensions of the war have re-assembled.

The Sri Lankan Tamil diaspora

The significance of the overseas Sri Lankan Tamil population to the civil war lies in three factors. The first is its size, which as of 2001 is estimated at 600,000–800,000, accounting for between one-quarter and one-third of the global Sri Lankan Tamil population. The second is its location, spread across North America, Western Europe, Asia and Australia, which renders it of considerable strategic, economic and political value. As of 2001, there were an estimated 250,000 Sri Lankan Tamils in North America (the large majority in Canada), 200,000 in Western Europe, 150,000 in India and 30,000 in Australia.[10] The third factor is its close emotional proximity to events in Sri Lanka. The diaspora is itself largely a consequence of the war, consisting mainly of war-related exiles and refugees, and many of its members retain vivid memories of the traumatic circumstances that forced them to leave.

The most significant expression of the political involvement of this sizeable and strategically located diaspora is in terms of its visible support for the LTTE, a fact that has rendered it an important and perhaps even a distinct party to the conflict. Many of the recognisable overseas Sri Lankan Tamil organizations in North America, Europe and Australia have been openly sympathetic to the LTTE. Pro-LTTE organizations regularly host marches, meetings, sports events and cultural functions attracting hundreds, and often thousands, of supporters. Through the 1990s, outside of its military presence in the north-east of Sri Lanka, the LTTE's existence as an organization was visible mainly in terms of the location of its international offices in London and Paris, its international lobbying campaign, and its 'mass' presence at public rallies held in cities from Toronto to Melbourne. LTTE sympathizers have operated a persistent and sophisticated media network disseminating news and views over at least a dozen pro-LTTE websites, several radio stations, a Tamil cable television network, numerous publications in Tamil and English, and consistent lobbying with national governments, international organizations (UN human rights and minority rights fora) and with international NGO solidarity networks.

This is not to suggest a simplistic conflation of the diaspora with the LTTE, as there exists considerable diversity within the various overseas Tamil communities in terms of political sympathies and even in terms of predisposition towards politics at all. The available ethnographic evidence indicates that the political, cultural and social space that the LTTE occupies parallels the marginalization of diaspora communities from these very spaces abroad due to their vulnerable existence as national minorities or asylum-seekers.[11] But nevertheless, the diaspora has undeniably emerged since the late-1980s as the most important and visible constituency of support for the LTTE. The reasons for this are not difficult to understand – Sri Lanka's domestic Tamil population in the 1990s consisted of those living either under great insecurity in the war-torn north-east (often as internal refugees) or those living as a minority in the south, often subject to heightened surveillance. Under these circumstances, the diaspora has occupied a unique space with respect to the conflict, and in the absence of a peace process during the 1990s has formed the only available locus of open political activity for the LTTE.

The LTTE-diaspora nexus

It is widely alleged that the LTTE uses its international support network embedded within the diaspora for three specific functions: fund-raising, arms procurement and international advocacy. The involvement of overseas Tamils in these activities has received wide press coverage internationally since the mid-1990s,[12] and has led the Sri Lankan conflict to be dubbed a 'diaspora-funded war'. Not surprisingly, disrupting the LTTE-diaspora nexus has subsequently become the single most important pre-occupation of Sri Lankan foreign policy in the 1990s. In addition, recent reports from the media and intelligence establishment suggest that the LTTE operates a number of businesses around the world that it uses to raise and channel resources. These are said to include a deep-water shipping fleet, and even a business empire in construction, real estate investments, jewellery shops, international money transfers, cable television, and telecommunications. The LTTE is also said to have established covert bases in a number of south-east Asian countries, particularly in Thailand and Myanmar, in order to coordinate logistics, procurement and shipments to Sri Lanka (Davis 2000) While the scale and nature of the LTTE's international advocacy campaign can be more easily verified, the inherently clandestine nature of the business investments, arms procurement and fund-raising functions has meant that there is actually little beyond anecdotal or circumstantial evidence of these activities publicly available. What little exists is often speculative or attributed to national intelligence or police agencies in the context of their attempts to characterize the LTTE's international network as an international terrorist threat. For example, a report published by the Canadian Security Intelligence Service alleges that:

> The majority of financial support comes from six main areas, all of which contain large Tamil diasporas: Switzerland, Canada, Australia, the UK, the US, and the Scandinavian countries. (Chalk 1999)

The US State Department says:

> The LTTE also uses its international contacts to procure weapons, communications, and any other equipment and supplies it needs. The LTTE exploits large Tamil communities in North America, Europe, and Asia to obtain funds and supplies for its fighters in Sri Lanka. (US Department of State 2000, Appendix B)

Meanwhile, Gunaratna (2000) writes:

> About 80% of the LTTE annual budget, estimated at $82 million, is generated from diaspora contributions and revenue from international trade, enterprise and investments.

This is not to dismiss the existence of such a link between the diaspora and the LTTE, which the LTTE itself appears to readily admit to. Indeed, the diaspora-funding link plausibly exists simply by the fact of the considerable economic significance of overseas Tamils, and the extent to which they contain a sizeable element that is clearly pro-LTTE. But it is important to recognize that the most interesting inferences that can be drawn from the recent exposés of the LTTE-diaspora nexus lie not just in the raw content of the scarce and often partial information publicly available, but in terms of the global context, the political identities and the strategic compulsions of those seeking to gather and publicize such information.

International advocacy

During the 1980s external diplomatic advocacy for the Sri Lankan Tamil cause took place at one level through emerging international NGO networks, as it fit in within existing preoccupations over human rights, minority rights and conflict. But at the same time, the most important diplomatic interventions took place at the official level, primarily through the Indian government, Indian diplomatic missions and Indian delegates to international state-level meetings such as the UN Commission on Human Rights and the Subcommission on Prevention of Discrimination and Protection of Minorities. But such support from India at the official level ended with the Indo–Sri Lanka Accord in the late-1980s, leaving the Tamil Eelam movement without official diplomatic patrons. In this vacuum, the focus of the LTTE's international advocacy has fallen back on the unofficial or NGO level, which by the early 1990s, had been accorded a new space and legitimacy within international policy.

The elevation of NGOs to the centre of the international social policy debate in the 1990s is well documented and signified in the high profile role they have played in the deliberations of United Nations conferences on the environment (1992) human rights (1993) population (1994) social development (1995) women (1995) habitat (1996) and racism (2001). Most such UN and multilateral conferences have resulted in two separate concluding declarations: the first an official document negotiated by the state-entities; and the second a parallel 'NGO declaration' that intended to counter the perceived conservatism and inadequacy of the official programme of action.

The rapid incorporation of this often nebulously defined category of NGOs within such policy deliberations in the 1990s has provided a legitimate avenue for non-state entities to gain a foothold, albeit a marginal one, within the realm of international diplomacy, which had previously been monopolized entirely by internationally recognized state entities. As such, the changing external dimensions of the conflict in Sri Lanka are also reflected in the transformation of the inter-state diplomatic confrontation in the 1980s between India and Sri Lanka into a new confrontation between Sri Lanka in the official forum, and pro-Eelam activists in the NGO forum. This new configuration was evident, for example, in the September 2001 World Conference Against Racism (WCAR) in Durban, South Africa, held in the final months of Eelam War III. The Sri Lankan government delegate, participating in the official plenary session of the WCAR, made a remark apparently in an oblique reference to the LTTE, attempting to locate the group within the preoccupations of the conference: 'In my country extremist groups often use tribalistic rhetoric ostensibly to achieve communal aspirations and some engage in violence and terror.'[13] Meanwhile, the alternative NGO declaration from the same conference acknowledged a considerably different reality in Sri Lanka:

> Acknowledging 50 years of ethnic conflict in Sri Lanka which has resulted in death, disappearances, rape, torture and destruction and affirming the right to self determination of the Tamil minority.[14]

International diplomacy

The replacement of Tamil Nadu by the Sri Lankan Tamil diaspora as the most important political constituency of external support for the Tamil Eelam movement has meant that the external political dimensions of the conflict have effectively expanded from a regional to an international context. Alongside this, there has been a parallel shift in the diplomatic efforts of the Sri Lankan government, from one that centred around lobbying cold war allies in opposition to India, to one that centres around seeking out post-cold war allies to disrupt Tamil diaspora activism and the LTTE's international network.

While Sri Lanka's efforts in the 1980s were largely unsuccessful, those of the 1990s were more so, because of two key reasons. Firstly, in the 1990s Sri Lanka did not encounter any counter-lobbying at the state-level. Despite the fact that the LTTE mounted a persistent and well-resourced NGO campaign, and benefited from strong organizational networks at important centres of international diplomacy such as Geneva, London and Paris, they were completely unrepresented and had no advocates within state-level institutions such as the UN General Assembly or the UN Commission on Human Rights. They did not enjoy any measure of diplomatic patronage by a state and no state has put the kind of hostile pressure on Sri Lanka in the 1990s that India did during the 1980s. Indeed, India has been supportive of the Sri Lankan government's international efforts against the LTTE in the 1990s.

Secondly, Sri Lanka's anti-LTTE diplomacy internationally has coincided with the growing spectre of international terrorism that has arisen independently in countries where the Tamil diaspora is resident. International terrorism had been nominated well before the events of 11 September 2001 as a global security threat of a magnitude that could replace the position previously accorded by the western powers to international communism. By December 1994 the nature of the new post-cold war era consensus on this issue was signified in the landmark UNGA resolution 49/60, 'Measures to eliminate international terrorism'.

The General Assembly had already passed nine resolutions between 1972–89 titled 'Measures to *prevent* international terrorism'. But these resolutions invariably included wording that recognized the necessity to address legitimate underlying causes of terrorism including colonialism, racism, violations of human rights and those involving alien domination and foreign occupation. In addition, each one included a re-affirmation of the right to self-determination. The 1994 resolution, which was deliberately re-named 'Measures to *eliminate* international terrorism', was considered a breakthrough in international state-level co-operation because for the first time it secured broad agreement on terrorism without having to make concessions on its causes, or make mention of the right to self-determination.

In Sri Lanka, the repercussions of this emerging global paradigm from the mid-1990s have been evident in the way that the government successfully registered the LTTE within the pantheon of international terrorist organizations, thus gaining powerful new allies and new avenues of legitimacy in the prosecution of an old war. The first tangible signs of this new alliance emerged in 1994 when the US resumed arms sales to Sri Lanka. In the backdrop of an increasingly anti-LTTE rhetorical posture by the Clinton administration, media reports revealed in 1996 that the elite US 'Green Beret' corps were providing advanced training to the Sri Lankan security forces, albeit in camps located far from the actual conflict zone (Kaufman 1996). Since then, US military support for the government is reported to have expanded to include training missions by other highly specialized units such as the US Navy SEALs, the US Air Force Special Operations Squadron, and even the US Army's Psychological Operations or 'Psy-Ops' Group(Athas 2000).

In October 1997 the re-internationalization of the Sri Lankan conflict under new aegis was signified most vividly when the US State Department designated the LTTE as a 'foreign terrorist organisation' under the Anti-Terrorism and Effective Death Penalty Act (the 'Oklahoma City Law') of 1996 (US Department of State 2000, Appendix B). The provisions ban fund-raising and other tangible support for the LTTE from the US and block any existing funds of the organization held at US financial institutions. But beyond this, the indirect implications of the US ban have been in terms of the way it has delegitimized the LTTE's cause internationally, and has formed the basis upon which a number of other states have placed the LTTE's activities under greater surveillance.

In April 2001 a second, and potentially more influential international intervention into the war, occurred when Britain proscribed the LTTE under sweeping anti-terrorism legislation with provisions more restrictive than those of the 1997 US law. As the former colonial power and home to the LTTE's international headquarters, Britain's decision to proscribe the LTTE was arguably the most significant external political intervention into the conflict in the post-1990 period. In the months before the proscription order between December 2000 – February 2001, the pending, but yet unannounced, British decision on whether the LTTE would be proscribed briefly became the most important and carefully followed political issue in Sri Lanka. In a process that became emblematic of the internationalization of the conflict, an extraordinary lobbying effort came underway by both sides across the island and internationally, directed at the UK Home Office and the then Home Minister, Jack Straw.

On the one side, pro-LTTE organizations and numerous overseas Tamil organizations campaigned vigorously against proscription, organizing demonstrations and petitions around the world directed at the British Home Office. On the other side, the Sri Lankan government and Sinhala nationalist organizations demanded that the LTTE be proscribed, with similar petition campaigns organized in Sri Lanka and abroad to this effect. At an official level, there was intense diplomatic pressure by Sri Lanka on the British government. Foreign minister Lakshman Kadirgamar himself travelled to Britain to lobby for proscription, and used the strongest diplomatic language to convey how Britain's failure to proscribe the LTTE would be interpreted as 'an unfriendly act that would impose a considerable strain on our relations' (Associated Press 2001).

'Crouching Tiger, Hidden War'[15]

The internationalization of the conflict in this manner has made global perceptions and images of the war a potentially serious factor in affecting its outcome.[16] Consequently, both sides have come to pay closer attention to managing the external media coverage of the war, and have even accused each other of playing to the international media gallery. One of the most striking features of the international coverage of the war has been a considerable transformation in media sympathies towards the protagonists that is evident from the contrast between their coverage of events in the early-1980s and late-1990s. In the aftermath of wide media coverage of the anti-Tamil riots in 1983 and the subsequent refugee exodus, there was a wave of sympathy for the Tamils, and a demonization of the Sri Lankan state in international opinion. Gunaratna (1997) notes:

> Mid-1983 to mid-1987 witnessed Sri Lanka's international image at its lowest ebb. Despite having an open economy, a model democracy and a major tourist destination, Sri Lanka's international image suffered irreversibly. TULF propaganda branded Sri Lanka as a state guilty of discrimination and perpetrating genocide against its minority.

In contrast, international media coverage in the 1990s, and particularly after 1995, helped to rehabilitate the Sri Lankan state and to demonize the LTTE, which was held responsible for assassinating Sri Lankan President Premadasa and former Indian Prime Minister Rajiv Gandhi, unilaterally breaking a ceasefire in April 1995, conducting a suicide bombing campaign in Colombo that claimed hundreds of civilian lives in 1996–97, and recruiting child soldiers. By association, Sri Lankan Tamils overseas have themselves come under a cloud of suspicion as a group that funds bloodshed in their home country and that is involved in criminal and other undesirable acts abroad.[17]

A significant aspect of the international coverage of Eelam War III in the late-1990s has been the absence of what is known as the 'CNN effect'. At a time when graphic satellite television images of remote and exotic wars are increasingly commonplace, and are becoming instrumental in manipulating global public opinion, it is of interest to note that there were simply no such images available from the north-east of Sri Lanka. Between 1996–2000, the war in the north escalated to an unprecedented extent with several major military offensives both by the government (Operations Riviresa and Jaya Sikurui), and the LTTE (Oyatha–Alaigal) that resulted in thousands of military and civilian lives lost. Within the relatively small territory of north-eastern Sri Lanka, there were almost one million refugees by the late-1990s. But the virtual absence of international media coverage during this period means that there is virtually no visual record of this civilian tragedy lodged in the global public consciousness and consequently, diminished international public attention or political pressure to address or ameliorate it. In part, this is because of the tight government censorship and travel restrictions that placed the north-east out of bounds for both domestic or foreign journalists between 1996–2001. In contrast, there has been considerably more prominent international television and print coverage of the devastating bomb attacks in Colombo during 1996–97, the Temple of the Tooth in 1998, and Katunayake airport in 2001, all of which contributed towards the characterization of the LTTE internationally as a ruthless terrorist organization.

Conclusions

The ceasefire agreement of February 2002 formally ended Eelam War III and set the stage for an extended pause in hostilities. Despite the fact that the progress towards any political settlement since then has been extremely slow and has been disrupted by numerous unpredictable events such as the Tsunami of December 2004, it nevertheless represents the longest such absence of hostilities in two decades. As such, Sri Lanka is potentially in the midst of an important historical turning point that provides an opportune moment to revisit the causes and consequences of the conflict in better historical context.

This chapter has attempted to provide such a context by embedding the trajectory of the political conflict and civil war within changing global circumstances. Most importantly, the underlying dynamics of the conflict have been traced here to the larger changes that have taken place in the Sri Lankan economy and its relationship to the global economy. Despite claims to its ancient origins, the Tamil–Sinhala political conflict is an utterly modern one, and arose at a very specific moment in the island's economic history in the late-1950s at a time of rapid social, economic and demographic change. It similarly escalated into civil war at another crucial point of economic transition in 1977–83. Since then, the economy has undergone important structural transformations, often of a controversial nature during an extended period of civil war and displacement. Viewed together, the ethnic conflict in Sri Lanka, through its many phases from 1956–2001, has closely followed the changing integration of Sri Lanka into the global economy. The social repercussions and tensions arising in the context of this integration have been manifest and taken shape through the prism of domestic and international politics. In this paper, these have been viewed in terms of their temporal intersection with changing regional and global power interests, and to the making and unmaking of cross-border geographies of political solidarity and confrontation based on cultural, linguistic and national identity.

Notes

1. Thanks to Meghan O'Sullivan, Michael Ross, Valpy Fitzgerald, Frances Stewart, David Dunham, Danny Sriskandarajah and participants at two seminars in Oxford for helpful comments on earlier drafts.
2. At the time of writing, the war has effectively been in a state of suspended animation under the terms of ceasefire agreement (CFA) of February 2002.
3. For detailed accounts of the origins of the conflict, see De Silva (1998) Bose (1994) Manor (1984) Tambiah (1986) Wilson (1988) Manogaran (1987) Ponnambalam (1983)
4. In particular, see Gunasinghe (1984) Manor (1984) Tambiah (1986) Moore (1990) Herring (1994) Dunham and Jayasuriya (2001).
5. See for example, Ofstad (2002), Goodhand (2001).
6. See Herring (1994) Athukorala and Jayasuriya (1994).
7. See for example Obeyesekere (1984) Manor (1984) and Tambiah (1986).
8. See Tambiah (1992) Jayawardena (1985) Dharmadasa (1992) on contemporary Sinhala nationalism.
9. Quoted in Kearney (1973), p. 164.
10. Based on UNHCR statistics, media and NGO reports.
11. See for example Fuglerud (1999).
12. For example, see Davis (1996).
13. Statement by H.E. Mr Lakshman Jayakody, Special envoy of H.E. the President of Sri Lanka at the World Conference against Racism, Racial Discrimination, Xenophobia and Related Intolerance, Durban, South Africa, 1 September 2001, available at, http://www.un.org/WCAR/statements/srilE.htm.

14. WCAR NGO forum declaration, 3 September 2001, accessed 10 October 2001: http://www.hri.ca/racism/major/ngodeclaration.htm.
15. This was the title of a newspaper article, see - Steele (2001).
16. This is separate but related from the (not infrequent) inaccuracies in international reporting, and the highly problematic international media coverage of 'ethnic conflict'.
17. See Sriskandarajah (2001).

References

Arunatilake, N., S. K. Jayasuriya and S. Kelegama (2001) 'The Economic Cost of the War in Sri Lanka', *World Development*, 29, 1483–500.

Associated Press (2001) 'Sri Lanka Warns of Strained Ties If Britain Does Not Ban Tamil Tiger Rebels', *Associated Press*, 21 January.

Athas, I. (2000) 'Fighting Planned in LTTE's "Year of War"', *Jane's Intelligence Review*, 8 January.

Athukorala, P. and S. K. Jayasuriya (1994) *Macroeconomic Policies, Crises, and Growth in Sri Lanka, 1969–90*. Washington, DC: World Bank.

Bose, S. (1994) *States, Nations, Sovereignty: Sri Lanka, India and the Tamil Eelam Movement*. New Delhi: London: Sage.

Bullion, A. J. (1995) *India, Sri Lanka and the Tamil Crisis, 1976–1994: An International Perspective*. London/New York: Pinter.

Chalk, P. (1999) 'Liberation Tigers of Tamil Eelam's (LTTE) International Organization and Operations – a Preliminary Analysis', *Commentary, a Canadian Security Intelligence Service publication.*

Davis, A. (1996) 'Tigers Inc.', *Asiaweek*, July 26.

——(2000) 'Tracking Tigers in Phuket', *Asiaweek*, 29, June 16.

De Silva, K. M. (1998) *Reaping the Whirlwind: Ethnic Conflict, Ethnic Politics in Sri Lanka*. New Delhi: Penguin India.

Dharmadasa, K. N. O. (1992) *Language, Religion, and Ethnic Assertiveness: The Growth of Sinhalese Nationalism in Sri Lanka*. Ann Arbor, MI: University of Michigan Press.

Dunham, D. M. and S. Jayasuriya (2001) 'Liberalisation and Political Decay: Sri Lanka's Journey from a Welfare State to a Brutalised Society', Working Paper 352. The Hague: Institute of Social Studies.

Fuglerud, Ø. (1999) *Life on the Outside: The Tamil Diaspora and Long-Distance Nationalism*. London: Pluto.

Goodhand, J. (2001) *Aid, Conflict and Peace Building in Sri Lanka*. London: Conflict, Security and Development Group.

Grobar, L. M. and S. Gnanaselvam (1993) 'The Economic Effects of the Sri Lankan Civil War', *Economic Development and Cultural Change*, 41, 395–405.

Gunaratna, R. (1997) *International and Regional Security Implications of the Sri Lankan Tamil Insurgency*. Sri Lanka: Bandaranaike Centre for International Studies.

Gunaratna, R. (2000) 'Bankrupting the Terror Business', *Jane's Intelligence Review* 12 (8) (2000).

Gunasinghe, N. (1984) 'Open Economy and Its Impact on Ethnic Relations in Sri Lanka' in Committee for Rational Development (ed.) *Sri Lanka, the Ethnic Conflict: Myths, Realities and Perspectives*. New Delhi: Navrang.

Herring, R. J. (1994) 'Explaining Sri Lanka's Exceptionalism: Popular Responses to Welfarism and the "Open Economy"' in J. Walton and D. Seddon (ed.) *Free Markets and Food Riots*, New York: Blackwell.

Jayawardena, K. (1985) *Ethnic and Class Conflicts in Sri Lanka: Some Aspects of Sinhala Buddhist Consciousness over the Past 100 Years*. Dehiwala: Centre for Social Analysis.

Kadian, R. (1990) *India's Sri Lanka Fiasco*. New Delhi: Vision.

Kaufman, M. (1996) 'US Expanding Military Role in Sri Lanka', *The Dallas Morning News*, 30 June.

Kay, J. (2000) 'Grievance and Greed in Sri Lanka', *National Post*, June 19.

Kearney, R. N. (1973) *The Politics of Ceylon (Sri Lanka)*. Ithaca/London: Cornell University Press.

Krishna, S. (1997) 'Divergent Narratives: Dravidian and Eelamist Tamil Nationalisms' in M. Roberts (ed.) *Sri Lanka: Collective Identities Revisited*. Colombo: Marga Institute.

Manogaran, C. (1987) *Ethnic Conflict and Reconciliation in Sri Lanka*. Honolulu: University of Hawaii Press.

Manor, J. (1984) 'Introduction' in J. Manor (ed.) *Sri Lanka in Change and Crisis*. London: Croom Helm.

Moore, M. (1985) *The State and Peasant Politics in Sri Lanka*. Cambridge: Cambridge University Press.

Moore M. (1990), 'Economic Liberalisation versus Political Pluralism in Sri Lanka?', *Journal of Modern Asian Studies*, 24(2), 341–83.

Muni, S. D. (1993) *Pangs of Proximity: India and Sri Lanka's Ethnic Crisis*. New Delhi/London: Sage.

Obeyesekere, G. (1984) 'The Origins and Institutionalisation of Political Violence' in J. Manor (ed.) *Sri Lanka in Change and Crisis*. London: Croom Helm.

Ofstad, A. (2002) 'Countries in Violent Conflict and Aid Strategies: The Case of Sri Lanka', *World Development*, 30, 165–80.

Ponnambalam, S. (1983) *Sri Lanka: National Conflict and the Tamil Liberation Struggle*. London: Zed.

Samarasinghe, V. (1996) 'The Tyranny of Space: A Socio-Economic Analysis of the Spatial Dimensions of the Ethnic Conflict in Sri Lanka' in P. A. Groves (ed.) *Economic Development and Social Change in Sri Lanka: A Spatial and Policy Analysis*. New Delhi: Manohar.

Shastri, A. (1990) 'The Material Basis for Separatism: The Tamil Eelam Movement in Sri Lanka', *Journal of Asian Studies*, 49, 56–77.

Sriskandarajah, D. (2001): 'Devious Diasporas and a War without Witness: The Global Landscapes of the Conflict in Sri Lanka,' MacArthur Foundation Conference: Regional Security in a Global Context.

Steele, J. (2001): 'Crouching Tiger Hidden War', *The Guardian*, 4 May.

Tambiah, S. J. (1986) *Sri Lanka: Ethnic Fratricide and the Dismantling of Democracy*. Chicago: University of Chicago Press.

Tambiah, S. (1992) *Buddhism Betrayed?: Religion, Politics, and Violence in Sri Lanka*. Chicago, IL: University of Chicago Press.

United States Department of State (2000) *Patterns of Global Terrorism*. Washington, DC.

Wilson, A. J. (1988) *The Break-up of Sri Lanka: The Sinhalese–Tamil Conflict*. London: Hurst.

11
Conclusions

Valpy FitzGerald, Frances Stewart and Rajesh Venugopal

Global influences, self-determination and linkage mechanisms

Through case studies and overviews, this volume has explored a diverse cross-section of self-determination movements and uncovered the operation of an equally diverse constellation of global influences. Our most important finding is that the global dimension is a critical component of all SDMs and must be factored into the analysis of contemporary internal conflicts. This stems from the wide range, complex nature and pervasive operation of global influences on SDMs, forces which are enmeshed in the origins and dynamics of contemporary political conflicts. A second finding is that *both* economic and cultural influences are critical in framing each SDM and influencing its course, particularly through their interaction. Taken separately, neither the purely culturalist understanding of a 'clash of civilizations' (Huntington 1996, 2002), nor the purely economic instrumentalism of 'greed' (Collier and Hoeffler 2000) are particularly helpful – indeed both are capable of generating deeply problematic and counter-productive policy solutions. Conflict analysis must go beyond such limitations and embrace a genuinely multidisciplinary approach.

Global influences over SDMs range from commodity prices to *hawala* networks, from satellite TV to multinational companies, from international regulatory bodies to INGOs, from the United Nations to the war on terrorism. Global economic forces are closely linked to the factors provoking socio-economic discontent, while global ideologies inform and influence the ways in which such discontent is channelled into particular ideo-political and organizational forms. The presence of global forces thus informs the conditions within which SDMs come into being, adopt specific forms of action and formulate alternative notions of statehood. Even in cases such as Burma, where the government has deliberately followed a policy of insulating society from external influences, the fear of the outside world plays a vivid role in the regime's self-legitimation. This is not to suggest that globalization has become an all-powerful juggernaut that has swept away all local influences and conditions, as global influences at each stage interact with specific local conditions which together account for the trajectory of each SDM. As a result the presence of the same kinds of global influences can generate different outcomes in different cases, and even within the same case at different points in time.

In sections 2 to 4 we summarize our findings of the relationship between global influences and SDMs in relation to three themes set out in Chapter 1: the linkages between SDMs and the global economy; the local influence of (and reaction to) a globalizing culture; and the emergence of a single – yet fiercely contested – hegemonic global ideology. We have classified the global influences over SDMs into two categories: first, global economic dimensions, including the structure of international trade and financial flows (both legal and illegal), international regulatory institutions, market reform policies, foreign aid, commodity prices, and multinational corporations; and secondly, global cultural dimensions, which encompass global cultural pathways such as diaspora, media, transnational political and solidarity movements, international norms, international law, ideological and religious affinities. There are strong connections between the two, which makes it impossible to understand either in isolation from the other. For example, multinational corporations not only form an important aspect of global economic influences but also have a major cultural impact, challenging previous local cultures and sometimes provoking a reaction. Moreover, global cultural ties, like religious communities or diaspora networks, are often the pathways along which economic networks and SDM financing take place.

The importance of global influences of both kinds is powerfully shown by the way in which changes in the global system have been reflected in changes in the nature of SDMs. Understanding the importance of global influences on SDMs – and the complex interactions between economic and cultural factors – is thus central to the design of development policy. This we address later in this chapter, in sections which propose the elements of a new policy approach in the context of the changing global political environment. We identify both elements of alternative approaches to economic and cultural policy design and the corresponding implications for the reform of the global institutions responsible for coordinating such policies.

Designing appropriate policies is complex, partly because of these global–local interactions, but also because all policy-makers – whether global or local – are part of the problem and not outside it. They themselves have political and economic agendas and cannot be assumed to be 'above the fray'. A further problem is the issue of the legitimacy of SDMs, particularly when they involve violent conflict. Although violent struggles have characterized almost every nation's history – with their emancipation from repressive regimes and external oppression forming part of the common national cultural identity, the policy recommendations made below assume that the aim is to reduce the incidence of violent conflict, both by SDMs and the states that they oppose, while ensuring proper representation for oppressed groups and protection of the vulnerable.

The context of the globalizing economy

While many of the economic inequalities and injustices described in this volume had their origin in colonial patterns of development, these were often continued by post-colonial governments and accentuated by global forces. The displacement of local small scale cultivators by plantations owned by outsiders in Algeria, Somalia and even Colombia were all the outcome of colonial-era patterns of economic development. Yet global influences in the post-colonial era mostly continued in the same direction – as in Somalia where agricultural policies, supported by aid agencies, further accentuated the divisions between landowners and others. Moreover, the post-colonial context frequently generated new sources of economic inequality and impoverishment, again encouraging SDMs.

Prolonged impoverishment and marginalization of large sections of the population in Somalia, the Congo and Algeria have led to a situation in which many had little to lose from violent conflict. The emergence of high levels of unemployment among educated or semi-educated youth created a potential pool of violent opposition – even when overall economic growth improved, as in Algeria and Sri Lanka. Moreover, aid flows were distributed to elites in a way that enabled them to create their own private power-bases, often used (as in the cases of Somalia and Sierra Leone) for factionalized violence.

Economic globalization has reduced the economic role of the state generally, and both this and globalization itself have important implications for SDMs. On the one hand, the reduced role of the state in the economy and in the provision of services ruptured the implicit social contract, contributing to the quest for alternate state forms. On the other hand, the increasing globalization of transactions and diminished regulation have made it easier for SDMs to benefit from global markets and evade state regulation (Duffield 2001). SDMs have, as a result, increasingly relied on commodity trade, such as diamonds, drugs, hardwoods and so on, for finance (Chapter 2). In this way, market sources of support, as well as those from diasporas, partly replaced the official flows forthcoming during the cold war.

The adverse economic conditions that provided fertile soil for SDMs were not, of course, solely due to global influences. Indeed, at one extreme, economic stagnation in Burma was mainly due to the government's isolationist policies. In general, global and local influences interacted, as local decision-makers with their own agendas and capacities acted in the context of global conditions. However, global markets and financial flows, aid and adjustment policies, provided the opportunities and constraints in which local decision-makers operated, often with little autonomy. Of course, the countries considered here were selected because they had suffered violent conflict and therefore we have omitted countries that have flourished politically and economically in the same global context. We are not, therefore, seeking to generalize about the consequences of globalization as such. Rather we are exploring the ways in which in the parts of the world where violent conflict emerged, the major global economic influences prevalent were associated with worsening economic conditions of a kind that helped provoke conflict.

Global cultural pathways

We have identified three important global cultural pathways by which global cultural influences operate – international migration and diaspora links, the global media, and transnational social and political movements. Individually and in conjunction with each other, these three pathways have played a significant role in SDMs, although the impact varies across cases. In each pathway, globalization has increased the connections.

Diasporas play an important role in some conflicts, particularly where migration is the consequence of the same political persecution or economic grievances that underlie the conflict. In some cases, the diasporas are very large – for example, more than one in five Sri Lankan Tamils lives outside Sri Lanka and one in three Kurds lives outside the area claimed as Kurdistan. The Irish diaspora, whoses numbers exceed the population of Ireland itself, has a large presence in Britain – an important party to the conflict – as well as in the United States.

Diasporas have frequently been cast in a negative light as extreme nationalists who finance and prolong the violence that they themselves are safely removed from. However, we have found the role of diasporas to be more subtle, differentiated and country-specific. For example, Sri Lankan Tamils overseas support self-determination at home through cultural and political activities, as well as a variety of forms of financial support. In the case of Somaliland, the diaspora is not heavily politicized, yet family remittances contribute to revenue and political stability in the nascent state structure. The Irish diaspora has contributed through political influence over US government policy, as well as finance. In contrast, in Algeria the diaspora has not assumed such a distinct political role in the conflict.

One of the most vivid examples of the spread of contemporary transnational political/cultural influences is political Islam. In Algeria, for example, the ideas that shaped the development of Islamist groups such as the FIS and GIA were partly transmitted through the influence of Egyptian teachers linked to groups such as Al-Ikhwan Al-Muslimun (Muslim Brotherhood) – and were later reinforced through the influence of returning *mujahideen* volunteers who had fought in Afghanistan in the 1980s.

Transnational political activism took new forms in the 1990s with the increased space and legitimacy provided under the rubric of 'civil society', and with the rise of issue-specific international pressure groups and international non-governmental organizations (INGOs). The influence of INGOs ranges from campaigns over human rights abuses and child soldiers to the provision of services to affected populations. The spread of new media sources such as satellite television in the 1990s has also been of critical importance to the changing nature of self-determination in the post-cold war period. The ability of television to convey evocative images and messages to a mass audience has turned it into an important medium in the creation and manipulation of public opinion, and many satellite channels have consequently become objects of heavy controversy. In 1999 British authorities revoked the licence of Med-TV, a London-based Kurdish satellite channel on the grounds that it was broadcasting messages inciting violence against Turkey. Qatar-based Al-Jazeera television has been accused of promoting Islamic fundamentalism and anti-American violence, while US-based Fox News has been charged with anti-Arab and anti-Muslim bias. The 1990s also gave rise to what is called the 'CNN effect', in which the transmission of disturbing images of war and suffering have become a source of heightened pressure for external intervention. For example, in November 1991 vivid video footage of a massacre in East Timor by Indonesian soldiers was broadcast around the world and subsequently catalyzed a powerful and successful campaign of international activism.

The changing global political environment

The influence of over-arching ideo-political global paradigms provides identity, legitimacy, diplomatic allies and material resources to both state and non-state entities. But it has also been a source of distortion and external manipulation. During the cold war, numerous SDMs found themselves drawn to, and even trapped within, the ideo-political confines of a global superpower rivalry within which they became expendable foot soldiers. The importance of the cold war in sustaining or suppressing SDMs is evident from the way its demise in 1989–91 marked the end of numerous conflicts – such as the long-standing insurgent wars in Mozambique, Ethiopia, Namibia, El Salvador and Cambodia – and the beginning, or a new phase, in others, including Somalia, Algeria and the Democratic Republic of Congo. In Afghanistan, Sri Lanka and Colombia, the end of the cold war did not signify an end to the conflict, but nevertheless marked an important turning point.

Following the end of the cold war, a new axis of confrontation slowly took shape under the 'international terrorism' paradigm, with a new divide between those states identified as opposing terrorism and those identified as supporting terrorism (which includes a few states and many non-state entities).

This distinction was sharpened following 9/11. International cooperation among governments to tackle violent non-state actors has been a central feature of the changing power relations between states and SDMs, many of which were then labelled as international terrorist organizations and banned under new legislation in the US, UK and other countries. Banned organizations include the Fuerzas Armadas Revolucionarios de Colombia (FARC) and Ejercito de Liberacion Nacional (ELN) from Colombia, Partiya Karkeren Kürdistan (PKK) from Turkey, Groupe Islamique Armé (GIA) in Algeria, Liberation Tigers of Tamil Eelam (LTTE) in Sri Lanka, Hamas in Israel/Palestine, Hezbollah in Lebanon, and Harkat al-Ansar in India/Pakistan.

On balance, the rising emphasis on the international terrorism paradigm has strengthened incumbent states and weakened SDMs both materially and psychologically. SDMs have come under heavy pressure to accept power-sharing compromises rather than more profound changes, and pursue parliamentary or federalist solutions rather than armed struggle, while armed repression of dissident groups and violations of human rights by states have become more acceptable internationally.

In the post-cold war environment, external sources of political support, financial resources and legitimacy can be a source of both strength and weakness for self-determination movements. The case of Burma demonstrates the mixed effects of the heightened opportunities for political expression, media contact and access to communications technology wrought by globalization. On the one hand, the growth of transnational politics and solidarity movements during the 1990s provided better opportunities to publicize the actions of the pro-democracy movement and to coordinate solidarity actions on an international scale. On the other hand, the benefits they gained from situating their actions within international solidarity networks has arguably come at the expense of their diminished internal relevance and impact within Burma itself. Globalization has weakened the economic role of the state, as noted above, yet the state remains a critical entity in international norms and the international legal system. International norms of state sovereignty and the attendant material benefits of international recognition have helped to prevent the rise of self-determination movements and to perpetuate a weak, ineffectual state in the case of the Congo, while the absence of such global influences permitted the innovation of what appears to be a much more functional state apparatus in Somaliland.

The space for constructing an alternative policy towards SDMs

Because of the potential power of global forces in the development of SDMs, global actors can alter conflicts over self-determination and help to reduce the incidence of violence. To achieve this, the aim should be to reduce the resentments and provocations that give rise to violence, so that the actors themselves determine that violence is undesirable. International policies should also be designed that limit the means of violence while recognizing that unless the fundamental causes of SDMs are addressed, such policies may well be undesirable and will almost certainly be ineffective.

Broadly speaking, the global 'drivers' identified in this volume can be categorized into two types. The first comprises the more disaggregated and informal forces of economic and cultural globalization, comprising the growth of cross-border trade and financial links, the strengthening of global cultural pathways such as migration, the spread of media and communications technology and solidarity networks. The unregulated and cross-border nature of these forces has tended to promote the rise and sustenance of self-determination movements. The second comprises the conscious policy response to the 'disorder' inherent in the global system: multilateral regulatory authorities, inter-governmental co-ordination, global norms and international law. While the first driver works in the direction of weakening state capacity, facilitating conflict finance, promoting SDM identities, and co-ordinating international solidarity, the second works towards propping up weak states, preserving colonial-era borders, prohibiting conflict finance, and preventing and policing refugee flows. Much of this new co-ordinated global response is packaged within an external intervention regime which includes – in an uneven and highly political way – military intervention and humanitarian and economic aid as well as support for 'fragile' states.

There are two possible scenarios in the resolution of these conflicting drivers. First, global military–political–economic repression of SDMs could become more generalized. This is already happening to some extent under measures designed for the suppression of international terrorism. This is weakening international norms on minority and human rights, and undermining the authority of weaker states when they are viewed as facilitating 'terrorism'. Secondly, global socio-economic policies to ameliorate the root causes of SDMs, including policies to deal with rising inequalities and poverty, could be implemented, thereby reducing the root causes of many SDMs.

Which outcome occurs depends on the strengths and long-sightedness of governments. At first sight, there seems little space for alternative global policies in the present 'unipolar moment', when the US exercises military and geopolitical hegemony. Its ruling elite seems disposed towards 'preemptive action' in order to ensure national security as a permanent doctrine (Mann 2004) and has limited disposition to make serious efforts to reduce vulnerability and impoverishment in developing countries (Suskind 2004).

However, the present stage of globalization is not just a new version of colonialism. First, although military power is effectively unipolar, economic power is widely dispersed in terms of production, trade and finance. Under these circumstances a binding system of rules is in the interest of all countries, even the largest players, as is illustrated by the emergence of the WTO.

Second, colonial powers exercised effective sovereignty over the developing world by relying on their own populations to provide officers, police and local administrators, while controlling the activities of their national firms in the colonies. The US cannot exercise this kind of control: dependent governments are not always reliable supportrs of the hegemonic power and the US is unable/unwilling to recruit sufficient soldiers to maintain effective power across the world, while multinational corporations are responsive to their shareholders rather than the US government.

The costs of sustaining a hegemonic position, and the emergence of countervailing powers – as Europe and Japan recover their economic dynamism, and Russia and China emerge as geostrategic actors – will probably be sufficient to convince the US electorate that world peace cannot be achieved by military force and that cooperation within international institutions is necessary for its own security. The following policy recommendations are based upon this premise.

Elements of an alternative economic approach

The dominant view today is that a combination of suppression by force and eliminating the oxygen provided by global financial support is the most effective way to tackle SDMs. Such measures are inherently ineffective in combating terrorism because of the provocative consequences of the use of force and the systemic problems in regulating the global financial system. The ineffectiveness of such policies confirms the view that the underlying structural causes of violent SDMs have to be tackled. Our alternative emphasises the need to tackle the underlying inequalities that provoke violent SDMs.

Our review of the various sources of finance for SDMs that arise from globalization itself, including trade in commodities (such as diamonds and drugs) and financial flows from diasporas and elsewhere, shows that in most cases some progress has been made in identifying the problem and defining suitable regulations. In some areas (especially diamonds and timber) NGOs have played a vital role in identifying the problem, providing pressure for regulation, and monitoring compliance. In contrast, governments have taken a lead where they see themselves as directly affected – notably in relation to drugs and finance, and in sanctions against 'undesirable' regimes. But in no case have such policies been fully effective and mostly they have been broadly ineffective; where goods are concerned illicit trading networks continue (as with drugs and diamonds); financial flows find new channels; and sanctions are evaded, or hurt the vulnerable. Hence action is needed to address the root causes of violent SDMs.

From an economic perspective, the policies that are likely to reduce the root causes of violent SDMs have three elements: first, those that reduce economic stagnation and increase employment for all social groups; second, those that improve the goods and services provided by the state to all citizens; and third, policies which reduce ethnic and religious inequalities in access to political and economic resources and lead to inclusive systems. Global policies to support these objectives need to focus aid and trade on those parts of the world that have been impoverished during globalization – which includes most of Africa and least developed countries elsewhere. One way of achieving this is for a massive redirection of aid resources to these poor countries with a renewed commitment to the Millennium Development Goals in terms of universal primary health and education, as well as redesigning development strategies and poverty reduction targets to ensure the reduction of horizontal inequality. Current stabilization and adjustment approaches of the IMF and World Bank need radical rethinking to make the avoidance of stagnation and growth of employment prime objectives; to avoid rapid liberalization of trade where this threatens these objectives; and to extend rather than reduce the state's role in the social provision of such services as health, education, transport and housing.

The requirement of inclusiveness and reduced horizontal inequalities imposes demands on the economic system which neither the market nor the state necessarily fulfills. Both need to be monitored and constrained to ensure that the economic system is a fair and inclusive one. This is true of the global economic system as well as within nations. Increasing global inequality and the exclusion of parts of the world from global prosperity virtually guarantees continued international terrorism and global conflict.

The objective of inclusiveness and the reduction of horizontal inequalities requires a review of political as well as economic policies. Democratic systems involving simple majority rule and political parties – the leading model supported by international actors – can lead to ethnic exclusion where one ethnicity is in a majority, while political parties frequently exploit and enhance ethnic divisions. Hence constitutional settlements requiring respect for and empowerment of minorities are necessary to ensure minority rights – including, possibly, reserved positions for all major ethnic groups.

Elements of an alternative cultural approach

Global cultural pathways are even more difficult to regulate than economic ones. By their nature cultural influences are diffuse, generally the outcome of myriad actors. Moreover, devising relevant and appropriate policies is a much less well trodden path. Yet a central finding here is that cultural pathways interact with economic influences to affect the trajectory of SDMs, so that economic changes alone may not be adequate especially since so many SDMs present themselves as primarily cultural.

Despite the difficulties in influencing cultural pathways, official discourse, laws and regulations do affect them – but at present often in a way that promotes violent SDMs, for example provoking opposition by policies to outlaw minority cultural practices, making diasporas an embittered and isolated group. There is a need to support cultural pathways that are supportive of peaceful democratic solutions. It will be necessary to influence attitudes and beliefs in the North as well as the South; to do so requires challenging official discourse, disseminating alternative views via the media and the education system and thereby shifting the dominant paradigms.

Two major cultural influences on the development of SDMs today are the international ideo-political system, and international norms of statehood. In our view both need changing to encourage the peaceful and democratic evolution of SDMs. On the one hand, the war on terrorism – which has become the overarching ideo-political norm – emphasizes the violent suppression of SDMs rather than a solution to the tensions that gave rise to them. This approach is highly unlikely to lead to a permanent solution, and may result in prolonged and extended violence. If the 'war on terrorism' paradigm could be replaced by one which genuinely supports the rights of peoples to determine their own destiny in a peaceful way, it would be likely to generate more lasting and peaceful solutions to separatism which in the longer term would also reduce international terrorism. On the one hand, the dominant norm of respecting current state boundaries and avoiding separatism needs to be questioned. Many violent separatist movements are the product of artificial states created by colonial powers. Separatist solutions may be the democratic and peaceful answer. The norm of protecting states therefore needs to be replaced by one that protects human rights, including the right to political and economic participation in every political system. There is also a need to support pro-peace global connections at the non-governmental level. This includes support for INGOs to work with local groups to monitor human rights abuses. and support for pro-peace internet channels.

Based upon the principles of international law agreed between democratic states, Rawls has argued that 'peoples have a duty to assist other peoples living under unfavourable conditions that prevent their having a just or decent political and social regime' (Rawls 1999, p. 37). This justifies support for the right to self-determination, albeit with an important qualification: 'no people has the right to self-determination, or a right to secession, at the expense of subjugating another people' (Rawls 1999, p. 38).

The presence of diasporas in a country gives rise to considerable possibilities for influencing them and through them the evolution of SDMs – yet this opportunity is rarely taken. Diasporas can contribute to the accentuation of identity politics, as well as the financial support of violent SDMs; alternatively, they can contribute to peaceful solutions through lobbying and interactions with the home country. Diaspora choices can be influenced by the way they are treated in their host country. If they are treated as aliens, with suspicion, in a racist way, their identity scorned or ignored, they are likely to identify strongly with their country of origin and provide support for violent SDMs. In contrast, if well treated in the host country, integrated into employment, provided with benefits and treated with dignity, they may be less persuaded by identity politics and become more open to alternative political solutions.

The implications for the reform of global institutions

A first step is to recognize that people have legitimate reasons for self-determination and minorities need to have room to manage their lives and not be crushed by majorities – this is after all is what social democracy is about as a global project. The second step is to provide international support, which may occasionally include military intervention in order to make this principle effective.

In the spheres of both culture and the economy a policy of total *non*-intervention is an empty concept because global influences are *de facto* so widespread. None the less, there is a need for some clarity about the legal and ethical principles of explicit intervention in the struggles of other peoples. International support for solutions to SDMs should above all be directed at protecting vulnerable groups. In some contexts this requires economic interventions. Occasionally it justifies first diplomatic and then military action.

There is widespread agreement that any military intervention, justified according to the 'responsibility to protect', can only be legitimate if it is exercised through the United Nations Security Council. The primary responsibility for the protection of its people lies with their own state; but where a population is suffering serious harm as a result of internal war, repression or state failure, and the state in question is unwilling or unable to avert it, the principle of non-intervention yields to the international responsibility to protect (ICSS, 2001). This is the responsibility of the Security Council, under Article 24 of the UN Charter, and reflects the developing practice of states, regional organizations and the Security Council itself.

In the authoritative opinion of the International Commission on Intervention and State Sovereignty (ICSS) this has direct implications for SDMs: 'protective enforcement usually indicates sustaining or restoring forms of territorial self-government and autonomy'. Yet the Commission goes on to argue that

> the responsibility to protect is fundamentally a principle designed to respond to threats to human life, and not a tool for achieving political goals such as greater political autonomy, self-determination, or independence for particular groups within the country (though these underlying issues may well be related to the humanitarian concerns that prompted the military intervention). (ICSS 2001, para 5.23)

The UN Charter is also quite clear about the need for globally coordinated and progressive (in the sense of protecting the vulnerable) economic and cultural policies. Yet the founders of the UN created no effective institutions for world economic and social governance, nor for protecting the poor at a world level. Such institutions are needed because national governments do not fully take into account the economic impact of their actions beyond their borders, because international markets cannot be properly regulated by national governments, national governments cannot implement measures to prevent international disease, environmental destruction or crime prevention by themselves, and above all because there are worldwide agreements that extreme poverty should be ended, and yet many governments lack the resources, power or will to act. The present set of international institutions do not fulfill the functions needed at a world level and are not under the effective control of the UN (Stewart and Dawes 2003). Various organs of the UN, notably the General Assembly and ECOSOC, do have global social and economic functions, but in practice lack effective power.

We propose therefore an Economic and Social Security Council (ESSC) to cover economic, social and environmental arenas, with a role similar to that of the Security Council in security matters.[1] It would provide a flexible forum where urgent global issues could be considered at a very high level. The ESSC would operate by requesting action from existing institutions. For international institutions, including the World Bank, the IMF, the WTO and other UN specialized agencies, the directions of the ESSC would be mandatory. National governments could not be compelled to take action, though penalties could be applied if they systematically rejected requests. To be effective, membership would have to reflect the realities of global power, yet ensure representation for states at all levels of development.

Each particular SDM has its unique characteristics stemming from its own history and logic. None the less, global influences are pervasive. Hence, as well as an understanding of the local situation there are some general global actions that are required to help solve SDMs with peace and justice. This study has enabled us to sketch some of the major global changes that are urgently needed.

Note

1. This proposal is based on Stewart and Dawes (2003) where more details can be found of crucial aspects such as the voting system.

References

Brownlie, I. (1990) *Principles of Public International Law*. Oxford: Clarendon Press.
Collier, P. and A. Hoeffler (2000) *Greed and Grievance in Civil War*. Washington, DC: World Bank: 42.
Duffield, M. (2001) *Global Governance and the New Wars*. London: Zed.

Huntington, Samuel P. (1996) *The Clash of Civilizations and the Remaking of World Order*. New York: Simon & Schuster.
——(2002) *The Clash of Civilizations and the Remaking of World Order*. New York: Free Press.
ICSS (2001) *The Responsibility to Protect* (Report of the International Commission on Intervention and State Sovereignty, ICSS). Ottawa: International Development Research Centre.
Mann, J. (2004) *Rise of the Vulcans: the History of Bush's War Cabinet*. New York: Viking Penguin.
Rawls, J. (1999) *The Law of Peoples*. Cambridge, MA: Harvard University Press.
Reno, W. (2000) 'Liberia and Sierra Leone: The Competition for Patronage in Resource-rich Economies' in E. W. Nafziger, F. Stewart and R. Väyrynen (eds) *War, Hunger and Displacement: The Origin of Humanitarian Emergencies*. Oxford: OUP.
Stewart, F. with S. Daws (2003) 'Global Governance: The Case for a World Economic and Social Council', *Finance and Common Good*, 15, Summer.
Suskind, R. (2004) *The Price of Loyalty: George W. Bush, the White House and the Education of Paul O'Neill*. New York: Simon & Schuster.

Index